STUDENTS, INVESTORS, BUSINESS PEOPLE,
VIDEO GAME ENTHUSIASTS, COMPUTER HACKERS,
CONSUMERS, TRAVELERS, RESEARCHERS . . .

Expand your personal computer to the limit of its power and potential.

Tap into the resources of computer networks.

Know where to go for free software; business news; information on video games, electronic mail, and special consumer opportunities.

All this information and more is in

THE COMPUTER PHONE BOOK™

MIKE CANE has worked for the leading new electronic media market research firm and has also consulted on personal computers, data communications, and online database systems. He is currently researching another book on personal computer communications. He lives in New York City.

THE COMPUTER PHONE BOOK™

by
Mike Cane

A PLUME BOOK
NEW AMERICAN LIBRARY
NEW YORK AND SCARBOROUGH, ONTARIO

NAL BOOKS ARE AVAILABLE AT QUANTITY DISCOUNTS WHEN USED TO PROMOTE
PRODUCTS OR SERVICES. FOR INFORMATION PLEASE WRITE TO
PREMIUM MARKETING DIVISION, NEW AMERICAN LIBRARY,
1633 BROADWAY, NEW YORK, NEW YORK 10019.

Copyright © 1983 by Mike Cane
"The Computer Phone Book" is a trademark of Mike Cane
All rights reserved. For information address New American Library

ACKNOWLEDGMENTS
  The following companies and individuals have granted permission to reprint their copyrighted online prompts, menus, and illustrations: Bibliographic Retrieval Service, Inc.; Bill Blue; Capital Cities Communications Corporation; Ward Christensen & Randy Seuss; The CommuniTree Group; CompuServe Information Service, Inc.; Dialog Information Services, Inc.; Dow Jones & Company, Inc.; GameMaster Corporation; General Videotex Corporation; Matchmaker Enterprises; R. R. Bowker & Company, Inc.; Reader's Digest Association, Inc.; Joe Simon/Computer Services of Danbury, Inc.; Craig Vaughan/Software Sorcery, Inc.

(The following page constitutes an extension of this copyright page.)

Several trademarks and/or service marks appear in this book. The companies listed below are the owners of the trademarks and/or service marks following their names.

Ashton Tate: dBase II; AT&T/Bell System: Trimline; Apple Computer: Apple; William Bates, Publisher: The Computer Cookbook; Mike Cane: *The Computer Phone Book*; Ward Christensen & Randy Seuss: CBBS (Computerized Bulletin Board System); Commodore International, Inc.: CBM, Commodore, Commodore-64, VIC-20; CompuServe, Inc.: CompuServe Information Service; Compu-Board: Consumer Electronics Newsbase; Control Video Corporation: GameLine, Master Module; Dialog Information Services, Inc.: Dialog; Digital Research, Inc.: CP/M, CP/M-Net; Dow Jones & Company, Inc.: Barron's, Corporate Earnings Estimator, Dow Jones News/Retrieval Service, Dow Jones News Service, Dow Jones Quotes, News/Retrieval Sports Report, News/Retrieval Weather Report, The Wall Street Journal, The Wall Street Journal Highlights Online, Wall Street Week Online, Weekly Economic Survey, Weekly Economic Update; GameMaster Corporation: GameMaster; General Videotex Corporation: Delphi; J. Norman Goode: Micro Moonlighter; LICA (Long Island Computer Association): InstaPoll; Little Computer Store, Inc.: Komputer Klassified; Matchmaker Enterprises: Dial-Your-Match, Fantasy Plaza; Max Ule & Company, Inc.: Tickerscreen; McGraw-Hill Book Company: Electronic Bookshelf; Microhouse Corporation: Microline; Lance Miklus, Inc.: Mouse-Net, ST80; PARTICIPATE Systems, Inc.: PARTICIPATE; Books in Print; Reader's Digest Association, Inc.: The Source, SourceMail, SMail; Sangar Media, Inc.: Sangarnet; Small Business Systems Group: Forum-80; Software Sorcery, Inc.: ABBS; Softworx: Softworx; Tandy Corporation: Color Computer, TRS-80; Taylor Electronics, Inc.: MicroShare; Telephone Software Connection, Inc.: Telephone Software Connection; Texas Instruments, Inc.: TI/994A; Warner Communications Inc.: Atari, Atari VCS; WUI, Inc.: Mailgram, Western Union.

LIBRARY OF CONGRESS CATALOGING IN PUBLICATION DATA

Cane, Mike.
   The computer phone book.

   Includes index.
   1. On-line data processing—Directories.   2. Information storage and retrieval systems—Directories.   3. Data libraries—Directories.   4. Computer networks—Directories.   I. Title.
   QA76.55.C36   1983   025'.04   83-17305
   ISBN 0-452-25446-9

PLUME TRADEMARK REG. U.S. PAT. OFF. AND FOREIGN COUNTRIES
REGISTERED TRADEMARK—MARCA REGISTRADA
HECHO EN WESTFORD, MASS., U.S.A.

SIGNET, SIGNET CLASSIC, MENTOR, PLUME, MERIDIAN and NAL BOOKS are published *in the United States* by New American Library, 1633 Broadway, New York, New York 10019, *in Canada* by The New American Library of Canada Limited, 81 Mack Avenue, Scarborough, Ontario M1L 1M8

First Printing, November, 1983

   3 4 5 6 7 8 9

PRINTED IN THE UNITED STATES OF AMERICA

For my mother

The Computer Phone Book is continually being updated to provide the best possible future edition. If you would like to receive a monthly update of this book, you can subscribe to The Computer Phone Book Update™ by sending a check or money order for $20 U.S./Canada; $30 overseas, made payable to The Computer Phone Book, to:

    Mike Cane
    The Computer Phone Book
    175 Fifth Avenue, Suite 3371
    New York, New York 10010, USA.

Contents

Preface	xiii
1. How to Make Your Computer Communicate	1
2. Overview of Online Systems	12
3. How to Use the Online Systems	26
4. Directory Section: United States National Networks	138
5. Directory Section: United States Local-Area Services	165
6. Directory Section: United States Bulletin-Board Systems	174
7. Directory Section: Canadian Bulletin-Board Systems	351
8. Directory Section: Overseas Bulletin-Board Systems	354
9. Special Services: Domestic and Foreign	359
APPENDIX 1. Bulletin-Board System Help Files	362
APPENDIX 2. State, City, Area Code Guide	388
APPENDIX 3. Downloadable Software	401
APPENDIX 4. Special Interests: Computers/Miscellaneous	412
APPENDIX 5. 1200 bps Systems	426
APPENDIX 6. United States National Networks	429
APPENDIX 7. United States Local-Area Services	430
APPENDIX 8. A Sampling of Communications Software Suppliers	431
APPENDIX 9. Bulletin-Board System Listing Form	433
INDEX	437

Preface

Somewhere in the back of your mind there is probably a term you have read in a book, magazine, or newspaper but have set aside. That term is "microcomputer telecommunications." You may have put it aside while you struggled to learn BASIC on your computer, or to play games on your computer, or to juggle the quarterly earnings estimates on your computer. It is a concept you should now take the time to explore and learn about.

When you bought your computer system, you followed a simple formula: Computer plus storage device (floppy disk drive or cassette tape) plus monitor (or TV) equals system. Microcomputer telecommunications can be similarly described in a formula: Your system plus modem plus telephone equals telecommunications. It is that simple. That is why each year an increasing number of computer owners are walking into stores and buying the one small device that will ensure them of a complete system—a modem.

These people are parents who want their children to have access to information that cannot be found in school libraries, couples who want to be able to place just one phone call to compare prices among a multitude of competing products, business people who have realized that it takes information and knowledge as well as overtime to get ahead in business, and individuals who want to find a new friend. These people are, in fact, just like you.

All of them started out as you are now, being told about something that will allow their computer to do more than compute, about something that will allow their computers—and them—to communicate.

Microcomputer telecommunications is the largest-growing segment of the entire microcomputer industry. Soon, it will become commonplace to hear phrases such as "online," "videotex," and "modems" in conversations.

All of this adds up to what has been called the Information Age. But, unlike anything else you may have read, this book does not tell you that the Information Age is coming. This book tells you that it is here—and how you can join it.

CHAPTER 1
How to Make Your Computer Communicate

Welcome to the directory of the Information Age—*The Computer Phone Book*™.

Since you probably already know something about using your computer for telecommunications, you can use *The Computer Phone Book* as a guide to increase your knowledge in this new world where you will meet people and learn new things. If you are already telecommunicating, you may want to skip this chapter and go to the system listings in the directory section. I suggest, however, that you review Chapter 3, which may provide some new tips and act as a refresher course.

The purpose of *The Computer Phone Book* is to bring to your attention the many systems and services available to you. In it you will find an overview of what you need to go *online*, that is, to call the many systems; what is available to you once you are online; some salient points and tips about how to use the systems and services to their fullest; and, most importantly, a directory of over 400 systems and services that you can access.

Once you assemble what you will need to go online and your knowledge of systems and how to use them increases, you can use *The Computer Phone Book* as a reference source. Use *The Computer Phone Book* as you would your personal phone book. If a system has a new offering or service, make a note of it in this book. Should a system *go down*, which means that it is no longer available for use, cross out that particular listing. If you discover a new system, for example, one that came online after this book was published, make a note of it. This will help to keep you current until you can get the next regular update of this book, which will include all of the new systems. You will also be assured that all of your necessary information concerning your online activities will be in *one* place: in *The Computer Phone Book*.

In terms of the equipment you will need to go online, I must make a cautionary note: Since the number of brands of personal computers is enormous and grows each month, it is beyond the scope of this book to discuss what is needed for any one brand. You will have to use and adapt your computer according to its capabilities. For example, if you find that your computer does not have a *serial port* into which you can plug a modem (a device to allow your computer to "talk" over the telephone; explained shortly), you will need to purchase an RS-232C interface, which will provide your computer with a serial port.

A similar caution is given in regard to modems and communications software packages. It is impossible to cover every available modem and every possible feature of a communications software package. Some computers can only be used with a specially made modem (of the same brand), whereas others can use virtually any commercially available modem that will plug into a serial port. Communications software can sometimes be limited to a specific brand of computer or a specific operating system and may require a certain amount of memory. Also, the software may require a modem with certain features or may be particular about the type of printer it will work with.

These caveats mean that you will have to do a bit of homework. It is not as difficult as it may sound, however. A good dealer and articles and reviews in computer magazines can help you. Since you probably already own a personal computer, I assume you have used it enough and read enough about it to know what is best and available for it.

In general, all available modems and communications software offer the same basic features. Available and useful special features will be discussed at the end of this chapter.

Of all the uses to which you can put your personal computer, none are as exciting or as broadening as *telecommunications*, that is, using your computer as a communications service. Any investigating you may have to do to make your system function will be worth it.

I assume that you have a system that is composed at least of a personal computer, a storage device (either a cassette recorder or a disk drive), and (optional but very handy) a printer. You must also have a telephone. In addition, you will need a modem and a communications software package.

A *modem* is a device that you connect to your computer and the telephone line. The word "modem" is a truncation of *mod*ulator–*dem*odulator, which describes its function. Simply put, your modem takes the signals generated by your computer and translates them into signals that your telephone can understand and transmit.

Modems come in a wide variety of shapes and sizes. The least-expensive type is an *acoustic-coupled modem*. It has two rubber cups into which you place a telephone handset. The telephone handset must be a conventional one, such as found in offices or pay phones; Trimline[tm] handsets will not fit into the cups.

Another type of modem is a *direct-connect* modem. It plugs either into the telephone itself or the telephone wall jack. In order to use this type of modem, you must have a telephone that uses the Bell System modular jacks (RJ11 is their exact name). Ideally, it should also be a push button not a dial telephone, although some modems can use either or both. Direct-connect modems come in two categories: on-board or standalone modems. An *on-board modem* is a collection of chips on a printed circuit board that fits into one of the slots inside of a computer's casing. A *standalone modem* is connected to the serial port of a computer and sits beside it (sometimes it is large enough to sit right under the telephone to which it is connected).

There are advantages and disadvantages to each type. An acoustic-coupled modem may be prone to interference from room noise. The earpiece of the telephone handset is not made to receive and hold a single-tone transmission, such as a carrier signal, and will eventually jam and lose the signal. The solution to this is to bang the handset gently against a hard surface such as a desk; but if you are online for several hours, you run the risk of being disconnected abruptly. Although a direct-connect modem is not subject to these problems, you may find it inconvenient to have to connect the modem to the telephone or the wall jack when you want to telecommunicate and then remember to reconnect the telephone for normal use. There are direct-connect standalone modems that allow you to switch from data use to regular voice use of the telephone with the flip of a switch. You could also get a second telephone line to simplify matters.

Your computer operates by a series of electrical impulses that are represented by zeros (∅) and ones (1). Each zero or one is called a *bit,* which is the smallest unit of information that your computer can handle. It takes eight bits, in unique combinations, to form any character (such as 1, 2, A, B, #, @, *) that appears on your screen. The eight bits that form a single character is known as a *byte*. This way of operating is known as *digital processing*.

Each computer generates its electrical signals differently. There are variations in current, voltage levels, and so forth. Also, some computers do not generate the same combinations of bits to form a character. For example, pressing the A key on one computer will not necessarily produce the same combinations of zeros and ones as will pressing the A key on another computer. Fortunately, two standards exist that can bring together the incompatible electrical signals and convert every computer's digital alphabet into understandable code. These standards are RS-232C and ASCII (ask-ee).

RS-232C is used to standardize the electrical signals being sent out of a computer's serial port. With it, a computer can "talk" to a printer, modem, or (in some cases) a disk drive in understandable, common electrical signals.

ASCII is a standard manner of arranging the zeros and ones so that when you press your A key, a computer receiving your zeros and ones will know they stand for an A. The majority of personal computers are equipped with ASCII-generating keyboards. The computers that generate non-ASCII characters have them translated into ASCII by an appropriate communications program. You need not worry about whether or not your computer has an ASCII or non-ASCII keyboard. If there is a modem available for your computer, chances are it will come with a communications program to translate the non-ASCII into ASCII symbols.

Both RS-232C and ASCII pertain to digital operations. Your telephone, however, works by transmitting sound, which is an *analog* signal. This is where your modem fits in. It converts the digital signals into sounds and *modulates* them. Any computer with which you communicate over the telephone will be equipped with a modem that will *demodulate* the sounds, converting them back into digital signals that the computer can comprehend.

A modem will transmit and receive these signals at a certain rate of speed, known as *bits per second* (bps). You may have also heard this rate of speed described as *baud* or the *baud rate*; these terms are not entirely accurate. It actually takes a mathematical formula to convert bits per second into baud. Bits per second is the precise term used to describe the rate of speed; any time you come across the term baud, bits per second is probably what is meant.

Modems for personal computers generally transmit and receive at one of two speeds: 300 bps or 1200 bps. (In addition, 110 bps is sometimes available, but it is too slow and is generally not used.) Here again a standard must be used to ensure that what the modem transmits can indeed be carried by the telephone line. The standard for 300 bps modems is Bell 103, and the standard for 1200 bps modems is Bell 212A. (There is another Bell standard for 1200 bps modems, Bell 202. It is unlikely, however, that you will want a Bell 202 modem, and I caution you to look for a Bell 212A standard modem when purchasing a 1200 bps modem.)

If you can afford it and there is one available for your computer, it may be best to purchase a dual-speed (300/1200 bps) modem. After using 300 bps for any great length of time, you will long for a faster speed. The 1200 bps modem is also preferred if you intend to transmit and receive a lot of text or programs (a process that will be discussed shortly). If you cannot afford a dual-speed modem or if one is not available for your computer, a 300 bps modem will suffice.

The directory listings in *The Computer Phone Book* cite the bits-per-second speeds of the systems that are available for you to call. You need only read the bits-per-second specification and set your modem accordingly to either 300 or 1200 bps. For the time being, have your modem set for 300 bps.

A modem can also transmit and receive in full- or half-duplex. *Full-duplex* allows your computer to talk at the same time as the other computer you are calling. This feature is important because it will allow you to "interrupt" the computer you are calling and issue a command. *Half-duplex* permits only one computer at a time to talk. For a technical illustration of this concept, think of a CB radio on which one person must signify that he or she is through transmitting by saying "over" so that the other person can then transmit a reply. Half-duplex is handy in situations in which long files of information are being transmitted. Half-duplex is the *only* duplex available for a Bell 202 standard 1200 bps modem.

In full-duplex, what your computer transmits is *echoed* by the receiving computer. For example, if the computer you have called asks you to type in your name, you will see your name appear on your screen as you type it in. Each letter that you typed in was sent to and received by the computer you called. It was also sent back to your computer, which is how it appears on your screen. Echoing is a good way to see if what you are sending is getting through to the other computer. Let's say I was online and typed in my name; instead of getting "Mike," I got "M@$o" on my screen. I would know that something was wrong. Generally, when something such as this occurs, it means that the telephone connection has noise on it. If the problem were to persist, it would be best to terminate the session and call again.

In half-duplex, the receiving computer does *not* echo what you have sent, and what you type in will *not* appear on your screen. Should you accidentally have your modem set to half-duplex when you are calling a system designed for full-duplex operation, you will get a very confusing result. In the example about typing in my name, I would get double letters: "Mike" would become "MMiikkee." Don't worry if this happens to you. You are not ruining your modem or damaging the other computer. Simply reset your modem for full-duplex.

Unless otherwise noted, the directory listings in *The Computer Phone Book* are for systems operating in full-duplex. Simply set your modem to transmit and receive in full-duplex.

The last modem setting you will be concerned with has to do with which computer is calling which. Since you will mainly be calling other computers, set your modem for *originate*. The modem setting, *answer*, would be used, for example, if a friend was going to call your computer with his or her computer. Your computer would have to "answer" the phone, just as you would if your friend were calling you.

A communications software package is the next piece of equipment you will need in order to go online. Such software will instruct your computer to act as a *terminal*; that is, a device connected to the computer that may access information.

Most modems used with personal computers require a communications program. You may find that the modem you purchase for your computer includes such software. If so, it will most likely be a simple program, lacking many of the features you will need to have later. Nonetheless, it will allow you to call another computer and become comfortable with telecommunications. That is all that matters in the beginning.

Once again we come across a question of standards. Not every system you will call transmits and receives information in precisely the same way. Differences exist because of what the systems have to offer and the purposes for which they were designed. This is where your communications program fits in. Each system you will call requires a *communications protocol*. This is simply a way of assuring that your computer is speaking the same language as the one you are calling, that is, transmitting and receiving in the same manner. Your communications software will allow you to set the communications protocol you will need. The protocol consists of three things: word length, parity, and stop bits.

The Computer Phone Book cites the communications protocols for the systems listed in its directory. Although you could just enter the protocol needed, it would be best if you first know something about what you are doing.

The first setting is called *word length*, but that is somewhat misleading. It does not actually mean the length of a word; rather, it means the number of bits that comprise a single character. The ASCII code uses seven bits, with an extra bit (a zero) at the beginning of the seven. This first bit is known as a *start bit*. It lets the receiving computer know that the seven bits following it comprise a single character. Some systems you will call will not want this start bit; others will. Therefore, it is necessary for you to set your word length to either seven or eight, as required.

The second setting, *parity*, refers to a single bit that is transmitted with the seven or eight word bits. It is transmitted at the end of the seven or eight bit cluster and acts as an error-checking mechanism, mainly in the transfer of long files of text or programs. This specification would be set in your software to even, odd, or none (abbreviated in the directory section as E, O, and N), as required.

After your computer has sent a cluster of word bits (and a parity bit, if needed), it may also have to send one or more *stop bits*. These are bits that, in effect, tell the receiving computer the following: "You have just received all of the word bits that comprise a single character." The computer will then know that it has received one character and will be ready to accept the next stream of bits representing the next character. In your program, you would set the stop bit to zero, one, two, or more, as needed. Your communications program is now ready to be used.

In review, you have set your modem as follows:

- Speed: 300 bps
- Duplex: Full
- Mode: Originate

You have set your communications program as follows:

- Word length (7 or 8)
- Parity: Even, odd, or none
- Stop bits (0, 1, 2, or more)

You are almost ready to telecommunicate!

The next steps you will have to take to get online depend on how your communications software works and the type of modem you are using. Before taking these steps, however, read the next two chapters, or you will not know what to do if you happen to find yourself online with a system.

If your communications software has a dialing program in it, follow the instructions in your manual and enter a system phone number in your local area from the directory in *The Computer Phone Book*. If you are using an acoustic-coupled modem, or if your software lacks a dialing program, you will have to dial the number yourself.

After you (or your software) have dialed a system number, the system you are calling will pick up and emit a *carrier signal*. This is a high-pitched single-tone whine. If you are using an acoustic-coupled modem, you will have to place the telephone handset in the twin cups quickly, making sure it fits snugly. If you are using a direct-connect modem, you may hear part of the carrier signal through your computer's speaker or the modem itself. Depending on your modem and software, you may see "CONNECTED" or "ONLINE" on your screen, or you may see an indicator light on your modem come on. Whichever way it happens in your system, you are now online!

One of the things you may want to do online, as mentioned earlier, is to transmit or receive text or programs. This is one of the most exciting aspects of telecommunications. Many features of systems are listed in the directory section of *The Computer Phone Book*; among them are *messaging* and *program downloading*. Although all of the features that systems offer will be covered later, I will now focus on these two aspects because they affect the type of communications software you may need.

Messaging will enable you to read notices, questions, comments, and replies to other such messages posted by users of the systems you call. At one point, you may find yourself reading a question someone had posted to which you know the answer. It may be a question that involves a long answer. You will not be doing your phone bill any good if you sit at your computer, type in the reply one letter at a time, and have to edit your mistakes. Or you may find that after you have started to type in your reply that you cannot collect your thoughts as completely or quickly as you had hoped. In the meantime, you are tying up your phone, tying up the system, and wasting time and money. What you will want is a way to compose your reply (and any other future messages you may have) while you are *offline* (off the phone) and then be able to transmit the completed reply to the system at the touch of a single key.

Similarly, one day you will discover that a system you have called has a free program that you can use. You would like to have that program very much, but what do you do? Do you sit there and meticulously write down the program on paper as it scrolls across your screen? You would risk making errors—especially by the time you reached line 1000! You would also risk eyestrain, writer's cramp, having to decipher your frantic shorthand, and a huge phone bill.

Instead, you will want a way of receiving that program so that you can review it at your leisure while you are offline, or print it out (this is an example of how a printer comes in handy), or save it on a cassette or disk to run it later. Both of the above situations can be handled swiftly and easily if you purchase the proper communications software.

Although all communications programs are known as *terminal emulators* and allow your computer to act as if it were wired to the computer with which it is communicating, there are two kinds of terminals: dumb and smart. A *dumb terminal* is only able to display the information it retrieves while online. A communications program that emulates such a terminal will only allow you to go online with a system and read the output on your screen. Unlike your computer, a dumb terminal cannot manipulate or store information because it does not have a brain (central processing unit—CPU) or memory (RAM).

To be able to get the most out of the systems you will call, you will have to purchase a communications program that emulates a *smart terminal*. Depending on your particular computer system, a smart terminal program may allow you to use your printer while you are online, capture what you are looking at on your screen so you can save it to a cassette tape or floppy disk, and transmit previously composed text. In short, it literally allows you to have information at your fingertips. Information can be virtually anything: regular text (such as a message), a program that you can run on your computer, or (in limited instances) graphics.

When you are transmitting information *to* another computer, the process is known as *uploading*. When you are receiving information *from* another computer, the process is known as *downloading*. Uploading and downloading are accomplished by using a communications program that has a buffer. As you may know, when you load a program into your computer, it resides in memory. When you load the appropriate communications program, it will take a portion of your computer's available memory and set it aside as a space where you can put other information. This space is called a *buffer*. For example, if you have a computer with 64K of memory, you could get a communications program that will set aside 32K of the memory into which you could type a message to upload to another computer later. Or you could use that 32K to download information (text or a program) from another computer. The type of communications program that you buy depends on the type of computer that you have, your computer's memory size, and what you intend to do when you are online.

For your convenience, *The Computer Phone Book*'s Appendix 2 lists suppliers of communications software for personal computers. If you do not see your computer listed in this appendix, you will certainly find advertisements for suitable software in most of the popular personal computer magazines.

In addition to uploading and downloading, communications software may include options and features such as a *directory* into which you can place frequently called system phone numbers; an *online timer*, which keeps you alerted as to how long you have been online (one program even calculates how much the phone call has cost you or how much your connect-time charge was for that session); a simple *text editor* so you can make certain that your precomposed messages are free of typos; an *auto-logon* feature, which permits you to store your account number and password so you can sign on to a system with just the press of a key; an *addressable cursor*, a nice feature to have if you are calling a university timesharing system or playing an online game that can take advantage of it; *command storage*, which lets the program execute frequently used system commands at the touch of a key or automatically while unattended; and the option of uploading information in a *continuous stream* or just *line by line*.

These are just some of the many options available. You may find that your computer's available communications programs do not have many of the above features. Remember, though, that not all of the features are needed for every online system. There are very few smart terminal programs that are not useful. It is a good idea to shop around, ask questions, and read reviews of programs available for your computer.

Regardless of your computer, modem, and communications software, you can have an exciting time online by using the many systems and their services covered in Chapter 2.

CHAPTER 2
Overview of Online Systems

An often asked question in regard to telecommunications systems is, Why should I pay for that? Indeed, Why?

This question is certainly reasonable, but the answer is usually not well thought out. Telecommunications systems deliver information and services in a certain form. The form of the information is electronic, and it is primarily delivered over the telephone lines.

The type of information and services being delivered is somewhat similar to existing ones. Let's consider news as an example. You can get news from several existing sources: a newspaper, a radio, or a television. In each of these cases, you are paying for the information and service. You buy a newspaper directly; you buy products advertised on radio and television, which provides advertising revenues to support those media.

The difference between those three forms of news and electronically delivered news is that the latter is available *when you want it*. You don't have to wait for a truck to deliver a newspaper or for a certain hour to listen to or watch the news on radio or television. By using a telecommunications system, you just make a phone call and you can have all the news you want *when you want it*. That is what you are paying for—the privilege of having what you want *when you want it*. All else is a bonus.

In addition to electronic news, there are other things that may interest or excite you, such as electronic mail. There is no need for you to wait several days to receive a letter through the postal system. You can call the telecommunications system to which you subscribe and your mail will be displayed on your screen. You may reply to it immediately and that reply will be instantly transmitted to its recipient. There is no need for you to rely on the physical movement of paper for your written communications. You can have mail *when you want it*.

Another area that might interest you is banking. Suppose that you work an irregular shift and never have the opportunity to get to your bank. You have been banking by mail, but it has been taking too long for your paycheck to clear. Your bills are getting backlogged, your checkbook is a mess, and you do not even have any clear idea of how much is in your account. If you are a subscriber to a telecommunications system, you can just make a phone call and instantly see how much is in your bank account, which checks are in the process of clearing, and which bills have been paid. You may also choose to pay your bills by transferring the funds from your account to your creditor's account directly. You do not have to lose a wink of sleep, lick another stamp, or stand in line waiting to be served by a teller or a banking machine. You can have banking *when you want it*.

The above examples illustrate the three types of services available to you on a telecommunications system: information, communications, and transactions. *Information* ranges from news to reference libraries; *communications* range from simple electronic mail to live electronic conversations with many people at once; and *transactions* range from banking to shopping from an online catalog that allows you to comparison shop and get the best available price. All three are available to you in the comfort of your own home, any time of the day or night, and are no farther away than your telephone.

When the telephone was invented and began to be placed in offices, people had to deal with new words such as "operator," "dial," and "receiver," as well as the word "telephone" itself. Similarly, telecommunications systems have their own buzzwords, separate from the ones you had to learn when you started to use your personal computer.

The first word is database. A *database* is simply a collection of information in electronic form. For example, a collection of information would be your printed telephone directory; it would be a database once it has been put into electronic form.

Network is a word you are probably familiar with, living in the age of television. Like a TV network, a telecommunications network is available across the nation. The actual network that delivers information and services to you is the existing telephone wires that are spread throughout the world.

Value-added network (also known as *packet-switched network*) is a special telephone network designed to handle data communications (in other words, computer-to-computer communications). It enables you to make long-distance data phone calls without the expense of long-distance voice-grade phone calls.

Value-added carrier is the actual company that owns a value-added network. Value-added carriers for data communications are companies such as Transcanada Telephone System (offering DataPac), GTE Telenet (Telenet), Tymnet, Inc. (Tymnet), and British Telecom International (PSS).

Information utility is the actual collection of computers that store and make available to you information, communication, and transaction services. The computers are called *mainframes*. Since they are offering you the service, they are also called the *host*.

Connect-time is the phrase used to describe the per hour fee most information utilities charge you for *access*, that is, for the amount of time you are using them.

In summary, in computer talk, you will access a database on an information utility by using a value-added network and be charged for your connect-time. Or, in English, you will call a local number and use your personal computer and modem to use a variety of services that are priced at a rate that is described as an hourly increment.

There are three types of telecommunications systems: National Networks, Local-Area Services, and Bulletin-Board Systems. The above is true for only one of these types, *National Networks*. When you subscribe to a National Network, you will be furnished with a local phone number that will enable you to use a value-added network. In general, there will not be an additional charge for using a value-added network. Connect-time rates of national networks are divided into two categories: prime time and non-prime time. *Prime time* is generally from 8 AM to 6 PM, weekdays. *Non-prime time* is from 6 PM to 8 AM weekdays and includes weekends and most holidays. You will generally use non-prime time, as it is less expensive and is priced to be used by the average home computer owner.

With *Local-Area Services*, you will most likely pay a flat monthly fee and have unlimited connect-time. A Local-Area Service can best be described as the electronic equivalent of a local newspaper, featuring information and services of a regional interest.

Bulletin-Board Systems (BBSs) are operated on microcomputers and are mostly maintained by computer hobbyists and some businesses. They can handle only one user at a time, which means that you will get a busy signal if someone else is using the system when you call it. If you live in a one-BBS town, you might have to wait quite a while before you can get through to the system. Some *system operators* (*sysops*) have therefore instituted time limits of anywhere from 20 to 60 minutes to allow more callers a chance to use their systems.

When you call any one of these three types of systems, you will be presented with one of three ways of accessing information and services. The first way is by a series of menus. A *menu* is a list of choices available to you; each choice may or may not be numbered. If they are numbered, you simply type in the number that corresponds to the selection you want. If they are not numbered, you have to type in either the first letter of the selection or the entire word, depending on the system.

The second way is by using keywords. A *keyword* is either a word or a unique group of letters that you have to type in to get what you want. Instead of a menu, systems that use keywords will provide a user's manual containing a list of keywords for access. These systems also contain an online list of existing keywords and new keywords as they appear.

The third way of accessing the contents of a system is by direct commands. A *direct command*, which is similar to a keyword in some cases, will usually contain another word, such as a verb, that will tell the system to take a specific action.

Menu-driven, keyword-driven, and *command-driven* are the ways in which a system's method of accessing is described. Although these ways may sound confusing at the moment, the examples of each in Chapter 3 will clarify them for you. To orient you for Chapter 3, a brief description of some systems follows; comprehensive descriptions of available systems appear in the directory section of this book.

NATIONAL NETWORKS

BRS After Dark is from Bibliographic Retrieval Service (BRS), a company that has primarily provided databases to businesses, universities, and libraries. In late 1982, BRS instituted its After Dark service, offering several of its databases to the general public at a fraction of the cost its professional clients pay. As its name implies, BRS After Dark is available during non-prime time.

BRS After Dark is mainly a research tool; it has databases that will provide you with information about reports and articles from magazines, professional journals, industry publications, government studies, and other printed sources in the categories of Science & Medicine, Business & Financial, Reference, Education, Social Science & Humanities, and Energy & Environmental. Some databases provide a summary (called an *abstract*) of the printed versions. BRS After Dark is, in effect, a vast storehouse of information that will provide you with seed material for any research you may need to do for school, business, or personal reasons.

BRS After Dark uses a menu structure to help you select the databases you need. It then allows you to enter your own keywords on subjects you would like information about. Its main menu offers you the following choices: Search Service (which allows you to access databases in the categories previously mentioned), Newsletter Service, Software Service, Electronic Mail Service, Swap Shop, Sneak Preview, and the ability to change your password.

At the time *The Computer Phone Book* was being written, BRS After Dark had implemented only the Search Service portion of its system. As the titles of its other services suggest, BRS After Dark will be offering an online newsletter; a software purchasing and downloading service; an electronic mail service to permit users to communicate among one another privately; and a Swap Shop, which will be a bulletin board on which users can post notices for others to read and respond to.

In summary, BRS After Dark is designed to be a research tool to help you to gather and sort through large quantities of information efficiently and effectively.

The *CompuServe Information Service* was started in 1979 as a personal computer timesharing service called MicroNET. CompuServe (the parent company) had timesharing mainframes standing idle after business hours and decided to put them to use by offering the power of a mainframe at a price the general public could afford. MicroNET consisted of downloadable programs, electronic mail, online file storage, and mainframe computing languages. In July 1980, CompuServe wrapped their Information Service around MicroNET and have been building upon it ever since.

The CompuServe Information Service is a menu-driven system with information arranged in frames called *pages*. Each page is 32 characters wide by 16 lines deep and is formatted to take advantage of what was, at the time, the lowest-priced video terminal available to the general public: the *TRS Videotex* terminal. On CompuServe, you press a number on your keyboard that corresponds to your menu choice, flipping through a series of menus until you arrive at the information you are seeking. Some CompuServe sections are command driven as well.

CompuServe's main menu is divided into six categories: Home Services, Business & Financial, Personal Computing, Services for Professionals, User Information, and Index. These broad categories encompass sub-menus with as many as 23 choices. From the deceptively few choices on the main menu, CompuServe branches out to a staggering array of services, the most notable of which are the CB Simulator and Special Interest Groups.

The CB Simulator is similar to a CB radio in that many people can talk on it at one time. In addition, people use handles instead of their real names. The difference between CompuServe's CB and CB radio is, of course, that everyone "talks" by typing on his or her computer's keyboard. The CB Simulator is one of CompuServe's most popular services, and there are subscribers to the system who never venture beyond using CB.

Special Interest Groups (called SIGs) are virtually miniature CompuServes themselves, offering a bulletin board for messaging, databases for text files and downloadable software, and its own version of the CB Simulator. There are over 30 SIGs on CompuServe, ranging in interest from family topics, working at home, and education to individual SIGs for users of specific brands of personal computers, for example, an Apple SIG for users of Apple Computers. In each SIG, you will be surrounded by experts and novices alike, all willing to help you with any questions you may have. No other national network comes close to offering what CompuServe does in its SIGs.

There is virtually something for everyone on CompuServe. If you do not see what you want on the system, chances are it will show up soon. CompuServe adds new services and databases almost every week.

Connexions is a national network that you can use to look for a job in high-technology professions. Connexions allows you to scan online classified advertisements for job positions. It is a menu-driven system on which a series of qualification questions leads you to positions that meet your requirements. You can place your resume online in a file and send it electronically to potential employers. If you are looking for a job or are thinking of changing your present job, Connexions is a resource you may want to tap.

Delphi™, from General Videotex Corporation, is a newcomer to the ranks of national networks, having started operation in February 1983. Prior to that, it was the first online encyclopedia made available to the general public. General Videotex built upon their encyclopedia much as CompuServe built upon MicroNET.

Delphi is another menu-structured system, but unlike CompuServe you do not press a number key to make a selection. Instead, you will have to type in the first one or two letters of the selection's title. Also, you can set the length of the menus that appear on your screen, a feature that allows you to learn at your own pace and that, among national networks, is unique to Delphi. You may choose, for example, to see a full menu, a one-sentence question, or a one-word prompt.

Delphi has 17 selections on its main menu, more than any other menu-driven national network. Some of these selections will lead you directly to a service, whereas others will take you to another menu or series of menus. The main menu choices are Appointment Calendar, Banking, Bulletin-Boards, Conference, Delphi-Oracle, Exit (to leave the system), Games, Guided Tour, Help, Infomania, Library, Mail, News, Online Markets, Profile, Travel, and Writer's Corner.

A highlight of Delphi is Conference, which, like CompuServe's CB Simulator, is a real-time multiuser talk program. You will become familiar with it in Chapter 3.

Guided Tour, another feature that is unique to Delphi, is what you will see when you access Delphi for the first time. As its name suggests, you are given a guided tour of the system by which you will learn its navigational commands and will set the system's output so it will format itself for your computer's individual screen size.

Infomania, at the time *The Computer Phone Book* was being written, only offered one of its six planned services, Collaborative Novel. Here you write a *chapter* (one or more paragraphs) of one of several novels in progress (or create your own), and other users add to it. The results can be surprising and are often hilarious.

Library offers you an online encyclopedia and connections, called *gateways*, to the ITT-Dialcom and Dialog® Information Retrieval Service networks. Please note, however, that the Dialog gateway does not offer the Knowledge Index service (which is also from Dialog), described later in this chapter.

Although a good deal of Delphi had not yet been implemented as *The Computer Phone Book* was being written, Delphi's plans are to emerge as a strong contender in the national network race.

Dow Jones News/Retrieval Service®, from Dow Jones & Company, Inc., started in 1974 and has more subscribers than any national network currently operating. Designed primarily for business users, its success is due to the fact that it focuses on timely and comprehensive financial information and news.

Dow Jones News/Retrieval, although primarily keyword and command driven, also offers a Master Menu that will help to orient you once you are online. The user's manual for the service contains all of the information you will need in order to use the updated portions of the news and financial databases. A separate manual, described in Chapter 3, is needed to use the historical news database.

If you want to track the financial status of corporations or your personal investments, Dow Jones News/Retrieval will offer you the most efficient and effective way to do so.

EIES, pronounced "eyes" and meaning *Electronic Information Exchange System*, is from the New Jersey Institute of Technology.

EIES is primarily a conferencing system. Unlike the conference systems on CompuServe and Delphi, EIES's conferencing is not live; this means that you do not have to be online at a certain time to discuss topics with others. Instead, EIES can best be described as a bulletin-board-like system, with its messages arranged in a logical order and time progression.

Although it is menu and command driven, EIES can be very confusing to a new user, more so than any other national network. This confusion arises from the many options that are available on the system. The system requires intense study to become adept at using it.

EIES is not for the casual user. It is intended as a serious forum for the exchange of ideas and opinions on a variety of political, technological, aesthetic, and philosophical topics.

Knowledge Index, like BRS After Dark, is a research tool. That is all it is. You will not find services such as electronic mail or bulletin boards on it. Knowledge Index, provided by Lockheed-Dialog Information Services, was established in late 1982 to offer subsets of the databases available on Dialog Information Retrieval Service, the largest collection of commercially available information in the world.

Knowledge Index is command driven and sifts through millions of records according to subject keywords you supply. Dialog provides you with a comprehensive user's manual that is designed to help you use the service with the least amount of online time possible. An extra service provided by Knowledge Index is the ability to order copies of articles that are summarized on the system; for an additional fee, the article will be mailed to you, saving you a trip to a library.

Categories of information available on Knowledge Index include Agriculture, Business Information, Computers & Electronics, Corporate News, Education, Engineering, Government Publications, Magazines, Medicine, News, and Psychology. These represent a collection of over 10 million records from over 10,000 different sources. All of this is made available at a flat hourly charge and allows you to have the full power of a professional, prime time, search service at your disposal.

NewsNet, which started operations in 1981, is the first network dedicated solely to providing newsletters in electronic form. There are over 120 newsletters available. Most of them are online editions of printed products; several are only available electronically on NewsNet.

Newsletter categories include Advertising & Marketing, Aerospace, Automotive, Building & Construction, Chemical, Corporate Communications, Education, Electronics & Computers, Energy, Entertainment & Leisure, Environment, Farming & Food, Finance & Accounting, General Business, Government & Regulatory, Health & Hospitals, International, Investment, Law, Management, Manufacturing, Metals & Mining, Office, Politics, Public Relations, Publishing & Broadcasting, Real Estate, Research & Development, Social Sciences, Taxation, and Telecommunications.

NewsNet will be of interest to you if you need more than historical information and want to keep on top of late-breaking developments in a wide range of fields without the expense of subscribing to several thousand dollars' worth of newsletters.

OAG EE, the *Official Airline Guides Electronic Edition*, is a single database that is an online version of the printed *Official Airline Guides*. Although OAG EE is available on other systems, the advantages of subscribing to it separately are quicker access to flight information and not having to wade through or be distracted by unwanted material. OAG EE will allow you to comparison shop among airlines, thereby getting the lowest available flight fares for business or personal trips.

Photonet, although mainly for professional photographers, is included in *The Computer Phone Book* because it is a communications network, not simply specialized information retrieval, and its rates are competitive with other networks available to the general public. Photonet is a menu-driven service that started operating in July 1983. It primarily offers bulletin boards, electronic mail, an online magazine, and databases that are of interest to those in the photographic profession.

Bulletin-board categories include Ad Agencies, Stock Photo Agencies, Professional Photographers, Model & Talent, Film & TV Producers, Book & Magazine Publishers; Graphic Designers, and Printers.

The Source[sm] is the old timer of national networks aimed at the general public. It was the first to go online and was designed for novice users. The Source was created by the Telecomputing Corporation of America in 1979, and was bought by the Reader's Digest Association in 1980.

First designed and offered as a command-driven system, under the guidance of Reader's Digest, The Source had an optional menu structure grafted onto it. This has made it easier for first-time users to find their way around the system and also acts as a road map for users who happen to get lost at command level.

The Source's main menu is divided into eight categories of information and services: News & Reference Resources, Business/Financial Markets, Catalogue Shopping, Home & Leisure, Education & Career, Mail & Communications, Creating & Computing, and Source* Plus.

Highlights of The Source include the most powerful and flexible electronic mail system of any national network. Among the features of SourceMail (or SMail, as it is known) is the ability to send letters to a mailing list you have created and placed online in your personal filespace, to send carbon copies or blind carbon copies of letters to others, to forward received letters to others, to send Mailgrams, and to file your mail. You can also use its powerful text editor to format your letters and correct typos.

POST is The Source's bulletin-board facility, which contains more subject categories than any other national network. In *The Computer Phone Book* directory listing of The Source, you will find a complete list of POST categories. POST is where most things happen on The Source. It also acts as an industry grapevine. If something is happening in the world of personal computers, you are almost certain to find out about it first on POST.

User Publishing, or PUBLIC, is another interesting feature of The

Source. Subscribers may publish electronic online journals and earn a royalty from the connect-time their publications generate. There are a variety of interests represented, although the quality of the material varies.

Finally, The Source's PARTICIPATE system is where users gather to hold conferences in a manner similar to that of EIES. The quality of discussion and topics vary from conference to conference and person to person, but you are able to start your own conference if the topic (or topics) that interests you are not being covered.

Travelhost Network is another newcomer to the national network roster, having come online in April 1983. The publishers of the in-hotel *Travelhost* magazine have made this network available in hotel rooms. The Travelhost network uses a custom-designed terminal with special function keys that allow one-button access to information and services.

To use the Travelhost network in a hotel room, you need not become a regular subscriber; all you need is a valid credit card to which connect-time charges may be billed.

The Travelhost network offers electronic mail, a national restaurant guide, an online catalog shopping service, UPI Unistox, the Official Airlines Guides Electronic Edition, a library of text games, a job opportunity and resume-sending service, a database for the Travelhost Travel Club, and a travel service for advance booking of flights and hotel reservations.

Travelhost has plans to offer their system to home users, which may be available by the time you are reading this.

LOCAL-AREA SERVICES

A-T Videotext, based in Tiffin, Ohio, is a general-purpose system run by the *Tiffin Advertiser-Tribune* newspaper. It is a keyword-driven system available at a flat monthly rate with no hourly connect-time charges.

Buy-Phone started operations in 1983 and serves the Los Angeles, California, area. The menu-driven Buy-Phone is touted as being an "electronic yellow pages," offering over 10,000 listings of local merchants and services. System access, which is supported by local merchant advertising, is free.

CLEO, an acronym for *Computerized Listings of Employment Op-*

portunities, is a database of high-technology employment listings. Access to this menu-driven system is free.

DataPost, another free system, is located in Columbus, Ohio, and started operations in 1982. It offers DataPost, a general-interest bulletin board; Scan, a library of text files of different subjects; the *Columbus Business Journal,* the only service on the system that requires a fee; and AtariPost, a bulletin-board facility for owners of Atari home computers and videogames.

DEC-Line, also free, is located in Woodland Hills, California. This menu-driven system offers a general-interest bulletin board and a real-time multiuser conferencing facility.

GameMaster™, located in Chicago, Illinois, started operations the same day as The Source. It has the distinctions of being the oldest local service and of offering more multiuser computer games than any other system, local or national. Designed as an electronic mansion, GameMaster offers both text and graphic games, as well as a real-time multiuser conferencing program. A menu structure is available for new users. There is an hourly connect-time charge.

Harris Electronic News, in Hutchinson, Kansas, is a keyword-driven service offering general-interest and specialized business information. There is a flat monthly fee for use and no hourly connect-time charges.

MicroShare, located in Milwaukee, Wisconsin, started in 1982. It charges an hourly fee for access to its huge library of public-domain CP/M™-format programs. The system also offers a large selection of online text games.

StarText Metro serves the MetroPlex area of Fort Worth and Dallas, Texas. This system, which is keyword driven, charges a flat monthly fee for use. It is the largest local-area service of its type.

BULLETIN-BOARD SYSTEMS

Bulletin-Board Systems use a variety of software formats and microcomputers as hosts. Just as there is no standard National Network or Local-Area Service, there is no one standard BBS.

Among the packaged systems software you will come across are *ABBS (Apple Bulletin-Board System), AMIS (Atari*™ *Message and Information System), Bullet-80* (all -80 suffixes indicate a TRS-80-hosted system), *CBBS*™ *(Computerized Bulletin Board System), Connection-80, Conference Tree, Dial-Your-Match*™, *Forum-80*™,

Net-Works, *PMS (People's Message Service)*, and *RCP/M (Remote CP/M;* generally coupled with a CBBS or RBBS—Remote BBS). You will learn the differences among these various BBS formats in Chapter 3 and in Appendix 1 at the back of *The Computer Phone Book*.

Although you have seen the word "videotex" in the brief overview of systems, no definition of the word has been given. Actually, there are two terms that need to be defined—videotex and teletext.

Videotex is generally used to describe a system that relies heavily on graphics as part of the information and services it offers. In the strictest sense, a *videotex system* is one that uses a non-ASCII coding format to transmit and display text and graphics. The major coding standards (at this time there is not just one standard) for videotex are Prestel (the first standard devised; it originated in Great Britain), Telidon (from Canada), and PLP (Presentation-Level Protocol; from AT&T in the United States). All of these standards are meant to be used with specially designed terminals or decoder boxes that can accept and display the color graphics on a monitor or TV screen. Like the system you will be calling, videotex is usually transmitted over telephone lines, although there have been tests of sending it over cable TV. Unlike the systems you will be calling, the transmission speed of videotex is usually 1200 bps from the host and 75 bps to the host. As you can see, that is quite different from the 300/300 and 1200/1200 bps speeds personal computers presently use, as discussed in Chapter 1.

Although some systems listed in *The Computer Phone Book* call themselves videotex systems, they are not since they are ASCII based, contain no graphics, and may be accessed by any sort of personal computer or terminal. At the time *The Computer Phone Book* was being written, only two videotex systems qualified to be listed; they will be described shortly.

Teletext is a service that is transmitted over regular broadcast television; the broadcast signal may also be picked up and carried on cable TV. Like videotex, it relies on graphics to accompany the information it offers, and you need a special decoder box to receive it on your TV. Teletext cannot be accessed by personal computers, and there are no teletext systems listed in *The Computer Phone Book*.

SPECIAL SERVICES

Special Services are ones that do not fall under the general category of microcomputer telecommunications. *Citylink* is such a service and is based on the Prestel videotex standard. Based in and serving Boston, Massachusetts, Citylink started operation in Fall 1983 and offers information and services for the general business public. It may be accessed by personal computers using special communications software.

GameLine™ is a service that falls between the cracks of conventional telecommunications definitions and systems. It is a system for the downloading of videogames into Atari VCS™ (and VCS-compatible) videogame consoles. A special Master Module™ cartridge is used to receive and temporarily store the downloaded game.

Prestel World Service, based in Great Britain, is the oldest videotex system in existence. Although geared primarily to business users, Prestel has recently added a service called Micronet 800 (no relation to CompuServe's former MicroNET area) that features information and downloadable software for owners of personal computers.

Now that you have had an overview of the many telecommunications systems that are available, you are ready to see how some of them operate and how you can use them to your best advantage. It all starts in Chapter 3.

CHAPTER 3

How to Use the Online Systems

The first feeling you will have when you subscribe to a system such as a National Network or Local-Area Service is excitement. When your account number and password are given to you (either by purchasing it in a computer store, ordering it with your credit card over the telephone, or having it sent to you through the mail), you will feel a mounting eagerness to get on the system you have chosen and to join the thousands of other people across the country who are busily telecommunicating.

On the other hand, your first feeling when you actually sign on to a system—be it national, local, or bulletin board—may be sheer terror. Not having had any prior experience in using such a communications medium, you may be afraid of making a mistake or of looking like a dolt who hasn't the native intelligence to understand which button to press. Worse, you may fear breaking the system you are using and having to pay several million dollars for the banks of computers you destroyed by pressing the wrong key on your computer.

Since computers are made to help you, not frighten you, this chapter is designed to give you a solid understanding of how the systems listed in *The Computer Phone Book* work and to allay any anxiety you may have. In principle, if you learn how to use *one* system, you can easily learn how to use *any* system, whether you start out by using a BBS and then subscribe to a National Network or vice versa. All systems share ways of doing things. Although all systems are similar in principle, however, there are stylistic differences. Therefore, just showing you how one system operates will not do. By seeing a broad range of systems, you will have a better understanding of what you will need to do when you go online.

National Networks and Local-Area Services provide their subscribers with user's manuals that give full details and illustrations of how their particular system operates. This chapter is not meant to act as a substitute for those user's manuals. Instead, you should think of this chapter as a sneak preview of what is available to you, allowing you to see what awaits you at the other side of your computer's modem without you having to go online to find out.

On the BBS level, you will generally not be furnished with a user's manual. However, the majority of BBSs offer complete *documentation* (user's manuals) online. If you don't have a communications program to download this or a printer to make a copy for yourself, you will find yourself reading nothing but instructions for anywhere from 15 minutes to 1 hour. As you can imagine, this is not fun despite the fact that BBSs are made to be fun. To save you from this frustration, *The Computer Phone Book* contains the instruction files from several BBS software formats. Thus, before you go online with a BBS, you can simply review the instructions reprinted here.

When you are seated in front of your computer's screen, you will see text moving from the bottom to the top. This is called *scrolling*. There will be times when you will need to read carefully and absorb what is scrolling on your screen. If you are a slow reader or the material is very long or involved, you will want a way of temporarily stopping the scrolling so that you can either catch up with it or review it again. Similarly, there will be times when you have made a mistake in your selection and want to stop the text output and start all over again.

Control functions enable you to stop and restart scrolling, as well as to interrupt output. On your computer keyboard, you will see a key marked Control or Ctrl or Ctl. This key, when pressed in conjunction with one of several letter keys, sends a command to the system you are on, telling the system to perform one of several actions. These actions include pause output, resume output, redisplay the characters you have entered, skip text at high speed, stop the current operation and be ready to accept a new selection or command, erase the characters you have entered, and more. Although each system is particular about which Control commands it will accept, commonly used ones are as follows:

Control-C: This interrupts the current command the system is executing and returns it to a state of readiness so you can enter a new command or make a new selection.

Control-G: This sounds a bell on your computer. Not all systems permit this.

Control-H: This moves your cursor back one space so that you may erase a letter you have typed in and replace it with the correct one.

Control-O: This tells the system to skip through the text it is sending you and stop at the end.

Control-P: This function is similar to Control-C. Some systems use both, whereas some only accept Control-P.

Control-Q: This will resume output, restarting the scrolling of paused text.

Control-R: On some systems this function redisplays the line you have typed into the system. On a printing terminal, this command is handy if you have overwritten your text by overusing Control-H and need to see the text clearly.

Control-S: This causes a pause in output, stopping the scrolling of text so you can read it without feeling rushed.

Control-U: This erases the entire line you have typed into the system and allows you to type in a new one.

Control-V: This is a function similar to Control-R. Some systems use this instead of Control-R.

Control-Z: On some systems, this function indicates *end of file*, a command that is used to tell the system that the file you have typed in or uploaded is completed and should be stored.

All of the above functions are executed by you pressing your Control key and the letter next to it *at the same time*. Think of the Control key as being similar to the Shift key: When you want a capital letter, you hold down Shift and the letter. The same method is used in executing a Control function.

If you are using a TRS-80® computer, you will have to press your Shift key, down arrow key, and the function letter *all at the same time* in order to execute any of the Control functions. Depending on the type of communications software you are using, you may have to use different keys to execute these functions on a Commodore computer. Check your user's manual.

Aside from Control functions, there are other commands that you may have access to on your computer's keyboard: Escape (or Esc), Delete (or Del), Rub Out (or Rbout), and Break (or Brk).

Much like Control-C and Control-P, Escape and Break are generally used to interrupt a function. Delete and Rub Out are used in place of Control-H to move the cursor one space to the left to erase a character.

One other key you will need to use is labeled either Return or Enter on your keyboard. If you are using a Sinclair ZX-80, 81, or a Spectrum, this key will be labeled Newline. This key is what you will press after entering a command, making a selection, or typing in anything to a system except a Control function. Until you press this key, what you have typed in will not be executed by any National Network or Local-Area Service. This is not the case on some BBSs, which will be explained later in this chapter.

All of these keys place the system at your beck and call. The system is working for you, not the other way around. These keys give you flexibility in accessing what you want and allow you to correct any typing mistakes.

When you are using systems and encounter anything that is alien to your online experience, such as a system that seems to be acting strangely or malfunctioning altogether, you should blame the system, not yourself. Hundreds of thousands of people have already used the systems listed in *The Computer Phone Book*. If the systems were prone to fail at the slightest touch of the wrong key, this book would not be possible. Don't worry: *There is nothing you can do to accidentally break a system.*

NATIONAL NETWORKS

Having learned the keyboard functions available to you, you are now ready for a preview of the various systems. Following the order of presentation in Chapter 2, the first system you will get a peek at is BRS After Dark.

BRS After Dark

BRS After Dark provides an excellent user's manual that is filled with sample screens from each database available on the system, shows a sample *query* (*search question*) you might ask, and gives the format in which each database presents its information. After you have called your local number for a *packet-switched* network (provided in the user's manual) and entered your account number and password, you will be given the following instructions:

WELCOME TO BRS AFTER DARK
PLEASE TYPE IN SCREEN LINE LENGTH (20, 40 or 80)

After you reply accordingly by typing in one of those numbers, you are asked:

IF YOU ARE USING A VIDEO TERMINAL, ENTER THE NUMBER OF LINES ON YOUR SCREEN. (EG 20, 21, 22).

You type in the number that is suitable for your terminal. If you are using a printing terminal, respond to this by just hitting your Return key. After this, you will see the following:

TONIGHT'S MENU IS:

NUMBER	ITEM
1	LOOKING FOR INFORMATION? . . . SEARCH SERVICE
2	WANT TO HEAR THE LATEST? . . . NEWSLETTER SERVICE
3	NEED A PROGRAM? . . . SOFTWARE SERVICE
4	KEEP IN TOUCH! . . . ELECTRONIC MAIL SERVICE
5	LET'S MAKE A DEAL . . . SWAP SHOP
6	WANT A SNEAK PREVIEW? . . . COMING ATTRACTIONS
7	WANT TO CHANGE YOUR SECURITY PASSWORD? . . . SECURITY

TYPE IN MENU ITEM NUMBER THEN HIT ENTER KEY FOR DESIRED SELECTION

Before the above is explained to you, you should understand the significance of the first two items you responded to at signon. The above list is formatted for an 80-column screen, that is, a screen that can fit a line that is 80 characters in length. If your computer's screen is fewer than 80 columns, you would need to specify that, so that what you will see on your screen is not confusing or scrambled. If you have a 20-column screen, for example, and said so when you signed on, the above would look like this:

TONIGHT'S MENU IS . . .

NUMBER   ITEM
   1   LOOKING FOR
          INFORMATION
          . . . . .SEARCH
          SERVICE

   2   WANT TO
          HEAR THE
          LATEST? . . . .
          NEWSLETTER
          SERVICE

and so on. On a 40-column screen, it would look like this:

TONIGHT'S MENU IS . . . .

NUMBER   ITEM
   1   LOOKING FOR INFORMATION? . . .
          SEARCH SERVICE
   2   WANT TO HEAR THE LATEST? . . .
          NEWSLETTER SERVICE

and so on. But had you left the material in 80-column format when using either a 20- or 40-column screen, it would look like this:

TONIGHT'S MENU IS:

NUMBER   ITEM

    1   LOOKI
NG FOR INFORMATION?
. . .SEARCH SERVICE
   2   WANT
TO HEAR THE LATEST?
. . .NEWSLETTER SERVI
CE

and this:

```
TONIGHT'S MENU IS:

NUMBER      ITEM

    1           LOOKING FOR INFORMATION?.
..SEARCH SERVICE
    2           WANT TO HEAR THE LATEST?.
..NEWSLETTER SERVICE
```

The even columns and the words are broken up. The results are not very easy for you to read or to understand.

The second specification you were asked to set, number of lines on your screen, tells the system to pause after it has transmitted the set number of lines. After it has sent them, the text will stop scrolling and the last line will read:

HIT ENTER FOR NEXT SCREEN

This means you are to press your Return or Enter key.

Now, back to the first screen of text.

```
TONIGHT'S MENU IS:

NUMBER      ITEM

    1           LOOKING FOR INFORMATION? ... SEARCH SERVICE
    2           WANT TO HEAR THE LATEST? ... NEWSLETTER SERVICE
    3           NEED A PROGRAM? ... SOFTWARE SERVICE
    4           KEEP IN TOUCH! ... ELECTRONIC MAIL SERVICE
    5           LET'S MAKE A DEAL ... SWAP SHOP
    6           WANT A SNEAK PREVIEW? ... COMING ATTRACTIONS
    7           WANT TO CHANGE YOUR SECURITY PASSWORD? ...
                SECURITY

TYPE IN MENU ITEM NUMBER THEN HIT ENTER KEY FOR DESIRED
SELECTION
```

The above list is called a *menu*. Like a restaurant's menu, you are presented with a list of choices. As the last line states, you simply press the number key on your computer, press Enter (or Return), and you are taken toward your goal.

As mentioned in Chapter 2, BRS After Dark had only implemented the Search Service when *The Computer Phone Book* was being written. To access the Search Service, you press your **1** key, hit Return, and will see:

```
YOU ARE NOW CONNECTED TO THE BRS AFTER DARK SEARCH SERVICE.
THE FOLLOWING CATEGORIES OF DATABASES ARE AVAILABLE FOR
SEARCHING.


CATEGORY        DESCRIPTION

    1           SCIENCE AND MEDICINE DATABASES
    2           BUSINESS AND FINANCIAL DATABASES
    3           REFERENCE DATABASES
    4           EDUCATION DATABASES
    5           SOCIAL SCIENCE AND HUMANITIES DATABASES
    6           ENERGY AND ENVIRONMENTAL DATABASES
TYPE IN CATEGORY NUMBER THEN HIT ENTER KEY FOR
CATEGORY OF DATABASES DESIRED
```

Again, you need only press the appropriate number, hit Return, and you will be led to your destination. In this case, you will choose Reference Databases, **3**.

```
REFERENCE DATABASES
* * * * * * * * * * * * * * * * *


DATABASE NAME                                   LABEL
BOOKS IN PRINT                                  BBIP
DISC                                            DISC

TYPE IN LABEL FOR DATABASE DESIRED:
```

In this case, you would not type in a number, but a keyword, called a *label* here. Let's try Books in Print.

After typing in its label **BBIP**, you will see:

```
ARE YOU A NEW AFTER DARK USER? PLEASE TYPE IN YES OR NO:
```

This is an important question because it will affect the way in which you are able to search the database. In this instance, you will type **YES** as the answer. Next, you will see:

WOULD YOU LIKE A DESCRIPTION OF THE DATABASE? (Y OR N)

If you typed in **Y**, what you would see, in any of the databases, is a description that is copied word for word from the user's manual. The option of a description is provided since it comes with a quote of the hourly price of each database, reminding you how much your connect-time is. In this instance, a description is not needed. What you want is to get to your needed information as quickly as possible. After responding with **N** to the above question, you will see:

TYPE IN SEARCH TERMS

S1 -->

to which you will respond by typing in a word that describes the information you need. If more than one word describes what you are looking for, you will have to separate the words by using a *connector*. The connector that will be used in this example is **AND**. A one-word search example would look like this:

S1-->**COMPUTER**

which will give you

5637 ITEMS FOUND

TYPE S TO CONTINUE SEARCHING, P TO PRINT FIRST ITEM,
      M TO RETURN TO MASTER MENU, D TO RETURN TO DATABASE
      MENU
OR   O TO SIGN OFF.

Yes, there are over 5000 books that either have the word "computer" in their title or as part of their subject matter, and that number is rapidly growing. Unless you have unlimited time and money, you will not want to read through over 5000 entries. Therefore, you will have to narrow your search, limiting the number of entries available to you by adding another word to your first search term. First, you will have to type **S** (to continue searching) and will see:

TYPE IN SEARCH TERMS

S2--> (and type in) **COMPUTER AND COMMUNICATIONS**

and get:

25 ITEMS FOUND

TYPE S TO CONTINUE SEARCHING, P TO PRINT FIRST ITEM,
      M TO RETURN TO MASTER MENU, D TO RETURN TO DATABASE
      MENU
OR   O TO SIGN OFF.

Although the addition of a second word, using **AND** as a connector, helped to narrow the field, you still may not be satisfied. Therefore, type **S** again, press Return, and you will get:

TYPE IN SEARCH TERMS

S3--> (and type in) **COMPUTER AND COMMUNICATIONS AND PHONE**
1 ITEM FOUND

TYPE S TO CONTINUE SEARCHING, P TO PRINT FIRST ITEM,
      M TO RETURN TO MASTER MENU, D TO RETURN TO DATABASE
      MENU
OR   O TO SIGN OFF.

If you are satisfied that you have found what you were looking for, type in **P**, press Return, and you will get:

ENTER S FOR SHORT PRINT FORM, M FOR MEDIUM PRINT FORM,
    OR HIT CARRIAGE RETURN FOR LONG PRINT FORM.

You hit your Return (or Enter) key and get:

ENTER DOCUMENT NUMBERS TO PRINT IN FOLLOWING FORM:
       1, 2, 3 ETC. OR 3-10 OR ALL.
    OR HIT CARRIAGE RETURN TO PRINT FIRST DOCUMENT.

Since there is only one item, you just hit Return and get:

```
ME CANE-MIKE
TI THE COMPUTER PHONE BOOK
ED ORIGINAL
PD OCTOBER, 1983
PR PAP TXT 00.00 0-0000-0000-0
PB NEW AMERICAN LIBRARY
SC ACTIVE ENTRY (AE).
SU  TECHNOLOGY: COMPUTERS AND COMPUTER TECHNOLOGY (00456X),
    MICROCOMPUTERS (00596668). COMPUTERS: HANDBOOKS, MANUALS,
    ETC. (00566366)
PG 250
```

The above is a fabricated example in the format of the Books in Print database. The BRS After Dark user's manual will show you what those two-letter abbreviations in the entry mean.

If you are thinking that the example given took too many steps, you are right. All of the search terms could have been placed on one line as follows:

TYPE IN SEARCH TERMS

S1-->**COMPUTER AND COMMUNICATIONS AND PHONE**

However, if you were starting out in your searching, typed in only the word **COMPUTER**, and then, after being presented with over 5000 entries, decided you wanted to narrow it down, you could do the following (after having typed **S** to continue searching and pressed Return):

TYPE IN SEARCH TERMS

S2-->**1 AND COMMUNICATIONS**

Each search request is *numbered* (as you probably have noticed): "S1," "S2," "S3," and so on. By simply typing in **1**, you are telling the system, Use the phrase from the previous search request with this new word (or series of words). It saves you from having to type **COMPUTER** again. After continuing the search to a third level, you could type:

TYPE IN SEARCH TERMS

S3-->**2 AND PHONE**

which would stand for **COMPUTER AND COMMUNICATIONS AND PHONE**.

AND, by the way, is not the only connector you can use. Others are listed in the BRS After Dark user's manual.

Before you started searching, you had to reply to the question:

ARE YOU A NEW AFTER DARK USER? PLEASE TYPE IN YES OR NO:

The example search session shown was for a new user. Once you have gained a familiarity with the BRS After Dark system, you can answer **NO** to that question. By doing so, the following command lines, known as *prompts*, will be changed:

TYPE S TO CONTINUE SEARCHING, P TO PRINT FIRST ITEM,
       M TO RETURN TO MASTER MENU, D TO RETURN TO DATABASE
       MENU
OR   O TO SIGN OFF.

to:

ENTER COMMAND

to which you may then reply with **S, P, M, D,** or **O**. Next,

ENTER S FOR SHORT PRINT FORM, M FOR MEDIUM PRINT FORM
    OR HIT CARRIAGE RETURN FOR LONG PRINT FORM

will become:

ENTER S, M, OR RETURN

The last prompt,

ENTER DOCUMENT NUMBERS TO PRINT IN FOLLOWING FORM:
    1, 2, 3 ETC. OR 3-10 OR ALL
    OR HIT CARRIAGE RETURN TO PRINT FIRST DOCUMENT.

will become:

ENTER DOCUMENT(S) OR RANGE.

As you can see, that is quite a time-saver. Instead of constantly being told what to do, you are given a few words. The best part is, if you forget what you should type in, all you have to do is hit your Return key and you are given the full prompt.

Another way to save time while using BRS After Dark is to hit your Break key (if you have one) while a menu is being printed. This will stop it and allow you to enter a command.

In terms of commands, you can go one better by using *command stringing*. This means you place all of your commands on one line. An example of this strategy is as follows:

TONIGHT'S MENU IS:

NUMBER	ITEM
1	LOOKING FOR INFORMATION?... SEARCH SERVICE
2	WANT TO HEAR THE LAT(break)

You have hit your Break key to interrupt output. You will not see (break) appear on your screen. You type in **1;3;BBIP**, which will take you directly to the Books in Print database. The number, **1**, selects the Search Service; **3** selects Reference Databases from the Search Service menu, and **BBIP** selects Books in Print from the Reference Databases menu.

You may also string commands when you are in the Books in Print database (or any BRS After Dark database you are using) as follows:

TYPE IN SEARCH TERMS

S1-->**COMPUTER**
5637 ITEMS FOUND
ENTER COMMAND (and you type in) **P; L; 1**

This will tell the system to print the first entry (P) in long form (L) with the range of documents only being the first (1).

If you have ever used a professional search service, you will know that you may have the entries printed out according to your specifications. For instance, you could print out the title, or title and author, or title and abstract (the summary). BRS After Dark does not allow this customized retrieval. In order to make the system easy to use for those who have never before used a professional search service, BRS has eliminated that option and replaced it with three types of entry forms: *short, medium*, and *long print forms*, which is what the following prompt means:

ENTER S FOR SHORT PRINT FORM, M FOR MEDIUM PRINT FORM,
    OR HIT CARRIAGE RETURN FOR LONG PRINT FORM.

The sample entry you have seen was in long print form. In medium form it would look like this:

ME CANE-MIKE
TI THE COMPUTER PHONE BOOK
PD OCTOBER, 1983
SU TECHNOLOGY: COMPUTERS AND COMPUTER TECHNOLOGY (00456X),
    MICROCOMPUTERS (00596668). COMPUTERS: HANDBOOKS,
    MANUALS,
ETC. (00566366)

In short form, it would look like this:

ME CANE-MIKE
TI THE COMPUTER PHONE BOOK
PD OCTOBER, 1983

One other tip when using BRS After Dark: The individual category menus are flexible. That is, they are only an overlay to point you to an individual database. But you do *not* have to type in the database label you are presented with. For example, say you accidentally chose **3** (Reference Databases) from the Search Service menu when you really wanted **1** (Science and Medicine Databases). If you don't have a Break key, you have no choice but to watch that wrong menu print out in its entirety. You do not want to go back and reprint the Search Service menu again, wasting more time and money. If you know the database label that you want (you may find it in the user's manual), you can just type it in at the end of the Reference Databases menu. You will be brought directly to that Science and Medicine database even though you were at the Reference Databases menu. As you can see, BRS After Dark is a powerful, professional quality search service that is very easy to use.

CompuServe Information Service

Next, let's take a glimpse at the CompuServe Information Service. CompuServe, like BRS After Dark, is menu driven. There are, however, some services on the system that are tricky to use.

After you have entered your account number or User ID (called a PPN on this system) and password and have responded to a signon message in regard to subscribing to the service, you will get the system's main menu:

```
CompuServe              Page CIS-1

CompuServe Information Service

1 Home Services
2 Business & Financial
3 Personal Computing
4 Services for Professionals

5 User Information
6 Index

Enter your selection number,
or H for more information.

!
```

This is one example of what a menu page on CompuServe looks like. Depending on your computer, it may appear in all upper case letters. As you can see, it differs from BRS After Dark in that it has a *page number* at the top, is formatted for a 32-column screen only, and the CompuServe prompt is ! (an exclamation point). But, just like with BRS After Dark, all you have to do is to press a number key on your computer, hit Return (or Enter), and you will be sent to a new page that will guide you on.

To acquaint you with CompuServe, I will give you a tour through one of the above choices. Pressing **1** on your keyboard and hitting Return, you will next see:

CompuServe   Page HOM-1

HOME SERVICES

1 News/Weather/Sports
2 Reference Library
3 Communications
4 Home Shopping/Banking
5 Groups and Clubs
6 Games and Entertainment
7 Education
8 Home Management
9 Travel

Last menu page. Key digit
or M for previous menu.

!

There are two things to notice about this menu: First, it has a page number that is prefixed not by "CIS" but by "HOM," indicating that you are now in the Home Services section of CompuServe. Second, at the bottom it says, "Last menu page," which lets you know that you must make a selection from the above list. All of the menu-structured and page-oriented portions of CompuServe are known as the DISPLA (display) section of the system.

Communicating on CompuServe is one of its most popular features and one of the portions of the system where things can get a bit tricky. Hitting the **3** key (for Communications) and pressing Return, you will see:

CompuServe   Page HOM-30

COMMUNICATIONS

1 Electronic Mail
  (user to user messages)
2 CB Simulation
3 National Bulletin Board
  (public messages)
4 User Directory
5 Talk to Us

6 Lobby Letters of America
7 Ask Aunt Nettie
8 CB Society

Last menu page. Key digit
or M for previous menu.

!

Electronic mail is something you will need to know how to use if you are going to get the most out of CompuServe, so press **1** on your keyboard, hit Return, and you will see:

CompuServe   Page HOM-26

Welcome to EMAIL, the user-to-
user message system from
CompuServe. EMAIL allows you to
communicate with other users of
the information service.
Instructions and options are
included on each page. You are
prompted for all required
information. If you are not sure
of what to do, key H (for Help)
and receive further
instructions.

Key S or ⟨ENTER⟩ to continue

!

For the purpose of this short tour, **H** will not be pressed for further information. When you are actually on the system, you may do so for your own information or curiosity.

Press the Return key to reveal the following:

CompuServe   Page EMA-1

   Electronic Mail Main Menu

1 Read Mail
2 Compose and send mail

Last menu page. Key digit
or M for previous menu.

!

You will notice that this page is prefixed "EMA." You are no longer in the Home Services section; instead, you have reached the first page of an actual service.

As you see, you have two choices. The first one is to read your mail. How do you know if you have any mail waiting for you? That is easy. Before the CompuServe main menu (CIS-1) is printed for you, you will see a notice that says:

You have EMAIL waiting

If you don't see that notice, you can dispense with checking for any mail. If you do check for mail, you will only be told on the next page that you have no mail waiting.

Instead, press **2** and the Return key to get:

CompuServe   Page EMA-4

CREATE a new message in your
temporary workspace using:
  1 FILGE editor
  2 ICS editor
  3 File from disk space
EDIT message in workspace using:
  4 FILGE editor
  5 ICS editor

  6 SEND message from workspace
  7 Information on FILGE
  8 Information on ICS

Last menu page. Key digit
or M for previous menu.

!

    Confusing, isn't it? CompuServe's EMAIL is not the easiest electronic mail service offered on a national network. To be able to use the FILGE and ICS editors to their fullest, you should order a *Personal Computing Guide* from CompuServe. It is not included in the elementary user's manual you will get when subscribing and is an extra expense. The *Personal Computing Guide* will show you how to use the FILGE and ICS editors as well as the Programmer's Area (formerly MicroNET; to be covered later in this chapter). However, to get a rudimentary understanding of FILGE and ICS, you could select both "7" and "8" (one at a time) from the above menu.

On this tour, I will show you how to compose a mail message using some of the FILGE commands. By pressing **1** and Return, you will get:

New file Z99EMA.TYP created—ready

That is all of the prompting you will get. What do you do? Easy, just type in your message, such as,

New file Z99EMA.TYP created—ready

**Thsi is a tsetof the mail system for myselff.
It will show me how esay it is to use EMail.**

There are a few typos there. Since you did not catch them in time to execute a Control-H (to move the cursor back over the wrong letter and type in the correct one), you may think that you are stuck with a note that looks like the creation of a poor typist. Not so. Watch.

New file Z99EMA.TYP created—ready

Thsi is a tsetof the mail system for myselff.
It will show me how esay it is to use EMail.
/T

On a new line, you type /T. FILGE, you see, is a *line-oriented* text editor. After you hit Return at the end of your second line, the FILGE line pointer was set at the third line, where you just typed in /T. /T is a command that tells FILGE to go to the first line (or *top*) of your file. The FILGE line pointer is now located at the beginning of your first sentence. FILGE, however, will *not* print that line of its own accord. You must command it to, as follows:

New file Z99EMA.TYP created—ready

Thsi is a tsetof the mail system for myselff.
It will show me how esay it is to use EMail.
/T
/P
Thsi is a tsetof the mail system for myselff.

The **/P** command tells FILGE, Print the line your pointer is located at. Since you had first moved it to the top (**/T**) of the file, then asked it to print (**/P**) what it saw, you were given your first sentence. All that you now need to do is to correct the typos. You can do that as follows:

New file Z99EMA.TYP created—ready

Thsi is a tsetof the mail system for myselff.
It will show me how esay it is to use EMail.
/T
/P
Thsi is a tsetof the mail system for myselff.
/C/Thsi/This
/P
This is a tsetof the mail system for myselff.

The command to change any text on the line that FILGE is pointing to is **/C**. **/C** means change. The format of this command is **/C/misspelled word/correctly spelled word**, and it tells FILGE to change what follows after the second slash (/) into what follows after the third slash (/). In other words, Change "Thsi" to "This." After you made the change, you then printed (**/P**) the line again to verify that it was made. It is always a good idea to print the line after you have made a correction to make sure that you told FILGE to point to the correct line and that the change you wanted was carried out without error.

Getting back to your letter, now that you know you have the correct line, you can make other needed changes.

New file Z99EMA.TYP created—ready

Thsi is a tsetof the mail system for myselff.
It will show me how esay it is to use EMail.
/T
/P

Thsi is a tsetof the mail system for myselff.
/C/Thsi/This
/P
This is a tsetof the mail system for myselff.
/C/se/es
/P
This is a testof the mail system for myselff.
/C/to/t o
/P
This is a test of the mail system for myselff.
/C/f./.
/P
This is a test of the mail system for myself.

You may have noticed that you skipped some steps. You did not tell FILGE to change "tsetof" to "testof." Instead, you just told it to change "se" to "es." If you look carefully at that sentence, you will see that the first occurrence of the letters "se" is in the word "tsetof." When you tell FILGE to make any sort of change, it looks for the *first occurrence* of the word or letters (called a *character string*) in the line it is positioned at. Therefore, you do not have to type in, **/C/tsetof/testof** since the first occurrence of "se" is within the word you want to change. Therefore, you only told FILGE to transpose those two letters, that is, "se" into "es."

Next, you wanted to place a space between "test" and "of." You accomplished this by telling FILGE to look for the first occurrence of the letters "to" and to place a space between them. Hence, you only typed **/C/to/t o** instead of **/C/testof/test of**.

Lastly, you told FILGE to delete an "f." But, had you just typed in **/C/f/**, you would have changed "of" to "o" since the first occurrence of the letter "f" is in "of," which is not the one you wanted to delete in "myselff." So, you *isolated* the "f" you wanted to delete by telling FILGE to look for the one that was followed by "." (a period).

Now that you have corrected the first sentence, you can finish your message by correcting the second sentence.

New file Z99EMA.TYP created—ready

Thsi is a tsetof the mail system for myselff.
It will show me how esay it is to use EMail.

/T
/P
Thsi is a tsetof the mail system for myselff.
/C/Thsi/This
/P
This is a tsetof the mail system for myselff.
/C/se/es
/P
This is a testof the mail system for myselff.
/C/to/t o
/P
This is a test of the mail system for myselff.
/C/f./.
/P
This is a test of the mail system for myself.
/N1
/P
It will show me how esay it is to use EMail.
/C/sa/as
/P
It will show me how easy it is to use EMail.
/T
/P100
This is a test of the mail system for myself.
It will show me how easy it is to use EMail.
%FLGEOF—end of file

To position FILGE at your second sentence, you told it to move down one line by typing /N1. Whenever you want FILGE to move *down* a file, you type /N and a *positive* number, such as /N1, /N2, or /N3. To get FILGE to move *up* a file, you type /N and a *negative* number, such as /N−1, /N−2, or /N−3. The number that you place after /N will correspond to how many lines up or down a file you want FILGE to move.

Once the line pointer was at your second sentence, you printed (/P) the sentence then transposed "sa" to make the word "esay" into "easy."

After you were through, you told FILGE to go to the top of the file (/T). Then you told it to print all of the file by typing /P and a number that was greater than the number of lines in your file. The sentence, "%FLGEOF—end of file," simply is a reminder that you are at the end of your text.

You may now continue typing in your message. The text will start on the third line of FILGE. Do not worry about "%FLGEOF—end of file" becoming a part of your text; it will not.

Suppose you have gone mail-happy and typed in 50 more lines. Once you are through, you decide that there is one word in all of that text that you want to change. You will not want to waste time by reviewing the entire file. Yet you want to find that one word quickly and change it. You can do this by issuing the **/L** command. First, go to the top (**/T**) of your file. Now type **/L/word that you want** and FILGE will stop at the line that contains that word. You will then print (**/P**) the line and make the change (**/C**) that you want. It is that easy.

All of the commands cited for FILGE—as well as any and all commands for National Networks and Local-Area Services—should be followed by pressing your Return or Enter key. It will quickly become a habit to do so.

Once you are through with your file, you will want to be able to get out of FILGE and send your letter. Let's review the text again.

```
This is a test of the mail system for myself.
It will show me how easy it is to use EMail.
/EX
```

The command to get out of FILGE and back to the EMail menu is **/EX** (followed by Return or Enter). Having typed that in, you will now get:

```
CompuServe            Page EMA-4

CREATE a new message in your
temporary workspace using:

  1 FILGE editor
  2 ICS editor
  3 File from disk space
EDIT message in workspace using:
  4 FILGE editor
  5 ICS editor

  6 SEND message from workspace
  7 Information on FILGE
  8 Information on ICS
```

Last menu page. Key digit
or M for previous menu.

!

You have just finished using **1** to create a message, so you don't need that again. Since you now know how to *edit* your message, you don't need to choose **4**. Choice **6** is the one you will choose to send your two sentences to a friend. Press **6** (and Return or Enter) to get:

CompuServe   Page EMA-8

Key ⟨ENTER⟩ to leave; ? for help

Send to User ID
:
Subject (32 characters max)
:
Your name (32 characters max)
:
Is this correct? (Y or N):

That is what Page EMA-8 looks like, but it is not filled in. You will have to supply all of the requested information.

If this is your first time on CompuServe and you do not know the PPN (User ID) of another person, you can send your test letter to yourself. This will give you the experience of composing, editing, and sending mail. When your letter arrives, you will have experience of reading mail and filing or deleting it.

Do the following:

CompuServe   Page EMA-8

Key ⟨ENTER⟩ to leave; ? for help

Send to User ID
:(type in *your* PPN:) **77777,778**
Subject (32 characters max)
:A MAIL TEST
Your name (32 characters max)
:(type in *your* name:)
Is this correct? (Y or N): **Y**

Message awaiting delivery.

Key ⟨ENTER⟩ to continue

!

Do not try to read your mail immediately. It will not be in your mailbox yet. Although electronic mail is supposed to be instantaneous, in CompuServe's case, there is a delay of anywhere from 15 minutes to 1 hour.

After you have finished sending your mail, hit the Return or Enter key and you will be back at Page EMA-8. Since you have already sent your message, you are finished using EMail.

You are now ready to learn a new feature of CompuServe. In DISPLA (any part of the service that uses ! as its prompt), you may move around by entering page numbers as direct commands. The page number must be prefixed by the command, **GO**, which may be abbreviated **G**. Instead of leaving Page EMA-8 by typing **M** for the previous menu and eventually moving back to Page HOM-30, at ! you may type in **G HOM-30** (or **G HOM30**; you may leave out the hyphen) to get:

CompuServe   Page HOM-30

COMMUNICATIONS

1 Electronic Mail
  (user to user messages)
2 CB Simulation
3 National Bulletin Board
  (public messages)
4 User Directory
5 Talk to Us
6 Lobby Letters of America
7 Ask Aunt Nettie
8 CB Society

Last menu page. Key digit or
M for previous menu.

!

Touring by the numbers, by selecting **2**, you will be transported to the CB Simulator, CompuServe's real-time multiuser conferencing program. The next page you see is:

```
CB Information          Page CB-10

    Citizens Band Simulator

 1 Instructions
 2 CB Etiquette
 3 CB Band A (Mainframe A)

 4 CBIG Special Interest Group
 5 CB Society: Cupcake's Column

Last menu page. Key digit
or M for previous menu.

!
```

If you have never been on CB before, you should read the instructions, by typing 1 (and using your printer, if you have one, to make a copy). Choice 2 will inform you of how you should conduct yourself when using CB. Choice 4 will place you in a SIG (Special Interest Group, to be covered shortly) where you may communicate with other CBers through a bulletin board. Choice 5 will give you a "gossip column" about CB happenings and users. Choice 3 will take you directly to CB. Due to the great popularity of CB, CompuServe is moving to expand the service through use of dedicated CB host computers. Choice 3, above, reflects that and as usage increases I am sure you will find a "Band B" and a "Band C" made available. In this tour, you will type **3** to get:

```
CB Information          Page CB-1

Request Recorded,
One Moment, Please
```

The CompuServe computers are switching you to the computer that is running the CB Simulator program. There will be a short delay, but soon you will see:

52 THE COMPUTER PHONE BOOK

Thank You for Waiting
CB Simulator Ver 3(51) Band A
What's your handle?

CB is asking you to type in the name under which you will be known when you use CB. Devise a pseudonym for yourself; it can be a fictional character, an animal, or any name that is not X-rated or designed to shock others. Hardly anyone on CB uses his or her real name. Anonymity is the rule, allowing conversations to be free and to permit everyone to have an equal say. It would be best if you always use the same handle so other CB users who you meet will be able to find you whenever you are on CB. After you have typed in your handle (**BROOKLYN** in this example), you will see:

CB Simulator Ver 3(51) Band A
What's your handle? **BROOKLYN**

(Channel) users tuned in
(1)16, (2)4, (3)1, (4)3, (7)2,
(9)3, (12)2, (17)2, (25)1, (33)5,
(35)2
Which channel:

You are being shown the active CB channels and the number of people using each one. Channel numbers are in parentheses, and you can see that channels 1, 2, 3, 4, 7, 9, 12, 17, 25, 33, and 35 are active. The numbers next to the channels are the number of people on each channel. Channel 1 has 16 users, channel 2 has 4 users, channel 3 has 1 user, and so on. Next, you select a channel that you wish to be on for CB. In this example, choose channel 2, which has four people on it. After typing **2** and pressing Return, you will be greeted with something like this:

(2, Jackrabbit) So, tell me where you are all from???
(2, ***ABC***) HE'S NOT LISTENING TO ME **SNIFF!**
(2,-QUERY-) WELL IF U PEOPLE R SO SMART, Y R U ALL HERE???
(2, V*A*M*P*I*R*E!) O shut up, Query!
(2,***ABC***) IM IN NEVADA JACK. WHERE R U???
(2,-QUERY-) YOU HAVE VERY BIG TEETH VAMPIRE
(2, Jackrabbit) I'm calling from +ALASKA+!!!!
(2, V*A*M*P*I*R*E!) And u'll get a bite if u don't behave, Query!!!

```
(2, ***ABC***) REALLY???!!!! HOWS THE WEATHER????
(2,-QUERY-) (((HOLDING UP CROSS!!!)))
(2, V*A*M*P*I*R*E!) GAK!!!
(2, ***ABC***) DONT HURT VAMPY, Q! I LIKE HIM!!!!
(2, Jackrabbit) It sure ain't no place for rabbits up here now!!!
(2,-QUERY-) Oh, OK, ABC. (((fingers crossed!!!))) heh-heh.
(2, ***ABC***) JACK---> HEHEHEHEHEHEHEHEHEHEHE
(2, OK) Is this as good as it gets here???? Geez!!!
(2, ***ABC***) HI OK!!!!! ((KISS!))
(2, V*A*M*P*I*R*E!) HO OK!! Long time no c!
(2,-QUERY-) %$¢$¢%$#$#@#%!!! OK, Where's that pgm u said u would send me???
```

Although the above exchange is made up, it represents what transpires on CB. As you can see, one-letter abbreviations are used whenever possible to speed up the conversation and each person's typing.

The first thing you should know about the above CB conversation is that the material inside the parentheses is the channel number and the person's handle. Thus (2,***ABC***) means channel "2" and a person whose handle is "***ABC***." When you type into CB, you do not have to type any of that; the CB Simulator will insert your channel number and handle automatically with each line that you type.

The second thing you should realize is that if you are using a screen that is fewer than 64- or 80-columns wide, the above exchange will scroll off your screen very quickly. Recall the two Control functions mentioned earlier in this chapter: Control-S to pause output and Control-Q to resume output. In your initial CB experiences, you will need to rely on these two functions to help you keep track of what is being said to whom and by whom. As you get used to CB, you will dispense with using these functions and will acquire the ability to carry on multiple conversations at one time.

Before you join this electronic repartee, try some of the commands available to you in CB. You can get these by typing /**HELP** anywhere in the program. Like FILGE, all CB commands are prefixed with a slash (/). Make sure that your keyboard is in the proper shifted mode or you will type ?**HELP** and get:

```
?CBXIVC—Invalid command.
For help, type: /HELP.
```

Having typed **/HELP** (do not worry if it was interrupted by CB banter on your screen, that will be covered in a moment) and pressed Return, you will see:

```
Prefix commands with a "/"
/TUN # - Tunes channel # (1-36)
/TALK # - Talk privately w/ job#
/MON 1,4 - Listen to extra channels
/UNM 7,3 - Unmonitor channels
/STA - Type channel status
/TIM - Type time, day, and date
/UST - User STatus typeout
/UST # - User STatus for Chan #
/EXI - Exit CB Simulator
/OFF - Exit CB and log off
/WHO - Type PPN of last talker
/HAN - Change handle
/SCR xyz - Scramble on key "xyz"
/SMC xyz - Scr & Monitor Clear
/XCL xyz - Xmt CLear; unscr rcvr
/UNS - Unscramble (both clear)
/SQU abc - Squelch handle "abc"
/SBU #,# - Squelch by User ID
/JOB - your job #
/HELP - Type this message
```

These are all of the CB commands at your disposal. Not all of them will be explained here; instead you will have fun in discovering them for yourself. Besides, there will be many others on CB who will be glad to give you a hand in learning and trying out new commands. It is, however, necessary for you to learn some commands so you can use CB the first time you enter it.

As you have probably noticed when you typed in **/HELP**, what you type in is bound to be interrupted by another person's transmission, no matter how fast a typist you may be. An example of this is shown below. It is formatted for a 40-column screen and illustrates what may occur when you try to type in the short greeting, **Hello, everyone! How's tricks?**

```
(2, ***ABC***) WELL WHAT DO U THINK OF TH
AT?
```

Hello, every (2,-QUERY-) Hey, where did t
he Vampire go to??**one! How's** (2, Jackrabb
it) I don't know what to make of it.**tric
ks?** (2, V*A*M*P*I*R*E!) Who rang for me???

It looks like alphabet soup. Your simple sentence was interrupted three times before you got it out. And this is a mild example. It is not unusual for you to be interrupted after just typing one letter. How would the above exchange look to another person tuned to channel 2? Like this:

(2, ***ABC***) WELL WHAT DO U THINK OF TH
AT?
(2,-QUERY-) Hey, where did the Vampire g
o to??
(2, Jackrabbit) I don't know what to make
of it.
(2, V*A*M*P*I*R*E!) Who rang for me???
(2, BROOKLYN) Hello, everyone! How's tric
ks?

Although what you typed in looked as if it were broken up, others are able to read you loud and clear on their screens. Once you have hit your Return key, everything that you type in is sent as one complete string, be it a word or a sentence. Therefore, ignore your broken-up words and sentences you see on your screen and merrily type away. The only limitation you have is that you must type in a line fewer than 80-characters long. If your sentence is longer than that, you must indicate it to others by ending it with ". . ." and starting the next part of the sentence the same way, that is ". . ." . If you try to type in a line longer than 80 characters, by choice or accident, you will be told that your line is too long, that it will not be sent, and that you must then retype it.

After you have been chatting away for a while (on channel 2, in this example), you will probably want to see how many other people have joined your group without announcing themselves. When you selected channel 2, you were shown that four people were on it. In CB, people hop from channel to channel looking for their friends or for an interesting conversation. While doing this, they do not always join in the conversation or make their presence known. These people are called *lurkers* in CB. To uncover lurkers, you may use the CB command, /STA, which means status. It gives you all of the CB channels in use as well as the number of users on each one. When you type /STA at the beginning of a new line, you will get:

(1)18, (2)7 #, (7)5, (12)5,
(17)3, (33)5

You will notice that some channels are no longer in use and that some have gained users. Looking at channel 2, you will see that three more people are on it than when you chose it and the "#" sign indicates that is the channel you are currently on. Of course, when you joined it, you added a person. Once you were on, you saw "OK" join in. In the meantime, someone else has tuned to your channel. To find out who that person is, you will need to get a list of the handles on your channel. You can do this by typing, on a line by itself, /UST 2 (for User STatus), and your channel number. You will then get a list of the users on your channel. It will look like this:

Job	User ID	Nod	Ch	Tlk	Handle
5	77777,19	POR	2		V*A*M*P*I*R*E!
27	77777,85	LAV	2		***ABC***
53	77777,891	NYC	2		BROOKLYN
6	77777,68	NOM	2		Jackrabbit
89	77777,900	IND	2		-QUERY-
100	77777,8	QAK	2		OK
127	77777,395	LOU	2		Pardner

At the bottom of the list, in this example, is your lurker: a user with the handle "Pardner." You can now tell Pardner that he or she should join in the conversation and not be shy.

The other information you see in Ustat (as it is commonly called) is "Job," "User ID," "Nod," "Ch," "Tlk," and "Handle," all of which are there to help you communicate with others more easily. "User ID" is each user's address for EMail. "Ch" is an abbreviation for Channel, and "Handle" is self-explanatory. "Nod" is short for Node, and, in most instances, indicates the city from which that user is calling. In this example, "POR" is short for Portland (Oregon), "NYC" for New York City, "IND" for Indianapolis, and so on. "Job" is short for Job Number, and will be covered in a moment.

Let's say that you become friendly with Jackrabbit and that he or she left channel 2 to move to another channel. You would like to locate Jackrabbit and have another chat. To do so, you would type—alone on a new line—**/UST** and would be given a list of *all* CB channels and their users. At times, this list can contain over 50 users and take about 2 to 3 minutes to scroll by at 300 bps, so it is not something that you would want to do often. As the list moves up your screen, you look for Jackrabbit and the channel he or she is on. Let's say it is channel 12. To move to channel 12, you would type **/TUN 12**, on a new line by itself, and will then be switched to channel 12 where you can speak to Jackrabbit. Jackrabbit has something private to talk about and asks:

(12, Jackrabbit) Let's /talk. What's your /job?

This means that Jackrabbit wants you to enter the CB private talk program and needs your Job number to page you. To find out your job number, you would type **/Job**. CB would then print out your Job number. You would give it to Jackrabbit and shortly thereafter you would see:

*** Please /TALK with Job 89 [77777,68] Jackrabbit

To talk privately, you would type **/TALK 89** (that is, enter the command **/TALK** and Jackrabbit's Job number, which is 89). Then, you would see:

Job 89 [77777,68] Jackrabbit now in contact

(Use ^P to break contact)

⟨Hi

The first line tells you that contact has been established in the talk program, the second line tells you that you should hit your Control and **P** keys to leave the program, and that "Hi" is from Jackrabbit. An example of a conversation between Jackrabbit and yourself would look like this:

*** Please /TALK with Job 89 [77777,68] Jackrabbit

/TALK 89
Job 89 [77777,68] Jackrabbit is now in contact

(Use ^P to break contact)

⟨Hi
⟩**Hi, Jackrabbit. What's up?**
⟨I wanted to know if you are going to be on tomorrow.
⟩**Yes, I think so. About what time, Eastern Time?**
⟨8 . . .
⟩**Oh, I**⟨ . . . or 9.
⟩**think that's too late.**
⟨OK. Maybe earlier?

The conversation can continue until either one of you issues the Control-P command to break contact. As you have noticed, your input in the Talk program can be interrupted just as it can be in CB. There is a trick to getting around that, both in CB and /TALK, in the form of two Control functions: Control-V and Control-U.

When you use Control-V, you will be able to have your interrupted line redisplayed. In the above example, it would look like this:

⟩**Oh, I**⟨ . . . or 9.^V
⟩**Oh, I**

Control-V would redisplay the line so you can continue typing it to its conclusion. The other person does not see this on the screen. Control-V is used a lot in CB, since it is the nature of that program to be constantly interrupted.

The other Control function, Control-U, erases the line you typed *before* you send it by hitting your Return key. If you have typed in a line that has many spelling mistakes or you were interrupted too many times to get it finished, you can issue a Control-U to erase it and then start fresh. A good way of remembering both of these commands is Control-View and Control-Undo.

You can leave the CB program by typing **/EX**. When you do that, you will see one of two things: either Page CB-10 again or a menu for a "multi-player host." (As *The Computer Phone Book* went to press, CompuServe was altering the CB Simulator and the exit procedure was still unwritten.) If the latter should occur, you will be given a menu of choices, some of which will be multi-player games.

How to Use the Online Systems 59

In this instance, let's use Page CB–10 to illustrate my next point. As Page CB–10 scrolls by, you will interrupt it by issuing a Control-P. It will look like this:

CB Information   Page CB–10

    Citizens Band Simulator

  1 Instruc^P

What you have done is to tell CompuServe, I don't want to see that again! Stand ready for a command! The ! prompt appears to wait for your command. You can issue a Control-P inside any CompuServe page, whether it is a menu page or a text page, to allow you to move to another section of the system without watching layers of menus go by.

In this case, we want to examine CompuServe's National Bulletin Board (BULLET). Recall that the page before CB–10 was a Communications menu and that the National Bulletin Board was one of the selections available on it. To return to that menu, type in **M** (which stands for previous menu) at the ! prompt:

CB Information   Page CB–10

    Citizens Band Simulator

  1 Instruc^P

^P Interrupt

!**M**

You will get:

CompuServe   Page HOM-30

COMMUNICATIONS

  1 Electronic Mail
    (user to user messages)
  2 CB Simulation
  3 National Bulletin Board
    (public ^**P**

^P Interrupt

!

Now that you are no longer wanting to scroll through the menu again, you issue another Control-P. At this page, you type in **3**, and will see:

CompuServe   Page HOM-23

    National Bulletin Board

At present you can post public
messages to other CompuServe
subscribers via the BULLET
program. You should have a
"CIS User's Guide"
before using BULLET. Type:
T⟨ENTER⟩ to return to the main
menu, or proceed to the next
page to enter BULLET.

Key S or ⟨ENTER⟩ to continue

!

Press your Return or Enter key to go on and see:

CompuServe   Page HOM-24

Request Recorded,
One Moment, Please

Thank You for Waiting

Notice: CompuServe reserves the right to review all
publicly posted information and to delete any which, in
its sole judgment, is inappropriate or offensive.
CompuServe will be indemnified against any loss or expense
arising out of the publication of advertisements,
including those resulting from claims or suits for
libel, violation or right of privacy, or publicity,
plagiarism or copyright infringement. CompuServe will

not be responsible for any loss or expense arising from
customer's use of posted information, without limitation.
CompuServe makes no warranties, expressed or implied.

Please enter HELP if you
need instructions

*

You are now in BULLET, CompuServe's National Bulletin Board system. In BULLET, * (an asterisk) replaces the ! prompt found in the DISPLA portion of the system. Type in **HELP** and you will see:

```
The CompuServe Information Service National
Bulletin Board is an information exchange
medium.
The following commands are implemented:
        SCAN        READ    INDEX   VIEW
        COMPOSE     POST    EDIT    ERASE
        CHECK       EXIT    AGE     OFF
Commands may be abbreviated to the first 3 letters.
For additional information about a command, type:
HELP command
For example:    HELP SCAN
```

By typing a **HELP** command, you will be able to retrieve instructions on how you can use the commands mentioned in the above list. BULLET is not the easiest bulletin board for a novice to use on a national network, but it is an extremely flexible and powerful system.

BULLET is divided into three broad categories: SALE, WANTED, and NOTICE. To post a message on it, type in **COMPOSE**. You will then be placed into the FILGE editor, the same one that you used earlier when composing an EMail message. When you finish typing in your message and exit COMPOSE with the /**EX** command, you will get the * prompt again. Then, you will type in **POST**, followed by the category (SALE, WANTED, or NOTICE) and a nine-letter word that describes your message (you will soon see examples of such words, called *keywords*).

In addition to posting a message, you may retrieve them in a variety of ways. To look at all of the messages posted on BULLET, you would type **SCAN** and see a longer version of the following list:

62 THE COMPUTER PHONE BOOK

```
*SCAN

#      From:         Date:         Keyword:

  4    77777,569     12-Oct-83     SOFTWARE
 10    77777,84      10-Oct-83     PIRACY
123    77777,448      8-Oct-83     BBS
130    77777,338      1-Oct-83     VOICE
133    77777,945      8-Oct-83     FREE!
141    77777,788     11-Oct-83     BBS
```

If you wanted to read, for example, message number 123, you would type **READ 123**. You would then see:

*READ 123
"The Computer Phone Book(tm)" lists over 300 systems worldwide that you may call using your personal computer and modem. National Networks, Local-Area Services, and Bulletin-Board Systems are listed in a directory section, along with descriptions of their offerings and a chapter on how to use them. Go to your local bookstore to buy this new Information Age directory published by New American Library. "The Computer Phone Book" is a trademark of Mike Cane.

** 123 [77777,448] 8-Oct-83 BBS

It's as easy as that.

But say you do not want to wade through a list of over 200 message headlines. You can therefore concentrate on one of the three categories by typing, for example, **SCAN NOTICE**, or you may search for messages by a particular keyword. If you were interested in finding messages about Bulletin-Board Systems, you could do a *selective view* in each of the three categories. You must realize, though, that a BBS can be described under several different keywords, for example, BBS, Bulletin, or New BBS. What you retrieve in a selective view will ultimately depend on the subject keywords supplied by the author of each message. Postings about BBSs are actually placed in the NOTICE category, so your selective view would appear this way:

```
*VIEW NOTICE BBS

#      From:         Date:         Keyword:

123    77777,448     10-Oct-83     BBS
—Read (X, Y, or RETURN)?
```

If you type **Y**, which means Yes, you would see the message's text; if you type **X**, which means Exit, you would be sent back to the Communications menu; RETURN means press your Return or Enter key to skip to the next message headline.

The final BULLET command that is useful is **AGE**. This command allows you to SCAN, READ, or VIEW messages that have been posted within a specified number of days. For example, you type **AGE 3** for messages that have been placed online within the past 3 days or type **AGE 1**, to have access to messages posted within the past 24 hours.

Now that you have seen CompuServe's facility for leaving messages to all subscribers, you can leave BULLET by entering **EX** at the * prompt. You will then return to the Communications menu. Issuing a Control-P to interrupt it, you type in **M** to get the previous menu from which you will select choice 5: Groups and Clubs. This will give you the following menu:

CompuServe   Page HOM-50

GROUPS AND CLUBS
1 CBers   10 Literary
2 HamNet   11 Educators
3 Netwits   12 Arcade
4 Orch 90   13 Games
5 Sports   14 Family Matters
6 Cooking   15 Good Earth
7 Golf   16 Work-at-Home
8 Space   17 Music
9 Issues   18 Food Buyline
      19 Instructions
      20 Descriptions

Input a number or key
⟨ENTER⟩ for more choices

!

As you can see, there are quite a few subjects covered. Groupings of people with similar interests are called *Special Interest Groups*, or *SIGs* for short. We will take a look at the Work-at-Home SIG, choice 16. After you have typed in **16**, you will see:

CompuServe   Page HOM-146

Request Recorded,
One Moment, Please

64 THE COMPUTER PHONE BOOK

Thank You for Waiting

Your name:

Type in your name; after you have done so, you will see:

Do you wish to be added to the
member list at this time?

If you have an interest in the particular SIG's subject matter, type in **Y**. It is not necessary to join a SIG to be able to look through it, although you may not be permitted to post any messages of your own. If you do post a message in a SIG that allows nonmembers to do so, you will not be able to have any replies it has generated automatically retrieved or flagged for you when you next look in; this is only something you can get if your name is in the SIG's membership roster. If you reply **N** to the above, you will be given a brief invitation to join the SIG. In the example, I will reply **Y**, and you will see:

Inserting name and ID; please stand by...

Welcome to Work-at-Home, V. 1A(52)

Name: Mike Cane 77777,448
Last on: 10-Oct-83 00:12:22
High msg#: 0

You are user number 15756
System contains messages 4985 to 5369
Brief Bulletin:

You will then see a message welcoming me to the SIG and a brief summary of how to get help on the various commands. The following list of options will then be shown; you will see the same list, even if you did not join the SIG:

Function menu:

1 (L)   Leave a message
2 (R)   Read messages
3 (RN)   Read new messages

How to Use the Online Systems 65

```
5  (B)    Read Bulletins
6  (CO)   Online Conference
9  (OP)   Change your SIG options
0  (E)    Exit from this SIG
```

Enter Selection or H for help:

CompuServe's SIGs programs are the most complex feature of the system, and many users get lost when they first use it. It is for this reason that CompuServe has published and sells a manual just for the use of the SIGs. Even though I will show you a way to use SIGs, you should obtain a copy of the manual so you may see all of the options available to you. I will also show you a way to get detailed information from the SIG itself later in this chapter (you need a printer for this method).

Although the menu structure of a SIG will help you to use it, very few people use this method. Most people operate on an *expert level*, and this is what I will show you how to do in the following example.

The first selection you will make in the above menu is **OP**, which stands for User Options. It will give you the following menu:

```
T      - return to Function level
ST     - stop between messages
NS     - don't stop between messages
LL     - change line length (80
BR     - set brief mode, which suppresses
           repetitious display of options
NB     - clear brief mode
PC     - change prompt character
TWM    - type waiting messages
MWM    - mark waiting messages
CN     - change name
DS     - set default login Section
RNS    - RN command skips messages you left
RNT    - RN command types all messages
P      - make options permanent
MEN    - use menus instead of command prompts
```
User option:

At the "User option:" prompt, type, in the following order, these choices: **ST, BR, TWM, RNS**—and if you have a screen with fewer than 80 columns, **LL** and your screen width at a "New line width:"

subprompt—and finally **P**, and **T**. After each selection, until the last, the "User option:" prompt will repeat itself. On your screen it will look like this, including the **LL** option:

User option: **ST**
User option: **BR**
User option: **TWM**
User option: **RNS**
User option: **LL**
New line length: **40**
User option: **P**
User option: **T**
Function:

ST will pause after you have read a message and give you a prompt; **BR** will do away with repetitive prompts and shorten the ones you do see; **TWM** will automatically retrieve and type out any messages that are addressed to you in the SIG; **RNS** will skip messages you have posted (such as replies you have typed in to your waiting messages) when you read new (RN) messages, thus saving you time; **LL** will format the text of SIG messages to fit your screen, making them easier to read (the figure **40** above is just an example); **P** makes these options permanent (that is, you do not have to reset them each time you enter the SIG, but you may change them any time you wish by using **OP** again); and **T** returns you to the command level of the SIG, which is now no longer a menu but a one-word prompt: "Function:." You are now set at expert level, which will save you time and let you start to use the SIG immediately.

At the expert level, you can access messages in one of three ways: Quick Scan (**QS**), Scan and Display (**SD**), or running through them all, with Read New (**RN**), pausing when you want by using Control-S and Control-Q. Let's briefly examine each of these options.

The first way of accessing messages is by Quick Scan. At the "Function:" prompt, type in **QS**, to quickly scan the messages. You will then be asked:

System contains messages
4895 to 5369
Starting message (N for new):

If you type in **N**, you will be given *all* of the messages. Since this is your first time in the SIG, all of the messages are "new" to you. You can also just hit Return and the default will be the first message, or you could have typed in the command string, **QS; N**. The quick scanning will look like this:

4895:	Databases help 1 reply	Sec. 0 - General Interest
4996:	IRS query	Sec. 2 - Questions & Answers
4999:	Home Businesses	Sec. 1 - Wanted
5002:	Conf. tomorrow	Sec. 4 - Member meetings

and so on, through as many messages as you want, until you interrupt with a Control-C. This method of scanning messages is useful if you have a printer; you can just run through the whole list of available messages then sign off the system and read your hardcopy, choosing which messages you will read when you next sign onto the SIG. Or you may choose to write the message numbers down on a sheet of paper, pausing the scroll intermittently with a Control-S and resuming with a Control-Q. This latter method is slow, however, and the SIG already provides something similar called Scan and Display.

The second way of accessing messages is by Scan and Display. Scan and Display is activated by typing **SD** at the "Function:" prompt. You will again be asked which message you would like to start with. You can hit your Return key or type **N** in reply. You will then see:

```
#:    4895     Sec. 0—General Interest
Sb:   Databases help
      9-Sep-83 03:32:52
Fm:   Mike Cane, 77777,448
To:   All

      ⟨R⟩ead ⟨T⟩op:
```

"⟨R⟩ead ⟨T⟩op:" is another prompt, asking you if you would like to read this message (type **R**), return to the "Function:" prompt (called "Top," type **T**), or pass up this message (hit Return). In this example, choose to read it by typing **R**:

```
#:    4895     Sec. 0—General Interest
Sb:   Databases help
      9-Sep-83 03:32:52
```

Fm: Mike Cane, 77777,448
To: All

⟨R⟩ead ⟨T⟩top:**R**

You have all found out how CompuServe can help you to meet new people and form helpful networks. Now you can learn about many other electronic information services by reading "The Computer Phone Book(tm)" published by New American Library and written by yours truly. Coming soon to your local bookstore!
"Tm" = trademark of Mike Cane.
* Reply:
5110

(C RE T):

"* Reply: 5110" tells you that someone has replied to this message, which you may then retrieve separately. "(C RE T)" is a prompt, with "C" meaning Continue, although you may just press Return to continue; "RE" stands for Reply, and will place you in a text entry mode; "T" will place you back at the "Function:" prompt. As you can see, you may just go through message headers with Scan and Display, selectively reading messages. You will not have to bother with reading a Quick Scan transcript or your own handwritten notes.

The third way of accessing messages is by Read (**R**). Typing **R** at the "Function:" prompt will give you a "Subcommand:" prompt. Typing **H** at the "Subcommand:" prompt will give you the options available in reading messages:

Subcommand: **H**

⟨A⟩bort
⟨F⟩orward
⟨I⟩ndividual
⟨M⟩arked
⟨N⟩ew
⟨R⟩everse
⟨S⟩earch

Subcommand:

You may use the command **R** with any of these options; for example, **RN** will Read New messages and **R; I** will Read Individual messages.

You will be asked for a starting message number for most options, except RN. The messages will print out in their entirety, and you will get the "(C RE T)" prompt after each one. If you just want to run through all of the messages from a certain point, without pausing, type **NS** (No Stop) after the first "(C RE T)" prompt.

The final messaging ability of a SIG that you will need to know about is replying (RE) to messages. By typing **RE** at the "(C RE T)" prompt at the end of a message, you will be able to type in a reply to that message. On your screen, it will look like this:

(C RE T): **RE**

1:

The SIG automatically places your name and PPN (User ID), as well as the person the message is meant for and the message's original title ("Subject:"), into the message header. All you need to do is to type in your message. The only limitation you have in entering text is that you must type in lines that are fewer than 80-characters long. If you surpass that length, you will have to retype the entire line. As long as your lines are from 20 to 79 columns, the SIG software will automatically reformat your message so that it may be easily read on any size screen.

You may remember that Control-H can be used to backspace for correction, Control-V (Control-View) will redisplay your current line, and Control-U (Control-Undo) will erase your current line. But there are other ways to correct an error. Let's look at an example of editing a reply. First, type in your message:

(C RE T): **RE**

1: **Hi, Mike. I saw your message about The**
2: **Computer Phone Book and I'd like some**
3: **mre information. Can do? Thanks. Jack.**
4:

Now that you have finished your message with line 3, you will get a prompt for line 4. Since you are through, just hit your Return key. You will then get the "Leave option:" prompt. To get a list of your options, type in **H**, and you will see:

Leave option: **H**

A - abort   C - continue
D - delete   E - edit
I - insert   L - list
P - preview   R - replace
S# - Store to Sec #
SP# - Store Prvt to Sec #

Briefly, "A" will ask you if you want to erase the message and will do so if you affirm; "C" will put you back at the line "4:" prompt so you may add more text; "D" will ask you which line of the message you wish to erase; "E" will be explained shortly; "I" will ask you between which lines you wish to place a new line of text; "L" will reprint all of your lines of text with the number prompts; "P" will allow you to see your text without line numbers; "R" will ask you which line you want to exchange with a new line of text; and "S#" and "SP#" will be explained shortly.

At the moment, you are concerned with fixing the typo in line 3 of your text. Therefore, at "Leave option:," you type in **E** for edit:

3: mre information. Can do? Thanks. Jack.
4:

Leave option: **E**

Line # to edit:

Since your mistake is in line 3, you type in **3**.

Line # to edit: **3**

Line 3 reads:
mre information. Can do? Thanks. Jack.
String to replace:

You will recall that when you used FILGE, I told you that any collection of characters, whether a word or a sentence, was called a string. Here, you are being asked, in effect, What is it you want to change? Type it in. You want to change "mre" to "more," so you reply with:

String to replace: **mre**
Replacement string:

This is saying, Please type it in the right way this time. So, you type in **more** as follows:

Replacement string: **more**
more information. Can do? Thanks. Jack.
OK?

As you can see, both your line to edit and the original line are reprinted for you automatically. If you accidentally chose the incorrect line to edit, you simply press Return in response to the prompts until you get "OK?" At that prompt, you would type in **N** and the edit would be aborted, placing you back at the "Leave option:" prompt to start again. Right now, though, you have corrected your mistake, so you reply with **Y** and are then sent back to the "Leave option:" prompt from which you may continue.

Now that you have finished your message, you have to decide whether your message is something that may be read by all SIG users or just the individual you are replying to. If your message has no general interest for other SIG users, you should make the message a *private* one. As you will discover after you have read many SIG messages, some of them do not have any practical information in them. This will help you realize the importance of making such messages private.

To make the reply in this example private, type **SP** at the "Leave option:" prompt. You then get:

Message # 5370 Stored

Function:

The same would occur had you just typed **S** to save the message in a public mode.

When you compose an original message (as opposed to a reply), you type in the **L** (leave msg.) command at the "Function:" prompt. You are then asked for the person you want to address it to and the subject. If anyone may read it, address the message to **ALL**. If you want a particular person to receive it, type in that person's name and

PPN. If you just enter the name without the PPN, the person may miss the message. The PPN is each person's name on CompuServe; that is, the number is how the system knows each person. The text entry mode for original messages is the same as the reply example shown here. Once you are through and ready to store the messages, you must type **S** or **SP** followed by the Section number. If you type **S**, and leave off the required number, you will be prompted for it. Then you may just type the number. If you type **SP**, however, and leave off the number, you will have to retype **SP** plus the number. I cannot emphasize this enough: If you do not type **SP** a *second* time with the Section number, your message will *not* be private and anyone can read it. Here is an example:

Leave option: **SP**

Section # required
0 - General Interest
1 - Wanted
2 - Questions & Answers
3 - Member Meetings

Leave option: **SP2**

Your message will be stored as private (in Section 2 in the above example), and you will be placed back at the "Function:" prompt.

After you are through reading and posting messages, you may want to take a look at the databases available to you in a SIG. SIG databases are mainly text files with information to help you use the SIG or news of interest to members. To access them, you would type **X** and a Section number at the "Function:" prompt. Each database contains contents that correspond to the name of each Section.

Another sort of database available to you in a SIG is called ACCESS. At the "Function:" prompt, you type **XA** and a Section number. You then get the prompt, "SIG/Access:" and a notice telling you which Section you have accessed. Pressing Return will give you this list of available commands:

SIG/Access:

Valid Commands:

PUB - retrieve from Public ACCESS
NOR - normal SIG access

```
XA    - change to a new database
CAT   - catalog
TYP   - type a file
DOW   - download a file
KEY   - search keyword list
SUB   - submit a file
DEL   - delete a file
EXI   - exit from ACCESS
HEL   - explains ACCESS
? xxx-explain command xxx
```

SIG/Access:

To get a full explanation, you can order the CompuServe SIG manual or have your printer type what you will get after you enter **HEL** and the prompt. You may also get explanations of each command by typing, **? xxx**, where **xxx** stands for one of the three-letter commands, for example, **? PUB**. For now, it will be enough for you to know the **CAT** and **TYP** commands.

"CAT" is short for CATalog, and will allow you to get a list of the available files in the database. An entry will look like this:

SIG/Access: **CAT**
- - - - - - - - -
[77777,1239]

WORK.DAT   09-Jul-83   11800   Accesses: 36   1-Oct-83

It shows you the PPN of the person who submitted it, the file's title ("WORK"), the kind of file it is (".DAT," which means data or a regular text file), the date it was placed in Access, how many bytes it is ("11800," almost 12K), how many people have accessed it, and the date of the last access. What is the file about, though? To get that information, you will have to use the **CAT** command with a second command: **/DES**, which is short for DEScription. The entry would then look like this:

SIG/Access: **CAT/DES**
- - - - - - - - -
[77777,1239]

WORK.DAT   09-Jul-83   1180Ø   Accesses: 36 1-Oct-83
   Keywords: HOME WORK BUSINESS TAXES EQUIPMENT
   This file explains the various aspects of working at home and contains a checklist.

If you wanted to read this file, you respond to the prompt as follows:

SIG/Access: **TYP WORK.DAT**

and the file would then scroll up your screen. The format for printing a file is, **TYP filename.extension**; in this case it is **TYP WORK.DAT**. The majority of the files available in the SIG/Access sections are in text, whether they are information files (.DAT, .TXT, or .DOC) or program listings (.XTN, .BAS, .ASC). Most can be retrieved by using the **TYP** command. The exception to this are files with the extension .IMG. These files are in binary format and cannot be TYPed. To retrieve them, you must have a CompuServe terminal program called an Executive, and use the DOWnload (**DOW**) command instead of TYPe (**TYP**). **DOW** will download the file into the terminal program's buffer using a special communications protocol.

To leave ACCESS, you type **EXI**; this will return you to the "Function:" prompt. Remember, if you have any problems using a SIG, you can always leave a message addressed to **SYSOP** (no PPN is needed) and you will get a reply to your questions.

The last method of communication available to you in a SIG is the **CO** (COnference) command, which will place you in a version of the CB Simulator where you may chat with other SIG members. Unlike CB, though, Conference is not usually occupied by users. If you want to find out if Conference is occupied or find another SIG member to chat with, you will have to type **UST** at the "Function:" prompt. On your screen, you will see:

Function: **UST**

```
31   77777,7779      T03NRK      USTAT
37   77777,80        T05LAN      WAHSIG
41   77777,395       T07QAK      ACCESS
```

The first number, "31," is the user's Job number; it is followed by their PPN, node, and current SIG activity. "USTAT" shows that you have executed the **UST** command; "WAHSIG" shows that the second user is in the SIG bulletin-board section; "ACCESS" shows that the last user is in the SIG/Access program.

You will not be able to interrupt the user who is in the SIG/Access section (the program prevents that so you do not interrupt someone who is downloading a file), but you can page the other user by typing **SEN** at the "Function:" prompt. The format for this command is **SEN JOB # message.** For example, in response to the prompt "Function:" you can type:

Function: **SEN JOB 37 Hello, care to go into CO?**

You will know that your message has been sent once the "Function:" prompt reappears. Then, you can either go directly to the Conference section and wait for that person or you can wait a few moments and type **UST** to see if that person is now listed as being in CB. In the latter case, type **CO** to join the person. If you do not get any response from the person, do not feel slighted. The person may be a new user and may not know how to use all of the SIG options.

Now that you have had a tour of CompuServe's SIG facility, you are ready to learn the shortcut I mentioned earlier to get more details about SIG operations without waiting for your manual to arrive in the mail. At "Function:" type **I,** for Instructions. You will get a very long file that details the SIG commands. It will help you to become acquainted with the various SIG commands while you wait for your manual.

To leave the SIG, type **EX** at the "Function:" prompt. You will get a brief message that shows you the highest message number you have retrieved. (If you became a member, the same message will reappear the next time you sign on to the SIG.) You will now be back at Page HOM-50, the Groups and Clubs menu.

You are now ready to learn a shortcut to get through the CompuServe menus and pages that, when coupled with a generous use of Control-P, will get you into the sections of the system you want with the least amount of time. In the short user's manual that you received with your CompuServe membership, you will notice an Index. This index lists all of the page numbers that will bring you to the various information services on the system. You do not have to wade through a series of menus to get to where you want to go; you simply type in the page number preceded by **GO** or **G** (for example, **GO CIS-1** or **G CIS1**) at any ! prompt. At the ! prompt at Page HOM-50, you type in **PRO** (or **MIC**). This is not a page number, but a direct command to take you to the Programming Area, formerly known as MicroNET. After pressing Return, you will either get a "Request Recorded, One Moment Please" notice or be transferred directly to the Programming Area. Once there, you will see:

OK

That is the prompt that indicates you are now in the Programming Area. If you wish, type **HELP** to get a list of information files to read, although these are not to be thought of as a replacement for the *Programming Area Guide* that CompuServe sells.

In the Programming Area, you will have access to high-level programming languages and a variety of text editors. You have already learned about FILGE, and that is the primary text editor you will probably use here. To invoke FILGE so that you may create a file, type **FIL filename. Filename** is whatever name you care to give your file; you may wish to append an **.extension** to it so you can later tell what type of file it is. Say that you have named your file **List** and added the extension **.dat**. It would look like this on your screen:

OK
FIL List.dat

NEW FILE List.dat created—ready

Since you have already used FILGE in creating an EMail message, I will not give you another example of creating and editing a file. You may type in your file or you may upload it using a smart terminal program. Although it is not necessary, you may want to investigate the purchase of a CompuServe Executive terminal program that will allow you to upload to FILGE and download from Access using a special communications protocol that can help prevent errors in transmission.

Once your file is completely typed in or uploaded and you have closed your file by typing the **/EX** command, you will see the "OK" prompt reappear. To read your file, use the **TYP** command that was available to you in SIG/Access.

OK
TYP List.dat

Your file would then scroll up your screen.

To get a catalog of your files, type **CAT** and you will see the titles of your files.

OK
CAT

LIST.DAT

OK

To get details, such as the file size, creation date, and protection level, request your directory by typing **DIR**:

OK
DIR

LIST.DAT   1920   9-Oct-83   (4)

OK

Recall that one of the options of the EMail main menu was to create a message using a file from your disk space, choice 3. Your file above, List.dat, would be such a file. In EMail, you would select **3** and then be asked to "Name the output file:" to which you would reply **List.dat**. You would be told that it was loaded (provided that it was less than 4000 characters in length; beyond that you would have to edit it or split it into two files), and you would then send it like any piece of EMail, as shown in the example earlier.

To exit the Programming Area, you either type **R DISPLA** (Request DISPLA) or enter a direct page number. For now, type in **G EMA**.

CompuServe   Page EMA-1

Electronic Mail Main Menu

1 Read Mail
2 Compose and send Mail

Last menu page. Key digit
or M for previous menu.

!

Remember the letter you sent to yourself earlier? You are going to read it, so type in **1** to get:

CompuServe   Page EMA-3

1 Me/Mail Test

Last menu page. Key digit
or M for previous menu.

!

Type in **1** again.

CompuServe   Page EMA-5

10-Oct-83 21:07 Mn 77777,779
This is a test of the mail system for myself.
It will show me how easy it is to use EMail.

Key ⟨ENTER⟩ to continue

!

Press your Return key.

CompuServe   Page EMA-5

1 File this message, then
delete from mailbox
2 Delete from mailbox
3 Display the message again

Last menu page. Key digit
or M for previous menu.

!

If you were to select **1**, you would see:

CompuServe		Page EMA-9

Name the output file, ? for help
or ⟨ENTER⟩ to delete message.
:

You would then have to type in a file name. Let's say you call it **Test.dat**.

: **Test.dat**

Message filed in DSK:TEST.DAT
and deleted from your mailbox.

Key ⟨ENTER⟩ to continue

!

Press Return.

CompuServe		Page EMA-3

                Read Mail

           No Mail Waiting

Last page. Key M for menu.

!

You have now seen the most outstanding aspects of the CompuServe Information Service: EMail, FILGE, the CB Simulator, the National Bulletin Board, a CompuServe Special Interest Group, and the Programming Area. Although some of these particular services may seem confusing, they will become easy to use with practice. CompuServe's menu structure enables you to access all parts of the system easily.

Delphi

The next National Network you will get a look at is Delphi from General Videotex Corporation.

When you sign on to Delphi for the first time, you will be taken on a guided tour of the system. At this time you will set your terminal's screen width and depth and be told about the system and how it works. When you are through with that, you will be given the main menu:

```
MAIN menu:
APPOINTMENT-CALENDAR
BANKING
BULLETIN-BOARDS
CONFERENCE
DELPHI-ORACLE
EXIT
GAMES
GUIDED TOUR
HELP
INFOMANIA
LIBRARY
MAIL
NEWS
ONLINE-MARKETS
PROFILE
TRAVEL
WRITERS-CORNER
MAIN)What do you want to do?
MAIN)
```

As you can see, the selections available to you from Delphi's main menu are not numbered as they are on both BRS After Dark and the CompuServe Information Service. In using Delphi, you must type in either the first one or two letters of a selection, depending on your selection's uniqueness within a menu. For example, if you wanted to choose "BANKING" from the menu, you could not type in just the letter **B** since "BULLETIN-BOARDS" also begins with B. You would have to type in **BA**. Don't worry if you make a mistake; Delphi will let you know that your one-letter entry defines more than one available service, and you will be able to make a correction.

Delphi is not completely established but is still under construction. Therefore, it is not possible to give you as detailed a tour as I gave you for BRS After Dark and CompuServe. There is only one program in Delphi that is likely to remain the same by the time you are reading this book: Delphi's Conference program.

Like CompuServe's CB Simulator, Delphi's Conference program is a real-time, multiuser discussion system. In my opinion it is, in fact, superior to the CB Simulator and you will see why shortly. From the main menu, type in C to get:

```
Welcome to the DELPHI Conference System
Conference Menu:
    WHO 〈list users〉
    PAGE 〈user〉
    JOIN 〈group〉
    NAME 〈nickname〉
    EXIT
CONF〉What do you want to do?
CONF〉
```

Unlike CompuServe's CB, you are not asked for a handle since your *membername* (User ID) will perform that function (represented in this example as "YOURNAME") nor are you given a list of available channels that you may enter. Most of the Delphi subscribers use their real names as membernames. Instead, you must perform the equivalent of CompuServe CB's /UST (User STatus) command. This command is **WHO** at the "CONF〉" prompt (**/WHO** within the Conference program itself), and it will give you:

```
CONF〉Who
GROUP LIST:
-1
    AKIRA, BABE, WAYNE
-PRIVATE
    STAN, JOE, *JIM
-idle
    YOURNAME
AVAILABLE LIST: * = operator ( ) = talking
    SHARI, (AKIRA), (BABE), (WAYNE), (STAN), (JOE), (*JIM), YOURNAME,
WENDY, WES, LINDA
```

Under "GROUP LIST" you will see group names in capital letters written as numbers or preceded by a hyphen ("-"). "Idle," which is in lower case, is *not* a group name; it indicates a user who is at the "CONF〉" prompt. You can see two active groups above, "1" and "PRIVATE." Under each group, you can see the membernames of those talking. "AKIRA," "BABE," and "WAYNE" are in group "1." "STAN," "JOE," and "JIM" are in the group "PRIVATE."

You, as "YOURNAME," are "idle," that is, sitting at the "CONF⟩" prompt. "AVAILABLE LIST" shows you all of the users currently on the Delphi system. Those within parentheses, such as "(AKIRA)," are currently talking in Conference; those not in parentheses, such as "SHARI," are somewhere else in the system. The asterisk ("*") next to "JIM," indicates that he is a member of the Delphi staff.

Now that you know there are people in the Conference system, you will want to join them and get to know them. To join those in group "1," at the "CONF⟩" prompt type **Join 1** and the screen will show:

CONF⟩**Join 1**

You will then see:

** YOURNAME just joined 1 (4 members now) **
(Type CONTROL/Z to exit back to menu)

The "** YOURNAME just joined..." notice will be seen by all within group "1," letting them know that you are now among them. Unlike CompuServe's CB, a user cannot lurk in Delphi's Conference system, listening to conversations without being immediately noticed. To leave the Conference system, execute a Control-Z or type **/EX** on a line by itself. Now that you are in a group, a conversation will look like this:

AKIRA⟩ I'm new to this system. How about you, Wayne?
BABE⟩ I think this is neat!
WAYNE⟩ Me, too. I learned about it from the Computer Phone Book. You guys come here often?
AKIRA⟩ It sure is, Babe. Hello, YOURNAME! Welcome!

To respond to AKIRA with, **Hi, Akira. Hello, everyone**, you just type it in. On your screen, it will look like this:

Hi, Akira. Hello, everyone.
YOURNAME⟩ Hi, Akira. Hello, everyone.

You will immediately notice two things: First, your input was *not* interrupted as it was when you were typing into CompuServe's CB

Simulator, and, second, your line was repeated with your membername preceding it. You were allowed to type without interruption because Delphi's Conference program is *buffered*; that is, all output to you is suspended until you have finished your input and have pressed your Return key. Then your input line is repeated, verifying its transmission and letting you know how it appeared. Any output that was halted during your typing is now resumed with no loss of text. This method makes Delphi's Conference system superior to CompuServe's CB. You can use it *immediately*, without being confused by interruptions from other users. You can also type in over 200 characters at one time instead of fewer than 80 as on CompuServe's CB.

By typing **/HELP**, you will see the following on your screen:

```
Immediate Commands:
/Answer    /Cancel     /Echo     /Exit    /Gname (name)
/Help      /Join (group)         /Menu (1, 2, 3)
/Name (nickname)       /Page     (user) /Reject
/Send (name-list) (msg)          /Time /Who
```

Using these commands will show you how flexible the Delphi Conference system can be. The most useful ones will be explained here.

"/Page" allows you to notify another user on the system that you would like him or her to join you in Conference. You may page anyone listed as available in Conference. The format is **/Page membername**. For example, if you wanted "SHARI" to come to Conference to chat with you, you would type **/PAGE SHARI**. The Conference program would then tell you:

SHARI being paged

When SHARI gets to the "CONF)" prompt, she will see:

CONF)Would you like to talk to YOURNAME?

If SHARI decides to chat, she is automatically placed in your group. If she is too busy or does not want to chat, SHARI could use the **/REJECT** command, which cancels the page and informs you:

SHARI cannot talk now.

"/Join" allows you to enter an existing group, as well as permits you to create your own. You may give it any name (except an obscene one). The format is **/JOIN name**. You can create a group called YOURNAME'S PLACE by typing, **/JOIN YOURNAME'S PLACE**. You will then be told:

You have just created group YOURNAME'S PLACE

If you want it to be a private group that other users can join only if you page them, include the word **private** in the group name. You can change the name of any group you have created or are in by using the **/GNAME** command followed by a new group name. Therefore, you can make your group private by typing:

/GNAME YOURNAME'S PRIVATE PLACE

The secret weapon of Delphi's Conference system is the **/Send** command. Much like a CompuServe SIG's **SEN** command, Delphi Conference system's **/SEND** command allows you to transmit a private message to an individual user. The format is **/SEND membername message**. To send a private message to SHARI who is very busy, you would type:

/SEND SHARI Sorry to have interrupted you.

You may also use this command to chat privately with a user within a group without other users knowing it. There is no need for you and another user to create and join a private group— just **/SEND** to each other!

Most of the Delphi Conference commands may be abbreviated to their first letter. The exceptions are **/ECHO** and **/EXIT**, since both have an E as their first letter.

These are just a few of the commands that will help you to use Delphi's Conference system like an expert. In Conference, you may ask old timers of the system to explain other commands and help you use them.

Dow Jones News/Retrieval Service

Dow Jones News/Retrieval Service features comprehensive business and financial news, historical news, and information and transactional services.

How to Use the Online Systems

After you have logged onto the system, you will see a brief signon message and copyright notice. Then you will see:

TYPE //MENU FOR A DATA BASE LIST

Typing **//MENU** will give you:

> MASTER MENU
> COPYRIGHT (C) 1983
> DOW JONES & COMPANY, INC.

TYPE   FOR

- A   DOW JONES BUSINESS AND ECONOMIC NEWS
- B   DOW JONES QUOTES
- C   FINANCIAL AND INVESTMENT SERVICES
- D   GENERAL NEWS AND INFORMATION SERVICES

You will not see a prompt asking you to type one of the above four choices. Instead, the cursor on your screen will sit in one spot. Selecting **A** will give you:

> DOW JONES BUSINESS
> AND ECONOMIC NEWS SERVICES

TYPE   FOR

- //DJNEWS   DOW JONES NEWS
- //FTS   FREE-TEXT SEARCH OF DOW JONES NEWS
- ///UPDATE   WEEKLY ECONOMIC UPDATE
- //WSJ   WALL STREET JOURNAL HIGHLIGHTS ONLINE

FOR HELP, TYPE CODE AND HELP.
(EXAMPLE: //DJNEWS HELP)

A highlight of Dow Jones News/Retrieval is the ability to get excerpts of the *Wall Street Journal*'s past issues and of the same day's issue at 6 AM. Let's take a look at that by typing in **//WSJ**:

```
    THE WALL STREET JOURNAL
       HIGHLIGHTS ONLINE
        COPYRIGHT (C) 1983
     DOW JONES & COMPANY, INC.

  THIS DATA BASE ENABLES YOU
  TO VIEW ONLINE HEADLINES AND
  SUMMARIES OF MAJOR STORIES IN
  THE WALL STREET JOURNAL. FOR
  DETAILS ON THESE AND OTHER
         STORIES, PLEASE SEE
         MONDAY'S JOURNAL.


  PRESS     FOR
     A   MONDAY'S EDITION
     B   PREVIOUS EDITIONS
```

Pressing **A** will give you

```
WSJ 10/10/83
      THE WALL STREET JOURNAL
      THE EDITION FOR MONDAY,
          OCTOBER 10, 1983.


  PRESS      FOR

     1    FRONT PAGE
     2    EDITORIALS
     3    FRONT PAGE--SECTION 2
     4    MARKET NEWS
     5    BACK PAGE
```

Selecting any of the above choices will give you a menu with headlines and corresponding numbers with which to select each. To get back to the News/Retrieval Master Menu, type **//MENU** at any text page in the system. You can also type any command prefixed by two slashes (//) to move around the system from any menu or text page.

Go back to the Master Menu, so you can take a look at one aspect of the News/Retrieval Service's quote services. By typing, **B** for "DOW JONES QUOTES," you will see:

           DOW JONES QUOTES

     TYPE   FOR

    //CQ   CURRENT QUOTES
    //DJA   HISTORICAL DOW JONES
                  AVERAGES
    //HQ   HISTORICAL QUOTES

FOR HELP, TYPE CODE AND HELP.
(EXAMPLE: //CQ HELP)

Typing //**CQ** will show you:

CURRENT DAY QUOTES BEING ACCESSED
ENTER QUERY

"ENTER QUERY" means you are to type in a three- to four-letter company code that will enable you to see the most current stock price quote for that company. The News/Retrieval user's manual contains a list of all companies and their stock codes; all you have to do is look up the company, type in the code, and press your Return key. You will then be given the stock's closing bid; its open asking price; its high, low, and last quote; and its trading volume.

Move back to the Master Menu by typing //**MENU.** Type **C** to get a glimpse of "FINANCIAL AND INVESTMENT SERVICES." Its menu looks like this:

           FINANCIAL AND
         INVESTMENT SERVICES

     TYPE   FOR

    //DSCLO   DISCLOSURE II
    //EARN   CORPORATE EARNINGS
                 ESTIMATOR

//MEDGEN   MEDIA GENERAL
//MMS   MONEY MARKET SERVICES

FOR HELP, TYPE CODE AND HELP.
(EXAMPLE: //DSCLO HELP)

All of the above databases are *value-added services*, meaning you will have to pay a fee above the usual connect-time for accessing other parts of the Dow Jones News/Retrieval Service. Current rates for these services may be found on the system itself by typing **//INTRO** for the system's free information newsletter.

The last menu you will take a look at here is accessed by going back to the Master Menu and selecting choice **D**, "general news and information services." On your screen you will see:

GENERAL NEWS AND
INFORMATION SERVICES

TYPE   FOR

//INTRO   FREE INFORMATION ABOUT
              NEWS/RETRIEVAL
//ENCYC   ENCYCLOPEDIA
//MOVIES   MOVIE REVIEWS
//NEWS   WORLD REPORT
//SPORTS   SPORTS
//STORE   COMP-U-STORE
//SYMBOL   SYMBOLS DIRECTORY
//WTHR   WEATHER
//WSW   WALL $TREET WEEK

FOR HELP, TYPE CODE AND HELP.
(EXAMPLE: //INTRO HELP)

The first selection, **//INTRO**, is where you will find news about the Dow Jones News/Retrieval Service and current connect-time rates. **//SYMBOLS** will allow you to retrieve any three- or four-letter company symbol you may need in order to use the quote service (described earlier); this is very handy if you are using the system and do not have your user's manual with you. //WSW will allow you to get full transcripts of the previous weeks' and current week's PBS-TV program, *Wall $treet Week.*

Although the Dow Jones News/Retrieval Service's user's manual is imposing when you first thumb through it, the service itself is actually very easy to use. You may choose to be guided to your needed information by a series of menus, or you may directly enter double slash (//) commands. The only portion of the system you may have difficulty with is the Free-Text Search Service.

Like BRS After Dark (and Knowledge Index, described next), the Dow Jones News/Retrieval Service's Free-Text Search system is an information retrieval database in which you use subject keywords to locate and display items of interest. Dow Jones provides a separate manual for this portion of their service, and I strongly suggest that you do not try to use the Free-Text Search service without it. It is a very powerful and flexible service, but it does not have a command protocol that can be learned through blind trial and error. You can call Dow Jones News/Retrieval Customer Support and order the Free-Text Search manual. It is free to all subscribers and will allow you to take full advantage of the service.

Knowledge Index

Knowledge Index, from Dialog Information Services, is the next National Network on our electronic itinerary. Knowledge Index is a powerful tool that you can use to retrieve information swiftly with just a handful of simple commands, making it a powerful resource for information gathering.

After you have entered your account number and password into the system, the following will appear on your screen:

WELCOME TO KNOWLEDGE INDEX

For instructions on how to use
Knowledge Index, enter HELP KI or ?
Otherwise enter your commands.
**Type BULLETIN for exciting news!!
?

? (a question mark) is the prompt character used in the system. Unlike the menu-driven systems you have just seen, Knowledge Index places you at a command level at all times. No matter which database you eventually access, you may execute any "HELP" command at any ? prompt. As the above notice tells you, you can type in either **HELP** or **?** to get a file that will give you some of the commands you can use on the system. Not every command that is listed in the large Knowledge Index manual is documented in online files, however, and the **HELP** or **?** command will actually point you to individual files you can read for each available command. The online help files contain enough commands to allow you to use the system the first time you logon.

Knowledge Index contains 16 databases under 11 categories of information. Typing **HELP SECTIONS** will give you the list of categories, databases, and database keywords (which is similar to BRS After Dark's database label).

Basically, there are three commands you use to locate and retrieve information: Begin, Find, and Display. **Begin** switches you to an individual database. To search, for example, the Microcomputer Index database (its keyword is **COMP3**), you type in:

?BEGIN COMP3

FIND tells Knowledge Index to search for the information you have specified with keywords. A typical search statement would look like this:

?FIND COMPUTER

or like this:

?FIND COMPUTER AND PHONE AND BOOK

As on BRS After Dark, **AND** is not the only connector you may use in searching; others are listed in the manual.

DISPLAY commands the database to print out any number of total entries it has found. There are three subcommands that may accompany **DISPLAY**, separated by a slash (/). They are a **SET** number, which specifies which search statement you want the database to act upon; **S, M,** or **L**, which tells the database you want the retrieved information to be displayed in Short, Medium, or Long form; and a number or range of numbers (such as **1, 1,2,3,** or **1-3**) specifying how many of the retrieved entries you want displayed. As you can see, this is very similar to the print options you can use on BRS After Dark. A **DISPLAY** could appear in the following forms:

?DISPLAY S1/S/1

which means, Display from my first search statement, in short form, the first (or only) available entry.

?DISPLAY S3/M/1-3

which means, Display from my third search statement, in medium form, items 1 through 3, with a pause between each item.

?DISPLAY S5/L/1, 2, 3, 4

which means, Display from my fifth search statement, in long form, items 1 through 4 without a pause between each item.

Combining what you have seen so far into an example of an actual Knowledge Index search would look like this on your screen:

?BEGIN COMP3
  10/10/83 18:25:36 EST
Now in COMPUTERS & ELECTRONICS (COMP) Section
  Microcomputer Index (COMP3) Database
  (Copyright 1983 Micro Info. Serv. Inc.)

?FIND COMPUTER AND PHONE AND BOOK
                4987 COMPUTER
                 79 PHONE
                988 BOOK
                 5 COMPUTER AND PHONE AND BOOK
?DISPLAY S1/S/1, 2
              Display 1/S/1
020638   8100604
    Computer Phone Book (— book review —)
              Display 1/S/2
020638   8100604
    The Electronic World of Mike Cane
?

In the above example, you entered the Microcomputer Index (COMP3) database (**BEGIN COMP3**), asked it to search for Computer Phone Book (**FIND COMPUTER AND PHONE AND BOOK**), and were told there were five entries that contained those three words ("5 COMPUTER AND PHONE AND BOOK"). You then told the database to print in short form the first two entries without a pause between them (**DISPLAY S1/S/1, 2**), which were then displayed for you. Each of these commands may be abbreviated to one letter; that is, **B** for Begin, **F** for Find, and **D** for Display.

Although the entries shown in the above example are totally fictitious, they are in the form they would appear in that particular database. Some databases, however, will give you up to three to four lines in a short print form.

In the above example, you can then print out more of the five entries in short form, print the first two short entries in long form, start another search by entering a new **FIND** command with subject keywords, or switch to an entirely different database by issuing the **BEGIN** command with a database name. You will not have to wade through menus or prompts, allowing you maximum speed and flexibility in locating and displaying information.

One other command you will be interested in is **COST**, which allows you to see how much you have spent during a search session thus far. After the above search example, you could type in **COST** to see:

?COST
  10/10/83 18:25:55   EST
 Session total: 0.019 Hours $ 1.00 User X99999

This cost printout is a rough estimate in this example.

Another feature of Knowledge Index is the ability to place an online order to get a duplicate or original copy of any article that has been indexed in any of the databases. It will be mailed to you, freeing you from a trip to your local library. There is an additional charge for this service.

The Knowledge Index user's manual is one of the largest I have seen for a service affordable by the general public. It is designed and written for the purpose of helping you to get into Knowledge Index and get out with the least amount of connect-time. Many examples of searches are shown with multiple options, allowing you to get a sense of the system before you logon.

The Source

The final National Network you will get a peek at is The Source, a broad-based information and communications system.

The Source, like Dow Jones News/Retrieval Service, gives you the option of being led through the system by a series of menus or of jumping directly to command level, where you may enter one-word commands or command strings to access databases and services directly.

When you have finished entering your account number and password and the signon notices have scrolled by, you will see The Source's introductory menu, which looks like this:

WELCOME TO THE SOURCE

1 USING THE SOURCE
2 TODAY
3 BUSINESS UPDATE
4 THE SOURCE MAIN MENU
5 WHAT'S NEW
6 COMMAND LEVEL

Enter item number or HELP

Choice "1" will give you a brief tutorial on using the system (which is not needed if you have the excellent user's manual); "2" will give you a choice of daily articles on different topics; "3" will place you in a database that features late-breaking news; "4" will place you in the menu structure; "5" will give you a selection of news about services and improvements added to the system; and "6" will place you at command level ("->"), where you may enter information and services directly.

Not every feature of The Source will be covered in this chapter. What we will do first is choose **6** and jump directly to command level, foregoing menus. Should you ever get lost at command level, however, just type **MENU** at any -> prompt and you will immediately return to the menu structure. At command level, you will see an arrow on your screen:

->

This arrow indicates command level in the system and the system's readiness for you to enter a command. The first thing you should type in is **CHAT -OFF**. This will prevent you from being interrupted by other users while you explore the system (full details will be presented later).

-> **CHAT -OFF**

Like our tour of the CompuServe Information Service, the first item we will examine on The Source is the electronic mail facility, called SourceMail or SMail. At the -> prompt, type in **MAIL** to see:

-> **MAIL**
Version 6.47 SOURCEMAIL
Do you want instructions?

If you have the excellent user's manual provided by The Source free to all new subscribers, you may dispense with instructions. If you are new to the system, and your manual has not yet arrived in the mail, answer **Y** to the above question. In this tour, we will bypass the instructions. Typing **N** will reveal:

⟨S⟩end, ⟨R⟩ead, ⟨SC⟩an, ⟨D⟩isplay, or ⟨Q⟩uit?

These are the commands available to you in using SMail. Even though you are at command level, The Source will still provide you with prompts in some of the services and databases "⟨S⟩end" will place you in text entry mode (shown shortly); "⟨R⟩ead" will start showing you all of your mail currently waiting (new letters and any letters you have not filed or deleted); "⟨SC⟩an" will show you the headers of any letters waiting for you (or still in your mailbox); "⟨D⟩isplay" will show you your mail files (although you will have to read these with an entirely separate and different command); and "⟨Q⟩uit" will return you to the command level prompt (->). All of these commands, which are displayed with their first letters in "⟨ ⟩," may be entered by just typing in the angle-bracketed letter(s). Since it will be highly unlikely that you will have mail waiting for you when you sign on to The Source for the first time, you can begin by learning how to send mail. Typing in **S** for ⟨S⟩end, you will see:

To:

This indicates that you must enter the User ID of the person to whom you wish to send mail. Unlike EMail on CompuServe, this is the first step you must take, not one of the last. Since you may not know anyone else on The Source, send a letter to yourself. This will allow you to gain experience in using SMail and help you to become confident in using the system. At the prompt, you will type in your User ID and then get a response, as follows:

To: **DEF123**
Subject:

Again you can see a difference between SMail and EMail: All of the information you placed *last* in EMail is *first* in SMail. Enter your subject, and you will see:

To: DEF123
Subject: **SMail test**
Enter text:

You are now in text entry mode. Just go ahead and type away.

Enter text:
This is a tsetof the mail system for myselff.
It will show me how easy it is to use SMail.

Once again, in your enthusiasm to send a letter, you have made the same typographical errors you made when you were writing your EMail message on CompuServe. You now have to do some editing and will discover the similarities and differences between *text editing* on CompuServe and on The Source.

Unlike CompuServe's FILGE, you are not in the file editor when you enter text in SMail. You must invoke the text editor in SMail by issuing a separate command. All active commands within SMail are preceded by a . (period) and are commonly called *dot-commands*. To call up the editor, you will have to type in **.ED**. It will look like this on your screen:

To: DEF123
Subject: SMail test
Enter text:
This is a tsetof the mail system for myselff.
It will show me how esay it is to use SMail.
.ED

You will then see the word "EDIT" on the next line:

Enter text:
This is a tsetof the mail system for myselff.
It will show me how esay it is to use SMail.
.ED
EDIT

You are now in the text editing system of SMail. Unlike FILGE on CompuServe, SMail editor commands are not preceded by a slash (/). Like FILGE, however, the SMail text editor is a line-oriented editor, and similar navigational commands are used. The first of these is **T**, to go the Top of your file. In the SMail editor, however, this does *not* take you to your first line of text, as you will soon see. Also as in FILGE, to move the line pointer *down* a line, you type **N** plus a *positive* number (such as, **N1**); to move it *up* a line, you type **N** plus a *negative* number (such as, **N−1**). **P**, like in FILGE, displays the current line. Again, although the same basic navigational commands are used, *none* of them are to begin with a slash (/) in the SMail editor. Let's look at what happened after you told the editor to move to the top (**T**) of your file and print (**P**) the first line:

This is a tsetof the mail system for myselff.
It will show me how esay it is to use SMail.
.ED
EDIT
T
P
.NULL.

What happened to your first line of text? Actually, nothing happened to it. There is always a blank, or *null*, line placed in any text file you create on The Source, whether it is a SMail letter, a text file typed in online, or a file that you have uploaded into the system.

How to Use the Online Systems 97

You need not worry about having lost any text when you see that first ".NULL." notice. It is probably obvious to you that if your letter starts with a blank line your first line of input text is actually the *second* line. Therefore, instruct the line pointer to move down one line, by typing **N1**. It will look like this on your screen:

This is a tsetof the mail system for myselff.
It will show me how esay it is to use SMail.
.ED
EDIT
T
P
.NULL.
N1
This is a tsetof the mail system for myselff.

You will notice that you did *not* have to move the line pointer down and then issue a separate print (**P**) command. One of the differences between FILGE and the SMail editor is that when you tell the line pointer to move to a line, it does not just simply move to that line—it moves to it and *displays* it.

Now that you can see the line that needs editing, do the same things you did when you edited your EMail letter in CompuServe's FILGE. Like FILGE, **C** is the command for changing text, but remember, you do not have to type in that first slash (/). Your editing of the displayed line will look like this:

This is a tsetof the mail system for myselff.
C/se/es
This is a testof the mail system for myselff.
C/to/t o
This is a test of the mail system for myselff.
C/f./.
This is a test of the mail system for myself.

To edit the second line, issue the **N1** command to move the line pointer down one line to display it automatically. Then edit the sentence.

C/f./.
This is a test of the mail system for myself.

N1
It will show me how esay it is to use SMail.
C/sa/as
It will show me how easy it is to use SMail.

Like in FILGE, to redisplay the entire message, tell the editor to go to the top (**T**) of the file, then tell it to print a greater number of lines than the file contains. It will appear this way:

C/sa/as
It will show me how easy it is to use SMail.
T
P100
.NULL.
This is a test of the mail system for myself.
It will show me how easy it is to use SMail.
BOTTOM

"BOTTOM," like FILGE's "%FLGEOF—End of File" notice, indicates that you are at the last line of your text. Your first SMail letter is finished! To get back to the regular SMail text entry mode, press your Return key *twice* and you will see:

.NULL.
This is a test of the mail system for myself.
It will show me how easy it is to use SMail.
BOTTOM
(you pressed Return here)
(you pressed Return here)
Enter text:

Although blank lines are not shown in this example, I will explain how to insert them. First note that you may not insert a blank line in any mail or text file by just pressing your Return key. As you have seen in this example, the use of the Return key placed you back into SMail's text edit mode. In order to skip a line of text—say, to make a new paragraph—you will first have to press your space bar to insert a blank space on the blank line. The program will read that space as a character, not as a ".NULL." line. You then press Return to start a new line of text. This rule is the same for uploading files, in most cases, and will be covered later.

If you are through with your letter, you may now send it. The basic sending function of SMail, which is all you need to be concerned with in this example, is executed by typing **.S**. This will speed your letter on its way with this notice:

DEF123—SENT

You will then be returned to the prompt:

⟨S⟩end,⟨R⟩ead,⟨SC⟩an,⟨D⟩isplay, or ⟨Q⟩uit?

Type in **Q** to return to command level ("->").

You have just seen an elementary demonstration of SMail. In reality, SMail is the most powerful and flexible electronic mail system offered by any of the national networks listed in *The Computer Phone Book*. At any point within SMail, you may issue the **.HELP** command to get a list of options available to you. Similarly, when you are in the SMail editor, you may type **.HELP** to get a complete list of navigational commands. SMail is an easy-to-use way of keeping in touch with other users of The Source.

One of the ways to meet other Source users is Chat, a real-time conferencing program. Unlike CompuServe and Delphi, at the time *The Computer Phone Book* was being written, The Source did not have a real-time multiuser conferencing program such as CB Simulator or Conference. Chat, on The Source, is a medium for one-to-one communication, not one-to-many conferencing.

To locate someone to chat with, you must first have a list of users currently online. You can get this by issuing the equivalent of CompuServe CB's /UST (User STatus) or Delphi Conference's /WHO commands. On The Source, this command is **ONLINE**. At command level, type in **ONLINE** and see:

DEF123 DEF234 DEF456 DEF789 DEF980 GHI231
GHI521 GHI766 GHI900 PQR111 PQR223 PQR359
PQR556 PQR613 PQR650 PQR789 PQR888 PQR979

This is a facsimile of a list of users on The Source at the same time as yourself.

To chat with one of these people, you first have to enter the command **CHAT -ON** at command level. Recall that one of the first commands I told you to type in when you initially logged onto The Source was **CHAT -OFF**. This command prevented you from being interrupted by chat requests from other users. Had you gotten one while you were looking around the system, you may have become confused by it. Now that you want to learn Chat you will allow yourself to be interrupted and to talk to other users. After you have typed in **CHAT -ON** and gotten another command level prompt, choose any of the User IDs you saw in the "ONLINE" list. Let's use PQR979 as an example. At command level, you will type:

->**CHAT PQR979**

If PQR979 has issued **CHAT -OFF** on his or her end, you will then see:

->CHAT PQR979
NOT AVAILABLE FOR CHAT

If, however, PQR979 has **CHAT -ON**, activated, you will see:

->CHAT PQR979

Enter:

You may now type in a one-line invitation to chat, such as:

->CHAT PQR979

Enter:
Hi, there. Have a few moments to chat?

Do *not* follow up with a second line immediately. PQR979 is probably busy in another section of the system and may not be able to finish what he or she is doing right away. It would be best and courteous to wait 3 to 5 minutes before giving up. If PQR979 is available to chat, you will shortly see on your screen:

** CHAT FROM PQR979   ***
SORRY FOR THE DELAY. WHAT'S UP?

You may then go ahead and type away. Like CompuServe's CB, however, your lines of dialogue will interrupt each other if both of you are not careful. On The Source, the proper Chat protocol is to indicate you are through "talking" by hitting your Return (or Enter) key *twice*. This will let the other person know that you are through and that it is his or her turn to send a reply.

When you are through chatting, you can end your session by hitting your Escape key. If you do not have an Escape key, use Break or Control-P. With an Escape key, the other person will get a "BYE BYE" message. In this example, let's say that PQR979 has an Escape key. On your screen, you will see:

BYE BYE...FROM PQR979

By using either Break or Control-P, you will merely get the command level prompt (->) again.

Perhaps you were not satisfied with the chat you had with PQR979 and would like to try to learn more about the person. You could look into The Source's User Directory, called Disearch, which is a voluntary listing of User IDs, first names, and interests. The listing is contributed by users who want to establish contact with other users who have similar interests. At command level, you will type in **DISEARCH** and will see:

->**DISEARCH**
Send any problems to TCA088. Thank you.
Do you want a description of this program?

We will dispense with this part in our example. Instead, type **N** and you will see the following:

On which keyword(s) do you wish to search:
Account name (A), First name (F), State (S), or
Interests (I). (other options are "STOP", "ALL",
or "SI")?

"STOP" will take you out of the program and return you to command level. "ALL" consists of over 1000 entries (not all of which are still active accounts). Therefore, you would not want to type in "ALL," unless you have a large bank account, a lot of paper for your printer, and a very good communications program. "F," for First name, will give you a long list of people with the first name you input. "S," for State, is useful, if you are looking for people who are in your immediate area or some other specific place. "I," for "Interests," is very useful, allowing you to search through thousands upon thousands of possible interests. In this example, "A," for Account name, will do. Type in **A** and see:

Keyword(s):

Then type in the User ID, **PQR979**, and after a few moments, you will see:

Keyword(s): **PQR979**
PQR979/NY/BARBARA/APPLE II+/NETWORKS/MUSIC/DATING/LITERATURE

The first entry is the User ID, the second is the two-letter post office state abbreviation, the third is the user's first name, and everything following are her interests. Had PQR979 *not* been listed in Disearch, you would have been told:

Keyword(s) :**PQR979**
No match.
More?

If you were not interested in looking up anyone else, you would reply **N** and be placed back at command level.

In Disearch, you may look for more than one User ID by separating them with a space between each one. You may also search for Interests in the same fashion. Since Disearch contains so many entries, it may take up to 5 minutes to complete a search. You may exit the program during that time by hitting your Escape or Break keys or by issuing a Control-P. Should you wish to enter yourself in Disearch, type **DIRECTADD** at command level.

Like CompuServe, The Source has a bulletin-board system. It is called Post, and by typing **POST** at command level, you will see:

->**POST**
Do you want instructions?

Again, in this example, we will skip that and type **N** instead to reveal:

⟨R⟩ead, ⟨PO⟩st, ⟨PU⟩rge, ⟨S⟩can, or ⟨H⟩elp:

"⟨R⟩ead" will allow you to go through complete message headers and choose which individual message you would like to read according to the additional items you will specify in the next prompts. "⟨PO⟩st" will place you in text entry mode, prompting you for a subject and, after you have composed your message, a category into which the notice will be placed. "⟨PU⟩rge" will allow you to delete any notices you have placed. "⟨S⟩can" will be the item used in this example, and typing **S** will reveal:

⟨C⟩ategory, ⟨U⟩ser ID, ⟨D⟩ate, ⟨K⟩eyword:

"⟨C⟩ategory" will allow you to specify one or several of the over 75 Post categories. (For your convenience, the entire list is printed in the directory listing of The Source in *The Computer Phone Book*.) "⟨U⟩ser ID" will scan all of the Post categories for postings made by the one or more User IDs that you will specify. "⟨D⟩ate" will scan all Post categories within the time frame you specify. "⟨K⟩eyword," like on CompuServe's BULLET, will scan subject headers for the keyword or keywords you may enter. In this example, you will scan according to categories. By typing in **C** you will get:

Categories or ⟨H⟩elp:

You may now enter a single Post category or several categories separated by spaces. For example:

Categories, or ⟨H⟩elp: **ART BOOKS**

Post will now do a scan of the categories "ART" and "BOOKS":

Categories, or ⟨H⟩elp: ART BOOKS
Searching . . .

No notices found for ART
1 notice found for BOOKS
1 notice valid.

Post has told you that no one has posted anything under the category, "ART," and that only one notice has been posted under the category, "BOOKS." It will then ask you:

⟨N⟩arrow, ⟨E⟩xpand or Return for all:

Although the above prompt may seem ludicrous, had you searched, for example, under the category "APPLE," you would have been presented with over 50 valid notices. If you did not want to wade through all of them, you could narrow your search by keyword, User ID, or date. In this example, though, you press Return and get:

1   10 OCT DEF111 COMPUTER PHONE BOOK(TM) (BOOKS)
Enter item(s), ⟨H⟩elp, or Return for all:

The first line is giving you the notice's scan number ("1"), the date it was posted ("10 OCT"), the User ID that posted it ("DEF111"), the subject ("COMPUTER PHONE BOOK(TM)"), and the Post category ["(BOOKS)"]. The prompt is asking you if you would like to read the above item(s) and, if so, to type in the scan number(s). Typing **1** will give you:

Category: BOOKS
Subject: COMPUTER PHONE BOOK (TM)
From: DEF111
Posted: 10 OCT 4:28 pm

⟨N⟩ext, ⟨PO⟩st, or Return for text-

Although you have already told Post, Yes, I want to read that, you are again asked if you want to read it or skip to the next notice (if there is one). Pressing your Return key will give you the message's text:

Has anyone seen this book in the store yet?
If you've read it, let me know. SMail DEF111.
Thanks.
- End -

"- End -" signifies that you have arrived at the last posting under your search requirements. Type **Q** to quit and return to command level.

The next thing you will learn in this tour of The Source is how to read mail. The command to see if you have any mail waiting for you is, **MAILCK**. Typing this at command level will show you:

->**MAILCK**
1 Unread

To read your letter directly, without the previous prompts, type in **MAIL R** and you will see:

->**MAILCK**
1 Unread

->**MAIL R**
Version 6.47 SOURCEMAIL
From: DEF123   2-Lines
On:10 OCT 1983 At: 16:55
To: DEF123
Subject: SMail Test

—More—

"—More—" is a prompt with several options, and you can get a list of them by typing **H** or **?** To read your letter, you merely have to type **Y**.

This is a test of the mail system for myself.
It will show me how easy it is to use SMail.

Disposition:

"Disposition:" is another prompt with several options that you can list by typing **H** or **?** in response. In this example, it is not necessary for you to save your letter, so type in **D** for delete, to get:

Disposition:**D**
No more mail.

Before exiting the system entirely, you should know that you may invoke the Source's text editor at any time at command level by typing **ED**. This will allow you to create a text file while you are in the editor mode. Remember, though, that you should not insert blank lines in the text without first keying in a space as a null character. If you have a file that you wish to upload that does contain blank lines (ones that you cannot remove without a great deal of trouble), at command level, type in **RCV**. This will allow you to upload files no matter what their format may be. You may then edit them as you would any other sort of file.

Although this has been a very brief tour of The Source, you can now see how easy it is to use. The number and types of databases and services available to you on the system are enormous, and what you do on and with the system is limited only by your imagination.

The Source is the last of the National Networks looked at in this chapter. The brief tours that have been presented should give you an idea of what is available to you and the ease with which you may use the various networks.

LOCAL-AREA SERVICES

The next type of system to be examined will be Local-Area Services. Since you have already seen how a menu-structured system operates, we will skip menu-driven local services and look at a keyword-driven system and a unique system.

StarText Metro

A good example of a keyword-driven system is StarText Metro, based in Fort Worth, Texas. StarText Metro began as most of the other keyword-driven local systems listed in *The Computer Phone Book*—by using a Tandy Videotex Host system. StarText has since upgraded its system and written new software. It is now the largest Local-Area Service in the nation, with local phone lines serving the cities of Fort Worth and Dallas.

After you have entered your User ID and password into the system, you will be greeted with a message such as:

```
10-Oct-83    22:02:19

GOOD EVENING NEW
SUBSCRIBER
WELCOME TO
S.T.A.R.T.E.X.T.
```

SINCE 10/1/83 YOU
HAVE BEEN ON THE
SYSTEM 5 TIMES FOR
A TOTAL OF 90
MINUTES. YOU HAVE
ACCESSED 56 KEYWORDS
AND HAVE 0.00 IN
OTHER CHARGES. THE
LAST TIME YOU WERE ON
THE SYSTEM WAS
09-OCT-83 AND YOUR
SUBSCRIPTION EXPIRES
ON 01/03/84.
OCT 10 22:40:20
Cloudy skies, a high
near 50 and a chance
of showers are
forecast for Tuesday.
Low near 40.

REQUEST:

"REQUEST:" is the prompt used in the system; it asks you to enter a keyword. You will be provided with a user's manual and a list of keywords as part of your subscription.

StarText Metro has features other Local-Area Services do not offer. You can set system parameters for seven different screen sizes, allowing you to tailor the system's output to suit your particular computer. You can define a clear screen character so your screen will go blank and the next *page* (screenful) of text will start on a clear screen. You can define the length of a pause between pages so that your screen does not go blank before you have finished reading the text. You can tell the system which of your keys you want to use as output-suspend and output-resume function keys.

The most important feature of the system (especially if you plan to call it long distance) is called Profile. This allows you to create a file with up to nine subject keywords in it. Your file will automatically mark news stories in the system's database that contain your keywords. At the "REQUEST:" prompt, you will only have to type **PROFILE** to have the captured stories automatically called up on your screen. You may combine this with an automatic disconnect function. In essence, using a communications program that can capture data, you may have your computer automatically call the system in the morning, logon, execute the "PROFILE" command, download the news stories, and be disconnected from the system. You could then read the stories, offline, at your leisure. This makes StarText Metro the equivalent of an electronic newspaper.

When you are on the system, you may get an index of current keywords by typing **INDEX** and a list of keywords that have not yet been sent out as a printed update by typing **NEWKEYWORDS**.

StarText Metro has a flat monthly subscription rate and a wide variety of databases.

GameMaster

The second Local-Area Service that deserves special attention is as old as The Source. In fact, it coincidentally opened for business the very same day The Source did. Based in Evanston, Illinois, and serving the metropolitan Chicago area, is the Local-Area Service, GameMaster.

GameMaster was the first online service devoted to providing something other than information or communications. It was created to provide fun. The system itself is designed to function like an Adventure-type game, and afficionados of such computer games will feel right at home on the system. Here is the signon procedure:

```
The Mansion awaits.
hit RETURN
[GM Doorkeeper]
"GREETINGS TO ALL OLD AND NEW MEMBERS!"
ARE YOU A REGISTERED MEMBER OF THE
GAMEMASTER SYSTEM?Yes
```

Typing **NO** will give you information on signing up:

```
THE MANSION AWAITS...
['PLEASE IDENTIFY YOURSELF']
ACCOUNT NUMBER?
PASSWORD?
```

```
MONDAY, OCT 10, 1983 06:15:31
CURRENT CREDIT BALANCE = 3,811
YOU HAVE THE MANSION TO YOURSELF...
WELCOME, MIKE.


------------------------------------
[P.A.]
'MEMBER JUST WALKED IN'
------------------------------------


CHECKING MAILBOX NUMBER = = > 16
Sorry, nothing new in the box!
DO YOU WANT TO SEE WHO IS
IN THE HOUSE RIGHT NOW?
```

Type in **YES** to see:

```
*  G a m e M a s t e r     GUEST BOOK  *
>>MIKE CANE
= = = = = = = = = = = = = = = = = = =

DO YOU WANT TO SEND A MESSAGE ON THE
P.A. SYSTEM TO ALL THOSE IN THE HOUSE?
```

Typing **YES** will give you

```
OK, YOU WILL NOW BE ALLOWED TO SEND ONE
MESSAGE OF UP TO 80 CHARACTERS TO ALL IN
THE MANSION.
INPUT YOUR MESSAGE NOW.
```
Hello to all from The Computer Phone Book(tm)!
```
LOOK RIGHT?—Hello to all from the Computer
Phone Book(tm)!
```

Typing **YES** reveals:

```
PLACING MIKE CANE IN GUEST BOOK.

-------[FOYER ENTRY P.A. SYSTEM]------

Hello to all from The Computer Phone Book(tm)!
= = = = = = = = = = = = = = = = = = =
```

YOU ENTER UPON A GRAND FOYER. THERE ARE
DOORS ON EITHER SIDE OF YOU AND A HALL
IN FRONT OF YOU. THE STAIRWAY TO THE
SECOND FLOOR IS UP FROM HERE.
IF YOU'RE NOT SURE HOW TO USE THE SYSTEM
YET OR IF YOU NEED ASSISTANCE, TYPE HELP
WHEN ASKED FOR CHOICE IN THE FOYER.

What would you like to do
in the FOYER?

Typing **HELP** will give you:

IF THIS IS YOUR FIRST VISIT TO THE
GAMEMASTER'S MANSION HERE ARE A FEW
HELPFUL HINTS.
1) YOU CAN MOVE AROUND THE HOUSE EITHER
BY WALKING OR ACTIVATING THE PORTAL
DEVICE WHICH WILL "TRANSPORT" YOU FROM
ANY "ROOM" TO ANOTHER "ROOM". THE WALK
COMMANDS ARE FORWARD, BACK, LEFT, RIGHT,
UP, AND DOWN. THIS IS INPUT WHEN ASKED
FOR "WHICH DIRECTION WOULD YOU LIKE TO
MOVE?" TO USE THE PORTAL, TYPE PORTAL
FOR A DIRECTION WHILE IN A ROOM. THE
FOYER IS CONSIDERED A ROOM FOR USING THE
PORTAL DEVICE. IT IS ALSO RECOMMENDED
THAT YOU HAVE A MAP OF THE HOUSE WHICH
WILL GREATLY HELP IN LOCATING INDIVIDUAL
ROOMS.
2) A LIST OF ALL THE ROOMS AND THEIR
STATUS CAN BE FOUND BY MOVING DOWN ONCE
YOU'RE IN THE MAILROOM. THE MAILROOM
CAN BE ACCESSED BY MOVING "RIGHT" FROM
HERE.
3) A DETAILED LISTING OF EACH ROOM
IS LOCATED IN THE LIBRARY WHICH IS ON
THE SECOND FLOOR. YOU CAN REACH THE
LIBRARY BY MOVING UP, THEN LEFT WHEN YOU
REACH THE TOP OF THE STAIRS AND THEN
TURN RIGHT WHEN YOU REACH THE END OF THE
HALL, OR YOU CAN PORTAL DIRECTLY TO THE
LIBRARY. THE LIST IS TO THE LEFT.
MOVING TO THE RIGHT, THERE ARE "BOOKS"

WHICH CONTAIN INFORMATION ON USING THE
FUNCTIONS OF THE HOUSE AND IN PLAYING
THE GAMES.
4) IF YOU ARE STILL HAVING TROUBLE, CALL
THE HOTLINE (328-9009) OR LEAVE A NOTE
IN THE GAMEMASTER'S MAILBOX OFF THE LEFT
IN THE MAILROOM.
5) THERE IS ALSO A LIST OF SPECIAL FOYER
FEATURES THAT ARE SEEN BY LOOKING "DOWN."
What would you like to do
in the FOYER?

Typing **DOWN** reveals:

```
............................
********F O Y E R   M E N U********
............................
(F)ORWARD     = = MOVES DOWN THE HALL
(B)ACK        = = LEAVE THE HOUSE
(L)EFT        = = ENTER PARLOR
(R)IGHT       = = ENTER MAILROOM
(U)P          = = MOVE UPSTAIRS
(P)ORTAL      = = ACTIVATE THE PORTAL
(PA)P.A.      = = TURN YOUR P.A. OFF
(G)UEST       = = CHECK ON OTHER GUESTS
(H)ELP        = = GET HELP INFORMATION
(C)ALL        = = REQUEST FOR HELP SENT
                  TO GM STAFF MONITOR
(S)EE         = = GET FOYER DESCRIPTION
(T)IME        = = TIME SPENT IN HOUSE
(X)PERT       = = TOGGLE EXPERT/NOVICE USER MODE
(HAN)DLE      = = CHANGES YOUR P.A. NAME
(M)AIL        = = FOR OPENING YOUR MAILBOX
(DIP)LO       = = FOR DIPLOMACY PLAYERS
```
What would you like to do
in the FOYER?

To get a good idea of what the GameMaster mansion is like, type in **S** to (S)EE the "Foyer."

You are now in the Foyer. The oriental
rugs covering the slate floor are
beginning to wear thin as the foyer
prepares to get an overhaul during the

month-long house cleaning. The marble walls were some leftover slabs from the Acropolis which the GameMaster picked up during one of his many trips to the Mediterranean. You might notice that a simple sheepskin rug has replaced the bear skin there in front of you. Are you familiar with the paintings of Ancient Greece? Those two on the west wall are early Athenians.

Before you, the grand stairway leading to the second floor and beyond. To the East, the mailroom; to the West, the Parlor; behind you, the front door. Step into the beam of light to activate the portal or feel free to walk and discover the numerous treats that await. You will be able to move around the house by inputting commands such as forward, backward, right, left, up, down, or portal.

What would you like to do in the FOYER?

Before we leave the mansion in this tour, try typing in **PORTAL**.

E N E R G I Z E ! !
[PORTAL ACTIVATED]
WHAT ROOM ARE YOU THINKING OF?

You simply type in the name of an available room and you will be whisked there immediately. Or you can "walk" through the mansion, discovering its pleasures on your own.

As mentioned in the above output from the system, the GameMaster documentation contains a map of the house, showing all of the available game rooms and what they contain. Full details and instructions on each game room are also included, as are regular updates.

If you subscribe to the system, make sure that your subscription contains the proper documentation. Some low-cost memberships give you only the barest of information, leaving you to rely on the online help files. No matter which type of subscription you choose, the

GameMaster system often holds contests and competitions, allowing its members to win free time on the system.

GameMaster offers more multiplayer games than any other system, including the large National Networks. In addition, the system features electronic messaging (not exactly electronic mail, more like electronic notes) for game players to keep in touch, a real-time multiuser conferencing program (in the "Parlor"), private "Conference Rooms" in which only two people may talk, and a variety of multiplayer games that allow you to test your skill against an actual human being, not a computer.

If you are looking for computer games that go beyond the limitations of a floppy disk, investigate GameMaster.

Bulletin-Board Systems (BBSs)

The next kind of system you will examine is run on a microcomputer, is called a Bulletin-Board System (or BBS), and offers a virtually limitless variety of information and services. Apple Bulletin-Board System, abbreviated ABBS, heads the alphabetical list of this type of system. But do not be confused by its title. Although it runs on an Apple microcomputer, you may call it no matter what brand of computer you are using. This rule holds true for any BBS listed in the directory section of this book: No matter what brand of computer is running the BBS you are calling, you will be able to use the system. You may not find downloadable programs for your computer on a system hosted by another brand, but even this rule is falling by the wayside as many TRS-80-based systems are beginning to offer downloadable software for a variety of brands (such cases will be noted in the individual directory listings).

When you call an ABBS (and almost any other BBS), press your Return or Enter key several times after you have gotten the carrier signal. For systems running at more than one bits-per-second rate, this will set the BBS to operate at your bits-per-second rate and to begin operation. Depending on the version of ABBS software the individual system is running on, you will see the following on your screen:

TYPE ⟨C/R⟩
TYPE ⟨C/R⟩

This may mislead you. Although it seems to be telling you to type in the three characters "C/R," what you should actually do is press your Return or Enter key. You will find that "C/R" and "carriage return" mean to press your Return or Enter key. Next, you will be asked:

WHAT IS YOUR FIRST NAME?
WHAT IS YOUR LAST NAME?

Only one question at a time will appear, of course. Just type in this information. If you intend to use the system regularly, you may need to get a password to allow you access to all of the system's features, and the *sysop* (*system operator*) will need to know your name. The only place your name will appear is in the *userlog*, which is a list of those who have called the system. Also, should you leave a message on the system, your name will automatically be placed on the message to indicate who it is from. If you use a silly pseudonym, you may cause yourself some embarrassment, so it would be best for you to use your real name. After you have typed in your name, you will be asked:

WHERE ARE YOU CALLING FROM
(CITY, STATE)?

It is standard practice to type in the full name of your city and the two-letter post office abbreviation of your state. Most systems will not accept the entire state name, and you will be asked to re-enter the information. This information will also be added to the userlog. Next, you will be asked:

WHAT IS YOUR PHONE NUMBER?
(XXX-XXX-XXXX)?

The format for typing in your phone number is area code, exchange, number (for example, 555-555-5555), even if you are in the same area code as the system. This will *not* appear in the userlog, so do not worry about getting calls in the dead of night. Your phone number will be printed out on the sysop's end. Should the system go down while you are using it, the sysop may want to give you a call to ask what happened so he or she can correct what might be a recurring problem. In the event that you have applied for a password for the system, the sysop will call you to verify that you are who you said you were. Some systems will not allow you to progress further without supplying this information. If you have any qualms about giving out your home phone number, type in your work number. In the several hundred times that I have left my home phone number on a system, however, I have yet to be bothered by unwanted calls.

After entering this information, the system will repeat it, so you may see if it was received correctly:

```
HELLO MIKE CANE CALLING FROM NEW YORK, NY
HAVE I MISSPELLED ANYTHING (Y/N)?
```

If your name is not as you had typed it or if you made a mistake, type **Y** as a reply and the process will start over, giving you another chance. If you pressed the right keys but consistently get the wrong letters on your screen, you may have a noisy phone line (as mentioned in Chapter 1). Just hang up and try your call again.

Answering **N** to the above will reveal:

```
IS THIS YOUR FIRST TIME ON THIS SYSTEM
(Y/N)?
```

If it is, type **Y**. You will then get a brief explanation of the commands available to you, information about the system itself, and whatever else the individual sysop thinks you should know to help you use the system easily. On your second call, you can type **N**, which is what I will do in this example. You will then see:

```
TIME IN: 01:46:16
YOU ARE CALLER #11451
LOGGING MIKE CANE TO THE DISC....
```

This means your name is being placed in the userlog. Then you will see:

```
        WELCOME TO THE

APPLE BULLETIN BOARD SYSTEM

          VERSION 4.1
```

You may then see "System Bulletins," notices about the system's performance, who sponsors it, its operating hours, and other such information. Eventually, you will see:

```
FUNCTION:
(A, B, C, D, E, G, H, K, L, N, Q, R, S, T, V, W, X,
DOWNLOAD, UPLOAD, NEWS, CONF?)?
```

What do you do now? On virtually *all* systems, when you are presented with a prompt such as the above (or a one-word prompt such as "FUNCTION:"), you may type in **?** (a question mark) to get a brief explanation or a menu. Typing in **?** to the above will show you:

```
FUNCTIONS SUPPORTED:

A  =  APPLE 40 COLUMN
B  =  PRINT BULLETIN
C  =  CASE SWITCH
D  =  DUPLEX SWITCH (ECHO/NO ECHO)
E  =  ENTER MESSAGE INTO SYSTEM
G  =  GOOD-BYE (LEAVE SYSTEM)
H  =  HELP WITH FUNCTIONS
K  =  KILL (ERASE) A MESSAGE
L  =  LINE FEED (ON/OFF)
N  =  NULLS (SET AS REQ'D)
Q  =  QUICK SUMMARY OF MSG'S
R  =  RETRIEVE MSG
S  =  SUMMARY OF MSG'S
T  =  TIME OF DAY
V  =  TOGGLE VIDEO/PLAYER TERMINAL MODE
W  =  PRINT WELCOME MESSAGE
?  =  PRINTS FUNCTIONS SUPPORTED
DOWNLOAD = DOWNLOAD SOFTWARE TO YOUR APPLE
UPLOAD = UPLOAD FILES/SOFTWARE TO THIS SYSTEM
NEWS = INFO OF INTEREST TO SYSTEM USERS
CONF = SWITCH CONFERENCES

FUNCTION:
(A, B, C, D, E, G, H, K, L, N, Q, R, S, T, V, W, X,
DOWNLOAD, UPLOAD, NEWS, CONF,?)?
```

This is the function menu of an ABBS. Not all ABBSs will have features such as download, upload, news, or conference; it depends on how much software and equipment the particular sysop has invested in. Typing **H** at the above prompt will give you the system's help files, which are detailed explanations of each function. For your convenience, this material is reprinted in Appendix 1.

Now that you have seen the list of commands available to you on an ABBS, how would you use the system? It depends on you. When you first sign on to it (or any other BBS), you may choose to read all of the messages on the system. Or you may be selective by doing a quick scan and writing down the numbers of interesting message headers on a sheet of paper. You can retrieve them later en masse. Since an ABBS does not have keyword search on the subject field of messages, this latter method, illustrated below, is the fastest way to go through the message base.

FUNCTION:
(A, B, C, D, E, G, H, K, L, N, Q, R, S, T, V, W, X,
DOWNLOAD, UPLOAD, NEWS, CONF,?)?

To dispense with this long prompt, type in **X**, for expert user; you will then get the following as a prompt:

FUNCTION:?

Now enter **Q**, for quick scan, and get:

FUNCTION:?**Q**

STARTING MSG # (2500/2597)?

Instead of entering **2500** as the starting message, you may enter **1**. The system will then start at the first available message, like so:

MSG #2500 SUBJ: SYSTEMS GALORE!
DATE: 10/01/83
MSG #2501 SUBJ: PIRACY
DATE: 10/01/83
MSG #2503 SUBJ: ABORTED MESSAGES
DATE: 10/01/83
MSG #2509 SUBJ: APPLE II+
DATE: 10/01/83
MSG #2510 SUBJ: STILL HERE! ⟨PRIVATE⟩
DATE: 10/01/83

and so on, until you reach message number 2597. You will not be able to read any message marked as "⟨PRIVATE⟩." After you have scanned all of the messages and have made notes of the message numbers you want to read, you can retrieve them individually like so:

FUNCTION:?**R;2500**

You will now be able to read message number 2500, which looks like this:

```
MSG #2500
SUBJ: SYSTEMS GALORE!
TO: ALL
FROM: JIM
DATE: 10/01/83
```

If you are looking for more BBSs to call than just this one we have in town, you should get The Computer Phone Book by Mike Cane. It has literally hundreds of BBS listings and descriptions! Plus, it gives examples of how to use a good many of them. I just bought it yesterday and I'm sure my phone bill will never be the same!

You will then be prompted with:

MSG# TO RETRIEVE (2500/2597)?

You can now type in the next message you wish to retrieve or you could retrieve several as a group, like so:

FUNCTION:?**R;2510, 2515; 2519; 2530**

Remember, these are just two examples of how to retrieve messages, reading them all or typing **Q** for a quick scan. Take some time to experiment with the various ways of retrieving messages and pick the way that suits you.

If you want to leave a message on the system, type **E**, for enter message. You will then see:

```
FUNCTION:?E
THIS WILL BE MESSAGE #2598
SUBJECT?
```

Type in the message's subject:

SUBJECT?**Thanks**
TO?

Type in either **ALL**, if it is a message to be read by all users of the system, or a name, if it is a message for just one person:

TO?**Jim**
LOCK (Y/N)?

If you do not want the message to be erased by anyone else but you, answer **Y**:

LOCK (Y/N)?**Y**
PASSWORD FOR ERASE (4 CHARS. MAX.)?

Type in any four letters, but make sure you write them down so you will not forget them:

PASSWORD FOR ERASE (4 CHARS. MAX.)?**TEST**
MARK AS PRIVATE MAIL?

Unless you have given the other person the message's password, he or she will not be able to read the message. In this example, I will answer **N** for no:

MARK AS PRIVATE MAIL?**N**
YOU MAY NOW ENTER UP TO 20 LINES OF
UP TO 64 CHARACTERS OF TEXT PER LINE
1?

"1?" is the prompt for you to start typing in your text, like so:

1?**Jim: Thanks awfully much for the parise on my**
2?**Computer Phone Book. I really appreciate**
3?**it. Mike Cane.**
4?

After line 3, I hit Return and got prompted for a fourth line of text. I simply press Return again, and get:

4?

(A, C, D, E, L, R, S, ?)?

Typing in **?** will give

ENTRY FUNCTIONS:

A = ABORT
C = CONTINUE ENTRY
D = DELETE A LINE
E = EDIT A LINE
L = LIST LINE(S)
R = RESTART FROM BEGINNING
S = SAVE MESSAGE TO DISC
(A, C, D, E, L, R, S, ?)?

On line number 1, I made a mistake, so I must correct it. Choosing **E**, for edit, I am asked:

EDIT WHICH LINE?**1**
LINE 1 CURRENTLY IS:

Jim: Thanks awfully much for the parise on my

NEW LINE? (C/R TO LEAVE THE SAME)

On some systems, to correct a mistake on one line, you will have to retype the entire line. On ABBS (as its documentation in Appendix 1 states), there is a line editor similar to those on the National Networks. Editing the typo will look like this:

/parise/praise
LINE 1 CURRENTLY IS:

Jim: Thanks awfully much for the praise on my

NEW LINE? (C/R TO LEAVE THE SAME)

Next hit Return and get:

(A, C, D, E, L, R, S, ?)?

Type in **S**, to save the message onto the system and get:

(A, C, D, E, L, R, S, ?)?**S**
SAVING MSG TO DISC....

FUNCTION:?

If you wish, you may read your message to make sure that all is well.

Once you have finished using the system, log off using the appropriate menu selection. *Never, never* hang up on a system to leave it. *Always* terminate a session by issuing the proper command. If you were to hang up on a system, you might leave the system unable to be used by other callers until the sysop notices and corrects the problem. On some systems, the software can automatically recover, but it takes several minutes until it can ready itself to serve a new caller. This is so important, in fact, that increasing numbers of systems are instituting safeguards to make note of who hangs up on their systems. Those who do hang up may one day find themselves permanently banned from a system because they *exited with prejudice*, meaning just hanging up their phone.

On an ABBS, the proper exiting procedure is to type **G**, for goodbye. You will then see:

FUNCTION:?**G**

GOOD BYE, MIKE

THANKS FOR CALLING...

TIME OUT: 01:58:59
TIME ON SYSTEM: 00:12:43

++++END OF CONNECTION++++

The system will automatically hang up the phone on its end and you will have concluded your first BBS session.

Of all the BBSs you can call, none are as easy for a first-time caller as is ABBS. If there is an ABBS in your area and you have never before gone online, you would be doing yourself a great favor by practicing on an ABBS.

Most BBSs offer much the same things as the ABBS does, so there is no need to present an example of each type of system. There is, however, documentation for the most popular systems in Appendix 1. The rest of this chapter will present brief illustrations of four types of systems, three which are not similar to most BBSs and one which is (it is included to illustrate a function of other systems).

The next type of BBS you will learn about is actually not a BBS. It is a *conferencing system*, aptly called Conference Tree. Conference Trees, which are not too widespread, are intellectual systems, allowing you to read and participate in conferences that are, in effect, debates of topical issues or detailed discussions of individual topics. Subjects can range from disarmament to the latest rumors of new microcomputers.

Conference Trees are very easy to use, as you will see from this illustration. After establishing contact, you will see:

```
WELCOME TO THE CONFERENCE TREE
TERMINAL LINE LENGTH (20–80,
OR CARRIAGE RETURN FOR 80)?
LOWER CASE OK (C/R = YES)?

TYPE "READ HELP" ANY TIME
OR "READ CONFERENCES" TO START
"S" KEY TO PAUSE OR RESUME PRINTING

COMMAND?
```

"COMMAND?" is the system prompt. In the brief system notice above, you were given just enough information to start using the system. At "COMMAND?," type **READ CONFERENCES** and you will see something similar to this:

COMMAND? **READ CONFERENCES**

```
*** CONFERENCES          0-JAN-80

    PARENT = NONE              USAGE1500

CURRENT CONFERENCES ON THIS CONFERENCE TREE SYSTEM ARE:

        +++ SUBMESSAGES +++

HELP                 16-JUL-81
ANNOUNCEMENTS        20-JUL-81
FLAGSHIP             20-JUL-81
SYSOP                20-JUL-81
USERS                21-JUL-81
```

How to Use the Online Systems 123

```
SOFTWARE-REVIEWS      23-JUL-81
HARDWARE              25-JUL-81
```

COMMAND?

To read any of the above, all you have to do is type, **READ** and the conference's name, for example, **READ SOFTWARE-REVIEWS** (you must type the conference name *exactly* as it appears). Any comments added to that conference will be listed as "SUBMESSAGES." It will look something like this:

COMMAND? **READ SOFTWARE-REVIEWS**

```
*** SOFTWARE-REVIEWS         23-JUL-81

    PARENT = CONFERENCES           USAGE = 1300

THIS IS WHERE YOU ARE TO PLACE YOUR PERSONAL REVIEWS OF
SOFTWARE FOR ANY TYPE OF MACHINE. PLEASE BE AS DETAILED
AS POSSIBLE IN YOUR REVIEWS. --SYSOP

        + + + SUBMESSAGES + + +
APPLE-SOFTWARE               23-JUL-81
COMMODORE-SOFTWARE           23-JUL-81
IBM-PC-SOFTWARE              23-JUL-81
TRS-80-SOFTWARE              23-JUL-81
```

To read any of these conferences, type in **READ** followed by the conference's name.

A very useful command on a Conference Tree is **INDEX**. This command allows you to see just how much discussion is going on in any one conference. As an example, I will show you an index of the conference "HELP."

COMMAND? **INDEX HELP**

```
HELP                         16-JUL-81
  HELP-COMMANDS              16-JUL-81
    HELP-COMMANDS-2          16-JUL-81
HELP-OPTIONS                 16-JUL-81
HELP-ADDTO                   16-JUL-81
  EDITOR                     16-JUL-81
MISC-HELP                    16-JUL-81
SYSTEM-PASSWORD              16-JUL-81
```

As you can see, it looks like an outline, which is exactly what it is. "INDEX" shows you the logical progression of all of the "SUB-MESSAGES" under any given conference. You may read any of the submessages individually by issuing the **READ** command and the submessage's title.

Both the **READ** and **INDEX** commands may be abbreviated to their first letter. With just these two commands at your disposal, you will be able to use a Conference Tree the first time you call it. To get the most out of this type of system, however, you should thoroughly familiarize yourself with all of the system commands, printed in Appendix 1. A Conference Tree is worth a long-distance call, a distinction and blanket recommendation I cannot give to other types of systems.

The next type of system you will get a peek at is called Dial-Your-Match (commonly referred to as DYM). Its sole purpose is *matchmaking*. Matchmaking can mean finding a person of the opposite sex who shares your interests to finding a person of the same sex to get together with on a weekend. The audience of any one DYM is determined by its individual sysop; the individual DYM listings in the directory section of *The Computer Phone Book* make note of each system's audience.

When you call a DYM, you will see something like this:

```
         -> HOW MANY NULLS? (0-50)=>
     =* =* =* =* =* =* =* =* =* =* =* =* =* =* =*
      *                                         *
     =*          WELCOME TO     TM             _*
                                                =
     =*          DIAL-YOUR-MATCH#1             _*
                                                =
     =*          THE ONLY WORLD-WIDE           _*
                                                =
     =*       COMPUTER MATCHING SERVICE        _*
                                                =
     =*    (C)  1982 MATCHMAKING ENTERPRISES   _*
                                                =
     =* =* =* =* =* =* =* =* =* =* =* =* =* =* =*

        -> DIAL-YOUR-MATCH WILL NOW ONLY ALLOW
        -> YOU TO STAY ON FOR UP TO 25 MINUTES
```

The time limit, by the way, varies from system to system, and each system's listing specifies the time limit, if any.

```
675 CALLERS NOW IN THE DATE-A-BASE!
YOU ARE CALLER #51345
LOGGED ON AT 02:45 on 10/10/83
HAVE YOU CALLED DIAL-YOUR-MATCH BEFORE?
=>
```

If you have never before called the system, answer **N**. If you answer **Y**, you will have three chances to type in your password. Since you will not have a password as a first-time user, you will be disconnected after three tries and will have to call the system back—an expensive proposition if you are calling long-distance. Answering **N** will give you:

```
=*=*=*=*=*=*=*=*=*=*=*=*=*=*=*=*=*=

BEFORE YOU CAN DIAL-YOUR-MATCH, YOU

MUST ANSWER A QUESTIONNAIRE GIVING THE

COMPUTER INFORMATION ABOUT YOURSELF.

THE COMPUTER WILL THEN BE ABLE TO

MATCH YOU TO OTHER COMPATIBLE CALLERS.

=*=*=*=*=*=*=*=*=*=*=*=*=*=*=*=*=*=

WARNING!! ALL INFORMATION IN THE

FOLLOWING QUESTIONNAIRE MAY BE

RELEASED TO ANYONE CALLING THIS SYSTEM.

REMEMBER! NONE OF YOUR PERSONAL

INFORMATION IS CONFIDENTIAL AND

YOU MUST COMPLETE A QUESTIONNAIRE

TO BE ALLOWED ON THIS SYSTEM.
```

=> DO YOU WANT TO CONTINUE?
=> (YES/NO) =>

Answering **Y** to the above begins the process.

=*=*=*=*=*=*=*=*=*=*=*=*=*=*=*=*=*=*=

=*   QUESTIONNAIRE   *=

=*=*=*=*=*=*=*=*=*=*=*=*=*=*=*=*=*=*=

WHAT IS YOUR FIRST NAME (OR HANDLE):
=> **MIKE**
WHAT CITY ARE YOU CALLING FROM:
=> **NEW YORK**
WHAT IS THE 2-LETTER POST OFFICE
ABBREVIATION OF THE STATE YOU ARE
CALLING FROM:
=> **NY**
YOUR FIRST NAME IS: MIKE
YOU'RE CALLING FROM: NEW YORK, NY
IS THAT CORRECT? =

Then the actual questions will begin, for example,

WHAT IS YOUR SEX?
   A. MALE
   B. FEMALE
=> **A**
YOU PICKED: A. -> MALE
CORRECT? => **Y**

No answer will be tallied until you have verified that you have replied correctly. Take your time in filling out the questionnaire, which consists of about 25 questions (keeping in mind that your system time limit is 25 minutes).

Once you are through with the questionnaire, you will be assigned an "Address Code." This is a User ID that consists of your first name (or handle) and three numbers; it will enable you to receive private mail from anyone who is later matched to you on the system. You will also be assigned a password, so you will not have to fill out a questionnaire the next time you call in. *Make sure that you imme-*

How to Use the Online Systems   127

diately write both of these items down (preferably in the individual DYM directory listing in *The Computer Phone Book*!). You will be asked if you have written them down. If you answer **Y**, your screen will go blank and you will be asked to *type them in* so that the system will know that you have written them down properly.

Next, you will be given the following menu:

```
-> DIAL-YOUR-MATCH COMMANDS <-

B --> BROWSE QUESTIONNAIRES
C --> CHAT WITH THE MATCHMAKER
G --> GOODBYE
M --> MATCHMAKER, MAKE ME A MATCH
N --> SET NULLS
O --> OTHER DIAL-YOUR-MATCH SYSTEMS
P --> PUBLIC MESSAGE BOARD
R --> READ PRIVATE MAIL
S --> SEND PRIVATE MAIL
? --> HELP WITH COMMANDS

MIKE, WHAT NOW?
-> ?, B, C, G, M, N, O, P, R, S => 
```

The above is pretty much self-explanatory. There is only one command that I will illustrate here: "M." Typing in **M** will give you:

```
MIKE, WHAT NOW?
-> ?, B, C, G, M, N, O, P, R, S =>M

MATCHMAKER, MAKE ME A MATCH
-> COMPLETE SEARCH TAKES 7 MINUTES
```

Actually, the search time varies from system to system, depending on how many callers are in the "Date-A-Base." Systems with few callers will only take 2 to 3 minutes to complete a match.

```
*NOW SEARCHING FOR YOUR PERFECT MATCH*
    P TO PAUSE, S TO STOP
```

You will eventually see something like this:

ADDRESS CODE	%	AGE	ST	PREF
ALI000	64%	18 - 20	CA	HETERO
BETTY000	57%	31 - 40	CA	HETERO
CATHY000	53%	13 - 17	NV	BI
DEVON000	55%	21 - 25	OR	HETERO

and so on, showing you the "Address Codes" of the individuals in the system, the percentage of matches between their answers and yours, and their age range, state, and sexual preference ("HETERO" for heterosexual, "BI" for bisexual).

The next step you take depends on you. You can either immediately send mail to those you have been matched with, or you can look at the answers they gave in their questionnaires to see if you are compatible. To do the latter, type **B**. You will then have the option of reading either each person's answers or the questionnaire questions and the answers. When you use **B** you will also get statistics such as how many times that person has called the system, how many days ago his or her last call was, and if the person has any open mail slots so you can send him or her mail.

Several matchmakers, as well as female callers to DYM, have told me that women callers are put off by getting electronic mail that is, to be blunt, graphic in its description of a certain social activity and its various configurations. Please exercise good taste.

In the 1960's, there was a flurry of hype about the arrival of computer dating services. Dial-Your-Match is a true computer-dating service, and the best part of it is that it is only the price of a phone call.

The next system to be discussed here is PMS (People's Message Service). I will use it to illustrate a feature you will find on other BBSs—*marking messages*. I have chosen PMS to illustrate this feature because on PMS this task is easier and faster than on any other system, including National Networks. Once you have established contact, you will see:

```
PMS—SANTEE, CA
USERID (N=NONE) :
```

If you do not have a User ID, reply **N**. You may get a User ID by requesting one from the sysop before you log off. Typing **N** will give you:

YOUR FULL NAME ?**Mike Cane**
City, St. ?**New York, NY**
Phone number ?**212-555-5555**
You are Mike Cane from New York, NY
Is that right ?**Y**
Logging caller #75655 at 16:32 Pacific

Notice how PMS switched from sending all upper case letters to upper and lower case when I typed in lower case. After the system has logged your name onto the disk, you will see:

Type "N" for system news.
Type "?" for commands.
Command ?

Remember, on virtually any system that you can call, typing a **?** (question mark) will give you a menu or help file. In this case, you will get:

---->> System Commands

```
E    = Enter a message into system.
F    = Features, articles, excerpts
G    = Goodbye. Leave system. (Hangup)
H    = Help with various functions.
I    = Information about system.
K    = Kill a message from the files.
M    = Message alert. Messages for you?
N    = News—System news.
O    = Other systems current summary.
Q    = Quickscan of all message headers.
QP   = Quickscan of private msg headers.
R    = Retrieve a message from the files.
S    = Scan of all message headers.
SP   = Scan of private message headers.
SR   = Selective message retrieval.
T    = Time, date and connect time.
U    = User modifiable system functions.
```

X   = eXpert user mode. (On/Off toggle)
Z   = Continue message entry after abort.
?   = Prints this list of commands.
*   = Flagged message memory retrieval.
TALK = Lets you talk to the Sysop.
TEST = Modem continuous test loop.
NEWCALL = Information for new callers.
ALT = Switch message bases.
GENERAL14 = File Transfer—Download files.
GENERAL15 = File Transfer—Upload files.

Command ?

The PMS help file, reprinted in Appendix 1, details all of the above options. Be sure to study them before you use a PMS so you can take advantage of its many built-in ways to save you time in long-distance calling.

Two tricks to save you time will be presented here: the **SR** and **Q** commands. **SR** means Selective Retrieval and, as it implies, is a way to search the subject fields of messages according to any keyword you may supply. It would look like this:

Command ?**SR;BBS**

I have just told the system to look through all of the messages currently on the system and to "selectively retrieve" all of those that have the three letters "BBS" in the subject field. As you can see, I did all of this in one step—by command stringing and separating the two commands with a ; (semicolon). The actual search would look like this:

Command ?**SR;BBS**
Msg# 248 on 10/09/83 @23:28 (2)
Subj: BBS???, To: All
From: Akira Fitton, New York, NY

Has anyone found a BBS that specializes in the Commodore-64 computer??

Msg# 275 on 10/10/83 @16:55 (3)
Subj: C-64 BBSs, To: Akira Fitton
From: Mike Cane, New York, NY

Yes, Akira, there are plenty of such BBSs. All
you need to do is to buy "The Computer Phone Book
(tm)" at your local bookstore. (Plug!)

and so on. As you can see, PMS retrieved messages with the string "BBS," regardless of other characters surrounding those three letters. It is quite a time saver, allowing you to go through a message base without having to scan or quickscan every message header to find what you are looking for.

In the above two sample messages, you will notice that on the first line there are numbers within parentheses, such as "(2)" and "(3)." These are the number of lines each message contains. This information is helpful in determining how long you may be online reading when you do a quickscan (**Q**), as illustrated below:

Command ?**Q**
Msg# (240/490) ?**490**

PMS asked me at which message I should start the quickscan, and I specified the highest number in the system. This will cause PMS to run through the messages from the most recent to the earliest. I could have done a command string such as **Q;9999** to accomplish the same thing; however, not all PMSs have that ability and some will prompt you for a starting message number (this missing option is due to sysops not upgrading their software with regular updates). The quickscan will look like this:

Command ?**Q**
Msg# (240/490) ?**490**

Msg# 490 on 10/11/83 @21:05 (7)
Subj: VIC 20, To: All

Msg# 489 on 10/11/83 @20:20 (2)
Subj: Apple, To: All

Msg# 488 on 10/11/83 @20:15 (3)
Subj: Book??, To: All

Msg# 487 on 10/11/83 @19:57 (15)
Subj: User IDs, To: All

and so forth. Doing a quickscan will not save you any time, however, which is what I want to show you how to do here.

When you are doing a quickscan on a PMS, you can use a powerful subcommand while the message headers are scrolling up your screen. This subcommand is to press your **R** key, which will mark the messages you are interested in reading. In other words, the system will make a note of which messages you have expressed interest in and will retrieve these messages for you when you issue a second command. The time when you press the **R** key is during the printout of the *next* message header for the *previous* message header. In other words, if I had wanted to read message number 490, above, I would have pressed my **R** key while message number 489 was appearing on my screen. It would look like this:

Msg# 490 on 10/11/83 @21:05 (7)
Subj: VIC 20, To: All

Msg# 489 on 10/11/83 @20:20 (2)

I press my **R** key as this is printing out.

Subj: Apple, To: All
Ok <490>

The "**Ok** <490>" means that PMS has *marked* message number 490 for me so I may retrieve it when I am ready, using a second command. This second command is * (an asterisk). Using it would look like this:

Command ?*

Msg# 490 on 10/11/83 @21:05 (7)
Subj: VIC 20, To: All
From: Babe Stevens, New York, NY

```
::::::::::::::::::::::::::::::
:  looking for          :
:  other vic users      :
:  to trade pgms and    :
:  info with. call      :
:  555-5555. thnx       :
::::::::::::::::::::::::::::::
```

How to Use the Online Systems 133

There is no need for you to look at all of the message headers in the system and write their numbers down so you can later retrieve them individually. The system will bring all of them to you if you use the **R** and ***** commands. If most PMS users were to use this method, each system could handle more callers each day and you would be able to get on more often.

The last feature of a PMS that will be presented here is the message entry and editing procedure. Selecting **E** for enter message into system will look like this:

Command ?**E**
To: ?**Babe Stevens**
Subject ?**VIC-2Ø(!)**
C/r to end.

1
?**Babe: Long time no see. I didn't know you had**

2
?**goten a VIC! How do you like it? I have one,**

3
?**too. Give me a ring when you're able and we'll**

4
?**chat. Best, Mike Cane**.

5
?

Since I am finished with my message, I could press my Return key at the prompt for line 5 and get a list of options. If you already know the message editing and entry options, you can dispense with the options and enter them directly, preceded by a "." (period). It is the same as using the dot-commands on The Source in SMail. I made a mistake in line 2, so I will edit it as follows:

5
?**.E2**
line #2:
goten a VIC! How do you like it? I have one,

```
edit
?/goten/gotten
line #2:
gotten a VIC! How do you like it? I have one,
edit
?
```

I have corrected the error on line 2, am certain that the message is as I want it, and will save it. Since the message is to a particular person and has no interest to other users of the system, I will save it as a *private message*—one that only the person it is meant for can read. To do this, I must first issue the **.S** command to save the message:

```
?.S
Password (4 Chrs. max.) ?LOCK
```

"LOCK" is not the message's password, it is a command to the system to store the message as a private one. Then:

```
Password (4 Chrs. max.) ?LOCK
Password?VIC
Msg# 491....saved
```

VIC is the password I chose for that particular message. When my friend signs on to the PMS, she will be able to read the message I left and delete it or reply to it. In the least amount of time, I was thus able to write and store a message on the system.

As a new user, you will need to know the PMS message entry and editing functions available to you. Here is the list:

(A, C, D, E, H, I, L, S, W, ?)?

---->> Message entry commands

```
A  = Abort message.
C  = Continue entry.
D  = Delete line (Dx).
E  = Edit line (Ex).
H  = Help with message entry functions.
I  = Insert a line (Ix).
```

L = List lines from specified # (Lx).
S = Save completed message to disk.<<<
W = reWrite an old message.

Again, it would be best for you to familiarize yourself with the details of each of the PMS commands, reprinted in Appendix 1.

The last type of system you will be shown is not as simple to use as other BBSs. In fact, when you call this type of system, you may not even get a BBS but just a file-transfer facility. I am speaking of RCP/M (Remote CP/M) systems. An RCP/M system is often, but not necessarily, linked with an RBBS (Remote BBS; or variations such as MINIRBBS, MINICBBS, or a CBBS itself) to allow its users to leave public messages. This type of messaging facility is easy to use. Its commands are similar to those of conventional BBSs. If you have never used CP/M, however, you will find it very difficult to use an RCP/M system.

When you call an RCP/M, you will be placed into either a messaging facility or the CP/M operating system directly. When the latter occurs (or you choose it from the messaging facility's menu), you will see a prompt like this:

A0⟩

There are variations of this prompt, but you are most likely to get this one. **A0⟩** means you are currently on Drive A, User 0. RCP/Ms are made up of *multiple drives* and, in most cases, the drives are segmented into *user areas* labeled 0 to 4. The drives themselves can range from A to D. It is on these drives that you will find free, public-domain, downloadable software for CP/M-based computers. To find out what resides on each drive and user segment, you will have to use a command to call up the disk's directory. This command is **DIR**. Typing **DIR** on Drive A, User 0 will give you something like this:

A0⟩**DIR**

RBBS.COM   35k : RCPM.COM 0k   : BYE.COM   3k: CHAT.COM 1k
LDIR.COM   7k : XMODEM.COM 6k : SYS.DQC   3k: DSK.DIR   5k
   Drive A, User 0 contains 60k in 8 files with 4k free.

This is a representative directory. If the first thing you saw when you logged onto the RCP/M is the **A0⟩** prompt, you should read the file labeled "SYS.DQC" (or any variants, "THISYS.DOC," "SYS.DOC," "HELP.DOC," and so forth). This file will tell you how to use the system. You can read it by using the **TYPE** command as follows:

A0⟩**TYPE SYS.DQC**

When files have the ".DQC" extension, you will have to type in **TYPESQ**. If this is the case, you will be notified when you sign onto the system. You will not be able to **TYPE** files with the extension ".COM." This is because .COM indicates a file that is runnable on the system; that is, most of the time a program that is the system itself (such as "RBBS.COM," "RCPM.COM," "BYE.COM," and "CHAT.COM" in the above directory).

To view the directories of other user areas on a disk, you must tell the system to change user areas with the **USER** command. Type **USER** and a number. For example, to go to User 1 on Drive A, type:

A0⟩**USER 1**
A1⟩

"A1⟩" indicates you are now on Drive A, User section 1. Most systems place a master disk directory on Drive A, User 1, which contains a catalog of all programs stored on the system. In the sample directory above, this file is labeled "DSK.DIR." You can **TYPE** that file, download it to your system, and read it offline. It will save you a considerable amount in phone costs if you are calling long distance.

If you want to see any public messages left on the system, you will have to enter the BBS program on the system. In the sample directory above, the BBS is called "RBBS," and you can get to it by typing its name (without extension) as follows:

A0⟩**RBBS**

If the message facility's title is "MINIRBBS," "MINICBBS," or "CBBS," you will have to type that instead. Once you are in the message base, you will find a menu selection, usually labeled "C" or "J," to get you back into CP/M.

To switch from Drive A to Drive B in CP/M, you would type **B:** as follows:

A0>**B:**
B0>

"B0)" indicates you are now on Drive B, User section 0.

If you get stuck or confused on the system, return to Drive A, User 0 and type **CHAT** (if a file named CHAT.COM resides there). This will summon the sysop to his or her console, if available, and he or she will be able to help you.

Finally, to leave the system while you are in CP/M, type **BYE**. You will be logged off, and the system will reset itself for the next user. No matter how confused you become when you are on the system, do *not* just hang up! Type **BYE**.

Downloading from an RCP/M requires the use of a public-domain communications program called MODEM (and its variants, MODEM7, XMODEM, and so forth). This program can be obtained at any CP/M users' group meeting or by mail from a user group. It provides strict error checking to allow users to download long files with no chance of transmission errors.

If you are not a CP/M user, I suggest that you do not call an RCP/M. RCP/Ms are mainly designed for CP/M users to exchange programs and information about that operating system. There are plenty of other general-interest message systems in existence waiting to welcome you.

The examples presented here of how to use five types of BBSs illustrate enough elementary information to enable you to use any other sort of BBS with a minimum of anxiety and confusion. There are hundreds of systems available to you, just waiting for your call. You can learn about them in Chapter 4, which starts the directory section of *The Computer Phone Book*.

CHAPTER 4
Directory Section: United States National Networks

There is no existing set of guidelines you can use in deciding upon which National Network to subscribe to. Furthermore, I am not even certain that any set of rules developed would last because of the ever-changing nature of each system. Since, first and foremost, most systems are in the business of delivering information, a lot depends upon your particular interests.

If you are looking for a general-purpose network, your choice will be fairly easy. If you are looking for a research tool, your choice will be easier. If you are only looking for business information, your choice will be easier. There are only a limited number of networks that fit into these three categories, despite the claims of each network's respective marketing staffs.

Before you subscribe to any of the systems listed in this part of *The Computer Phone Book*'s directory section, request literature and study it carefully. You are bound to find information in greater detail than can be written here, as well as information about services that have been added since this book went to press.

After you have received the literature, have studied it carefully, and have a general idea of what you are interested in and looking for, visit your local computer dealer and request a demonstration of the system(s). More dealers than ever are recognizing the importance of modem sales and the attendant services their customers can go online with. If your dealer is unable to arrange for such demonstrations, however, look up a local user group, go to a meeting, and ask the members which services they are subscribing to, which they find the best, and why. You may even meet people who will gladly give you a demonstration of the system to which they subscribe.

Once you have made your decision, return to your local dealer to purchase the subscription package(s) for the system(s) you chose. If your dealer does not sell them, call the offices of the system(s) directly to arrange for a subscription. Most systems will bill your credit card, so have it handy.

After you have decided on a national network subscription and received your account number and password, you will be entering a world that has yet to be fully explored, so have your pioneer spirit ready.

The listings of National Networks in this section are in alphabetical order, according to the system's name. Each system listing is in the following format:

CPB number   bps rate(s)
System name   Protocol
Networks
Operating hours
Registration fee
Minimum
Connect-time
Billing
Contact
Contents
Comments

- *CPB number.* Each system listed in *The Computer Phone Book* has been assigned a system number prefixed with CPB (for Computer Phone Book, to indicate the assigned number's source), and the letter N for National Network, L for Local-Area Service, or B for Bulletin Board. In this edition of *The Computer Phone Book,* the system numbers are place holders and do not signify any specific information other than a sequential numbering. In most instances, the numbering is by tens to allow for future expansion. Eventually, a code will be developed to act as an identification number for each system, and the number itself will act as a shorthand form of basic information about each system. A similar coding standard is just now gaining acceptance in the microcomputer software marketplace. It is my hope that *The Computer Phone Book* will set a similar coding standard for all online systems available to the general public so that one day you will be able to get the latest information on systems in your own city or cities around the world from your own terminal.

- *bps rate*. This is the transmission speed(s) at which the system is available. It will generally be 300 bps, 1200 bps, or both.
- *System name*. This is self-explanatory. I must caution you, however, that some systems may undergo name changes for marketing purposes.
- *Protocol*. This refers to the arrangement of bits your computer should be sending. The format is word length/stop bits/parity. For example, a setting of 7 word bits, Ø stop bits, and no parity would appear as 7/Ø/N.
- *Networks*. This cites the packet-switched networks through which the system is available. In most cases, this will mean you will only have to make a local call to a number (or numbers) furnished to you by the system when you subscribe. Some cities may be served by only one packet-switched network, some by all, some by none. Although this information should not be a major factor when choosing a system, remember that a long-distance call can contribute considerably to the price of using a system.
- *Operating hours*. Most systems available on a part-time basis are moving toward round-the-clock service, and you should check with the system itself. In cases in which the system is available 24 hours a day, the hours will be divided into the appropriate prime-time and non-prime-time format. Note that "local" means your local time.
- *Registration fee*. This is what you are required to pay in order to have your account activated on the system. The fee usually includes any user manual you will need to help you use the system.
- *Minimum*. Most systems bill on a monthly basis. If you do not use the system during that 1-month period, you

are still billed a small fee. This fee ensures that your account remains active on the system.
- *Connect-time.* This is the cost of the system measured in a per-hour increment. For example, you are not billed for a whole hour if you only use the system for 5 minutes to check for waiting mail during non-prime time. During prime time, there may be a 1- or 2-hour minimum charge, and you should check with the system before such use.
- *Billing.* This is how you may go about paying for your connect-time. Some systems will only bill to a charge card, whereas others send a bill or invoice to individual or business customers. Check with the system to see how you may arrange payment.
- *Contact.* This cites the address and phone number to use for additional information or a subscription.
- *Contents.* It is not possible to give a complete list of what a system contains because each system is constantly adding or subtracting from its roster. Additionally, some systems contain several hundred different services.
- *Comments.* The comments are what, if anything, I have to say about the system, good or bad, after having used the system. If I have not used a system, I will say so. In situations in which I have used a system, my comments will not have been derived from a set checklist of things I look for on a system nor will they necessarily be objective. I want to note that I have been using online systems for over 3 years, and although my opinions of systems are informed, they are to be taken as just that: *my* opinions.

Now that you understand the format of the listings for this chapter, you are ready to start on your search for a National Network that will allow you to venture into the world of microcomputer telecommunications.

CPBN00040   300/1200 bps
BRS After Dark   7/1/N

Networks: Datapac, Telenet, Uninet.
Operating hours: Mon–Fri, 6 PM local–4 AM Eastern; Sat, 6 AM local–

4 AM Eastern; Sun, 6 AM local—2 PM Eastern; Sun, 7 PM local–4 AM Eastern.

Registration fee: $50.

Connect-time: $6–15/hour at 300 bps or 1200 bps.

Billing: Credit card or direct billing with a one-time $250 deposit.

Contact: BRS, 1200 Route 7, Latham, NY, 12110, (518)783-1161.

Contents: BRS After Dark is divided into five sections: Search Service, which contains 25 databases of various topics (see below); Newsletter Service, produced by BRS and covering computer and online-related subjects; Software Service, for ordering and downloading microcomputer software; Electronic Mail Service, for personal communications; and Swap Shop, a bulletin-board system.

At the time *The Computer Phone Book* went to press, only the Search Service was available. It contained the following categories and databases:

SCIENCE AND MEDICINE

Agricola database, covering various aspects of agriculture. $8/hour.

BIOSIS Previews database, covering biological sciences. $13/hour.

Chemical Abstracts database, covering chemistry and related sciences. $15/hour.

DISC database, covering current microcomputer literature. $15/hour.

Health Planning and Administration database, covering economic, administration, and planning aspects of health care and hospitals. $6/hour.

Mathematical Reviews database, covering pure and applied mathematics. $13/hour.

Medlars database, covering medicine, nursing, and dentistry. $10/hour.

NTIS database, from the National Technical Information Service, covering government reports in all subject areas. $8/hour.

Pre-Med database, covering current clinical medicine. $6/hour.

BUSINESS AND FINANCIAL

ABI/Inform database, covering business management and administration. $15/hour.

Management Contents database, covering business planning and administration. $14/hour.

Patdata database, covering all patents registered through the U.S. Patent Office since 1975. $6/hour.

REFERENCE

Books in Print database, corresponds to the printed editions, covering all books in print. $14/hour.

EDUCATION

Bilingual Education Bibliographic Abstracts database, covering aspects of bilingual education. $6/hour.

ERIC—Education Resource Information Center database, covering education-related subjects. $6/hour.

Exceptional Child Education Resources database, covering education-related subjects pertaining to exceptional children. $11/hour.

School Practices Information File database, covering programs currently used in schools. $6/hour.

SOCIAL SCIENCES AND HUMANITIES

National Information Sources on the Handicapped database, covering organizations that aid disabled individuals. $6/hour.

Family Resources database, covering various aspects of family relations. $12/hour.

National Rehabilitation Information Center database, covering disability and rehabilitation topics. $6/hour.

Pre-Psyc database, covering current clinical psychology. $6/hour.

Psych INFO database, covering applied, clinical, and developmental psychology. $14/hour.

ENERGY AND ENVIRONMENTAL

Energy database, from the U.S. Department of Energy, covering all aspects of energy. $6/hour.

Comments: BRS After Dark is simple to use and quickly retrieves information sought. The databases it makes available are identical in content and scope to those offered to its corporate users. Being a writer interested in computers, the combination of Books in Print and DISC are irresistable to me, and I've spent quite a bit of time on both, sometimes just thumbing through them to see what I can discover.

CPBN00060 300/1200 bps
CompuServe Executive Information Service 7/1/E or 8/1/N

Networks: ComLink, Datapac, Telenet, Tymnet.
Operating hours: 24 hours/day, 7 days/week.
Registration fee: Not available at press time.
Connect-time: Not available at press time.
Billing: Credit card, direct billing to individuals and businesses.
Contact: CompuServe Executive Information Service, 5000 Arlington Centre Blvd., Columbus, OH, 43220, (614)457-8600.
Contents: Specifics were not available at press time, although I was told this service would be geared, at the outset, to business users of the IBM Personal Computer. Customized telecommunications software would be made available for the IBM PC so that subscribers would be able to interact with special *decision support* databases. A demographic and statistical analysis database would be part of the decision support services, and users would be able to download the information and manipulate it while offline. Also available on the system will be several news databases and financial and stock market databases; Infoplex software will be used for electronic mail. This service will be announced and made available on October 1, 1983. Contact CompuServe for details.

CPBN00045 110/300/1200 bps
CompuServe Information Service 7/1/E or 8/1/N

Networks: ComLink, Datapac, Telenet, Tymnet.
Operating hours: Prime time: Mon–Fri, 8 AM–6 PM local. Non-prime time: Mon–Fri, 6 PM–5 AM local time; Sat–Sun, 8 AM–5 AM local time; holidays, 8 AM–5 AM local time.
Registration fee: Purchase of a CompuServe Starter Kit at any Radio Shack, Radio Shack Computer Center, or authorized computer dealer. Cost is $30 and includes 1 hour of free connect-time.
Connect-time: Prime time: $22.50/hour at 300 bps; $35/hour at 1200 bps. Non-prime time: $5/hour at 300 bps; $17.50/hour at 1200 bps.
Billing: Credit card, direct billing to individuals and businesses.
Contact: CompuServe Information Service, 5000 Arlington Centre Blvd., Columbus, OH, 43220, (614)457-8600.

Contents: CompuServe's main menu is divided into six choices. The last choice, Index, is an alphabetical listing of services on the system and their corresponding page numbers. The remaining five categories are further divided into sub-menus of anywhere from one to three layers. This structure, outlined below, shows the system's contents.

HOME SERVICES
News/Weather/Sports: The Washington Post, St. Louis Post-Dispatch, AP Viewdata Wire, NOAA Weather Wire, Official PGA Tour Guide, Hollywood Hotline.
Reference Library: Popular Science, movie reviews, U.S. government publications, New York Fashion Report, Health-Tex, the Victory Garden, video information, National Satirist, Belmont's Golf Association, parenting and family life.
Communications: Electronic mail, CB Simulation, national bulletin board, user directory, Talk to Us, Lobby Letters of America, Ask Aunt Nettie, CB Society.
Home Shopping/Banking: Compu-U-Store, electronic banking, the Athlete's Outfitter, documentation and art gallery, Music Information Service, Fifth Avenue Shopper, Primetime Radio Classics, AutoNet.
Groups and Clubs: CBers, HamNet, Netwits, Orchestra 90, Sports, Cooking, Golf, Space, Issues, Literary, Educators, Arcade, Games, Family Matters, Good Earth, Work-at-Home, Music, Food Buyline, Pets, Travel.
Games and Entertainment: Scorpia's Game SIG, Multi-Player Game SIG, Adventure, Golf, Multi-Player Casino, Civil War, Eliza, Kesmai, Multi-Player DECWars, MegaWars, New Adventure, Gomoku, Hangman, Lunar Lander, Multi-Player Space War, StarTrek, Scott Adams Adventure, House of Banshi, Backgammon, Concentration, Craps, Chess, Cube Solver, Furs, Hammurabi, Maze Maker, Mugwump, Othello, RT Trek, Roulette, Scramble, Wumpus, Astrology, Bridge, Single-Player Blackjack, Biorhythms, Football, FasterMind, Fantasy, Folie des Rois.
Education: Grolier's Academic American Encyclopedia, the College Board, the Multiple Choice, Clarke School for the Deaf.
Home Management: Balance your checkbook, calculate your next raise, calculate your net worth, amortize a loan, IDS Financial Services.

Travel: Official Airline Guides, Pan Am Travel Guide, Worldwide Exchanges, State Department Advisories, Travel Fax, Airport delays, FIRSTWORLD Travel Club, Norwegian American Cruises, TravelVision, Travel SIG.

BUSINESS AND FINANCIAL
News/Reports: Business Information Wire, the Business Wire, MMS Financial Analysis, Commodity News Service, Heinold Commodity Reports, Investment News and Views, Stevens Business Reports.
Investments and Quotations: MicroQuote, Quick Quote, Standard and Poor's, Value Line Data Base II.
Communications: Electronic mail, user directory, Talk to Us.
Brokerage Services: Unified Management Corporation, Tickerscreen ®.
Banking Services: First Tennessee Bank, Huntington National Bank, Shawmut Bank of Boston, Central Trade Bank of Memphis.
Discussion Forum: HiTech Forum (Columbus, Ohio Area Chamber of Commerce High Technology Group).
Travel: Official Airline Guides, Pan Am Travel Guide, Worldwide Exchanges, State Department Advisories, Travel Fax, Airport delays, FIRSTWORLD Travel Club, Norwegian American Cruises, TravelVision, Travel SIG.
Personal Finance: Checkbook balancing, calculating a loan payment, calculating your net worth, calculating your next raise, IDS Financial Services.

PERSONAL COMPUTING
News: RCA Newsletter, Tandy Newsletter, the Micro Advisor, Computers & Electronics, Commodore Newsletter.
Reference: Periodical Guide DataBase, software reviews, programming languages, text editors, word processing, utilities, mathematics and statistics, special features, terminal software.
Communications: Electronic mail, CB Simulation, national bulletin board, user directory, Access, Talk to Us.
Shop at Home: Softex, art gallery and documentation, Howard Sams Books, Heathkit Online Catalog.
Groups and Clubs (SIGs): CP/M, HUG (Heath), MAUG (Apple), MNET-11, MUSUS (Pascal), RCA, TRS-80 Color Computer, Panasonic, MNET80 (TRS-80), LSI Users, PowerSoft, Program-

mers, Computers & Electronics magazine, Software & Authors, Commodore VIC-20, Commodore-64, Commodore Business Machines, Atari, IBM PC, OSI, MicroSoft, Telecommunications.

Programmer's Area: personal disk space, text editors, languages (not a menu-structured section of the system).

SERVICES FOR PROFESSIONALS

Agribusiness: Commodity News Service, crop break-even analysis, Information Retrieval Service.

Aviation: ASI Newsletter, NWS Aviation Weather, EMI Flight Planning, AVSIG (Aviation SIG), Official Airline's Guide, Peak Delay Guide, aircraft insurance, FAA Rule Changes/NTSB Cases.

Engineering/Technical: FireNet (Firefighter's SIG), Communications Industry Forum (SIG), Mine-Equip, Information Retrieval Service.

Environmental: NWWA–Waterline, Environmental Forum (SIG), Information Retrieval Service.

Legal: Lawyer's SIG.

Medical: AAMSI Medical Forum (SIG), American Society of Computers in Medicine and Dentistry (SIG), FOI Newsline–FDA Information, AAMSI Communications Network (SIG), Veterinarian's Forum (SIG).

User Information: What's New; command summary and usage tips; FEEDBACK, Manuals, Products; changing terminal defaults; changing your password; reviewing your charges; changing credit card info; telephone access numbers; current rates; CompuServe Viewpoint; Electronic Bounce Back.

Comments: CompuServe has services to suit virtually any interest. Of particular interest to me are the Special Interest Groups (SIGs), which can help me get answers to almost any technical question I might have; Hollywood Hotline, which places the Nielsen ratings at my fingertips; video information, which keeps me on top of developments in that field; the Business Wire, which allows me to read press releases every day from a virtual Who's Who of corporate America; and the Periodical Guide DataBase, which allows me to search for topics relating to microcomputers from a publication index that spans several years. I am not fond of EMail because it does not offer receipts for delivered letters or an express sending option. It took me a whole day to learn how to use FILGE, but every minute was worth it. You are not likely to have many problems with CompuServe; it has an acceptable response time (the length of time between your entry of a command and the system's execution of it). One word of caution, though: On Friday and Saturday nights, CompuServe is *very* busy and response time becomes frustratingly slow. If you can avoid using the system during these peak-use periods, you will find the service to be quite speedy.

CPBN00075   300/1200 bps
Connexions

Networks: Telenet, Tymnet.
Operating hours: 24 hours/day, 7 days/week.
Registration fee: $15; includes 2 hours of connect-time.
Minimum: None.
Connect-time: $15 for each additional 2 hours.
Billing: Credit card; direct billing to individuals.
Contact: Connexions 55 Wheeler St., Cambridge, MA, 02138, (617)492-1690.
Contents: Employment positions online; online resume creation, storage, and sending; electronic mail.
Comments: I have not used the service. You may call the system at (617)938-9307 or via Telenet at C 60366 for a demonstration; in both instances logon with the User ID, JOB12345.

CPBN00100   300/1200 bps
Delphi   7/1/N

Networks: Telenet, Tymnet.
Operating hours: Prime-time: Mon–Fri, 8 AM–6 PM local time. Non-prime time: Mon–Fri, 6 PM–8 AM local time; Sat–Sun, 24 hours/day; holidays, 24 hours/day.
Registration fee: $49.95.
Minimum: None.
Connect-time: Prime time: $20/hour at 300 bps*; Non-prime time: $6/hour at 300 bps*. (*Prime-time charge does not include network surcharge; non-prime-time charge includes $1/hour network surcharge. Contact system for 1200 bps rates.)
Billing: Credit card; direct billing to businesses.
Contact: General Videotex Corporation, 3 Blackstone St., Cambridge, MA, 02139, (617)491-3393, 1-(800)544-4005.

Contents: Delphi was still undergoing construction when *The Computer Phone Book* went to press. There will be more available on the system than is indicated by the system's menu outline below.

APPOINTMENT-CALENDAR
Appointment-Calendar: For placing your schedule online.

BANKING
Banking: Enables you to conduct business with your local bank online from your home.

BULLETIN BOARDS
Computers: Apple, Atari, Commodore, CP/M, DEC, Heath/Zenith, IBM, Northstar, Osborne, Other-Computers, S-100, Sinclair, TRS-80, Xerox.
Delphi: Member-Service, Operations, Suggestions, System.
General: Gossip, Miscellany, Personals.
Reviews: Books, Hardware, Software.
Special Interest: Business-Use, Games, Word-Processing.

CONFERENCE
Conference: Multiuser real-time conferencing system.

DELPHI-ORACLE
Delphi-Oracle: A panel of experts in a variety of fields who will attempt to answer any question you may have.

GAMES
Adventures: Colossal-Cave, DND, Seawar, Star-Trek, Zork.
Board Games: Backgammon, Hexapawn, Othello, Qubic.
Delphi Casino: Craps, Darts, Poker, Russian-Roulette, Wheel-of-Fortune.
For the Younger User: Animal, Bagels, Bug, Chief.
Logic: Alien, Chomp, King, Pirana, Rocket, Super-Wumpus, Tower, Wumpus.
Multiplayer Games: Conquest, Parsec, Scales of the Gods, Timelords.
Sports: Baseball, Boxing, Football.
Games for VT52 Terminals: Blackjack, Gammon, Hobbit, Master-Mind, Trek.

GUIDED-TOUR
Guided-Tour: The first thing you see when you sign on to Delphi as a new user; a quick tutorial on how to use the system.

INFOMANIA
Authors: User-written text files.
Collaborative Novels: Each chapter is written by a different user.
Member's Choice: Interactive programs from users.
Newsletter: User publishing.
Poll: User-created opinion polls.
Punchline: User-submitted jokes.

LIBRARY
Dialcom: Gateway to the ITT-Dialcom network.
Librarian: Online searching performed by a researcher.
Lookup: Electronic encyclopedia.
Research-Library: Gateway to the Dialog Information Retrieval Service.
XREF: Cross referencing of indexed items from the electronic encyclopedia.

MAIL
Mail: Electronic mail system.

NEWS
News: Electronic news and wire clipping service.

ONLINE MARKETS
Bazaar: User-submitted items for sale.
Catalog: Online shopping from various firms.
Comp-U-Store: Online catalog of over 50,000 items that may be ordered online.
Garage-Sale: User-submitted items for sale.

PROFILE
Profile: Terminal and system parameter settings; user directory (IamWhois).

TRAVEL
Travel: Transportation and accommodation arrangements from a travel agent.

WRITERS CORNER
Writers Corner: Online file creation and maintenance; programming languages; teletypesetting service.
Comments: Less than 1 year old, Delphi has shown great promise in its innovative handling of services such as multiuser real-time

conferencing, user publishing, a user-directory, and (to an extent) bulletin boards. Delphi has the best user directory and conferencing program of any National Network. Its electronic mail system and bulletin boards could use some improvement and, from what I have been told, such improvement is on the way. The system has quick response time, is constantly being upgraded, and is very easy to use. All of this makes Delphi a system with a bright future.

CPBN00125 300/1200 bps
Dow Jones News/Retrieval Service (DJNRS) 8/1/N or 8/2/N

Networks: Datapac, Telenet, Tymnet.
Operating hours: Prime time: Mon–Fri, 6 AM–6 PM local time. Non-prime time: Mon–Fri, 6 PM–4 AM local time; Sat–Sun, 6 AM–4 AM local time; holidays, 6 AM–4 AM local time.
Registration fee: $50 or purchase of a Dow Jones News/Retrieval package at an authorized dealer for a Standard Subscription. (*Notice:* DJNRS offers three types of subscription plans. The Standard Subscription rates are the only ones quoted here. Contact Dow Jones for other rates.)
Minimum: None.
Connect-time: Prime time: $36–$72/hour at 300 bps. Non-prime time: $9–$12/hour at 300 bps. (Connect-time at 1200 bps is 1.7 times 300 bps rates.)
Billing: Credit card; direct billing to businesses.
Contact: Dow Jones & Company, Inc., P.O. Box 300, Princeton, NJ, 08540, (609)452-1511, 1-(800)257-5114.
Contents:
DOW JONES BUSINESS AND ECONOMIC NEWS

Dow Jones News, from the Wall Street Journal, Barron's, and the Dow Jones News Service. $72/hour prime time, $12/hour non-prime time.

Wall Street Journal Highlights Online, contains front page news, front and back page features, market pages, editorial columns, and commentary. $72/hour prime time, $12/hour non-prime time.

Free Text Search, contains news from June 1979 to the present. $72/hour prime time, $12/hour non-prime time.

Weekly Economic Update, contains reviews of economic events. $72/hour prime time, $12/hour non-prime time.

FINANCIAL AND INVESTMENT SERVICES

Corporate Earnings Estimator, earnings, forecasts for 2400 companies compiled from over 50 major brokerage houses. $72/hour prime time, $54/hour non-prime time.

Disclosure II, contains 10-K extracts and company profiles on 8500 publicly held companies. $72/hour prime time, $54/hour non-prime time (plus database surcharge).

Media General Financial Services, contains financial information of over 3000 companies and over 150 industries. $72/hour prime time, $54/hour non-prime time.

Weekly Economic Survey, contains economic forecasts from over 40 leading financial institutions. $72/hour prime time, $54/hour non-prime time.

DOW-JONES QUOTES

Current Quotes; Historical Quotes; Historical Dow Jones Averages. $54/hour prime time, $3/hour non-prime time.

GENERAL NEWS AND INFORMATION SERVICES

Academic American Encyclopedia; News/Retrieval World Report; News/Retrieval Sports Report; News/Retrieval Weather Report; Cineman Movie Reviews; Wall $treet Week Online; Comp-U-Store. $36/hour prime time, $18/hour non-prime time.

Comments: Dow Jones News/Retrieval Service is the oldest online system designed for the average computer user. It started in 1974, and has more subscribers than any online system. I have used the service and find it to be a virtual treasure trove of news and business information. I have never had any problems with the system; it has a good response time, and the Free Text Search feature is marvelous. I only have one question, though: Why is it difficult to find the command to logoff the system in the manual? My first time on, I was stranded online for 5 minutes while I combed the manual for the proper command. Nevertheless, it is a service I find full of value. By the time you read this, the Official Airlines Guides will have been added to the system.

CPBN00200 300/1200
EIES 8/2/N, half-duplex
(Electronic Information Exchange System)

Networks: Telenet, Uninet.
Operating hours: 24 hours/day, 7 days/week.

Registration fee: None.
Minimum: None.
Connect-time: $75/month, flat fee; excludes network connect-time charges. (*Notice:* EIES has other subscription plans. Contact New Jersey Institute of Technology—NJIT—for details.)
Billing: Direct billing to individuals and businesses.
Contact: CCCC at NJIT, 323 High St., Newark, NJ, 07102, (201)645-5211.
Contents: Electronic mail; conferencing (not real time); notebooks (personal file space, with text editors).
Comments: Don't be fooled by the brief list of EIES's contents; there is a lot of information on the system. I can't present a list because the information is *volatile,* that is, subject to change too quickly to be captured in a book. I have not used EIES as much as other National Networks. My brief encounters with the system left me with a feeling of frustration. It is not a system that can be mastered in a few sessions. EIES offers a multitude of options online, and it is difficult to keep track of all of them in the beginning. System architecture aside, if you are looking to discuss serious issues, you could not find a better system with which to do so than EIES. EIES used to offer a public demonstration account for interested parties to logon to the system for a half-hour interval. This public account now requires a password furnished by NJIT. Call the above number to inquire about public access.

CPBN00350 300/1200 bps
Knowledge Index 8/1/N

Networks: Telenet, Tymnet.
Operating hours: Mon–Thurs, 6 PM–5 AM local time; Fri, 6 PM to midnight local time; Sat, 8 PM to midnight local time; Sun, 3 PM–5 AM local time.
Registration fee: $35.
Minimum: None.
Connect-time: $24/hour.
Billing: Credit card.
Contact: Knowledge Index, Dialog Information Services, Inc., Marketing Dept., 3460 Hillview Ave, Palo Alto, CA, 94304, 1-(800)528-

6050 ext. 415, 1-(800)352-0458 ext. 415 (in Arizona), 1-(800)528-0470 ext. 415 (in Alaska and Hawaii).
Contents: Knowledge Index is divided in 12 sections, each with the following databases:
  Agriculture: Agricola database.
  Books: Books in Print database.
  Business Information: ABI/Inform database.
  Computer and Electronics: Inspec database; International Software database; Microcomputer Index database.
  Corporate News: Standard & Poor's News database.
  Education: ERIC database.
  Engineering: Engineering Literature Index database.
  Government Publications: GPO Publications Reference File database; NTIS database.
  Magazines: Magazine Index database.
  Medicine: Medline 1980+ database; Medline 1973–79 database; Medline 1966–72 database; International Pharmaceutical Abstracts database.
  News: Newsearch database; National Newspaper Index database.
  Psychology: PsychInfo database.
Comments: Knowledge Index is fast. Within 1 or 2 seconds, literally, your search is processed. If the system is being used heavily and your request takes longer than 4 seconds to process, "PROCESSING" will be printed on your screen to reassure you that the system is still functioning and working on your search. Knowledge Index comes with a large manual designed to lead you through the system and to help you gather your information in the least amount of time possible. This is another system I have found myself just thumbing through to discover information. Knowledge Index is, indeed, a professional and exquisite system.

CPBN00500 300/1200 bps
NewsNet 7/1/E or 7/1/N

Networks: Datapac, Telenet, Tymnet, Uninet.
Operating hours: Prime time: Mon–Fri, 8 AM–8 PM local time. Non-

prime time: Mon–Fri, 8 PM–8 AM local time; Sat–Sun, 24 hours/day; holidays, 24 hours/day.
Registration fee: None.
Minimum: $15/month.
Connect-time: Prime time: $24/hour at 300 bps; $48/hour at 1200 bps. Non-prime time: $18/hour at 300 bps; $36/hour at 1200 bps. (*Notice:* These rates do not include a surcharge for reading newsletters. This surcharge varies with each newsletter.)
Billing: Direct billing to individuals and businesses.
Contact: NewsNet, Inc., Customer Service, 945 Haverford Rd., Bryn Mawr, PA, 19010, 1-(800)345-1301, (215)527-8030 (in Pennsylvania).
Contents: NewsNet offers electronic mail for communications with newsletter publishers and NewsNet; an online NewsNet Bulletin newsletter; a library of sample issues of newsletters for browsing; an electronic clipping service called Newsflash; and the ability to scan, keyword search, or read all newsletters available on the system. Available categories and newsletters include the following:
  Advertising and Marketing: Media Science Newsletter; Source.
  Aerospace: Satellite Week.
  Automotive: Electric Vehicle Progress; Runzheimer on Automotive Alternatives.
  Building and Construction: Construction Claims Monthly; Construction Claims Monthly Citator; Construction Computer Applications Directory; Construction Computer Applications Newsletter.
  Chemical: Hazardous Waste News; Sludge Newsletter; State Regulation Report; Toxic Materials News.
  Corporate Communications: The Corporate Shareholder.
  Education: Campus Exchange.
  Electronics and Computers: The Anderson Report; Computer Consultant; The Computer Cookbook®; Computer Market Observer; Consumer Electronics; Distributed Processing; Interactive Video Technology; Micro Moonlighter™; Mini/Micro Bulletin; Personal Computers Today; Reistad Monitor; S. Klein Newsletter on Computer Graphics; two/sixteen Magazine; UNIQUE: Your Independent UNIX/C Advisor.
  Energy: Coal Outlook; Coal Outlook Marketline; Daily Petro Futures; Energy & Minerals Resources; Petroleum Information

International; Solar Energy Intelligence Report; Today's Energy News Update.

Entertainment and Leisure: The Fearless Taster; The Gold Sheet; Video Week.

Environment: Air/Water Pollution Report; Clean Water Report; Ecology U.S.A.; Land Use Planning Report; Nuclear Waste News; World Environment Report.

Farming and Food: Agricultural Computer Developments; Agricultural Research Review; Agri-Markets Data Service; Computer Farming Newsletter; Farm Software Developments; Washington Farmletter.

Finance and Accounting: Bank Network News; Banking Regulator; Daily Bank Digest; Financial Management Advisor; Credit Union Regulator.

General Business: International Intertrade Index; Mergers and Corporate Policy; Preretirement Counseling; Update/The American States.

Government and Regulatory: Compliance Alert: Federal Register Digest; Compliance Management Report; Emergency Preparedness News; Government Training News; Grants and Contracts Alert; Grants and Contracts Weekly; Handicapped Rights & Regulations; PACs & Lobbies; U.S. Census Report.

Health and Hospitals: Health Benefit Cost Containment Newsletter.

International: Africa News; Daily Currency Report; Latin America Weekly Report; Latin America Commodities Report; Caribbean Regional Report; Southern Cone Regional Report; Andean Group Regional Report; Latin American Energy Report; Brazil Regional Report; Mexico and Central America Regional Report.

Investment: Biotechnology Investment Opportunities; Daily Industrial Index Report; Ford Investment Review; EPIC/Ford Data Base; Tax Shelter Insider; Technical Trends.

Labor: Fair Employment Report.

Law: Legal Bulletin of International Business.

Management: Altman & Well Report to Legal Management; The Entrepreneurial Manager; Executive Productivity; Office Technology Management.

Manufacturing: Hedging Report; Noise Control Report; Solid Waste Report.

Metals and Mining: Daily Metals Report.
Office: Advanced Office Concepts; The Seybold Report on Office Systems; Telehints.
Politics: The American Sentinel; F&S Political Risk Letter; Initiative News Report; Legislative Intelligence Week.
Power Generation: Fusion Power Report.
Public Relations: PR Newswire.
Publishing and Broadcasting: Hudson's Washington Directory; IIA Friday Memo; Link News Briefs; NAA Hotline; The Newsletter on Newsletters; NewsNet's Online Bulletin; Online Database Report; The Photoletter; Public Broadcasting Report; RadioNews; RadioNews Bulletin Service; The Seybold Report on Publishing Systems; Television Digest; Travelwriter Marketletter; Viewdata/Videotex Report; Worldwide Videotex Update.
Real Estate: Real Estate Intelligence Report; Real Estate Investing Letter.
Research and Development: Federal Research Report; Hi Tech Patents: Data Communications; Hi Tech Patents: Fiber Optics Technology; Hi Tech Patents: Laser Technology; Hi Tech Patents: Telephony; Research Monitor News; Research Monitor Profiles Index.
Social Sciences: Behavior Today; Church and Society; Marriage and Divorce Today; RFC News Service; Sexuality Today.
Taxation: Corporate Acquisitions & Dispositions; Employee Retirement Plans; IRS Practices and Procedures; Tax Notes Bulletin Service; Tax Notes Today; Taxes Interpreted.
Telecommunications: CableNews; Cellular Radio News; Communications Daily; DBS News; DataCable News; Data Channels; Fiber/Laser News; Fiber Optics and Communications Newsletter; Fiber Optics and Communications Weekly Newsletter; Inteltrade; ISDN News; International Videotex/Teletext News; Satellite News; Satellite News Bulletin Service; Telecommunications Counselor; Telephone Angles; Telephone News; Telephone News Bulletin Service; Telepoints; TeleServices Report; VideoGames Today; VideoNews; Viewtext.
Transportation: Public Transit Report; Toxic Materials Transport; U.S. Rail News.
Comments: I have not used NewsNet.

CPBN00575
OAG EE
(Official Airline Guides Electronic Edition)

300/1200 bps
8/1/E or 8/1/N

Networks: Datapac, Telenet, Tymnet, Uninet.
Operating hours: 24 hours/day, 7 days/week.
Registration fee: $50.
Minimum:
Connect-time: $6/hour (*Notice:* Service is billed on a per-information-unit basis. Connect-time cited does not include the additional fee.)
Billing: Credit card; direct billing to individuals and businesses.
Contact: Official Airline Guides, 2000 Clearwater Dr., Oak Brook IL, 60521, 1-(800)323-3537, 1-(800)942-1888 (in Illinois).
Contents: Flight schedules and comparative fare information for over 640 airlines worldwide. Updated daily.
Comments: I have not used OAG EE.

CPBN00625
Photo-1 Network

300/1200 bps
Not available (N.A.)

Networks: N.A.
Operating hours: N.A.
Registration fee: N.A.
Minimum: N.A.
Connect-time: N.A.
Billing: Credit card; direct billing to individuals and businesses.
Contact: Photo-1 Network, 170 Fifth Ave, New York, NY, 10010, (212)929-8030
Contents: Among planned features of the system are an electronic mail service; a bulletin-board system; a personal scheduling system/calendar; a database comprised of stock photo information; a marketing section with items of interest to photojournalists; online equipment support for cameras and equipment; The Photographer's Phone Book; indexed articles from trade publications; Photolog, a users' shared-file schedule/calendar; and a press credential service.
Comments: Photo-1 Network was still in Beta testing when I was given a tour of it by its principals. I was impressed by their unique

method of designing a system as well as their enthusiasm for their project. By the time you read this, Photo-1 may be ready for public access. Contact them for details.

CPBN00650 300/1200 bps
Photonet 7/1/E or 8/1/N

Networks: Dun's Net.
Operating hours: 24 hours/day, 7 days/week.
Registration fee: $49.
Minimum: $24/month.
Connect-time: $24/hour at 300 bps; $48/hour at 1200 bps.
Billing: Credit card; direct billing to individuals and businesses.
Contact: Photonet, 500 Park Ave, New York, NY, 10022, (212)750-1386.
Contents: Photonet is an information and communications medium for photographers and photojournalists. It contains the following:
   Communications: National bulletin board, regional bulletin boards, electronic mail, Photonet Express (a same-day delivery hardcopy mail service), Telex interconnect.
   News and Information: Photonet magazine, law database, Copyright database, photo agency database, new product information database.
   Photo Sources: Stock and assignment photo agency database.
   Resources and Services: Listings of mailing list, preproduction, and computer-generated slide companies, among others.
   Marketplace: Cameras, equipment, and accessories for sale by vendors.
Comments: I have not been on Photonet.

CPBN00800 300/1200 bps
The Source 8/1/N

Networks: Datapac, SourceNet, Telenet, Tymnet, Uninet.
Operating hours: Prime time: Mon–Fri, 7 AM–6 PM local time. Non-prime time: Mon–Fri, 6 PM–4 AM local time; Sat–Sun, 6 AM–4 AM; holidays, 6 AM–4 AM.

Registration fee: $100.
Minimum: $10/month.
Connect-time: Prime time: $20.75/hour at 300 bps; $25.75/hour at 1200 bps. Non-prime time: $7.75/hour at 300 bps; $10.75/hour at 1200 bps.
Billing: Credit card; direct billing to businesses.
Contact: Source Telecomputing Corp., 1616 Anderson Rd., McLean, VA, 22102, 1-(800)336-3366, 1-(800)572-2070 (in Virginia), (703)734-7500 (outside United States).
Contents: The Source contains more information and services than the brief outline below, which is drawn from following the system's menu structure.

NEWS AND REFERENCE RESOURCES

News and Sports: UPI News Service, The Editorial Page, UPI Sports.

Travel and Dining: Domestic flights, international flights, travel tips and specials, travel reservations, Guide to New York City, restaurant guides, wine, U.S. Hotel Guide.

Government and Politics: President's schedule (daily), Senate Committee, House Committee, political commentary.

Consumer Information: Consumer Corner columnists, buying wine, toll free numbers, restaurant guides, health guide.

Science and Technology: Electrical engineering, mechanical engineering, simulation, geography, statistics.

Bylines News Features: Various columnists.

BUSINESS/FINANCIAL MARKETS

Financial Markets: NYSE closing prices, AMEX closing prices, Unistox, Media General Stock Analysis, Commodity News Service.

Analysis and Computation: Raylux, Modell financial modeling, computational programs, Media General Stock Analysis.

News and Commentary: UPI business news, Raylux Financial Services, Management Contents.

Personal Finance: Computing interest, amortization of loans, annuity payments and analysis, bond accrued interest, tax computations.

Research and Reference: Information on Demand, Management Contents.

method of designing a system as well as their enthusiasm for their project. By the time you read this, Photo-1 may be ready for public access. Contact them for details.

CPBN00650
Photonet

300/1200 bps
7/1/E or 8/1/N

Networks: Dun's Net.
Operating hours: 24 hours/day, 7 days/week.
Registration fee: $49.
Minimum: $24/month.
Connect-time: $24/hour at 300 bps; $48/hour at 1200 bps.
Billing: Credit card; direct billing to individuals and businesses.
Contact: Photonet, 500 Park Ave, New York, NY, 10022, (212)750-1386.
Contents: Photonet is an information and communications medium for photographers and photojournalists. It contains the following:
  Communications: National bulletin board, regional bulletin boards, electronic mail, Photonet Express (a same-day delivery hardcopy mail service), Telex interconnect.
  News and Information: Photonet magazine, law database, Copyright database, photo agency database, new product information database.
  Photo Sources: Stock and assignment photo agency database.
  Resources and Services: Listings of mailing list, preproduction, and computer-generated slide companies, among others.
  Marketplace: Cameras, equipment, and accessories for sale by vendors.
Comments: I have not been on Photonet.

CPBN00800
The Source

300/1200 bps
8/1/N

Networks: Datapac, SourceNet, Telenet, Tymnet, Uninet.
Operating hours: Prime time: Mon–Fri, 7 AM–6 PM local time. Non-prime time: Mon–Fri, 6 PM–4 AM local time; Sat–Sun, 6 AM–4 AM; holidays, 6 AM–4 AM.

Registration fee: $100.
Minimum: $10/month.
Connect-time: Prime time: $20.75/hour at 300 bps; $25.75/hour at 1200 bps. Non-prime time: $7.75/hour at 300 bps; $10.75/hour at 1200 bps.
Billing: Credit card; direct billing to businesses.
Contact: Source Telecomputing Corp., 1616 Anderson Rd., McLean, VA, 22102, 1-(800)336-3366, 1-(800)572-2070 (in Virginia), (703)734-7500 (outside United States).
Contents: The Source contains more information and services than the brief outline below, which is drawn from following the system's menu structure.

NEWS AND REFERENCE RESOURCES

News and Sports: UPI News Service, The Editorial Page, UPI Sports.

Travel and Dining: Domestic flights, international flights, travel tips and specials, travel reservations, Guide to New York City, restaurant guides, wine, U.S. Hotel Guide.

Government and Politics: President's schedule (daily), Senate Committee, House Committee, political commentary.

Consumer Information: Consumer Corner columnists, buying wine, toll free numbers, restaurant guides, health guide.

Science and Technology: Electrical engineering, mechanical engineering, simulation, geography, statistics.

Bylines News Features: Various columnists.

BUSINESS/FINANCIAL MARKETS

Financial Markets: NYSE closing prices, AMEX closing prices, Unistox, Media General Stock Analysis, Commodity News Service.

Analysis and Computation: Raylux, Modell financial modeling, computational programs, Media General Stock Analysis.

News and Commentary: UPI business news, Raylux Financial Services, Management Contents.

Personal Finance: Computing interest, amortization of loans, annuity payments and analysis, bond accrued interest, tax computations.

Research and Reference: Information on Demand, Management Contents.

Directory Section: United States National Networks

CATALOG SHOPPING
Catalog Shopping: Data Bucks, Barter, books, records, tapes videotapes, radio recordings, classified ads, Comp-U-Store.

EDUCATION AND CAREERS
Education and Careers: Foreign languages, geography, mathematics, elementary education, Career Network.

MAIL AND COMMUNICATIONS
Mail and Communications: Mail, Chat, POST, PARTICIPATE, Mailgram® messages.

CREATING AND COMPUTING
Creating and Computing: Source manuals, text editor, programming, user publishing.

SOURCE*PLUS
*Source*Plus:* Management Contents, Commodity News Service, Media General Stock Analysis.

In addition to the above menu structure outline, The Source's user publishing section contains the following publications: Access Numbers, Apple City, Be Your Own Lawyer, Blind Pharoah, Classic & Exotic Cars, Dicheck, Elephant Walk Enterprises, Home Design, IBM PC Gazette, Legal Users Group (SIG), Mr. Software's Catalog, The Muses, Mylar's Warp, The National Challenge, Out of the Closet, Par Mt. Telegraph, Product Reviews, Public Access Systems, Real Times Magazine, Ridexchange, S.A.U.G. Magazine, S.A.U.G. Libraries, S.I.G.O.P. Library, Sorsex, SourceTrek, Today in History, Trashpoop, Tri-Weekly Trombone, Valut of Ages, W__I__N__K Magazine.

The Source's POST facility contains bulletin boards for the following: Aircraft, Antiques, Apartments-Rent, Apple, Art, Astrology, Atari, Automobiles-Domestic, Automobiles-Foreign, Aviation, Basic, Books/Publications, Bulletin-Board, Businesses, Cado, CBM/Pet-Computers, Chatter, Clubs, Collectibles, Commodore, Conferences & Meetings, CP/M, CPT, DEC, Documentation, Engineering, Fairs-and-Festivals, Fortran, Games, Gripes, Ham-Radio, Hardware-Rent, Hardware-Sale, Hardware-Wanted, Hayes, Heath, Help-Wanted, Hewlett-Packard, Hobbies-and-Crafts, HUG, IBM, Infox, Lanier, Library-Forum, Merchandise, Music, NEC, Novation, Office-Equipment, Osborne, OSI, Overseas, Parti, Pascal, Personal, Pets, Philips, Photography, Politics, Property/

Houses-Rent, Property/Houses-Sale, Property/Houses-Swap, Property/Houses-Wanted, Public-Files, Puzzles, RKO-Forum, Satellite-TV, Sayings, Services, Soap-Operas, Software-Sale, Software-Wanted, Source, Sports, Stereo/TV, Students-Corner, TI-99/4, Travel, TRS-80, User-Publishing, Video, Visicalc, Wang, Weekend-Getaway, Xerox, Zenith.

The Source also has a special network for Texas Instrument 99/4 and 99/4A owners, called Texnet.

The Source is developing its own packet-switched network, called SourceNet, and will have graphics software available to use online with the IBM PC and Apple II+ computers.

Comments: The Source, in its early days, was my favorite system. In recent times, unfortunately, response time has become unacceptable and a constant irritant, the system has bugs in it from the changeover to a new operating system, and it seems as if the sparkle it once had has faded. On the plus side, The Source has more bulletin boards than any other system, is filled with user-supplied information that cannot be found anywhere else, has the best electronic mail system of any network listed in *The Computer Phone Book,* and has a good stable of news and business services. Control Data Corporation (CDC) has purchased a minority interest in The Source. Should CDC decide to host the system on their Cyber series of computers, it could turn out to be one of the fastest systems in existence.

CPBN00875
Stewart/Finnco Stock/Option Databank

300/1200 bps
8/1/N

Networks: Tymnet.
Operating hours: 24 hours/day, 7 days/week.
Registration fee: $50.
Minimum: None.
Connect-time: $16/hour.
Contact: Douglas Stewart, Inc., c/o Finn Anderson, 76 Beaver St., New York, NY, 10005, (212)344-6630.
Contents: Preformatted and user-customized stock/option strategy screens that correspond to the markets. About 90 days of pricing data is available for all symbolized stocks, bonds, indices, groups, and options.

Comment: I have not used this system. You can see what it is like by calling its demonstration line at (212)543-9033 (see CPBB003280, page 466, for additional information).

CPBN00900
Travelhost Network

300/1200 bps
8/1/N

Networks: Uninet.
Operating hours: Prime time: Mon–Fri, 6 AM–6 PM local time; evening, Mon–Fri, 6 PM–1 PM local time; night, Mon–Fri, 10 PM–6 AM local time.
Registration fee: None.
Minimum: Prime time: $3 for 6 minutes of access; evening, $3 for 8 minutes of access; night, $3 for 12 minutes of access.
Connect-time: Prime time, $21.90/hour; evening, $15.48/hour; night, $11.16/hour.
Billing: Credit card.
Contact: Travelhost Network, 6116 N. Central, Ste. 1020, Dallas, TX, 75206.
Contents: The Travelhost Network uses a custom-designed terminal with special function keys to access services. Its special function keys are labeled and access the following:

Travel Club, a database of information for members of the Travelhost Travel Club.

Restaurants, a nationwide restaurant guide.

Shopping, a service for direct ordering of items online from a printed catalog.

Airlines, the Official Airline Guides (OAG EE).

Travel, a service for booking ahead room reservations and travel arrangements.

Messages, an abbreviated version of the ITT-Dialcom Intercomm electronic mail system.

Games, the Dialcom library of text games.

Stocks, the Unistox database.

Jobs, a job opportunity and resume-sending service.

Other, a wildcard key for entering direct commands from the keyboard.

Comments: I have not used this system. Travelhost has plans to offer many more databases than described above, and most of them should be online by the time you are reading this. In addition, Travelhost has plans of allowing their system to be accessed by users from home (instead of a hotel room). Check with Travelhost for new databases, access arrangements, and possibly a new connect-time rate schedule.

CHAPTER 5

Directory Section: United States Local-Area Services

Local-Area Services can be an inexpensive introduction to microcomputer telecommunications, providing you with reliable service and an easy, pressure-free way to get used to using an online system. If there is a Local-Area Service near you, it would be to your advantage to give it a try.

The systems listed in this section range from those run by newspapers to those that would be classified as bulletin-board systems (listed in Chapter 6) were it not for their having multiplexors to allow more than one user at a time online.

There are not enough Local-Area Services at present to require them being listed by state or locality. As with National Networks in Chapter 4, they are arranged in alphabetical order by system name.

The format for the individual system listings is not as standardized as in Chapter 4. Local-Area Services do not have the same pricing policies as National Networks, which is the primary cause for the difference in listings among systems. Despite this, a universal listing format has been developed. In *The Computer Phone Book* it consists of the following items:

CPB number
System name
Operating hours
Subscription fee
Minimum
Connect-time
Billing
Contact

bps rate(s)
Protocol

Contents
Comments

- *CPB number.* This has the same function as in the Chapter 4. In this chapter, L is part of the CPB prefix to indicate it is a Local-Area Service.
- *bps rate(s).* As in Chapter 4; 300 bps, 1200 bps, or both.
- *System name.* This is self-explanatory, although you should not be surprised if a system happens to undergo a name change. Some of the systems listed are quite new and were still under development when *The Computer Phone Book* went to press.
- *Protocol.* This indicates what you will set your communications software's word length, stop bits, and parity to in order to use the system. A setting, for example, of 8 word bits, 1 stop bit, and no parity will be abbreviated as 8/1/N.
- *Operating hours.* These may fluctuate as the systems are upgraded. It is rare to find a Local-Area Service that has prime-time and non-prime-time hours. In such cases, the hours will be duly noted.
- *Subscription fee.* Unlike National Networks, most Local-Area Services do not charge a fee that is separate from actual system access. In most cases, a monthly subscription fee is charged for unlimited use of the system during that month. When this is not so, it will be noted.
- *Minimum.* Since this is an exception, rather than a rule, it will only be listed if a system has such a requirement.
- *Connect-time.* This will only be listed if it is required. If this does not appear in a system listing, it means the monthly subscription fee covers all connect-time costs.
- *Billing.* As in Chapter 4, you may be billed automatically to your credit card or have a bill sent to you or your company. The procedure is specified in each listing.
- *Contact.* The address and phone number from which you may obtain additional information or immediately sign up for a subscription are given.
- *Contents.* This tells you what is on the system. Content descriptions will be very brief because of the nature of

Directory Section: United States Local-Area Services 167

the systems themselves. Most carry information that correspond to what is found in a local newspaper.
- *Comments.* This is what I have to say about the system, if I have used it, and what I found to be outstanding or disappointing.

Now that you have a thorough understanding of how the Local-Area Services are arranged in this chapter, you can begin your search for a Local-Area Service to guide you into the Information Age.

CPBL00050 300 bps
A-T Videotext 7/1/E or 8/1/O

Operating hours: 24 hours/day, 7 days/week.
Subscription fee: $6/month (*Notice:* you may also pay in 3-, 6-, or 12-month multiples.)
Billing: Direct billing to individuals or businesses.
Contact: A-T Videotext, 320 Nelson St., Tiffin, OH, 44883, (419)447-4493.
Contents: Local news, UPI national news, farm news, business and financial news, public service information, local school news, entertainment information, consumer information, advertising.
Comments: A-T Videotext was the first Local-Area Service with a monthly subscription fee and the first to use the Tandy Videotex Host system. The service has good response time, a variety of information, and is quite a bargain.

CPBL00150 300 bps
Buy-Phone 8/1/N

Operating hours: 24 hours/day, 7 days/week.
Subscription fee: Free of charge.
Contact: Buy-Phone, P.O. Box 29307, Los Angeles, CA, 90029, (213)474-2220.
Contents: An "electronic yellow pages" of West Los Angeles, containing over 10,000 listings covering all kinds of consumer products, services, and entertainment.

Comments: This is courtesy of Buy-Phone. You can call the service at (213)474-0270; the call is not free, but the information is. It can be a great help if you are going to travel to West Los Angeles and would like to find out what is available for entertainment and restaurants. Since the information is electronic, you can be assured of getting up-to-the-moment listings.

CPBL00250   300 bps
CLEO (Computerized Listings of Employment Opportunities)   7/1/N

Operating hours: 24 hours/day, 7 days/week.
Subscription fee: Free of charge.
Contact: CLEO, 2164 West 190 St., Torrance, CA 90504, (213)618-0200.
Contents: An online listing of employment available in high-technology fields in California.
Comments: CLEO is new and it is expanding fast. You can call it on your own, paying only for the phone call. CLEO has several phone lines:

Los Angeles	(213)618-8800
Orange County	(714)476-8800
San Diego County	(619)224-8800
San Jose/Santa Clara	(408)294-2000
San Francisco/Oakland	(415)482-1550

CPBL00300   300 bps
DataTrac Information Service   8/1/N

Operating hours: 24 hours/day, 7 days/week.
Subscription fee: Free of charge at press time.
Contact: DataTrac Information Service, 2848 Westerville Rd., Columbus OH, 43224, (614)476-5895, CompuServe ID 70001,1065.
Contents: The DataTrac Information Service consists of three systems in one. DataPost is an electronic messaging system, much like a bulletin-board system (BBS). Scan contains a variety of esoteric

text files. ATRPOST, or AtariPost, is an electronic messaging system (again much like a BBS) for users of Atari home computers and videogames.

Comments: At the time *The Computer Phone Book* went to press, DataTrac was undergoing a system overhaul and details on changes to the system were unavailable. Charges for system access may be imposed, so check with DataTrac. You may call the system, and, depending on the changes, may still get on for free or be presented with information on getting a paid subscription or account at (614)476-2035. The system is quite easy to use.

CPBL00350 300/1200 bps
DEC-Line 8/1/N

Operating hours: 24 hours/day, 7 days/week.
Subscription fee: Free of charge at press time.
Contact: N.A.
Contents: BBS list, mail, messaging, multiuser real-time conferencing, system information, userlog.
Comments: This is a multiplexed BBS. It is running on a DEC minicomputer with 80 megabytes of online storage. I used the real-time conferencing system to chat with another user and it worked fine. The sysops seem to be very creative and I suggest that you give this system a call to see what new features have been added. It can be reached at (213)346-1849.

CPBL00400 300 bps
Electronic Editions 7/1/E

Operating hours: 24 hours/day, 7 days/week.
Subscription fee: $19.95/month.
Billing: Credit card, prepayment, or direct billing to individuals and businesses.
Contact: Electronic Editions, Cowles Publishing Co., P.O. Box 2160, Spokane, WA, 99210, (509)455-6896.
Contents: Electronic Editions was still under development as *The Computer Phone Book* went to press. It will contain national and local news, information from several universities, information from

several farm magazines, a computer software column, and more. Contact Electronic Editions for details.
Comments: I have not used this system.

CPBL00450
Fantasy Plaza™

300 bps
7/1/E

Operating hours: 24 hours/day, 7 days/week.
Subscription fee: Free of charge.
Contact: Fantasy Plaza, P.O. Box, 6055, Burbank, CA, 91510, (213)840-8211.
Contents: Online catalog with computer software, firmware, peripherals, accessories; videogame software; general merchandise.
Comments: Give the system a call at (213)244-1100 and see it for yourself. Be sure to request a copy of the printed Fantasy Plaza catalog. You will not believe the photos in it!

CBPL00500
GameMaster

300 bps
8/1/N

Operating hours: 24 hours/day, 7 days/week.
Registration fee: $10 (includes 3 hours of system time plus 8 pages of documentation) or $40 (includes 8 hours of system access plus full documentation).
Minimum: $3/month.
Connect-time: $3/hour.
Billing: Credit card or prepayment.
Contact: GameMaster, 1723 Howard St., Ste. 219, Evanston, IL, 60202, (312)328-9009.
Contents: Electronic mail, multiuser real-time conferencing, messaging. Includes the following games: Airflight Simulator, All/None, Backgammon, Caverns, 18-Wheeler, GM-Air Freight, GameMaster Baseball, GameMaster's Den, GameMaster Football, Makin' Tracks, Mini Dungeon #1, Nuke Strike!, Oil Baron, PowerPlay, Rack-Up, Wonderful World of Eamon, Empyrean Challenge, and Starship Commander.
Comments: I have used the system quite a bit, but never in one long session. Consequently, I keep forgetting the appropriate com-

mands. It is my fault, not the system's, because I've met other users on the system who just swim through it like a fish in water. To get more information on GameMaster, call their ABBS at (312)475-4884. (See CPBB01820, page 250, for more information.)

CPBL00550 — 300 bps
Harris Electronic News — 8/1/N

Subscription fee: $5/month for basic news; $10/month for news plus Agritext or Monitor; $15/month for all three services. (*Notice:* you may pay in multiples of 3, 6, or 12 months).
Billing: Credit card, prepayment, or direct billing to individuals and businesses.
Contact: Harris Electronic News, 300 W. 2nd, P.O. Box 356, Hutchinson, KS, 67501, (316)662-8667, 1-(800)362-0283 (in Kansas).
Contents: Local and national news, weather, sports, technology news, advertising, home economics, farm news, grain and livestock prices.
Comments: There is plenty of information to be had by subscribing to all three services. If you are a farmer, you will find Agritext and Monitor of particular interest. The system has good response time and is easy to use.

CPBL00600 — TTY/300 bps
HEX2 — 8/1/N

Operating hours: 24 hours/day, 7 days/week.
Subscription fee: Free at press time.
Contact: N.A.
Contents: Feedback, mail, messaging, parameters, text files.
Comments: HEX stands for Handicapped Educational Exchange, and the 2 signifies this is the second incarnation of the system. It was originally one of the first four BBSs in existence. It has a special interest in aiding hearing-impaired individuals. There are text files on the system with information for the hearing impaired and a large message base covering a variety of subjects. This is a marvelous system; it is fast, has a nice format, and is worth a long-distance call. HEX2 can be reached at (301)593-7033.

CPBL00750
MicroShare

300/1200 bps
8/1/N

Operating hours: 24 hours/day, 7 days/week.
Registration fee: $10.
Minimum: $3/month.
Connect-time: $2.25/hour.
Billing: Credit card or prepayment.
Contact: MicroShare, P.O. Drawer 11N, Milwaukee, WI, 53201, (414)241-4321.
Contents: Several libraries of CP/M public-domain programs for downloading, Scott Adams Adventure games to play online.
Comments: If you can't get through to an RCP/M to fetch a program you need, MicroShare is the solution. It offers hundreds of CP/M programs ready to be downloaded to your computer. There are over 30 megabytes stored online. In between downloading software to your heart's content, you can try out your skill at a Scott Adams Adventure game. If you do not know what CP/M is or how to use it, wait until you do before trying this system.

CPBL00800
M-Net

300/1200
8/2/N

Operating hours: 24 hours/day, 7 days/week.
Subscription fee: Free of charge at press time.
Contact: N.A.
Contents: C programming language, conferencing, mail, messaging, Unix.
Comments: This system was fewer than 3 months old when I first accessed it. Aside from having a conferencing/messaging system that reminds me of Hypertext, it has a C shell and the full implementation of the Unix Operating System for hackers to dance through. It's a slick, fast, well-designed system that will probably have much more added to it by the time this description appears. There may even be a charge for access. Call it to find out, at (313)994-6333. It's located in Ann Arbor, Michigan.

CPBL00825   300 bps
Pantagraph Informant   8/1/N

Operating hours: 24 hours/day, 7 days/week.
Subscription fee: N.A.
Contact: The Pantagraph Informant, 301 W. Washington St., Bloomington, IL, 61701, (309)829-9411.
Contents: Local and national news, weather, sports, farm news, business and financial news, cultural and entertainment news.
Comments: This system was up in a test stage when *The Computer Phone Book* was going to press, and it is anticipated that a subscription fee will be charged for the service. Contact the company for details.

CBPL00950   300/1200 bps
StarText Metro   7/1/E or 8/1/N

Operating hours: 24 hours/day, 7 days/week.
Subscription fee: $7.95/month (*Notice:* May be subscribed to in 3-month increments.)
Billing: Prepayment.
Contact: StarText, P.O. Box 1870, Ft. Worth, TX, 76101, (817)390-7832.
Contents: National and local news, weather, sports, TV listings, business and financial news, computer user group newsletters, video-game reviews and news, entertainment and cultural news, special columnists.
Comments: StarText Metro is the largest Local-Area Service. It offers more information online than any local system and has the ability to be customized for screen output and information retrieval. It is the biggest bargain to be found in local systems. The system is fast, flexible, and very easy to use.

CHAPTER 6

Directory Section: United States Bulletin-Board Systems

This section of *The Computer Phone Book* represents the most accurate listing of operating BBSs available. To compile it, I called over 1500 phone numbers, got on over 900 operating systems, relied on over 100 lists of systems, awakened more people in the dead of night than I care to recall, and used my over three years of experience in calling such systems to weed out those I did not think would be operational within 6 months of my initial contact with them. Still, BBSs are ephemeral things; here today, into the Twilight Zone tomorrow. As the list stands now, I would not be surprised to learn that 10 percent of them disappeared from sight. But that is *all*, if any, I expect to have disappear; just 10%. I may have been wrong in some of my judgment calls in excluding systems; but I can live with that. It is better to compile and publish a list of too few numbers than it is to attempt a listing of "everything out there"; because, when you get down to it, "everything out there" *now* won't be "out there" six months (or even *three* months) from now. I would sooner put up with irate letters from disappointed sysops because their systems were excluded than I would put up with thousands of letters of complaint from purchasers of this book citing that 75 percent of the listings have netted them that infamous BBS farewell salute, "I'm sorry, but you have reached a number that has been disconnected or is no longer in service. If you feel you have reached this recording in error, please check the number and try your call again. Or call your operator for assistance." Of such recordings are the pillars of the Information Age eroded. I hope you sympathize and agree with my merciless manner of excluding systems. If you don't, not to worry. Virtually all BBSs

Directory Section: United States Bulletin-Board Systems 175

carry a list of other operating BBSs (I have noted this in the individual BBS listings). Remember, though, that when relying on other BBS lists, after you begin to hear the strains of "I'm sorry, but the number you have reached...," it is only in your imagination if you hear my voice in your *other* ear whispering, "I told you so!"

The systems in this section are arranged according to state, area code, city, and system name. If you wish to get to listings as fast as possible, the appendixes in the back of *The Computer Phone Book* will help you do so. Each system has been cross referenced in several ways allowing you to find *individual systems* as well as *individual parts* of systems.

Each system listing in this section is comprised of the following items, arranged as follows:

CPB number   Phone number
System name   bps rate(s)
City, State   Protocol
Access requirements   Software
Features
Special features
Special interests
Notice
Comments

- *CPB number.* B (for BBS) is added to the CPB prefix used in Chapter 4.
- *Phone number.* This is the number, with area code, you will call to connect to the system.
- *System name.* This is not as clearcut as the system names in Chapters 4 and 5. I cannot see the sense in calling a system by the name of its software and its location (such as, System X New York, NY) since, in most cases, the particular system is the *only* one in that location running brand system X software. In all situations in which a system is named by the software it is running and its location, I have dropped the location since it will appear as a separate item in the listing.
- *bps rate(s).* This is the speed at which the system can operate; usually 300 bps, 1200 bps, or both. In some

cases, particularly with RCP/Ms, a system will be able to operate between the speeds of 110 bps and 710 bps. This is accomplished by the use of a PMMI modem. If a PMMI modem is being used to offer more than just two bits-per-second rates, PMMI will appear as the bits-per-second rates.

- *City, State.* This is where the system is located—or claims it is located. If your local call turns out to be a toll call on your phone bill, petition your sysop to supply accurate location specifics. In situations in which no location information was supplied, I asked long-distance directory assistance to reveal the system's coordinates from its exchange.

- *Protocol.* This is what you set your word length, stop bits, and parity settings. In many instances, systems do not supply this information, and I have had to make a best guess. Again, petition your sysop to supply this information so it may benefit all users. An example of the format in a listing for 7 word bits, 1 stop bit, no parity is 7/1/N.

- *Access requirements.* "Open" in a listing indicates that you do not need a password to call the system as a new user; it does not, however, necessarily mean that your *second* call to the system will not require a password. In any situation where you are issued a password by a system or register a password of your own, *write your password down next to the system listing!* Sysops are not fond of users who think so little of their system (and their own time) that they don't take a few moments to put their password in a readily-available place. "Password required" in a listing will indicate that, while you may call a system without a password for the first time, you must either request or register a password for future access. This item is subject to change at a moment's notice on any system.

- *Software.* This is the software the sysop was running on the system when I accessed it for *The Computer Phone Book.* It is because of this item that all other items listed for any given system may change. Sysops usually try to

give their users the best service possible and are constantly upgrading or entirely changing their system software. For example, if a listing states that System ABC is running Y software, you may actually find it to be running Z software when you call it, such is life in the fast lane of BBSs. Make a note of any such changes in the individual system listing so you will have it for future reference. Appendix 1 contains help files from the most popular BBS software formats, and you should familiarize yourself with the particular commands of that software before you attempt any call.
- *Features*. This is the heart of a BBS; it is what it offers its users. A BBS can offer a variety of things, and the list below will explain the terms used to classify the standard features found on all types of BBSs.

CATALOG: A list of merchandise for sale, sometimes supplied by businesses running or sponsoring a BBS. Generally, the items offered for sale are computer-related. You may use your credit card to order items online.

CHAT: The ability to page the sysop and converse with him or her via your keyboard. On RCP/M–RBBSs, you must enter CP/M and look for CHAT.COM on Drive A, User Ø if a chat option is not offered on the RBBS menu. RCP/M–RBBSs are not listed as having chat capability unless Chat is a selection from the RBBS menu.

CONFERENCE: A sequentially or logically structured discussion system; found on Greene Machine and Conference Tree. This is not the same as messaging (see below) as, on Greene Machines, it is a separate menu selection (Discussions). On Conference Trees it is all the system is designed to do.

DOWNLOADING: Programs you can capture in the buffer of your terminal program, save to cassette tape or floppy disk, and run on your computer when you are offline. When possible, individual brands of computers will be specified (under Special features) as being served by downloadable software on individual systems.

FEEDBACK: The ability to leave a private message to the sysop before you are disconnected from the system.

Not all systems permit this, particularly those running Net-Works software.

GAMES: The system offers a selection of games you may play while you are online, such as Adventure-type text games. This is not to be confused with role-playing games on some systems that are carried out by an exchange of messages between the players. When possible, a list of available games will be listed under Special features.

MAIL: The ability to leave private messages for individual users on a system via a menu selection that is specifically labeled "mail"; such as that found on Net-Works systems. Color-80 systems, against all reason, have chosen to label their messaging system "E-Mail." *The Computer Phone Book* does not consider it to be true mail since public, as well as private, messaging is permitted from the same menu selection.

MATCHMAKING: An option available on systems such as Dial-Your-Match and MMMMMM. You fill out a questionnaire and your answers are compared to those of the opposite sex; the percentage of identical answers are shown.

MESSAGING: The ability to leave both public and private messages on a system. Some systems do not allow new users to post messages until their passwords have been validated. *The Computer Phone Book* does not always specify whether new users may leave messages on a system since this policy is not always apparent on systems. Private messages are not considered mail by *The Computer Phone Book* unless there is a menu selection specifically labeled as such (see Mail above).

PARAMETERS: The ability to control one or more aspects of the system's output to your computer. This can range from toggling a prompt bell to setting screen width, bits-per-second rate, and protocol.

SYSTEM INFORMATION: A text file that explains the hardware and software that comprise the system.

TEXT FILES: Various and sundry types of information provided by sysops and/or users. Text files are sometimes labeled "Bulletins" on systems, a practice *The Computer Phone Book* frowns upon. In the purest sense, Bulletins should only be a reprinting of signon messages, not text

Directory Section: United States Bulletin-Board Systems

files. When possible, the contents of text files on individual systems are specified under Special features.

TIME/DURATION: The ability to see the system's local time and how long you have been on the system. This is an important feature if you are calling long distance and wish to keep your phone costs to a minimum or find yourself on a system with a time limit.

USERLOG: Either a temporary list of recent callers to the system or a permanent list of regular users. No distinction is made between the two by *The Computer Phone Book*.

- *Special features*. When possible, details of available downloadable programs, games, and text files will be listed under this heading.
- *Special interests*. If the system is being run to suit a particular interest (such as the user of a particular computer or piece of software), it will be noted under this heading.
- *Notice*. If a system has a time limit, charges its users, is X-rated, or has an unusual policy, it will be noted under this heading.
- *Comments*. Although I have used every system listed here, I will not necessarily have something to say in any detail about all of them. Some systems are nothing more than general-interest message bases; their content is supplied solely by users.

Before you begin sampling the systems in this section, I have to tell you how you should conduct yourself on BBSs you will be calling. It may seem self-evident, yet it bears repeating: Foul language is neither appreciated nor tolerated in public messages. Remember, the system you will be calling is private property and resides in an individual's home or in a business. Sysops are not timid in defending their systems from crashers or abusers and have no qualms about calling in the phone company in such matters. Data lines *can* have traces placed on them just as easily as voice lines can.

Try to keep your online visits from 15 to 20 minutes. Remember, only one person at a time can use a BBS, and you'll never know how many people have gotten a busy signal from the system while you were on it. If a system has a policy of one call per user per day, abide by it.

Lastly, but most importantly, do *not* try to get the sysop's telephone number. If you want to communicate with the sysop, do so on the system by leaving him or her a message. When I originally planned *The Computer Phone Book*, I wanted to list the names of the sysops of each system. I thought it would be only fitting to give recognition to the men and women who were providing this splendid service for all to use and enjoy. My initial inquiries to sysops about this idea were met with reactions ranging from refusals with no reason given to sheer terror. After a while, I discovered the leitmotif running through the responses I was receiving. Most sysops did not want to be identified because it opens them up to harassment and unwanted phone calls from users of their systems.

Now that you know the "rules of the road," you can start going through the listings. At the dial tone up ahead, your next stop is the Bulletin-Board Zone.

Alabama (205)

CPBB00030 (205) 492-0373
Bama Bullet 300 bps
Gadsden, Alabama 8/1/N
Open Bullet-80

Features: BBS list, chat, downloading, feedback, games, messaging, parameters, time/duration, system information.
Special features: Over 150 download programs available. Games include biorhythm, craps, othello, and scramble.
Comments: A general-interest message system.

CPBB00040 (205) 272-5069
Forum-80 300/1200 bps
Montgomery, Alabama 8/1/N
Probationary Forum-80

Features: BBS list, chat, downloading, feedback, messaging, parameters, system information, text files, userlog.

Special features: Unspecified download programs. Text file is local club information.
Notice: Forum-80 has a policy of displaying a long (series of) signon bulletin(s) that you cannot bypass and of labeling all new users as "probationary," requiring the sysop to approve any messages new users post before other users may read them (if at all).
Comments: A general-interest message system. This system seems to be an online meeting place where members of the Central Alabama Computer Society can exchange messages.

CPB00050 (205) 343-1933
Forum-80 300/1200 bps
Montgomery, Alabama 8/1/N
Probationary Forum-80

Features: BBS list, chat, downloading, feedback, messaging, parameters, system information, text files, userlog.
Special features: Unspecified download programs. Text files contain information on a local user group.
Notice: Forum-80 has a policy of displaying a long (series of) signon bulletin(s) that you cannot bypass and of labeling all new users as "probationary," requiring the sysop to approve any messages new users post before other users may read them (if at all).
Comments: A general-interest message system.

CPBB00060 (205) 288-1100
Joe's Computer 300/1200 bps
Montgomery, Alabama 8/1/N
Password Required TBBS

Features: BBS list, downloading, mail, messaging, parameters, system information, text files, userlog.
Special features: Text file is a local club newsletter. Multiple message boards for Apple, Atari, Commercial, Commodore, Executive, Heath, IBM, Miscellaneous, NEC, Northstar, TI, TRS-80, Vector, Victor, Video, XXX.
Notice: You will have to register a password for regular use.

Comments: A general-interest message system with quite a few boards for various interests.

Alaska (907)

CPBB00070 (907) 278-4223
Abacus-by-Phone 300 bps
Anchorage, Alaska 8/1/N
Password Required Net-Works

Features: BBS list, chat, downloading, mail, messaging, parameters, text files, time/duration.
Special features: Text files on various topics.
Notice: Net-Works systems do not allow you to read past the first 10 messages or to access certain sections of the system until your password is validated. This system charges a fee for access.
Comments: The sysops of this system initiated a fee for access after the system was nearly killed by people posting harassing notices on it. Since this is the *only* reliably operating BBS I have found in Alaska, you'll have to pay the fee in order to see if the system lists any new Alaskan BBSs.

Arizona (602)

CPBB00090 (602) 957-4428
Arizona Bulletin-Board 300/1200 bps
Phoenix, Arizona 7/1/E
Open ACCESS

Features: BBS list, mail, messaging, parameters, time/duration.
Special interest: Multiple message boards for Amateur/CB radio, Automobiles, Bulletins, Clubs, Computers, Hardware, Miscellaneous, Real-estate, Software, TV/stereo, Wanted.
Comments: This is quite a busy system with a lot of message activity. Give it a call and join in.

CPB00100 (602) 998-9411
Cactus-Net 300 bps
Phoenix, Arizona 7/1/E
Open ACCESS

Features: BBS list, mail, messaging, parameters, time/duration.
Comments: Another system with a lot of activity. This one seems to have many teenagers on it.

CPB00110 (602) 931-1829
Conference Tree 300 bps
Phoenix, Arizona 7/1/E
Open Conference Tree

Features: Conferencing.
Special interest: Education.
Comments: This system is getting very little use for its intended purpose—discussing education. Give it a call and help the tree to grow.

CPBB00120 (602) 938-4508
Micro Systems Services 300 bps
Phoenix, Arizona 8/1/N
Open Original

Features: Catalog shopping.
Comments: This system is provided by a software/hardware supplier that is offering 20 to 25 percent discounts on most products for Apple, Atari, IBM, and CP/M-based computers. You can read comparative pricing (retail versus discount), get information on a product, and, if you want, order it online.

CPBB00130 (602) 458-3850
Forum-80 300 bps
Sierra Vista, Arizona 8/1/N
Probationary Forum-80

Features: BBS list, downloading, feedback, messaging, parameters, system information, text files, userlog.
Special features: Unspecified download programs and text files.
Notice: This system requires a $10 registration fee in addition to the usual Forum-80 policy of forced signon bulletins and probationary user status.
Comments: A general-interest message system. No outstanding features.

CPBB00140 (602) 746-3956
Tucson Computer Group 300 bps
Tucson, Arizona 8/2/E
Open Original

Features: Messaging, system information, text files.
Special features: Text file contains historical information about a local computer club.
Comments: A general-interest message system.

Arkansas (501)

CPBB00150 (501) 646-0197
Ft. Smith Computer Club 300 bps
Ft. Smith, Arkansas 7/1/E or 8/1/N
Open PMS

Features: Feedback, messaging, parameters, text files, time/duration.
Special features: Text files on various topics.
Notice: This is a *part-time* system. Hours of operation are 6:30 PM–9:30 AM weekdays; 2:30 PM Sat to 9:30 AM Mon EST.

Comments: A general-interest message system specializing in message exchanging between members of the Ft. Smith Computer Club.

CPBB00160 (501) 372-0576
Ark-Net 300 bps
Little Rock, Arkansas 8/1/N
Open PBBS

Features: Downloading, feedback, messaging, text files, time/duration, userlog.
Special features: Text files contain information on the Arkansas Computer Club, Central Arkansas Radio Emergency Network and software reviews.
Notice: This is a *part-time* system. Hours of operation are from noon to midnight, Mon to Thurs; noon Fri to midnight Sun EST.
Comments: This is the second part-time system in Arkansas, and one of the very few listed in *The Computer Phone Book*. This is a general-interest message system with a friendly sysop.

California (209)

CPBB00170 (209) 298-1328
Dial-Your-Match #26 300 bps
Clovis, California 7/1/E
Questionnaire/Password Required DYM

Features: BBS list, chat, feedback, mail, matchmaking, messaging.
Special feature: Matchmaking.
Notice: You cannot use a Dial-Your-Match system unless you fill out a questionnaire. This system asks you to leave your name, address, and phone number in order to get a permanent password. This is to "varify" (sic) all users. This is not a common practice among DYMs.
Comments: Throughout this encyclopedia of electronica, you will read of my chronicle to find The Perfect Match through DYM. As for this system, I did not bother to get a password. Any DYM system

that wants to pierce the anonymity of its users is not one *The Computer Phone Book* can recommend. Using a DYM always entails risk, but trying to lessen that risk by invasion of privacy is not something I can condone, sanction, or recommend. Use this DYM at your own risk.

California (213)

CPBB00180	(213) 842-3322
Dial-Your-Match #1	300 bps
Beverly Hills, California	7/1/E
Questionnaire/Password Required	DYM

Features: BBS list, chat, feedback, mail, matchmaking, messaging.
Special feature: Matchmaking.
Notice: Even to browse a Dial-Your-Match system, you must first fill out a questionnaire. All of your answers will be public, available to other system users. Depending on the individual sysop (called a Matchmaker), the questions could be quite explicit. This is a sexually oriented system.
Comments: Be still my heart! Alas, 'twas but a palpitation. The highest percentage match I was presented with was a disappointing 64 percent, to two women. One too young, one too old.

CPBB00190	(213) 840-8252
Dial-Your-Match #7	300 bps
Burbank, California	7/1/E
Questionnaire/Password Required	DYM

Features: BBS list, chat, feedback, mail, matchmaking, messaging, userlog.
Special feature: Matchmaking.
Notice: See the previous listing for DYM guidelines. This is a sexually oriented system.
Comments: From bad to worse it gets. On this system, I was matched to only three women, and the percentage of identical questionnaire responses was only 50 percent! DYMs can be cruel.

CPBB00200   (213) 366-1238
Mog-Ur HBBS   300/1200 bps
Granada Hills, California   8/1/N
Open   HBBS

Features: Chat, downloading, messaging, parameters, time/duration, userlog.
Special features: CP/M downloadable programs.
Special interest: Multiple message boards for Fantasy 1, Fantasy 2, Buy/Sell/Barter, Interplay/Dating/Chatter, Humor, Underground, Heath/Zenith, Aviation/Sailing/Recreation, Operating Systems.
Comments: This is quite an active system with plenty of interesting messages. It is worth a long-distance call.

CPBB00210   (213) 764-8000
Dial-Your-Match #28   300 bps
Hollywood, California   7/1/E
Questionnaire/Password Required   DYM

Features: BBS list, chat, feedback, mail, matchmaking, messaging, text files, time/duration.
Special features: Matchmaking, text files on various topics.
Special interest: Joke message board.
Notice: Even to browse a Dial-Your-Match system, you must first fill out a questionnaire. All of your answers will be public, available to other system users. Depending on the individual sysop (called a Matchmaker), the questions could be quite explicit. This is a sexually oriented system. This system has a 25-minute time limit.
Comments: "This system is not intended for those without a sense of humor," a signon message warns. If you proceed to the questionnaire, you'll come across such gems as these: "I would rather watch a movie: A) in the theatre, B) on television, C) in a 25-cent movie booth with a stack of quarters," and, "What style of dress do you prefer? A) I like to get dressed up, B) I like to dress casual, C) I like to dress in drag, D) I dress like a goddamn clown," and, "My belly button is A) an innie, B) an outie." This DYM is as much fun as watching *NBC News Overnight*! On the other hand, my

quest for the Perfect Match netted me three bisexual women, and the highest percentage of identical questionnaire responses was a crushing 57 percent. And so it goes. . .

CPBB00220 (213) 653-6398
Hollywood RCP/M RBBS 300/1200 bps
Hollywood, California 8/1/N
Open RCP/M RBBS

Features: CP/M, downloading, messaging.
Special features: Downloadable software for Kaypro computers, worldwide RCP/M list.
Special interest: Kaypro computers.
Notice: This system is the U.S. collection point for the international RCP/M list that is distributed to all RCP/M systems. If you are an RCP/M sysop, call and leave details of your system.
Comments: If you are looking for more RCP/Ms to call than are listed in *The Computer Phone Book* (for instance, those which operate on a part-time basis), give this system a call and capture the international RCP/M list. Also, if you are an owner or user of a Kaypro computer, give this system a call to exchange information with other users about hardware and software.

CPBB00230 (213) 980-5643
Oracle BBS 300 bps
Hollywood, California 8/1/N
Password Required Original

Features: Chat, matchmaking, messaging, parameters, text files, user-log.
Special features: Matchmaking, text files on gay sex topics.
Special interest: Gay sex.
Notice: This is a sexually oriented, and quite explicit, system. Matchmaking special feature is only available to privileged account holders.
Comments: If you are not gay, are not sympathetic in the least towards gays, do yourself (and the users of this system) a big favor and

refrain from calling this system. I'm sure the users have heard every epithet imaginable (and then some) and do not need to hear them repeated online. This is a very explicit system.

CPBB00240 (213) 589-0372
California/80 300 bps
Huntington Park, California 8/1/N
Open RATS/Greene Machine

Features: BBS list, chat, conference, download, feedback, parameters, system information, time/duration, userlog.
Special features: Unspecified downloadable programs, conferences on various subjects, Cryline advice column.
Notice: Regular users of this system should register a password for downloading access and other system features.
Comments: A general-interest message system. Access to Cryline requires a password.

CPBB00250 (213) 428-5206
Dragon's Lair 300 bps
Long Beach, California 8/1/N
Open Original

Features: Chat, feedback, games, messaging, userlog.
Special features: Games. Adventures: Atlantis, Building of Death, D&D Quest, Dogstar, Dungeon Escape, Dutchman's Gold, Elephant 1, Elephant 2, Island Escape, Mouse of Chicago, Nuke Sub, Sabotage Adventure, Sorceror, Troll Adventure. Simulations: B1 Bomber, Biorhythm, Lunar Lander, Midway, Nukewar, Planet Miners, Sea Raider.
Special interest: Games.
Notice: There is a 1-hour time limit on this system. Games are rotated at irregular intervals, so not all of the choices listed above may be available when you call.
Comments: All of the games on this system are text based. The purpose of this system is to allow callers to test drive game software

before they buy it. If you call the system long distance, that's not very cost effective; but if you've never tried any of these games before and don't want to have to buy one, you might want to risk a late-night call out of curiosity. (I found Mouse of Chicago to be particularly strange.) To get system policies, first select Instructions, then choose W from the second menu. Watch that phone bill!

CPBB00260 (213) 431-2274
TKM's Mini BBS 300 bps
Long Beach, California 7/1/E
Open Original

Features: BBS list, chat, downloading, messaging, system information, text files, time/duration, userlog.
Special features: Downloadable programs for the Apple II+ computer, text files on Apple-related subjects.
Notice: This system only understands UPPER CASE INPUT.
Comments: A very basic system, with a two-step message retrieval process that takes too much time. Long-distance callers can skip this one; it is mainly of local interest.

CPBB00270 (213) 336-5535
Coin Games Net 300 bps
Los Angeles, California 8/1/N
Password Required Net-Works

Features: BBS list, downloading, feedback, mail, messaging, parameters, system information, time/duration, text files.
Special features: Unspecified downloadable programs, text files on a variety of topics.
Special interest: Coin-operated games.
Notice: Net-Works systems do not allow you to read past the first 10 messages or access certain sections of the system until your pass-

word is validated. Your telephone number will become part of your password, so don't give a false one.

Comments: Although this system is supposed to focus on coin games (arcade video and pinball), the message base was primarily filled with general-interest messages.

CPBB00280 (213) 829-1140
Computer Conspiracy 300 bps
Los Angeles, California 8/1/N
Open Original

Features: Catalog, chat, messaging, parameters, system information, time/duration.

Special features: Online catalogs, including Apple business, Apple games, Apple word processing, Atari, CP/M, hardware, IBM PC, peripherals.

Comments: This system is primarily designed for reading a catalog of over 800 computer-related items—mostly software—that you can buy at discount prices.

CPBB00290 (213) 667-9011
Consumer Electronics Newsbase™ 300 bps
Los Angeles, California 7/1/E
Open FoReM

Features: Text files.

Special features: Text files. News about audio, home computers, video, videogames.

Comments: This is an interesting idea but not as good as it could and should be. When I accessed the system, news consisted mainly of (dated) press releases from various manufacturers. This system is a good idea and may grow into something worthwhile.

CPBB00300   (213) 345-1047
Dial-Your-Match #9   300 bps
Los Angeles, California   7/1/E
Questionnaire/Password Required   DYM

Features: BBS list, chat, feedback, mail, matchmaking, messaging.
Special features: Matchmaking.
Notice: This is an XXX-rated system. The questionnaire itself may be deemed offensive by some. Use at your own risk, you have been warned.
Comments: Kinky questionnaire aside, I achieved a 76 percent match to one of a list of women. I was wounded to the quick, however, after reading the woman's replies to the questionnaire. I was left with the distinct impression this DYM didn't know how to count. The search continues...

CPBB00310   (213) 360-5053
Granada Engineering   300 bps
Los Angeles, California   8/1/N
Open   RCP/M RBBS

Features: CP/M, downloading, messaging, parameters, time/duration.
Special features: Downloadable software for CP/M-based computers.
Special interest: CP/M.
Comments: This is a typical RCP/M RBBS system. If you are looking for free software or want to learn something about CP/M, give this system a call.

CPBB00320   (213) 370-2887
LA-KUG BBS   300 bps
Los Angeles, California   8/1/N
Open   RCP/M RBBS

Features: CP/M, downloading, messaging, parameters, userlog.
Special features: Downloadable programs for Kaypro computers.
Special interest: Kaypro computers.

Notice: A password is required to access the downloading section.
Comments: There weren't too many programs on this system when I called it but I had a fun chat with the sysop and the publisher/editor of Pro/Files magazine. By the time you read this, the system should be multiuser with several new features and plenty of programs. If you have a Kaypro computer, this will probably be *the* system for you to call.

CPBB00330 (213) 473-2754
Softworxsm 300 bps
Los Angeles, California 8/1/N
Password Required Net-Works

Features: Chat, downloading, mail, messaging, parameters, system information, text files.
Notice: A membership fee is required to use this system regularly and fully. Temporary passwords, issued online, are good for 14 days.
Comments: I did not see anything on this system to warrant a fee. It seemed to me to be just another general-interest message system.

CPBB00340 (213) 331-3574
PMS 300 bps
Los Angeles, California 7/1/E or 8/1/N
Open PMS

Features: BBS list, chat, downloading, feedback, messaging, parameters, system information, text files, time/duration.
Special features: Downloadable programs for the Apple II+ computer, text files on various topics.
Comments: A general-interest message system with a variety of good programs for the Apple.

CPBB00350 (213) 577-9947
RBBS PMMI (110–1200 bps)
Pasadena, California 8/1/N
Open RCP/M RBBS

Features: CP/M, downloading, feedback, messaging, parameters, userlog.
Special features: Downloadable programs for CP/M-based computers.
Special interest: CP/M.
Comments: A general-interest message system and CP/M file transfer facility.

CPBB00360 (213) 897-3012
Data Connection 300/1200 bps
San Fernando, California 8/1/N
Open HBBS

Features: BBS list, chat, downloading, messaging, parameters, system information, userlog.
Special features: Unspecified downloadable programs.
Notice: A password is required to access the downloading section of this system. Regular users should also register a password.
Comments: This is a general-interest message system with more menu options than most.

CPBB00370 (213) 390-3239
MMMMMM #1 300/1200 bps
Santa Monica, California 7/1/E
Questionnaire/Password Required MMMMMM

Features: BBS list, chat, feedback, mail, matchmaking, messaging, userlog.
Special feature: Matchmaking.
Notice: To gain access to this system, you must first fill out a questionnaire. All of your replies will be public; available to all system users. This is a sexually oriented system.

Comments: MMMMMM stands for Marc the Martian's Mixed-up Matching & Message Machine. This is the headquarters system. I achieved a 67 percent match with one of a list of women. She was hardly my Perfect Match. But then, these systems rarely ask the questions I would!

CPBB00380 (213) 783-2305
Dial-Your-Match #4 300 bps
Sherman Oaks, California 7/1/E
Questionnaire/Password Required DYM

Features: BBS list, chat, feedback, mail, matchmaking, messaging.
Special feature: Matchmaking.
Notice: Even to browse a Dial-Your-Match system, you must first fill out a questionnaire. All of your answers will be public, available to all system users. Depending on the individual sysop (called a Matchmaker), the questions could be quite explicit. This is a sexually oriented system.
Comments: Reaching through the electronic network that connects us all, I achieved a 61 percent match with one of a list of women. I guess very few women say that movie soundtracks are their favorite type of music.

CPBB00390 (213) 563-7727
L.A. Color Exchange (Color-80 #4) 300 bps
Southgate, California 8/1/N
Open Color-80

Features: BBS list, chat, downloading, graphics, messaging, parameters, system information, text files.
Special features: Downloadable programs for the Color Computer, online graphics for the Color Computer, text files on Color Computer-related topics.
Notice: To download programs and view online graphics, you must be using a Color Computer and a terminal program such as Colorcom/E.

Comments: If you own a CoCo, you can call this system to meet with other users to exchange programming tips, ask questions, and upload and download public-domain programs.

CPBB00400 (213) 367-0324
Interact 300 bps
Sylmar, California 7/1/E or 8/1/N
Open Original

Features: BBS list, downloading, mail, messaging, parameters, system information, text files, userlog.
Special features: Downloadable programs for Atari home computers, text files on various topics.
Comments: This is a general-interest message system. The sysops are trying to promote an atmosphere that will encourage the exchange of thought-provoking comments, opinions, and news. This system is worth a long-distance call.

CPBB00410 (213) 881-6880
Novation Modem Information 300 bps
Tarzana, California 7/1/E or 8/1/N
Open Original

Features: Mail, text files.
Special features: Text files. Nationwide BBS list, Novation modem and software product information, technical information.
Notice: If you happen to be asked for a password when you sign on, try **CAT**.
Comments: This system is run by Novation, Inc., a major personal computer modem manufacturer. Novation maintains a nationwide list of BBSs on this system, but be forewarned—once the list starts to print out, you cannot interrupt the output. Be ready, therefore, to spend some money if you decide to call this system long distance. Have your communications software's buffer ready.

Directory Section: United States Bulletin-Board Systems 197

CPBB00420 (213) 370-3293
South Bay RCP/M RBBS 300/1200 bps
Torrance, California 8/1/N
Open RCP/M RBBS

Features: CP/M, downloading, messaging, userlog.
Special features: Downloadable programs for the Kaypro and Tandy Model 100 computers.
Special interest: Kaypro computers.
Notice: You must request access to the section containing the Model 100 downloadable programs.
Comments: This was quite a new system when I called it. Against all prior experience, I'm listing it in *The Computer Phone Book* because the system struck me as being maintained by a dedicated sysop. Time will tell. Give it a call to see if I'm right.

CPBB00430 (213) 516-9432
Telephone Software Connection™ 300 bps
Torrance, California 7/1/E or 8/1/N
Open Original

Features: Downloading, feedback.
Special features: Purchasing of programs for your Apple II+ or //e computer that you can download.
Notice: This is a fee-based system. Most of the programs carry a price, although you may download one of a few sample programs for free.
Comments: Over 60 programs are available on this system in the categories of Business, Communications, DOS, Education, Games, Graphics, Miscellaneous, Programming Aids, and Time. You may also order Apple peripherals online (they will be mailed to you, not downloaded). Your Apple must be running Applesoft in order to download and use the programs. Inquire about TSC's Programmer's Pipeline service.

CPBB00440   (213) 306-1172
PatVac   300 bps
Venice, California   8/1/N
Open   RCP/M RBBS

Features: Downloading, messaging, parameters, userlog.
Special features: Downloadable programs for CP/M-based computers.
Special interests: CP/M, esoterica.
Comments: "Are you a Vagrant or a Loon:" is the first thing you will see when you sign on to this system. Seeing it as a philosophic way of asking, Are you a new user or a registered ID holder, I answered "V" since I was a new user. It worked OK. The weirdness didn't stop there, though, because the system itself contains a weirdness file on its main menu. A message on the system, from the sysop, should give you an idea of the system's personality: "To: All Vgrntloons (sic). Questions. Henceforth askers of stupid questions get eaten. Stupid answers remain OK. This is the time of year for this to happen. We are susceptible."

California (408)

CPBB00450   (408) 688-9629
Mines of Moria   300 bps
Aptos, California   8/1/N
Password Required   Net-Works clone

Features: Catalog, chat, downloading, mail, messaging, parameters, system information, text files, time/duration.
Special features: Unspecified downloadable programs, text files on various topics.
Special interests: Multiple message bases. Categories: Adventure Hints, Apple, Atari, Backup Hints, Bartering, Games Reviews, Public, Software Docs, VIC/Commodore.
Notice: Just like a real Net-Works system, you will only be allowed to read certain portions of the system and will not have full system access until you are granted a verifiable password.

Comments: Visit with the sysop, "Tamerlane of the Rings," in this system devoted to adventure gaming. Running on a 10-megabyte hard disk, there is room on this system for a lot of information and messages. Tamerlane plans to add plenty of unique features, so give the system a call to see what's new.

CPBB00460 (408) 475-7101
Conference Tree 300 bps
Berkeley, California 7/1/E
Open Conference Tree

Features: Conferencing.
Comments: As with any Conference Tree, the topics discussed are as varied as the system's users. One of the conferences gaining steam on this system was about starting your own religion. A Conference Tree is always worth a long-distance call, and this one is no exception.

CPBB00470 (408) 378-8733
Computer Systems Design 300/1200 bps
Campbell, California 8/1/N
Open RCP/M RBBS

Features: Catalog, chat, downloading, messaging, parameters, user-log.
Special features: dBase II™ demonstration.
Special interests: dBase II software.
Notice: You must have a terminal program that is listed on this system's menu in order to use the online dBase II demonstration.
Comments: This system is designed to exchange information about and distribute public-domain programs that enhance the use of Ashton-Tate's dBase II software.

CPB00480 (408) 253-5216
GFxBBS 300 bps
Cupertino, California 7/1/E or 8/1/N
Open AMIS

Features: Downloading, messaging, time/duration, userlog.
Special features: Downloadable programs for Atari home computers.
Special interest: Atari home computers.
Comments: If you are looking to meet other Atari owners or want to find a suitable public-domain program, give this system a call.

CPBB00490 (408) 263-2588
Colossal Oxgate #2 300 bps
Milpitas, California 8/1/N
Open RCP/M Oxgate

Features: BBS list, catalog, chat, CP/M, downloading, messaging, parameters, userlog.
Special features: Downloadable programs for CP/M-based computers.
Special interests: CP/M.
Comments: The sysop will put up any program you request from the PICONET library (volumes 1–33), SIGM (volumes 1–24), or CPMUG (volumes 1–79, although the CPMUG library is not complete).

CPBB00500 (408) 238-9621
DataTech Node 007/Servu 300 bps
San Jose, California 8/1/N
Open RCP/M RBBS

Features: BBS list, chat, downloading, messaging, parameters, system information, time/duration, userlog.
Special features: Downloadable programs for CP/M-based computers.
Special interests: CP/M.

Notice: There is a 1-hour time limit on this system weekdays, 4 PM to midnight; weekends noon to midnight (Pacific Time). You will be automatically disconnected from the system after 1 hour.
Comments: Another system for CP/M users.

CPBB00510 (408) 997-2790
Computers for Christ 300 bps
San Jose, California 8/1/N
Password Required TBBS

Features: Chat, downloading, feedback, messaging, parameters, system information, text files, time/duration.
Special features: Downloadable Christian religion programs for the Color Computer and TRS-80 Models I and III computers; text files cover Christian religion subjects.
Special interest: Christian religion.
Notice: A password is required to leave public messages.
Comments: This is the headquarters system for the Computers for Christ ministry. When I accessed this system, it was just recovering from a power surge that had erased the message base. There are quite a few programs and text files on the system that would be of interest to Christians. If you're looking for kindred spirits, this is a system for you to call.

CPBB00520 (408) 298-6930
IBBS 300 bps
San Jose, California 7/1/E
Open FoReM

Features: BBS list, chat, downloading, messaging, parameters, user-log.
Special features: Downloadable programs for Atari home computers.
Special interests: Atari home computers.
Notice: This system has a 30-minute time limit.
Comments: IBBS stands for Itsy-Bitsy BBS. There is a cute ASCII graphic of the Space Shuttle launching when you logon. Cuteness aside, this system has a double-jointed message retrieval system that is annoying. Long-distance callers can bypass this one.

CPBB00530 (408) 867-1243
Oxgate Message System 001 300 bps
Saratoga, California 8/1/N
Open RCP/M RBBS

Features: BBS list, chat, CP/M, downloading, feedback.
Special features: Downloadable programs for CP/M-based computers.
Special interest: CP/M.
Comments: This system features a large message base. When I called it, the hard disk had just died. I don't know how that will reflect on the number of programs available for downloading when you call. Otherwise, this is quite an active system and worth a long-distance call.

CPBB00540 (408) 773-6809
Color-80 #1 300 bps
Sunnyvale, California 8/1/N
Open Color-80

Features: BBS list, catalog, chat, downloading, feedback, graphics, messaging, parameters, system information, text files.
Special features: Downloadable programs for the Color Computer, online graphics for the Color Computer, text files on Color Computer topics.
Special interest: Color computer.
Notice: To download programs and view online graphics, you must be using a Color Computer and a terminal program such as Colorcom/E.
Comments: This is the headquarters system for Color-80, a marvelous BBS for the CoCo and, in my opinion, the best. Version 4.0 was running when I called; it seemed slower than earlier versions and was infested with bugs. Apparently, the author put up the system to do some interactive debugging. It will probably be all debugged and faster when you call it. Is it worth a long-distance call? Yes! Any Color-80 is.

CPBB00550 (408) 749-1872
Stuart II 300 bps
Sunnyvale, California 7/1/E
Open Original

Features: Conferencing.
Comments: This is a hierarchically structured system, somewhat along the lines of a Conference Tree but not as easy to use. You will have to spend some time on the system to learn the many commands. There are a variety of topics on this system. If you don't find a topic that interests you, just start your own discussion. This is a very fast system and worth a long-distance call.

California (415)

CPBB00560 (415) 845-9462
Blue Boss 300 bps
Berkeley, California 7/1/E
Password Required Original

Features: Catalog, messaging.
Notice: If asked for a password, logon with GUEST.
Comments: This is an odd system, with no frills whatsoever. One message from a user stated, "There is nothing interesting on here!" A plaintive exclamation, yet true. If you call this system, try to leave an interesting message.

CPBB00570 (415) 538-3580
Conference Tree 300 bps
Berkeley, California 7/1/E
Open Conference Tree

Features: Conferencing.
Special interest: The FORTH programming language.

Comments: If you have any interest in the programming language FORTH, this is *the* system for you. I have yet to find another public system (national, local, or BBS) that can compete with the wealth of information found here about FORTH. Well worth a long-distance call.

CPBB00580 (415) 991-4911
Dial-Your-Match #17 300 bps
Daly City, California 7/1/E
Questionnaire/Password Required DYM

Features: BBS list, chat, feedback, mail, matchmaking, messaging.
Special features: Matchmaking.
Notice: Even to browse a Dial-Your-Match system, you must first fill out a questionnaire. All of your answers will be public, available to all system users. Depending on the individual sysop (called a Matchmaker), the questions could be quite explicit. This is a sexually oriented system.
Comments: Need I say it? A measly 61 percent match was my highest on this system. Maybe I should lie and say that rock is my favorite music? Nah.

CPBB00590 (415) 488-9145
Mojo's Download-80 300/1200 bps
Forest Knolls, California 8/1/N
Password Required Download-80

Features: BBS list, chat, downloading, messaging, parameters, system information, time/duration, userlog.
Special features: Downloadable programs are claimed for CP/M, TRS-80, and Unix; not verified by *The Computer Phone Book*.
Notice: There is a 40-minute time limit on this system. A password is required to access the downloading section.
Comments: A general-interest message system. If its claims of having downloadable Unix programs are true, this system would be worth a long-distance call.

CPBB00600 (415) 651-4147
Aardwolf-Express 300/1200 bps
Fremont, California 8/1/N
Password Required TBBS

Features: BBS list, catalog, chat, downloading, feedback, mail, messaging, parameters, system information, text files, time/duration, userlog.
Special features: Unspecified downloadable programs; text files include an online magazine called *The Sonshine Gazette,* which features articles about local attractions and health subjects.
Special interests: Multiple message boards. Categories include Apple, Atari, Commodore, IBM, TRS-80.
Notice: This system has a 30-minute time limit. You must have a registered password to access the downloading section.
Comments: The sysop of Aardwolf-Express has been running a BBS for several years and is one of the most reliable and dedicated sysops in the United States. This is a general-interest message system with a constantly updated and verified local BBS list. This system is worth a long-distance call.

CPBB00610 (415) 948-1474
SACDF Conference Tree 300 bps
Los Altos, California 7/1/E
Open Conference Tree

Features: Conferencing.
Special interests: Arms control and disarmament.
Comments: SACDF stands for Stanford Arms Control and Disarmament Forum. This Conference Tree covers all aspects of arms control—political action, networking, research, and more. The flower children of the sixties are back; this time Vietnam is spelled n-u-k-e.

CPBB00620 (415) 965-4097
Piconet Node #1 PMMI
Mountain View, California 8/1/N
Open RCP/M RBBS

Features: CP/M, downloading, messaging, userlog.
Special features: Downloadable programs for CP/M-based computers.
Special interests: CP/M.
Comments: Another RCP/M.

CPBB00630 (415) 897-2783
Golden State BBS 300 bps
Novato, California 8/1/N
Password Required Greene Machine

Features: BBS list, chat, conferencing, downloading, feedback, mail, messaging, parameters, system information, userlog.
Special features: Conferencing on various topics; downloadable programs for the Color Computer and TRS-80 Models I and III.
Notice: A password is required to access the downloading section.
Comments: There wasn't much on this system when I called it. It's basically a general-interest message system.

CPBB00640 (415) 530-7886
Peace Net 300 bps
Oakland, California 7/1/E
Open Conference Tree

Features: Conferencing.
Comments: Don your antifallout gear and duck-and-cover into this system to see how a Conference Tree can be used effectively. Even if it is antinuke oriented, it is worth a long-distance call.

CPBB00650 (415) 452-0350
Sunrise Omega-80 300 bps
Oakland, California 8/1/N
Password Required Greene Machine

Features: Chat, conferencing, downloading, mail, messaging, parameters, time/duration, userlog.
Special features: Conferencing on various topics; unspecified downloadable programs.
Notice: A registered password is required to access the downloading section.
Comments: A general-interest message system that has been in existence for over a year. The sysop takes great pains to make his system interesting, and there were quite a few interesting conferences going on when I called.

CPBB00660 (415) 595-0541
DataTech Node 001 300/1200 bps
San Carlos, California 8/1/N
Open RCP/M RBBS

Features: Chat, CP/M, downloading, messaging, parameters, time/duration, userlog.
Special features: Downloadable programs for CP/M-based computers.
Special interest: CP/M.
Comments: This is the DataTech headquarters system.

CPBB00670 (415) 824-7215
Clearpoint 300 bps
San Francisco, California 8/1/N
Password Required Net-Works

Features: Mail, news, parameters, system information, time/duration.
Special features: International news.
Notice: There is a monthly subscription fee for this service. Complete information is online and you may browse the system contents for free.

Comments: This system provides summaries of international news gathered from short wave radio monitoring. Over 10 sources are monitored. If, after watching *NBC News Overnight,* you still hunger for foreign news, give this system a call.

CPBB00680 (415) 467-2588
Dial-Your-Match #10 300 bps
San Francisco, California 7/1/E
Questionnaire/Password Required DYM

Features: BBS list, chat, feedback, mail, matchmaking, messaging, time/duration.
Special features: Matchmaking.
Notice: This system has a 45-minute time limit for first-time calls and a 20-minute time limit for subsequent calls. Even to browse a Dial-Your-Match system, you must first fill out a questionnaire. All of your answers will be made public, available to all system users. Depending on the individual sysop (called a Matchmaker), the questions could be quite explicit. This is a sexually oriented system.
Comments: This system has the standard, harmless DYM questionnaire. Once again, I did not find my Perfect Match. The highest match I achieved was 65 percent. The woman herself did not have a passing grade with me.

CPBB00690 (415) 552-7671
Drummer Magazine 300 bps
San Francisco, California 8/1/N
Open RCP/M

Features: Messaging.
Special features: Private club message base.
Special interest: Gay sex.
Notice: This is a sexually oriented system for gays. If you are offended by the existence of gays or are not gay, do not bother to call this system. This is an X-rated system.
Comments: If you try to enter the private club database, you will be immediately logged off the system.

Directory Section: United States Bulletin-Board Systems

CPBB00700 (415) 565-3037
Living BBS 300 bps
San Francisco, California 7/1/E
Open LBBS

Features: Chat, conferencing.
Special interests: Computers in education.
Comments: LBBS is not an easy system to use. It is a hierarchically structured system, somewhat like a Conference Tree, but it takes longer to learn all of the available commands. If you are a teacher using, or thinking of using, computers in the classroom, you should call this system to share your thoughts on the subject.

CPBB00710 (415) 469-8111
South of Market 300 bps
San Francisco, California 8/1/N
Open Original

Features: BBS list, messaging, parameters, time/duration, userlog.
Special interests: X-rated topics.
Notice: This is an X-rated system for both heterosexual and homosexual users. If you are offended by explicit sexual material, *do not bother to call this system*.
Comments: Like all such X-rated systems, the messages on this one ranged from the hilariously ridiculous to the disgustingly grotesque. If you decide to call this system, be ready to laugh or lose it, depending on your sensibilities and/or interests.

CPBB00720 (415) 357-1130
CBBS Proxima PMMI
San Leandro, California 8/1/N
Open CBBS

Features: Feedback, messaging, parameters.
Comments: I love CBBSs. They always have a huge message base, filled with interesting and varied messages. Calling them is like

sitting down with a magazine to pass the time—quite enjoyable and thought provoking. This system is no exception and is clearly worth a long-distance call.

CPBB00730 (415) 895-0699
System/80 300/1200 bps
San Leandro, California 8/1/N
Open Original

Features: BBS list, chat, downloading, feedback, graphics, messaging, system information, text files, time/duration, userlog.
Special features: Downloadable programs for the Color Computer and TRS-80 Models I and III; graphics for the Color Computer; grafitti message base.
Notice: Grafitti message base has PG material.
Comments: A general-interest message system.

CPBB00740 (415) 481-0252
No-Name IBM RBBS 300 bps
San Lorenzo, California 7/1/E
Open PCRBBS

Features: Chat, downloading, messaging, parameters, time/duration, userlog.
Special features: Downloadable programs for the IBM PC.
Special interest: IBM PC.
Comments: This system had a small selection of messages when I called it. If you have an IBM PC and want to discuss the mysteries of BASICA with other users, give this system a call. This is quite a fast system, and is worth a long-distance call to IBM PC users.

CPBB00750   (415) 332-8115
Energy Tree   300 bps
Sausalito, California   7/1/E
Open   Conference Tree

Features: Conferencing.
Special interests: Alternative energy sources.
Comments: A conference on all aspects of energy is being held on this Conference Tree. If you have any interest in the subject, give this system a call and join in the discussion. It is worth a long-distance call.

California (619)

CPBB00760   (619) 434-4600
Dial-Your-Match #11   300 bps
Carlsbad, California   7/1/E
Questionnaire/Password Required   DYM

Features: BBS list, chat, feedback, mail, matchmaking, messaging, text files.
Special features: Joke message base, matchmaking, text files on various subjects.
Notice: Even to browse a Dial-Your-Match system, you must first fill out a questionnaire. All of your answers will be public, available to all system users. Depending on the individual sysop (called a Matchmaker), the questions could be quite explicit. This is a sexually oriented system.
Comments: When you signon the system, you will get the usual Have you called DYM #11 before? question. Answering "Yes" will have the system reply, "What's yer password, eh?" After entering it, you will then see, "Now to see if you're lying. . ." The text files on the system consisted of other DYM phone numbers (a usual fixture), Dial-A-Joke phone numbers, toll free 800 numbers, California beach report phone numbers, and an odd file called Flintstone Facts. Did you know that Wilma Flintstone had two maiden

names? Wilma Slaghoople and Wilma Pebble. The joke database contained outrageously funny jokes. A fun system, well worth a long-distance call, fighting busy signals, and getting a lousy 61 percent match as I did. The sysop should take a well-deserved bow.

CPBB00770 (619) 691-8367
CVBBS 300 bps
Chula Vista, California 8/1/N
Password Required T-Net

Features: Chat, download, messaging, parameters, system information, text files, time/duration.
Special features: Various computer-related text files.
Special interests: Multiple message boards. Categories include Apple, Atari, CP/M, D&D, Diplomacy (game), General, IBM & Commodore, Traveller (game), TRS-80.
Notice: You will need to register a password for full system access.
Comments: This is a *very* busy system. You'll notice there is an IBM & Commodore message base—one of the strangest combinations I have ever seen. Naturally, the C64 users have taken it over. Give this system a call, there's bound to be a message base you can use and find information on.

CPBB00780 (619) 561-7271
Online/PMS 300 bps
Lakeside, California 7/1/E or 8/1/N
Password Required Online/PMS

Features: BBS list, downloading, feedback, messaging, system information, text files, time/duration.
Special features: Dual-software system, running both Online and PMS software. Online: Unspecified downloadable programs. PMS: ALTernate message base, various text files.
Special interest: On PMS, the ALTernate message base is used for role-playing games.
Notice: When you connect to the system, you will be prompted with "ID#." If you want to enter the Online system, type **GUEST** in

response, then, in response to "PSWD:," type **PASS**. If you want to enter the PMS, type **PMS** in response to "ID#."

Comments: There won't be much you will be able to do on the Online system, so choose PMS when you first call this system. Online systems are usually for the benefit of the sysop and his computing buddies for file transfers. On PMS, you will find a general-interest message system. When I called PMS, an interstellar space war game had just concluded.

CPBB00790 (619) 748-8746
Dial-Your-Match #33 300 bps
Poway, California 7/1/E
Questionnaire/Password Required DYM

Features: BBS list, chat, feedback, mail, matchmaking, messaging.
Special features: Matchmaking.
Notice: This system has a 40-minute time limit. Even to browse a Dial-Your-Match system, you must first fill out a questionnaire. All of your answers will be public, available to all system users. Depending on the individual sysop (called a Matchmaker), the questions could be quite explicit. This is a sexually oriented system.
Comments: This DYM features the standard, innocuous questionnaire. Another round of disappointment: 61 percent, a tie between three women! Can you believe there is actually a woman out there named Cochise? Well, there is—and she was one of the three I was matched to!

CPB00800 (619) 271-8613
PMS—Datel Systems, Inc. 300 bps
San Diego, California 7/1/E or 8/1/N
Open PMS

Features: BBS list, chat, feedback, messaging, parameters, system information, text files, time/duration.
Special features: ALTernate message base; various text files.
Special interests: The ALTernate message base featured a D&D game on it.

Comments: I was hoisted by my own petard on this system. The sysop caught me in a bad habit I had developed in quick scanning and retrieving PMS messages. He gently showed me the faster way, as well as explained some of the finer points of PMS features I had not seen illustrated (except for now—because they are in this book). This is, otherwise, a general-interest message system. Of course it is worth a long-distance call. PMS's are hotbeds of information.

CPBB00810 (619) 280-1958
PMS—The Floppy House 300 bps
San Diego, California 7/1/E or 8/1/N
Open PMS

Features: BBS list, feedback, messaging, parameters, time/duration.
Special features: Various text files.
Comments: The Floppy House rents time on microcomputers. You can walk into their office and rent an hour on a computer, using a variety of software (or you can bring your own). This system contains a text file that explains their service. It is a service I would have taken advantage of many times had it been available in my area. This is, otherwise, a general-interest message system.

CPBB00820 (619) 283-3574
PMS—Gameboard 300 bps
San Diego, California 7/1/E or 8/1/N
Open PMS

Features: BBS list, downloading, feedback, messaging, parameters, text files, time/duration.
Special features: Unspecified downloadable programs, text files on role-playing games.
Special interests: Role-playing games.
Comments: If you are interested in role-playing games give this system a call if you want to see exactly what is on it. It may not be worth a long-distance call merely to play games.

CPBB00830 (619) 692-1961
Sabaline 300 bps
San Diego, California 7/1/E or 8/1/N
Password Required Online

Features: BBS list, chat, downloading, mail, text files, userlog.
Special features: Unspecified downloadable programs, various text files.
Notice: There is a 15-minute time limit for guest accounts. To log on this system, type **GUEST** in response to "ID#," and **PASS** in response to "PSWD."
Comments: As Online systems go, this one was pretty accommodating to guest accounts, with a number of text files to be read. Online systems, however, are pretty much for the benefit of the sysop and his friends. Long-distance callers are advised to look elsewhere for infotainment.

CPBB00840 (619) 273-4354
RCP/M 300 bps
San Diego, California 8/1/N
Open RCP/M RBBS

Features: CP/M, downloading, messaging, parameters.
Special features: Downloadable programs for CP/M-based computers.
Special interests: CP/M.
Notice: To logon this system, type **GUEST**. There is a 15-minute time limit for guest users; you will have an opportunity to apply for a User ID at termination.
Comments: This is an odd RCP/M system. Why is it odd? Give it a call and see.

CPBB00850 (619) 727-7500
PMS 300 bps
San Marcos, California 7/1/E or 8/1/N
Open PMS

Features: BBS list, feedback, messaging, parameters, system information, text files, time/duration.

Special features: Various text files.
Comments: A general-interest message system. When I called it, the users were rallying together to play a D&D game.

CPBB00860 (619) 561-7271
Online 300 bps
Santee, California 7/1/E or 8/1/N
Password Required Online

Features: Downloading, mail, userlog.
Special features: Unspecified downloadable programs.
Notice: To logon the system, in response to "ID#," type **GUEST**; in response to "PSWD:" type **NONE**.
Comments: As a GUEST account, all you can do on this system is send or receive mail from User ID holders and read the userlog. Long-distance callers can skip this one. It may hold interest for local callers, though.

CPBB00870 (619) 561-7277
PMS #1 300 bps
Santee, California 7/1/E or 8/1/N
Open PMS

Features: BBS list, chat, downloading, feedback, messaging, parameters, system information, text files, time/duration.
Special features: Downloadable programs for the Apple II+ and //e computers, text files on various topics.
Comments: This is the headquarters system of PMS (People's Message Service), one of the finest pieces of BBS software to be written. Bill Blue, its author, was the first person in the world to start compiling a national BBS list. This system is where you can get the latest updated version of that list, as well as alert Bill to new or disconnected numbers. If you are a BBS sysop, phone Bill's system to have your system added to the list (or deleted, if your system is taken offline). This system is worth a long-distance call.

CPBB00880 (619) 481-3942
Kaypro BBS 300 bps
Solana Beach, California 7/1/N
Open RCP/M RBBS

Features: CP/M, downloading, messaging.
Special features: Downloadable programs for Kaypro computers.
Special interest: Technical support for Kaypro computers.
Notice: In response to the question at signon, type **DDT**. To exit this system, you must enter CP/M and type **BYE**.
Comments: This system is run by Kaypro's Technical Support Group for the benefit of all Kaypro owners, users, and prospective customers. Have a technical question? Leave it here. Looking for free public-domain software for your Kaypro? Call this system. Possible additions to this system include a Kaypro 10 host and 300/1200 bps operation.

California (707)

CPBB00890 (707) 257-1485
6809 Morning Star BBS (Color-80 #3) 300 bps
Napa, California 8/1/N
Open Color-80

Features: BBS list, catalog, chat, downloading, feedback, graphics, messaging, parameters, system information, text files, userlog.
Special features: Downloadable software for the Color Computer, online graphics for the Color Computer, various text files on Color Computer-related topics.
Special interests: Color Computer.
Notice: You need a registered password to access the downloading section. To download programs, you must use a Color Computer and a terminal program such as Colorcom/E.
Comments: Catalog shopping was not installed on this system. I find it disappointing and rather odd that this Color-80 system requires a password for download access. I am not altogether in favor of

such a policy. Limited-access downloading lessens my recommendation that this system is worth a long-distance call.

CPBB00900 (707) 257-1101
Greene Machine 300 bps
Napa, California 8/1/N
Password Required Greene Machine

Features: BBS list, chat, conferencing, feedback, mail, messaging, parameters, system information, userlog.
Special features: Conferencing, unspecified downloadable programs.
Notice: To access the downloading section and all sections of the system, you must register a password.
Comments: Although the software is a tad slow, I like it.

CPBB00910 (707) 257-6502
Napa Valley RBBS RCP/M PMMI
Napa, California 8/1/N
Password Required RCP/M RBBS

Features: CP/M, downloading, messaging, text files.
Special features: Downloadable programs for CP/M-based computers; text files for Apple, Atari, CP/M, Osborne, and TRS-80 computers.
Special interests: CP/M.
Comments: This is a general-interest system with some interesting files on it. Give it a call.

CPBB00920 (707) 538-9124
Peanut Gallery BBS 300 bps
Santa Rosa, California 8/1/N
Password Required D&M BBS

Features: BBS list, chat, conferencing, downloading, feedback, messaging, parameters, system information, time/duration, userlog.
Special features: Conferencing on various topics; unspecified downloading programs.

Notice: A registered password is required to access the downloading section and all sections of the systems. This system has a 60-minute time limit.

Comments: This is a very s-l-o-w system. The conferences that were taking place on it were interesting enough to make it worth the call, though. Long-distance callers will have to use their own discretion in calling; as I said, the system is annoyingly slow and you may not have the luck I had in finding good conferences taking place.

CPBB00930	(707) 944-8002
Infoex-80	300/1200 bps
Yountville, California	8/1/N
Password Required	Unknown

Features: Catalog, chat, messaging, time/duration, userlog.

Comments: Apparently, Yountville is a hamlet that has not yet joined the Information Age in a big way. This system was in great need of messages when I called it. It could also use some better software, but that's up to the sysop.

California (714)

CPBB00940	(714) 774-7860
Anahug	300/1200 bps
Anaheim, California	8/1/N
Open	RCP/M CBBS

Features: CP/M, downloading, messaging, parameters, system information, userlog.

Special features: A CBBS instead of an RBBS.

Special interests: Heath/Zenith computers.

Comments: Anahug stands for Anaheim Heath Users' Group. This system is using a CBBS instead of an RBBS, so there are a lot more messages on this RCP/M than most others.

CPBB00950　　　　　　　　　　　　　(714) 952-2110
CSHC　　　　　　　　　　　　　　　300/1200 bps
Anaheim, California　　　　　　　　　　　　8/1/N
Password Required　　　　　　　　　　　Original

Features: Chat, downloadings, messaging, system information.
Special features: Unspecified downloadable programs.
Special interests: A private self-help club.
Notice: This is mainly a system for club members. Nonmembers will only have 30 minutes of access time and be able to read but not post messages.
Comments: CHSC stands for California Self-Help Club. I found nothing outstanding about this system except the sysop's assertion that the system allegedly has over 1000 downloadable programs.

CPBB00960　　　　　　　　　　　　　(714) 772-8868
PMS—*IF* Magazine　　　　　　　　　　　300 bps
Anaheim, California　　　　　　　　　7/1/E or 8/1/N
Open　　　　　　　　　　　　　　　　　　　PMS

Features: BBS list, feedback, messaging, parameters, system information, text files, time/duration.
Special features: *IF*'s member's-only video club; text files on a wide variety of subjects.
Special interests: Home video.
Notice: *IF* has set aside a portion of the system for a club devoted to home video. Access to this section requires the payment of a membership fee and details may be found on the system. Access to the rest of PMS is free of charge.
Comments: *IF* stands for the Imagination Factory, a video production house. This system is running on a 16-megabyte hard disk, and well it should, for it has more text files than any other PMS currently operating. *IF* surely lives up to its name with this system. Definitely worth a long-distance call.

CPBB00970 (714) 350-2668
Color Corner 300/1200 bps
Fontana, California 8/1/N
Open Original

Features: BBS list, chat, downloading, games, messaging, system information, userlog.
Special features: Downloadable programs for the Color Computer; games include Adventure, Eliza, Fish, Jumble, Mansion, Tic-Tac-Toe.
Special interests: Color Computer.
Comments: This is an OK system. It looks like Color-80 in some respects, but isn't as polished.

CPBB00980 (714) 524-1228
RACS V 300 bps
Fullerton, California 8/1/N
Password RACS

Features: BBS list, chat, downloading, feedback, messaging, parameters, poll, system information, text files.
Special features: Downloadable Orchestra 80/85 programs for TRS-80 Model I and III computers; polling of users.
Special interests: Multiple message boards. Categories include Apple, Atari, Commercial, IBM, Public, VIC-20.
Comments: RACS is a confusing system for new users. It has long and wordy menus and submenus. Selections are not presented in a logical order or in a consistent format. RACS can be slow, so be warned if you are calling long distance.

CPBB00990 (714) 530-8226
OCTUG 300/1200 bps
Garden Grove, California 8/1/N
Password Required Original

Features: Chat, downloading, messaging, system information.
Special features: A Young Person's BBS with BBS list, chat, system information, time/duration; unspecified downloadable programs.

Special interests: Multiple message boards in the Young Person's BBS. Categories include Advertising, Computers, Educational, High Game Scores, Science & Astronomy.
Notice: A registered password is required to access the downloading section.
Comments: OCTUG stands for Orange County TRS-80 Users' Group. This is another original piece of BBS software and although the format is unique, it has too many steps to go through to retrieve a message.

CPBB01000 (714) 824-2129
TBBS 300 bps
Highland, California 8/1/N
Password Required TBBS

Features: Catalog, chat, feedback, mail, messaging, parameters, system information, text files, time/duration.
Special features: Text files on various topics.
Special interests: Two message boards, one of jokes, one for kids only.
Notice: There is a 30-minute time limit on this system.
Comments: You can call this system and go through its joke board. If you're under 18, you can join the kids-only board.

CPBB01010 (714) 983-9923
Computers for Christ 300 bps
Ontario, California 7/2/E
Open Commnet-80

Features: Chat, downloading, feedback, messaging, parameters, system information, text files, time/duration, userlog.
Special features: Text files on various religious subjects.
Special interest: Christian religion.
Comments: This is a forum for discussing the Bible from the standpoint of the Christian religion. I would like to note that one of the

high points in compiling *The Computer Phone Book* was having an online chat with the sysop of this BBS.

CPBB01020 (714) 359-3189
Commnet-80 300/1200 bps
Riverside, California 8/1/N
Open Commnet-80

Features: BBS list, catalog, chat, downloading, feedback, games, messaging, system information, time/duration, userlog.
Special features: Downloadable programs for a variety of computers offered each week; games include Bomber, CIA, Mansion, Nukesub, Thunder.
Notice: In the games section there is a 30-minute time limit. Once you have reached that limit, you are automatically logged off the system and locked out from further use until the next day. This system may also be reached at (714)877-2253.
Comments: A general-interest message system with a good variety of downloadable programs and computer items to buy online. A cute feature is an Eliza-type program that is activated if you cannot get the sysop to chat (if you get stuck in that program, type **QUIT** to get back to the main menu).

CPBB01030 (714) 359-1586
Growth Net 300 bps
Riverside, California 8/1/N
Password Required TBBS

Features: Chat, downloading, feedback, mail, messaging, parameters, time/duration, userlog.
Special features: Downloadable financial programs for TRS-80 Model I and III computers.
Special interests: For-sale message board.
Comments: A general-interest message system.

California (805)

CPBB01040 (805) 964-4115
South Coast Bulletin-Board 300 bps
Goleta, California 8/1/N
Open Unknown

Features: Messaging, time/duration.
Comments: A simple system but it works.

CPBB01050 (805) 687-9400
CoCo Corner 300 bps
Santa Barbara, California 8/1/N
Open CoCo Corner

Features: BBS list, chat, downloading, messaging, system information, userlog.
Special features: Downloadable programs for the Color Computer.
Special interests: Color Computer.
Comments: A bit different from other CoCo BBSs but not as slick.

CPBB01060 (805) 682-7876
Computer BBS 300 bps
Santa Barbara, California 8/1/N
Open Unknown

Features: Messaging, time/duration.
Comments: Another simple but functional system.

California (916)

CPBB01070   (916) 971-1395
Bullet-80   300/1200 bps
Sacramento, California   8/1/N
Open   Bullet-80

Features: BBS list, catalog, chat, downloading, games, messaging, parameters, text files, time/duration.
Special features: Downloadable programs for Atari, Color Computer, IBM, TRS-80 Model I and III computers; games include Biorhythms, Jumble, Scramble, Tarot, Thunder.
Notice: A one-time monetary "donation" is required to access the downloading and text file sections.
Comments: This is a modified version of Bullet-80 software that runs almost as fast as a TBBS. When I called this system, there were over 40 downloadable programs available. The sysop is dedicated to having the largest public-domain downloadable program library available in California. He just might succeed, too.

CPBB01080   (916) 483-8718
SMUG   300 bps
Sacramento, California   8/1/N
Open   RCP/M RBBS

Features: CP/M, downloading, messaging.
Special features: Downloadable programs for CP/M-based computers.
Special interests: CP/M.
Notice: To gain access to this system, you must be able to answer the question, What is the name of Digital Research's standard debugger?
Comments: SMUG stands for Sacramento Microcomputer User's Group. The entry question is designed to discourage non-CP/M users from gaining access to the system.

Colorado (303)

CPBB01110 (303) 632-3391
Old Colorado City Electronic Cottage 300 bps
Colorado Springs, Colorado 8/1/N
Open TBBS

Features: BBS list, catalog, chat, downloading, feedback, mail messaging, parameters, system information, time/duration.
Special features: Downloadable programs for various computers; text files on computer-related topics.
Special interests: Multiple message boards. Categories include Apple, Commodore, Education, Osborne, Politics, TI, TRS-80, Writing.
Notice: There is a 25-minute time limit on this system.
Comments: This system is operated by Sourcevoid Dave, the first celebrity of an electronic network. It has Dave's distinct, individual mark on it, and it alternates from a free forum to a free for all. It is worth a long-distance call.

CPBB01120 (303) 343-8401
Aurora-Net 300 bps
Denver, Colorado 8/1/N
Password Required GBBS

Features: Chat, messaging, system information.
Comments: This Net-Works clone has a pretty active message base.

CPBB01130 (303) 781-4937
CNode PMMI
Denver, Colorado 8/1/N
Password Required CNode

Features: CP/M, downloading, feedback, messaging, text files.
Special features: Downloadable programs for CP/M-based computers.

Special interests: CP/M, multiple message boards. Categories include 16000, 68000, Actor Languages, Citadel, CNode, C User's Group, Error, Geneology, Ham/Packet Radio, IBM, Lobby, Mail, New Software, Osborne, Software Tools, XYZZY.
Comments: This is not a conventionally structured RCP/M. It features a unique structure that is difficult to describe. It is very easy to use if you have had prior experience with BBSs or if you read the system instructions *very* carefully. It's fun, interesting, and worth a long-distance call.

CPBB01140 (303) 423-3224
MUMon 300 bps
Denver, Colorado 8/1/N
Password Required Unknown

Features: Downloading, messaging, userlog.
Special interests: Heath/Zenith computers.
Notice: You must be a member of the National Heath User's Group to have full system access.
Comments: When I accessed this system, there was a notice stating that it would be changed to an RCP/M.

CPBB01150 (303) 690-4566
TBBS HQ 300 bps
Denver, Colorado 8/1/N
Password Required TBBS

Features: BBS list, catalog, downloading, feedback, mail, messaging, parameters, system information, time/duration.
Special interests: Multiple message boards. Categories include 6502, Atari, IBM PC, Orchestra 80/85/90, TRS-80, "Vince's Place."
Notice: There is a 30-minute time limit on this system.
Comments: This is the headquarters system of TBBS (The Bread Board System). The system is designed as an electronic hotel and the main menu below should give you an idea of what it is like:

Hotel TBBS Main Lobby
⟨R⟩egistration Desk

⟨I⟩nformation Desk
⟨W⟩estern Union (c)
⟨A⟩dvice from Ms. Goode-Wench
⟨M⟩essage Central
⟨S⟩eminar Rooms
⟨G⟩ift Shop
⟨O⟩ther Services
⟨D⟩irectory of other Hotels
⟨F⟩leamarket (Upload/Download)
⟨L⟩ength of Stay
⟨C⟩heckout

CPBB01160   (303) 741-4071
TBBS   300/1200 bps
Denver, Colorado   8/1/N
Password Required   TBBS

Features: BBS list, catalog, chat, downloading, mail, messaging, parameters, text files, time/duration.
Special features: Downloadable programs for TRS-80 Model I and III computers, text files of local user groups.
Special interests: Multiple message boards. Categories include Apple/Franklin, CP/M, IBM, Kaypro II, Osborne, TI Pegasus.
Comments: A general-interest message system. If you have a particular interest in the Texas Instruments Pegasus computer, this is a system dedicated to exchanging information about it.

CPBB01170   (303) 223-4305
Front Range Commodore Bulletin-Board   300 bps
Ft. Collins, Colorado   8/1/N
Password Required   CBMBBS

Features: BBS list, downloading, messaging, parameters, text files, time/duration, userlog.
Special features: Downloadable programs for VIC-20, Commodore-64, and Commodore Business Machines computers.

Special interests: Commodore computers.
Notice: To download programs, you need an authorization code and a special terminal program. Contact the sysop for details.
Comments: This is the first of several Commodore-specific BBSs in *The Computer Phone Book*. The software was designed by the author of the WordPro word processing program. It is an elegant piece of BBS software. This system is filled with information about Commodore computers in its message base. If you are a Commodore owner, this is definitely worth a long-distance call.

CPBB01180   (303) 278-4244
UFONET   300/1200 bps
Golden, Colorado   8/1/N
Password Required   TBBS

Features: Feedback, mail, messaging, parameters, polling, system information, text files, time/duration.
Special features: Polling of users; text files include information on parapsychology organizations, UFO research organizations, and a UFO researcher list.
Special interests: Multiple message boards. Categories include Apple, Atari, CoCo, CP/M, Game-Board, Garu, General, Grimric, Ham, Jolar, Labyrinth, Lazartol, Literary, Middle-Earth, Nasa, Portable, Psionics, Space, Technical, Telco.
Notice: There is a 15-minute time limit on this system.
Comments: If someone had described this system to me, I would not have believed that person. Words cannot do justice to it. There are so many choices and so many submenus, I cannot begin to list them all. The menu choices show a great deal of imagination and a lot of work. One *very* interesting feature of this system is the Telco sub-board, which has a Mountain Bell employee as the sysop, giving information and replying to questions about the local phone company. Is this system worth a long-distance call? You bet it is!

CPBB01190   (303) 985-1108
RCP/M   300/1200 bps
Lakewood, Colorado   8/1/N
Password Required   RCP/M RBBS

Features: CP/M, downloading, messaging.
Special features: Downloadable programs for CP/M-based computers.
Special interests: CP/M.
Notice: There is a 60-minute time limit on this system. When you log on as a new user, you are only allowed access to a *very user unfriendly* Drive A, User 0.
Comments: This system is only for die-hard CP/M users.

CPBB01200   (303) 232-8509
Petula   300 bps
Lakewood, Colorado   8/1/N
Password Required   Pet-Net

Features: BBS list, chat, feedback, mail, messaging, parameters, system information, text files, time/duration, userlog.
Special features: Text files on various topics.
Special interests: Commodore computers.
Comments: Although this system looks very much like Net-Works, I am somewhat fond of it. The sysops are very nice people and devoted to maintaining their system. Although this system isn't polished, it is fast. For Commodore computer owners, it is worth a long-distance call.

Connecticut (203)

CPBB01250   (203) 744-4644
Bullet-80 #1   300/1200 bps
Danbury, Connecticut   8/1/N
Open   Bullet-80

Features: BBS list, catalog, chat, downloading, games, feedback, messaging, parameters, system information, time/duration, userlog.

Special features: Downloadable programs for TRS-80 Color Computer, Model I and III computers; games include Biorhythm, Jumble, Scramble, Tarot, Thunder.
Special interests: Multiple message boards. Categories include Apple, CoCo, CP/M & S-100, General, IBM PC, TRS-80 Mod I/II.
Comments: This is the headquarters system of Bullet-80. This is a general-interest message system. Long-distance callers should be advised that Bullet-80 systems tend to run rather slowly.

CPBB01260 (203) 629-4375
Education-80 300 bps
Greenwich, Connecticut 8/1/N
Open Bullet-80

Features: BBS list, catalog, chat, downloading, feedback, messaging, parameters, system information, text files, time/duration, userlog.
Special features: Downloadable programs for TRS-80 Color Computer, Model I and III computers; text files on various educational topics.
Special interests: Computers in education.
Comments: If you have an interest in putting computers in your classroom, or have already done so, give this system a call to share your ideas, opinions, and questions.

CPBB01270 (203) 525-2081
Bullet-80 300 bps
Hartford, Connecticut 8/1/N
Open Bullet-80

Features: BBS list, catalog, chat, downloading, games, feedback, messaging, parameters, system information, time/duration, userlog.
Special features: Downloadable programs for the TRS-80 Color Computer, Model I and III computers; games include Biorhythm, Jumble, Tarot, Thunder.
Special interests: Multiple message boards. Categories include Apple, CoCo, CP/M & S-100, General, IBM PC, TRS-80 Mod I/III.

Notice: Club section may have a Model 100 downloading section that requires a fee for access.
Comments: A general-interest message system.

CPBB01280   (203) 966-8869
Connecticut PC   300 bps
New Canaan, Connecticut   8/1/N
Password Required   PCRBBS

Features: Chat, downloading, mail, messaging, parameters, text files, time/duration, userlog.
Special features: Downloadable programs for the IBM PC, text files on various topics.
Special interests: IBM PC.
Notice: This system has a 50-minute time limit.
Comments: This is a fast system with a variety of downloadable programs. If you own or use an IBM PC, give this system a call to meet others like yourself.

CPBB01290   (203) 746-5763
Telcom-7   300 bps
New Fairfield, Connecticut   8/1/N
Open   Bullet-80

Features: BBS list, catalog, chat, downloading, games, feedback, messaging, parameters, system information, time/duration, userlog.
Special features: Downloadable programs for the TRS-80 Color Computer, Model I and III computers; games include Biorhythm, Jumble, Scramble, Tarot, Thunder.
Special interests: Multiple message boards. Categories include Apple, CoCo, CP/M & S-100, General, IBM PC, TRS-80 Mod I/III.
Comments: A general-interest message system. One mildly interesting feature is a section where business men and women can leave their names, addresses, phone numbers, and descriptions of what they do.

CPBB01300   (203) 853-0816
Westico   300 bps
Norwalk, Connecticut   7/1/E
Open   Original

Features: Catalog, messaging.
Notice: Messaging feature is only to sysop.
Comments: This is an online catalog from Westico, a firm dealing in microcomputer hardware, software, and peripherals for a variety of brands. If you need to order something in the dead of night, pull out your charge card and give this system a call. You can also use this system to see what's available and comparison shop, although I'm sure the sysop would be pleased if you made a purchase.

CPBB01310   (203) 688-8467
Bullet-80   300 bps
Windsor, Connecticut   8/1/N
Open   Bullet-80

Features: BBS list, catalog, chat, downloading, games, feedback, messaging, parameters, system information, time/duration, userlog.
Special features: Downloadable programs for the TRS-80 Color Computer, Model I and III computers; games include: Biorhythm, Jumble, Scramble, Tarot, Thunder.
Special interests: Multiple message boards. Categories include Apple, CoCo, CP/M & S-100, General, IBM PC, TRS-80 Mod I/III.
Comments: A general-interest message system.

Delaware (302)

CPBB01330   (302) 762-3170
Forum-80   300 bps
Wilmington, Delaware   8/1/N
Probationary   Forum-80

Features: BBS list, downloading, feedback, messaging, parameters, system information, userlog.

Special features: Unspecified downloadable programs.

Notice: Forum-80 has a policy of displaying a long (series of) signon bulletin(s) that you cannot bypass and labeling all new users as "probationary," requiring the sysop to approve any messages new users post before other users may read them (if at all).

Comments: In all of Delaware, this is the only operating BBS. Although this is a general-interest message system, with no overt special interests, there was quite a bit of discussion about Commodore computers when I called.

District of Columbia (202)

CPBB01350 (202) 276-8342
Armudic 300 bps
Washington, District of Columbia 7/1/E or 8/1/N
Open Armudic

Features: BBS list, downloading, messaging, system information.
Special features: Downloadable programs for Atari home computers.
Special interests: Atari home computers.
Comments: What does Armudic mean? Spell out this system's phone number on your phone dial. This is not the only BBS in Washington, DC, but it is the only one I believe will still be operating when you read this. (If luck has it that it is not, BBSs in both Maryland and Virginia carry local BBS lists that include the 202 area code.)

Florida (305)

CPBB01390 (305) 427-6300
Personal Message System 300/1200 bps
Deerfield Beach, Florida 8/1/N
Password Required Original

Features: BBS list, catalog, chat, downloading, messaging, parameters, system information, text files, userlog.

Special features: Unspecified downloadable software; text files include local computer club newsletter.

Notice: A registered password is required to access the downloading section.

Comments: This system had one of the longest signon messages I have ever seen. It nearly put Forum-80's interminable bulletins to shame. If that wasn't bad enough, you cannot sequentially scan messages, only read them or do a keyword search. Keyword searching takes a very long time. Long-distance callers can skip this system.

CPBB01400   (305) 772-4444
Forum-80   300 bps
Ft. Lauderdale, Florida   8/1/N
Probationary   Forum-80

Features: BBS list, downloading, feedback, messaging, parameters, userlog.

Special features: Unspecified downloadable programs.

Notice: To receive a registered password for this system for regular use, you must purchase LDOS from the computer store running this system. Forum-80 has a policy of displaying a long (series of) signon bulletin(s) that you cannot bypass and labeling all new users as "probationary", requiring the sysop to approve any messages new users post before other users may read them (if at all).

Comments: If you have been reading these listings through in order, you will have noticed that each Forum-80 listing has the above warning about its policy. This system is ample proof of why I have included this warning. The signon bulletins are totally out of date, irrelevant, and dull. After you have been assaulted by all of them, you are then told that you cannot use the system regularly unless you have purchased a product!

CPBB01410
Colorburst/Trade-80 #1
Ft. Lauderdale, Florida
Password Required

(305) 525-1192
300/1200 bps
8/1/N
Trade-80

Features: Catalog, chat, downloading, messaging, parameters, system information, text files, time/duration, userlog.

Special features: Downloadable programs for Apple, Color Computer, TRS-80 Model I and III computers; text files on various computer-related topics.

Special interest: Color Computer (Colorburst).

Notice: There is a 30-minute time limit on this system; new callers may only download a maximum of four programs. This is a dual-system BBS. To enter the Colorburst system, follow the instructions at signon.

Comments: This is the Trade-80 headquarters system; it also runs a special-interest system for the Color Computer. Long-distance callers are warned that Trade-80 is rather slow and sends out too many linefeeds. Over 5 megabytes of downloadable programs are claimed (but not verified by *The Computer Phone Book*).

CPBB01420
Orlando Connection
Orlando, Florida
Password Required

(305) 644-8327
300 bps
8/2/N
TBBS

Features: Chat, downloading, feedback, mail, messaging, parameters, system information, time/duration.

Special features: Unspecified downloadable programs.

Special interests: Multiple message boards. Categories include Apple, Atari, CFCS-Clubs, CP/M, General, IBM PC, Max80/LDOS, Noah/Soap Box, Personal, TRS-80, Wanted/For Sale.

Notice: There is a 20-minute time limit on this system. A registered password is required for access to the downloading section.

Comments: When I called this system, the TBBS software had just been installed and the sysop was in the process of constructing the system.

CPBB01430 (305) 686-4862
The Notebook 300 bps
West Palm Beach, Florida 8/1/N
Password Required Micro-80

Features: Chat, messaging, text files, time/duration.
Special features: Text files on writing-related topics.
Special interests: Editing, writing, publishing.
Comments: This is a quite active system that serves as a forum for aspiring and published writers and those in the publishing field to get together and exchange news and ideas. The software is patterned after the CompuServe SIGs but is not as fast nor as flexible. Still, those of you who may be members of the CompuServe LitSIG will feel at home here.

Florida (813)

CPBB01450 (813) 969-0512
Alpha 300 bps
Tampa, Florida 8/1/N
Password Required Original

Features: BBS list, chat, game, mail, messaging, parameters, polling, text files, time/duration, userlog.
Special features: Polling of users; text files include interactive fiction, movie reviews, software reviews, user publications.
Notice: There is a 30-minute time limit on this system. New users should follow instructions at signon to enter system. Accounts on Alpha require the payment of a one-time fee; see details online.
Comments: Alpha has more in common with an information utility than it has with other BBSs. The sysop is constantly adding new features, improving old ones, and is always on the lookout for suggestions. Alpha recently added a joke database. Alpha is worth a long-distance call.

CPBB01460 (813) 645-3669
Apollo Chariot 300 bps
Tampa, Florida 8/1/N
Password Required Original

Features: Chat, games, messaging, userlog.
Comments: This system operates like a clone of Alpha but lacks both the speed and the panache. If imitation is the sincerest form of flattery, Alpha's sysop should feel proud. Apollo's sysop should add more features and speed up his system; it makes 300 bps look like 110 bps. Long-distance callers can skip this one.

CPBB01470 (813) 988-7400
Wild Goose Aerie 300 bps
Tampa, Florida 8/1/N
Open Unknown

Features: BBS list, chat, feedback, messaging, parameters, userlog.
Comments: Selections from the Goose Menu, all verbatim: Enter Goose Grams, Kill GGs, Loose Goose, Pigskin, Quack with the Goose, Zoo.

Florida (904)

CPBB01490 (904) 399-1926
Access Jax 300 bps
Jacksonville, Florida 7/1/E or 8/1/N
Open Unknown

Features: Unknown at press time.
Notice: System was down for reconstruction at press time.
Comments: I am including this listing because I spoke with the sysop and he advised me there would once again be an operating BBS at this number by the time you are reading this. Prior to the reconstruction, this system contained an online version of a computer

newsletter that is distributed free to all computer stores in the Jacksonville area.

CPBB01500 (904) 725-4995
JUG RBBS 300 bps
Jacksonville, Florida 8/1/E
Password Required RCP/M RBBS

Features: BBS list, CP/M, downloading, feedback, messaging, parameters.
Special features: Downloadable software for CP/M-based computers.
Special interests: Heath/Zenith computers.
Notice: Access to the downloading section is restricted to members of JUG; details are online.
Comments: JUG stands for Jacksonville User's Group. Although access to CP/M is restricted, nonmembers can call this system to post and read messages.

CPBB01510 (904) 264-0335
Colour-80 300 bps
Orange Park, Florida 8/1/N
Open Color-80

Features: BBS list, catalog, chat, downloading, feedback, graphics, messaging, parameters, system information, text files, userlog.
Special features: Downloadable programs for the Color Computer, online graphics for the Color Computer, text files on Color Computer-related topics.
Special interests: Color Computer.
Notice: To download programs and view online graphics, you must be using a Color Computer and a terminal program such as Colorcom/E.
Comments: Another fine Color-80 system. This one had more private messages than other Color-80s and the sysop was soliciting programs for non-CoCos to place in the downloading section. If you live in the area, give this system a call and see about submitting some public-domain programs.

CPBB01520   (904) 456-7195
Dr. D's CoCo Corner   300 bps
Pensacola, Florida   8/1/N
Open   Color-80

Features: BBS list, catalog, chat, downloading, feedback, graphics, messaging, parameters, system information, text files, userlog.
Special features: Downloadable programs for the Color Computer, online graphics for the Color Computer, text files on Color Computer-related topics.
Special interests: Color Computer.
Notice: To download programs and view online graphics, you must be using a Color Computer and a terminal program such as Colorcom/E.
Comments: This is another fine Color-80 system. It is worth a long-distance call.

Georgia (404)

CPBB01550   (404) 636-6130
Atlanta Computer Society CBBS   300 bps
Atlanta, Georgia   8/1/N
Open   CBBS

Features: Chat, feedback, messaging, parameters.
Special interests: Atlanta Computer Society.
Comments: Sponsored by the Atlanta Computer Society, this is a general-interest message system that always seems to be overflowing with interesting and newsworthy messages. The system is very fast, has a large message capacity, and is definitely worth a long-distance call.

CPBB01560 (404) 929-0680
Bulletin/68 300/1200 bps
Atlanta, Georgia 8/1/N
Open Bulletin/68

Features: BBS list, catalog, messaging, parameters, system information, userlog.
Special interests: Color Computer.
Notice: A software change was imminent on this system when accessed by *The Computer Phone Book*. As such, information contained in this listing is subject to change.
Comments: This system had a very large message base filled with information about the Color Computer. For CoCo users it would be worth a long-distance call.

CPBB01570 (404) 378-4410
CoCo Board II 300 bps
Atlanta, Georgia 8/1/N
Open CoCo Board II

Features: Chat, downloading, feedback, graphics, messaging, parameters, system information, userlog.
Special features: Downloadable programs for the Color Computer, online graphics for the Color Computer.
Special interests: Color Computer.
Notice: To download programs and view color graphics, you must be using a Color Computer and a terminal program such as Colorcom/E.
Comments: This is a particularly slow and inflexible system. The downloading section was small but there were plenty of messages to make up for it.

CPBB01580 (404) 252-9438
MultiLink BBS 300/1200 bps
Atlanta, Georgia 8/1/N
Open MLBBS

Features: BBS list, downloading, messaging.
Special features: Downloadable programs for the IBM PC.

Special interests: IBM PC.
Comments: This BBS is "operating on an IBM PC as a subtask under MultiLink . . . in a multi-user multitasking environment . . . (and) . . . occupies a 35K region" shared with two other users. A unique system, to be sure, but odd all the same. All commands must be prefixed with . (a period). It's different, it's fast, and it's worth a long-distance call.

CPBB01590 (404) 252-4146
N.F. Systems Ltd. 300/1200 bps
Atlanta, Georgia 7/1/E or 8/1/N
Password Required Hostcomm

Features: BBS list, catalog, chat, downloading, userlog.
Special features: Downloadable programs for the IBM PC.
Special interests: IBM PC.
Notice: If you are asked for a password at signon, type **IBMPC**.
Comments: Any system running Hostcomm software is strictly of interest to owners and users of IBM PCs. They are file transfer facilities mostly, and not much else.

CPBB01600 (404) 891-0136
Bulletin/68 300 bps
Ringgold, Georgia 8/1/N
Open Bulletin/68

Features: BBS list, messaging, parameters, system information, userlog.
Special interests: CoCo.
Notice: At signon, you may see a prompt asking you to type **BBS** to enter the system.
Comments: No downloadable programs, just messages.

Georgia (912)

CPBB01620 (912) 439-7440
Trade-80 Mini BBS 300 bps
Albany, Georgia 8/1/N
Open Trade-80

Features: BBS list, chat, messaging, parameters, system information, userlog.
Comments: A general-interest message system. For such a small system, it is faster than larger Trade-80 systems.

CPBB01630 (912) 233-0863
Dial-Your-Match #3 300 bps
Savannah, Georgia 7/1/E
Questionnaire/Password Required DYM

Features: BBS list, chat, feedback, mail, matchmaking, messaging.
Special features: Matchmaking.
Notice: This system solicits a fee. Even to browse a Dial-Your-Match system, you must fill out a questionnaire. All of your answers will be public; available to other system users. Depending on the individual sysop (called a Matchmaker), the questions could be quite explicit. This is a sexually oriented system.
Comments: This is the strangest Dial-Your-Match I have ever been on. This system seems to have more women on it than any other DYM in existence, and my printout of matches did run over a foot long. But only the last 5 questions are used to make a match and when you consider that a 3 out of 5 match gives you a 60 percent match to someone, you can see what a waste this is. I don't believe this system has all of the women it claims, and I'm particularly suspicious since this system asks for money. It has always been the case that men outnumber women on DYMs by a large ratio; so how did *this* system in Savannah, Georgia, of all places, get so many women on its system? All I read on my printout were names. It doesn't follow there is actually a *woman* for each of those names. Save your phone call. Save your money.

Hawaii (808)

CPBB01650 (808) 487-2001
Conference Tree 300 bps
Honolulu, Hawaii 7/1/E
Open Conference Tree

Features: Conferencing.
Comments: In the land of Hawaiian Eye, Hawaii 5-0, Magnum P.I., and Hawaiian Punch(?) is a thriving Conference Tree. Subjects range from computers to telecommunications to island restaurants. There is also a very good list of island BBSs. If you decide to call this system, be prepared to say "Aloha" to a big phone bill.

CPBB01660 (808) 487-8755
Heathkit RBBS 300/1200 bps
Honolulu, Hawaii 8/1/N
Open RBBS

Features: BBS list, catalog, chat, feedback, messaging, time/duration, userlog.
Comments: This is quite an active system, filled with messages. If you live on the mainland, you'd have to be a diehard to call it.

Idaho

There are no operating BBSs in Idaho.

Illinois (217)

CPBB01690 (217) 753-4309
Word Exchange 300 bps
Springfield, Illinois 8/1/N
Open MCMS

Features: Catalog, chat, downloading, feedback, messaging, parameters, system information, userlog.
Special features: Downloadable programs for TRS-80 Model I and III computers.
Comments: This system had just installed its MCMS software a few days before I called it. Consequently, there weren't many messages.

Illinois (312)

CPBB01720 (312) 972-6979
EL Division Bulletin Board 300 bps
Argonne, Illinois 8/1/N
Password Required RCP/M RBBS

Features: BBS list, CP/M, downloading, messaging.
Special features: Downloadable programs for CP/M-based machines.
Special interests: CP/M.
Notice: You must be granted permission by the sysop to access the downloading section.
Comments: This system is run by the Argonne National Lab, is very fast, and could use more messages from callers. When I accessed the system, there was an interesting file on Drive B called Works.

CPBB01730 (312) 897-9037
Aurora Computers 300 bps
Chicago, Illinois 8/1/N
Password Required TBBS

Features: Catalog, chat, downloading, feedback, mail, messaging, system information, time/duration.
Special features: Downloadable programs for Apple, Atari, IBM, and TRS-80 Model I and III computers.
Special interests: Multiple message boards. Categories include All Users, Apple/Franklin, Atari, For Sale, IBM, NEC, Need Help, Sinclair, TRS-80.
Notice: There is a 45-minute time limit on this system.
Comments: Unlike most TBBSs, this one does not require you to register a password to have downloading access. There is a friendly atmosphere in this system.

CPBB01740 (312) 326-4392
Bridgeport RCP/M PMMI
Chicago, Illinois 8/1/N
Open RCP/M Signon

Features: CP/M, downloading, messaging.
Special features: Downloadable programs for CP/M-based computers.
Special interests: CP/M.
Comments: A typical RCP/M.

CPBB01750 (312) 267-2066
Caverns of Appleville 300 bps
Chicago, Illinois 8/1/N
Password Required Net-Works

Features: Chat, mail, messaging, parameters, system information, text files, userlog.
Special features: Text files on various science-fiction topics.
Special interests: Multiple message boards. Categories include Adventure, Science-Fiction, Fantasy Gaming.

Comments: A BBS with over 53 messages in the Science-Fiction subboard? A *Dr. Who* Information Center? A *Dr. Who* TV Episode Guide? If you have any interest in the above subjects, this is the system for you. Rev up the TARDIS, say goodbye to Sarah, and grab K-9 as you zip across the country—electronically—to sit with the admirers and followers of the Time Lord. Let's hope this system is still online when you read this—or you really will need a TARDIS!

CPBBØ1759 (312) 545-8086
CBBS #1 300 bps
Chicago, Illinois 8/1/N
Open CBBS

Features: Chat, feedback, messaging, parameters, time/duration.
Comments: This was the *first* BBS in the world; it started the ball rolling and made all of the other systems listed in *The Computer Phone Book* possible. The system is still operating and, like all other CBBSs listed, it is definitely worth a long-distance call.

CPBBØ176Ø (312) 849-1132
CBBS/CPMUG 300 bps
Chicago, Illinois 8/1/N
Open CBBS

Features: Feedback, messaging, parameters, text files.
Special features: Text files are CP/M public-domain software catalogs.
Special interests: CP/M.
Comments: This is *the* system to call to learn about the availability, type, and quality of CP/M public-domain software.

CPBBØ177Ø (312) 622-4442
Greene Machine 300 bps
Chicago, Illinois 7/1/E or 8/1/N
Password Required Greene Machine

Features: BBS list, chat, conferencing, mail, matchmaking, messaging, system information, time/duration, userlog.

Special features: Conferencing on various topics; matchmaking.
Special interests: Multiple message boards. Categories include Open Discussion, X-rated, Couples.
Notice: This is a sexually oriented system. A registered password is required to access the matchmaking/X-rated sections.
Comments: A modified Greene Machine with matchmaking capabilities. I did not try the matchmaking feature. After all, Cupid has to rest, too.

CPBB01780 (312) 848-3669
TI BBS 300 bps
Chicago, Illinois 7/1/N
Open Original

Features: Chat, messaging, text files.
Special features: Text files contain local club news.
Special interests: Texas Instruments home computers.
Comments: This system is running on a TI 99/4A home computer. If you know anything about that computer, you'll know this is a supreme accomplishment. This is a no-frills system but it's fast, it works, and you should give it a call just to see what a TI can do when made to do it.

CPBB01790 (312) 882-2926
CODE 300 bps
Chicago, Illinois 7/1/E
Open ABBS

Features: Chat, messaging, parameters, text files, time/duration.
Special features: Text files about CODE.
Special interests: Consultants and consulting.
Comments: This is a professional BBS for the membership of CODE—the Consultants Occupational Directory and Exchange, a society to promote professional consulting. Full details about CODE may be obtained by reading messages 1 to 10 on the system.

CPBB01800   (312) 397-0871
Commodore Public Bulletin Board   300 bps
Chicago, Illinois   7/1/E or 8/1/N
Password Required   CBMBBS

Features: BBS list, chat, downloading, messaging, parameters, text files, time/duration.
Special features: Downloadable programs for VIC-20, Commodore-64, and Commodore Business Machines computers.
Special interests: Commodore computers.
Notice: To download programs, you need an authorization code and a special terminal program. Contact the sysop for details.
Comments: This is another fine CBMBBS. It has the largest downloading section of all operating CBMBBSs. It is so big, in fact, that all 500-plus of the Commodore educational public-domain programs are on the system. It's worth a long-distance call.

CPBB01810   (312) 243-1046
Dial-Your-Match #39   300 bps
Chicago, Illinois   7/1/E
Questionnaire/Password Required   DYM

Features: BBS list, chat, feedback, mail, matchmaking, messaging.
Special features: Matchmaking.
Notice: Even to browse a Dial-Your-Match system, you must first fill out a questionnaire. All of your answers will be public, available to other system users. Depending on the individual sysop (called a Matchmaker), the questions could be quite explicit. This is a sexually oriented system.
Comments: This time I was only matched with 4 women, the highest percentage was 58 percent to a woman between 21 and 25 years of age. The other 3 were in the 13 to 17 years of age range.

CPBB01820 (312) 475-4884
GameMaster ABBS 300 bps
Chicago, Illinois 7/1/E
Open ABBS

Features: Messaging.
Special interests: GameMaster system.
Comments: This system is run by the folks who bring you GameMaster (CPBL00500, page 170). If you are interested in getting information about what the GameMaster system is and how you may subscribe, call this system and read the first 10 messages.

CPBB01830 (312) 397-0360
KUG 300/1200 bps
Chicago, Illinois 8/1/N
Open CBBS

Features: Chat, feedback, messaging, parameters, system information.
Special interests: Kaypro computers.
Comments: This is, to the best of my knowledge (and records), the first BBS ever hosted on a Kaypro II and devoted to Kaypro computers. This system features more messages than any other Kaypro-dedicated system. There are, however, no downloadable programs. Nonetheless, there is a wealth of information to be found here. I was able to read an ongoing exchange of messages between two Kaypro users about interfacing a certain brand of daisy-wheel printer to their computers. This was a perfect illustration of the usefulness of a BBS: The two people from different states were discussing a piece of hardware they each owned, through a system located in a third state.

CPBB01840   (312) 252-2136
Logan Square RCP/M   PMMI
Chicago, Illinois   8/1/N
Open   RCP/M RBBS

Features: CP/M, downloading, messaging.
Special features: Downloadable programs for CP/M-based computers.
Special interests: CP/M.
Comments: The MiniRBBS section of this system had messages dating back to 1981. I wonder if their original authors know that their transient messages are still alive 2 years later?

CPBB01850   (312) 927-1020
MCMS CAMS #1   300/1200 bps
Chicago, Illinois   8/1/N
Password Required   MCMS

Features: BBS list, catalog, chat, downloading, messaging, parameters, system information, time/duration, userlog.
Special features: Unspecified downloadable programs.
Notice: A registered password is required for access to the downloading section.
Comments: This is the headquarters system of MCMS; it's a very active general-interest message system.

CPBB01860   (312) 882-5766
Multi Image Information Line   300 bps
Chicago, Illinois   7/1/E
Password Required   MCMS

Features: BBS list, chat, downloading, feedback, messaging, parameters, system information, time/duration, userlog.
Special features: Unspecified downloadable programs.
Special interests: Audio-visual, film, TV.
Notice: Only "approved" users may access the downloading section.
Comments: This is a general-interest message system. I have no idea what the sysop(s) mean by "approved" users.

CPBB01870 (312) 944-4847
P-Chicago 300/1200 bps
Chicago, Illinois 7/1/E
Open Hostcomm

Features: Downloading, messaging, parameters, system information, text files, time/duration.
Special features: Downloadable programs for the IBM PC.
Special interests: IBM PC.
Notice: This system may no longer be public by the time you read this. Or it may still be public. That's the way BBSs are.
Comments: A typical Hostcomm system.

CPBB01880 (312) 373-8057
PMS—CRT 300 bps
Chicago, Illinois 7/1/E or 8/1/N
Open PMS

Features: BBS list, downloading, feedback, messaging, parameters, system information, text files, time/duration.
Special features: ALTernate message base; downloadable programs for the Apple II+; text files on various topics.
Special interests: Serious discussions.
Comments: CRT stands for the Chicago Round Table, and this system is a cross between the Algonquin Round Table and the Knights of the Round Table. It is good to see a PMS being used for something other than general (or private) messaging. Not all of the messages here are meaty stuff, but that's OK. If you want to post a general-interest message on this system, choose the ALTernate message base or you will see your message summarily erased.

CPBB01890 (312) 376-7598
SW PC-Connection 300 bps
Chicago, Illinois 8/1/N
Open PCRBBS

Features: Downloading, messaging, parameters, system information, time/duration, userlog.

Directory Section: United States Bulletin-Board Systems

Special features: Downloadable programs for the IBM PC.
Special interest: IBM PC.
Comments: A typical PCRBBS.

CPBB01900   (312) 964-6513
PMS—SRT   300 bps
Downers Grove, Illinois   7/1/E or 8/1/N

Features: BBS list, feedback, messaging, parameters, system information, text files, time/duration.
Special features: ALTernate message base, text files on various topics.
Special interests: Serious discussions.
Comments: SRT stands for Suburban Round Table. When I called the system, the users had covered discrimination, taxes, government services, and libertarianism. The ALTernate message base had messages mainly of a very esoteric nature.

CPBB01910   (312) 469-2597
RCP/M   PMMI
Glen Ellyn, Illinois   8/1/N
Password Required   RCP/M RBBS

Features: CP/M, downloading messaging.
Special features: Downloadable programs for CP/M-based computers.
Special interests: CP/M.
Comments: You will not be able to get on this system unless you can answer its signon question: Who invented CP/M (the original author)? No, this isn't Twenty Questions. Get it right or get dumped.

CPBB01920   (312) 295-6926
PMS—IAC   300 bps
Lake Forest, Illinois   7/1/E or 8/1/N
Open   PMS

Features: BBS list, downloading, feedback, messaging, parameters, system information, text files, time/duration.

Special features: Downloadable programs for Apple II + and //e computers, text files on various topics.
Special interests: Apple computers.
Comments: IAC stands for International Apple Core, one of the largest Apple user's groups in existence. When I called this system it featured general-interest messages and plenty of downloadable programs.

CPBB01930 (312) 674-6502
Video King BBS 300 bps
Lincolnwood, Illinois 7/1/E or 8/1/N
Password Required CBMBBS

Features: BBS list, chat, downloading, messaging, parameters, text files, time/duration, userlog.
Special features: Downloadable programs for VIC-20, Commodore-64, and Commodore Business Machines computers.
Special interests: Commodore computers.
Notice: To download programs, you need an authorization code and a special terminal program. Contact the sysop for details.
Comments: If you've been reading these listings from the beginning, you already know that I love the CBMBBS software and that, for a Commodore owner, all of them are definitely worth a long-distance call.

CPBB01940 (312) 647-7636
A.B. Dick RCP/M RBBS 300/1200 bps
Niles, Illinois 8/1/N
Open RCP/M RBBS

Features: BBS list, chat, CP/M, downloading, messaging, parameters, time/duration, userlog.
Special features: Downloadable programs for CP/M-based computers.
Special interests: CP/M.
Notice: This system has a time-limit of 1 hour per day per user.
Comments: This system is running on an A.B. Dick Magna III personal computer. There were so many disclaimers on this system

Directory Section: United States Bulletin-Board Systems 255

that I had to wonder why the company was running it as a public system. As far as RCP/Ms go, this was a slow system, leading me to wonder if that was any indication of the power of the computer it was running on.

CPBB01950 (312) 359-9450
PBBS Something for Everyone 300 bps
Palantine, Illinois 8/1/N
Open Original

Features: BBS list, catalog, messaging, system information, time/duration, userlog.
Comments: This is a system I am fond of. It is a bit rough around the edges but it works and there are always a few messages on it to pique my interest. Give it a call and try it out.

CPBB01960 (312) 462-7560
PCMS 300/1200 bps
Wheaton, Illinois 8/1/N
Open MCMS

Features: BBS list, chat, downloading, feedback, messaging, parameters, system information, text files, time/duration, userlog.
Special features: Downloadable programs for TRS-80 Model I and III computers.
Comments: A general-interest message system. The sysop is a columnist for a Chicago-area computer publication.

Illinois (815)

CPBB01980 (815) 838-1020
JAMS 300 bps
Lockport, Illinois 8/1/N
Open MCMS

Features: BBS list, chat, downloading, feedback, messaging, parameters, system information, time/duration, userlog.

Special features: Downloadable programs for TRS-80 Model I and III computers.

Comments: JAMS stands for Joliet Area Message Service. This is a general-interest message system that had quite a large selection of downloadable programs available when I called it.

Indiana (317)

CPBB02000 (317) 255-5435
AVC—Commodore Bulletin Board 300 bps
Indianapolis, Indiana 7/1/E or 8/1/N
Password Required CBMBBS

Features: BBS list, downloading, messaging, parameters, text files, time/duration, userlog.

Special features: Downloadable programs for VIC-20, Commodore-64, and Commodore Business Machines computers; text files on various topics.

Special interests: Commodore computers.

Notice: To download programs, you need an authorization code and a special terminal program. Contact the sysop for details.

Comments: This was the first CBMBBS I had ever called and it was like finding an oasis in a spreading desert. Although there are other CBMBBSs, I'll always have a fond memory of this one, which introduced me to this superb piece of software. Definitely worth a long-distance call.

CPBB02020 (317) 787-5486
PMS 300 bps
Indianapolis, Indiana 7/1/E or 8/1/N
Open PMS

Features: BBS list, feedback, messaging, system information, text files, time/duration.

Special features: Text files on local user's group.

Comments: A general-interest message system. When I had signed on to this system for the first time for *The Computer Phone Book*, there were quite a few messages dealing with computer-related bills that had gone before the Indiana State Legislature. Unfortunately, on subsequent calls, the messages were no longer on the message base. It was a shame not to see such information placed in the system's Features section, so they could have a longer life.

Iowa (319)

CPBB02040 (319) 364-0811
CBBS 300 bps
Cedar Rapids, Iowa 8/1/N
Open CBBS

Features: Feedback, messaging, parameters.
Special interests: Computers in medicine.
Comments: This is a CBBS with fewer messages online at one time than other CBBSs. It has been in operation since 1981, making it virtually one of the founding fathers of hobbyist micro telecommunications. Like any other CBBS, small number of messages or not, it is worth a long-distance call.

CPBB02050 (319) 363-3314
Hawkeye—PC 300/1200 bps
Cedar Rapids, Iowa 8/1/N
Password Required PCRBBS

Features: Chat, downloading, messaging, parameters, system information, text files, time/duration.
Special features: Downloadable programs for the IBM PC; text files on various topics.
Special interests: IBM PC.
Comments: This system had a small number of messages when I called it, but like all PCRBBSs, it was very fast. If you have an IBM PC, this is another system to call to look for free software.

CPBB02060 (319) 353-6528
Apple Medical BBS 300 bps
Iowa City, Iowa 7/1/E
Open ABBS

Features: Messaging, parameters, time/duration.
Special interests: Computers in medicine; medical topics.
Notice: This system's hours are Mon–Thurs 5 PM–8 AM *Central Time*, and Fri 5 PM—Mon 8 AM *Central Time*.
Comments: This is another of the very few part-time systems to be listed in *The Computer Phone Book*. I am listing it because it is run by a *very* dedicated sysop. Although it has never had many messages on it and very few of the callers to it leave a message, the sysop has kept the system up and operating for at least 2 years. In the face of all odds, in the face of user disinterest, he has kept it going. This, in itself, deserves recognition. The system deserves your call.

Kansas (316)

CPBB02090 (316) 665-3985
Forum-80 300 bps
Hutchinson, Kansas 8/1/N
Probationary Forum-80

Features: BBS list, downloading, feedback, messaging, parameters, system information, userlog.
Special features: Unspecified downloadable programs.
Notice: Forum-80 has a policy of displaying a long (series of) signon bulletin(s) that you cannot bypass and of labeling all new users as "probationary", requiring the sysop to approve any messages new users post before other users may read them (if at all).
Comments: This system is another one which amply deserves the above notice. The bulletins are too long, out-of-date, dull, slow, and a waste of money to long-distance callers. Long-distance callers can skip this one. It's too bad Hutchinson only has this one system. It deserves better.

Kansas (913)

CPBB02110   (913) 432-5544
Dickenson's Movie Guide   300 bps
Mission, Kansas   7/1/E or 8/1/N
Password Required   Online

Features: BBS list, downloading, mail, parameters, text files.
Special features: Unspecified downloadable programs; text files, movie synopses/reviews, movie theater listings.
Special interests: Movie directory.
Notice: To logon this system, respond to the "ID#" prompt by typing **GUEST** and respond to the "PSWD:" prompt by typing **PASS**. A registered User ID is required to access the downloading section.
Comments: This is an online directory of movies playing in the Kansas City Dickenson chain of movie theaters. Synopses and principal cast lists of films are given, along with the local theater and playing times. There are also synopses of films not yet playing in theaters. Even if you don't live in the area, this system is worth a long-distance call to read synopses of films that have not yet appeared in your area. The synopses are concise and well written. Also available on this system are short articles that give background information on recent films. This is a very nice system and shows just how flexible a BBS can be and how its uses are only limited by the sysop's imagination.

CPBB02120   (913) 384-2196
Online Beta Sigma Phi   300 bps
Overland Park, Kansas   8/1/N
Open   Color-80

Features: BBS list, catalog, chat, downloading, feedback, messaging, parameters, time/duration, userlog.
Special features: Downloadable programs for the Color Computer; online ordering from the Beta Sigma Phi gift shop.
Special interests: Beta Sigma Phi.

Notice: To download programs, you must be using a Color Computer and a terminal program such as Colorcom/E.

Comments: This is another nice Color-80 system. It's strange to find it being used by—of all groups—Beta Sigma Phi. I would have thought they would have something running on an IBM PC at least.

CPBB02130 (913) 341-3502
PMS—Apple Bits 300 bps
Overland Park, Kansas 7/1/E or 8/1/N
Open PMS

Features: BBS list, downloading, feedback, messaging, parameters, system information, text files, time/duration.
Special features: Downloadable programs for the Apple II+ computer; text files on local user's group and various topics.
Comments: A lively system that seemed to be the electronic equivalent of a kaffeklatch than a cut-and-dried message exchange between strangers. Politics, personal issues, and other nonstandard BBS topics were being discussed on this system when I called it.

CPBB02140 (913) 341-0471
PMS—Your Computer Connection 300 bps
Overland Park, Kansas 7/1/E or 8/1/N
Open PMS

Features: BBS list, downloading, feedback, messaging, parameters, system information, text files, time/duration.
Special features: Downloadable programs for the Apple II+ computer.
Comments: This is a general-interest message system. It seems that it is being developed into a twin system, the second part of it being an online information service for a vendor of microcomputer products. This second part was not available when I called this system.

Kentucky

The Information Age has not been kind to this state. The one system I had planned to list for this state went offline before press time.

Louisiana (318)

CPBBØ22ØØ   (318) 861-1012
Apple-Gumbo   300 bps
Shreveport, Louisiana   8/1/N
Password Required   Net-Works

Features: BBS list, chat, downloading, mail, messaging, parameters, system information, text files, time/duration, userlog.
Special features: Unspecified downloadable programs, text files on various topics.
Notice: Net-Works systems do not allow you to read past the first 10 messages or access certain sections of the system until your password is validated. Your telephone number will become part of your password, so don't give a false one.
Comments: This is the revival of a once-popular Net-Works system. The sysop would like to bring it back to its former usefulness. Local callers, give it a ring and help it to thrive.

CPBBØ221Ø   (318) 635-8660
TBBS   300 bps
Shreveport, Louisiana   8/1/N
Password Required   TBBS

Features: Catalog, chat, downloading, feedback, mail, messaging, parameters, polling, system information, time/duration, userlog.
Special features: Downloadable programs for the Apple II+, IBM PC, and TRS-80 Model I and III computers, polling of users on various topics.

Special interests: Multiple message boards. Categories include Apple, CP/M, IBM, TRS-80.
Notice: There is a 60-minute time limit on this system.
Comments: A general-interest message system with a good selection of downloadable programs.

Louisiana (504)

CPBB02230 (504) 291-4331
LNW TBBS Southeast 300/1200 bps
Baton Rouge, Louisiana 8/1/N
Password Required TBBS

Features: Catalog, chat, downloading, feedback, mail, messaging, parameters, system information, text files, time/duration.
Special features: Unspecified downloadable programs; text files on LNW-related topics.
Special interests: LNW computers.
Comments: A message system of interest to owners and users of LNW brand computers.

CPBB02240 (504) 273-3116
RCP/M PMMI
Baton Rouge, Louisiana 8/1/N
Open RCP/M RBBS

Features: CP/M, downloading, messaging.
Special features: Downloadable programs for Atari home computers.
Special interests: Atari home computers, CP/M.
Comments: There were quite a few Atari programs available, representing different applications. If you have an Atari home computer, are familiar with RCP/Ms, and have a version of XModem communications software, give this system a call.

CPBB02250 (504) 926-0181
TBBS 300/1200 bps
Baton Rouge, Louisiana 8/1/N
Password Required TBBS

Features: BBS list, chat, feedback, mail, messaging, parameters, system information, text files, time/duration.
Special features: Text files contain information on local user's groups.
Special interests: Multiple message boards. Categories include Apple, Commodore, General, Model IV, Model 100, Politics.
Notice: There is a 30-minute time limit on this system.
Comments: A general-interest message system.

Maine (207)

CPBB02270 (207) 839-2337
Programmer's Anonymous 300 bps
Gorham, Maine 8/1/N
Password Required RCP/M RBBS

Features: CP/M, downloading, messaging.
Special features: Downloadable programs for Osborne computers.
Special interests: Osborne computers.
Comments: In the wilds of Maine, this is the only operating BBS in the entire state. This makes the sysop somewhat of a celebrity. I hope you'll give this system a call and show the sysop that it is needed.

Maryland (301)

CPBB02290 (301) 661-2175
BHEC RCP/M RBBS 300/450 bps
Baltimore, Maryland 8/1/N
Open RCP/M RBBS

Features: CP/M, downloading, feedback, messaging.
Special features: Downloadable programs for CP/M-based computers.

Special interests: CP/M; Heath/Zenith computers.
Notice: This system has a time limit of 1-hour per day per caller. To enter the CP/M downloading section, type **HEATHUSR** (in caps, as spelled).
Comments: BHEC stands for Baltimore Heath Electronics Center. This system had more messages on it than most RCP/M systems I've called. Follow the signon instructions to download .DOC files so you can use the system efficiently.

CPBB02300   (301) 344-9156
GASNet   300 bps
Beltsville, Maryland   8/1/N
Open   Unknown

Features: Feedback, messaging, parameters, text files, time/duration.
Special features: Text files on the space program.
Special interests: NASA, space program, space shuttle.
Comments: The GAS in GASNet is an acronym for Get-Away Special, otherwise known as private-sector payloads carried on the space shuttle. If you're someone who stares at the stars and longs to go into orbit, give this system a call to meet some kindred spirits.

CPBB02310   (301) 460-0538
Capital PC   300/1200 bps
Bethesda, Maryland   8/1/N
Password Required   PCRBBS

Features: Chat, downloading, messaging, parameters, text files, time/duration, userlog.
Special features: Downloadable programs for the IBM PC, text files on various topics.
Special interests: IBM PC.
Notice: This system has a 45-minute time limit.
Comments: Another fast PCRBBS. This one has a wide selection and variety of downloadable programs.

CPBB02320 (301) 948-5717
CPEUG & NBS/ICST 300 bps
Bethesda, Maryland 8/1/N
Open CBBS

Features: Feedback, messaging, parameters.
Special interests: Computer technology evaluation/review.
Comments: CPEUG stands for Computer Performance Evaluation User's Group, and NBS stands for National Bureau of Standards. I haven't the foggiest notion what ICST stands for; the system doesn't let on. This is a good place to exchange technical information about mainframe, mini, and microcomputers. Just a quick-scan of the message base makes interesting reading, and technical-oriented callers will have a virtual field day discussing bits, bytes, and bauds. Worth a long-distance call.

CPBB02330 (301) 565-9051
Tech-Link 300 bps
Forest Glen, Maryland 8/1/N
Open Original

Features: BBS list, chat, downloading, messaging, parameters, system information, text files, time/duration.
Special features: Text files on various technical topics.
Special interests: Technical information about computers.
Comments: This is a well-designed system that is very fast and very active. If you can get through despite the almost nonstop busy signal, you will be in for a treat. Worth a long-distance call.

CPBB02340 (301) 251-6293
Capital PC 300/1200 bps
Gaithersburg, Maryland 8/1/N
Password Required PCRBBS

Features: Chat, messaging, parameters, text files, time/duration, user-log.

Special features: Text files on various topics.
Special interests: IBM PC.
Notice: There is a 45-minute time limit on this system.
Comments: Another fast PCRBBS. There wasn't a downloading section on this one, but there were quite a few messages.

CPBB02350 (301) 587-2132
Computer Age BBS 300 bps
Silver Spring, Maryland 7/1/E or 8/1/N
Open Armudic

Features: BBS list, downloading, messaging, system information, text files.
Special features: Downloadable programs for the Apple II+ and Atari home computers; text files on local user groups and various topics.
Comments: A general-interest message system. Of interest mainly to users and owners of Atari home computers.

CPBB02360 (301) 599-1726
Color-80 #25 300 bps
Upper Marlboro, Maryland 8/1/N
Open Color-80

Features: BBS list, catalog, chat, downloading, feedback, graphics, messaging, parameters, system information, text files, time/duration, userlog.
Special features: Downloadable programs for the Color Computer, online graphics for the Color Computer, text files on various Color Computer-related topics.
Special interests: Color Computer.
Notice: To download programs and view online graphics, you must be using a Color Computer and a terminal program such as Colorcom/E.
Comments: This is quite an active Color-80 system. If you are a CoCo owner or user, give it a call and join the many others using it.

Massachusetts (413)

CPBB02380 (413) 733-1749
TBBS 300/1200 bps
Springfield, Massachusetts 8/1/N
Password Required TBBS

Features: Chat, downloading, feedback, mail, messaging, parameters, system information, time/duration, userlog.
Special features: Downloadable programs for TRS-80 Model I and III computers.
Special interests: Multiple message boards. Categories include Adventure, Swap, TRS-80.
Notice: There is a 30-minute time limit on this system.
Comments: There weren't too many messages on this system when I called it, leading me to believe one of two things: that it was a new system or that most of the action was taking place in the boards for registered users, where role-playing games could take place. If you want to find out: Get modem, call system, take inventory.

Massachusetts (617)

CPBB02400 (617) 470-2548
CNode 300 bps
Andover, Massachusetts 8/1/N
Password Required CNode

Features: CP/M, downloading, feedback, messaging.
Special features: Downloadable programs for CP/M-based computers; C programming language user group archives.
Special interests: C programming language, CP/M.
Notice: There is a 60-minute time limit on this system.
Comments: When I called this system, it was planning to implement Citadel as a message base. The sysop, who is very friendly, was still debugging the software. By the time you read this, Citadel should be up, making this system worth a long-distance call.

CPBB02410 (617) 646-6809
Color-80 #16 300 bps
Arlington, Massachusetts 8/1/N
Open Color-80

Features: BBS list, catalog, chat, downloading, feedback, graphics, messaging, parameters, system information, text files, time/duration, userlog.
Special features: Downloadable programs for the Color Computer, online graphics for the Color Computer, text files on various Color Computer-related topics.
Special interests: Color Computer.
Notice: To download programs and view online graphics, you must be using a Color Computer and a terminal program such as Colorcom/E.
Comments: Yet another fine Color-80 system. This one has a rotating menu of downloadable programs. If you have a CoCo, it's time for you to get it a modem!

CPBB02420 (617) 966-0416
RCP/M 300 bps
Bellingham, Massachusetts 8/1/N
Open RCP/M RBBS

Features: CP/M, downloading, messaging.
Special features: Downloadable programs for CP/M-based computers.
Special interests: CP/M.
Comments: A typical RCP/M system; plenty of downloadable programs.

CPBB02430 (617) 423-6985
BIN-EX 300/1200 bps
Boston, Massachusetts 8/1/N
Open M-Tree RCP/M

Features: Conferencing downloading.
Special features: Downloadable programs for CP/M-based computers.

Comments: BIN-EX stands for Boston INformation EXchange, a hierarchically structured conferencing system that bears a striking resemblance to a Conference Tree. It also offers an RCP/M. All sorts of topics are discussed on this system; the volatility of the information prevents my giving you any sort of a list except to mention that there is a permanent conference on the system about videotex and computer telecommunications. One of the sysop's plans is to add PLP standard graphics to the system and to allow multiple users. It is, indeed, worth a long-distance call.

CPBB02435 (617) 423-6300
Computer Advertising Network 300 bps
Boston, Massachusetts 7/1/E or 8/1/N
Open Unknown

Features: Advertising.
Special features: Two-part system, featuring entertainment advertising on one half, computer-related advertising on the other half.
Comments: If you are thinking of going to Boston or happen to be there with your computer, give this system a call to learn about some of the places you can visit. Every time I have called this system, it has been my unfortunate experience to have it crash.

CPBB02440 (617) 683-2119
Lawrence General Hospital 300 bps
Boston, Massachusetts 8/1/N
Open CBBS

Features: Feedback, messaging, parameters, time/duration.
Special interests: Computers in medicine, medical topics.
Comments: This was one of the first systems dedicated to exchanging information about physicians using computers in their practices. The sysop of this system has been very dedicated to keeping the system online and has done a superlative job of trying to educate his peers about the many uses a computer can have in medical practice. If you are in the medical field, get your computer a modem and give this system a call. You'll be helping to keep a noble cause

CPBB02450 (617) 256-8396
Chelmsford Exchange 300 bps
Chelmsford, Massachusetts 7/1/E
Password Required Original

Features: Chat, downloading, text files, time/duration.
Special features: Downloadable programs for the Apple II+ computer; text file of questions and answers on data telecommunications.
Special interests: Apple computers.
Notice: A registered password is required to access the downloading section.
Comments: There aren't any messages on this system, just a program downloading section. Before you sign off the system, try the selection, **MENU** (heh-heh).

CPBB02460 (617) 259-0181
The Outpost 300/1200 bps
Lincoln, Massachusetts 8/1/N
Password Required TBBS

Features: BBS list, chat, feedback, mail, messaging, parameters, system information, time/duration, userlog.
Special interests: Multiple message boards. Categories include Events, Jokes, Science-Fiction/Fantasy, Trading Post, Video/Movies.
Notice: There is a 45-minute time limit on this system.
Comments: A general-interest message system.

CPBB02470 (617) 334-6369
Dial-Your-Match #18 300 bps
Lynfield, Massachusetts 7/1/E
Questionnaire/Password Required DYM

Features: BBS list, chat, feedback, mail, matchmaking, messaging, time/duration.

Special features: Matchmaking.
Notice: This system solicits a $5 charge to grant a password. Even to browse a Dial-Your-Match system, you must first fill out a questionnaire. All of your answers will be public, available to other system users. Depending on the individual sysop (called a Matchmaker), the questions could be quite explicit. This is a sexually oriented system.
Comments: I was matched to only *one* woman, who was between 18 and 20 years old, with a 66 percent match. There were some interesting, and telling, statistics about the users of this system. Registered as users were: 208 male heterosexuals, 14 male homosexuals, 12 male bisexuals, 38 female heterosexuals, 1 female homosexual, 5 female bisexuals. These ratios are pretty much the same with all DYMs, except those located in San Francisco and New York City, where there are many more homosexuals. A 4 to 1 ratio of (heterosexual) males to (heterosexual) females is standard.

CPBB02480   (617) 478-4164
RCP/M   300/1200 bps
Milford, Massachusetts   8/1/N
Open   CBBS RCP/M

Features: CP/M, downloading, feedback, messaging, parameters.
Special features: Downloadable programs for CP/M-based computers.
Special interests: CP/M.
Comments: A general-interest messaging system running on an OSI.

CPBB02490   (617) 969-9660
Boston Computer Society   300 bps
Newton, Massachusetts   7/1/N
Open   Original

Features: Messaging, system information, text files.
Special features: Text files about the Boston Computer Society.
Special interests: Boston Computer Society.

Comments: Although the designers of this system may have started out to ape CompuServe, the result is a clumsy, repetitive, user-unfriendly system. Since there will be a few months delay between the time I called this system and your reading this, the BCS may have improved the system. If you absolutely have to get information on the BCS, my advice is to save the cost of a long-distance call and send a letter instead.

CPBB02500 (617) 531-9332
North Shore HUG BBS 300/1200 bps
Peabody, Massachusetts 8/1/N
Open C/80

Features: Downloading, feedback, messaging, parameters.
Special features: Downloadable programs for Heath/Zenith computers.
Special interests: Heath/Zenith computers.
Comments: A typical RCP/M system.

CPBB02510 (617) 899-6524
Computer Bargain Guide 300/1200 bps
Waltham, Massachusetts 8/1/N
Open TBBS

Features: Advertising, feedback, mail, messaging, parameters, text files.
Special features: Advertising, text files on various topics.
Special interests: Advertising.
Comments: I have a friend who is a teacher. Now, you may have recalled that, earlier this year, a study of our nation's school system said that we had a "rising tide of mediocrity" in education. My friend has witnessed this first hand and bought himself a computer as a stepping-stone out of his chosen profession. What does all of this have to do with the Computer Bargain Guide? It's simple, really, when you consider the sysop of this system spells "articles" as "articals," "ads" (plural) as "ad's" (possessive), "their" as "there,"

and "completed" as "compleated." As the saying goes, "You can run but you can't hide. . ."

Michigan (313)

CPBB02530   (313) 662-8303
Barton Data Line   300 bps
Ann Arbor, Michigan   8/1/N
Password Required   TBBS

Features: BBS list, catalog, chat, feedback, mail, messaging, parameters, polling, text files, time/duration.
Special features: Telex sending/receiving, text files on various topics.
Special interests: Multiple message boards. Categories include Advice, Apple, Atari, IBM, Otrona Attache, TRS-80, VIC-20.
Notice: There is a 30-minute time limit on this system. Telex service requires registration. Contact sysop for details.
Comments: This is a nice system with a lot to offer. The sysop plans to make it into a multiuser system. Worth a long-distance call.

CPBB02540   (313) 933-1425
Detroit Download   300 bps
Detroit, Michigan   8/1/N
Open   Unknown

Features: Chat, downloading, feedback, messaging, system information, time/duration, userlog.
Special features: Downloadable programs for the Color Computer and TRS-80 Model I and III computers.
Comments: A general-interest message system.

CPBB02550   (313) 343-0877
Bit Bucket   300 bps
Detroit, Michigan   8/1/N
Open   Original

Features: BBS list, chat, downloading, messaging, system information, time/duration, userlog.
Special features: Downloadable programs for the Color Computer and TRS-80 Model I and III computers.
Comments: This system had a microscopic message base when I called it; scanning messages is clumsy and cumbersome. It may be of use to local callers, but long-distance callers can skip it.

CPBB02560   (313) 846-6127
Technical CBBS   300 bps
Detroit, Michigan   8/1/N
Open   CBBS RCP/M

Features: CP/M, downloading, messaging, parameters.
Special features: Downloadable programs for CP/M-based computers.
Special interest: CP/M.
Comments: There were plenty of interesting messages on the MiniCBBS of this system. Type **MINICBBS** at the "A)" prompt.

CPBB02570   (313) 398-5293
Bullet-80   300 bps
Hazel Park, Michigan   8/1/N
Open   Bullet-80

Features: BBS list, catalog, chat, downloading, feedback, games, messaging, parameters, time/duration, userlog.
Special features: Downloadable programs for TRS-80 Model I and III computers; games include: Atlantis, Dutchman, Journey, King, Tomb.
Comments: A general-interest message system. Long-distance callers be advised that Bullet-80s tend to be slow.

CPBB02580   (313) 261-0885
Livonia Download   300 bps
Livonia, Michigan   8/1/N
Open   Unknown

Features: BBS list, chat, downloading, feedback. messaging, system information, time, userlog.
Special features: Unspecified downloadable programs.
Comments: There was a preponderance of private messages on this system when I called it, and the downloading section was offline. The sysop is looking for CoCo downloadable programs. If you have any, here's a place you can upload them. They must, of course, be public-domain ones.

CPBB02590   (313) 455-4227
GBBS   300 bps
Plymouth, Michigan   7/1/E
Password Required   Net-Works

Features: BBS list, chat, downloading, messaging, parameters, system information, text files, time/duration, userlog.
Special features: Unspecified downloadable programs; text files on various gay sex topics.
Special interests: Gay sex.
Notice: This is an X-rated system that caters to gays. If you are offended by the existence of gays or are not gay yourself, *do not bother* to call this system.
Comments: The sysop of this system goes by the moniker, "Tootsie." If you have any interest in the special interest of this system, give it a call. When you sign off, the system will say (so help me, it's the truth!), "Tootaloo..."

CPBB02600 (313) 459-8375
Good News BBS 300 bps
Plymouth, Michigan 8/1/N
Password Required Original

Features: BBS list, chat, downloading, messaging, system information, time/duration, userlog.
Special features: Unspecified downloadable programs.
Notice: A registered password is required to access the downloading section.
Comments: This is a general-interest message system with a cumbersome method of message retrieval. Long-distance callers can skip this one.

CPBB02610 (313) 274-3940
M.A.C.E. West 300 bps
Southfield, Michigan 7/1/E or 8/1/N
Open AMIS

Features: BBS list, chat, downloading, feedback, messaging, parameters, userlog.
Special features: Downloadable programs for Atari home computers.
Special interests: Atari home computers.
Comments: MACE stands for Michigan Atari Computer Enthusiasts. This is another system for users and owners of Atari home computers to call.

CPBB02620 (313) 754-1131
Tony's Place 300/1200 bps
Warren, Michigan 8/1/N
Password Required Original

Features: BBS list, downloading, feedback, messaging, system information, userlog.
Special features: Unspecified downloadable programs.
Comments: A general-interest message system.

CPBB02630 (313) 683-5076
Bullet-80 300/1200 bps
Waterford, Michigan 8/1/N
Open Bullet-80

Features: BBS list, catalog, chat, feedback, games, messaging, parameters, system information, time/duration, userlog.
Special features: Downloadable programs for Apple, Atari, CoCo, IBM, TRS-80 Model I and III, VIC-20 computers.
Comments: A general-interest message system with quite a selection of downloadable programs.

Michigan (517)

CPBB02650 (517) 485-6232
Babblenet 300/1200 bps
Lansing, Michigan 7/1/E
Open MCMS

Features: Chat, downloading, feedback, messaging, parameters, system information, text files, time/duration, userlog.
Special features: Downloadable programs for TRS-80 Model I and III computers, text files about local user groups.
Notice: There is a 30-minute time limit on this system.
Comments: Apparently, there is some sort of fee required to obtain a password to use this system regularly. Unfortunately, neither of the two text files dealing with this would print out for me. At any rate, this system is strictly for local use. Long-distance callers can skip it.

CPBB02660 (517) 339-3367
CompuNet 300/1200 bps
Lansing, Michigan 8/1/N
Password Required TBBS

Features: Chat, downloading, feedback, messaging, parameters, time/duration.

Special features: Unspecified downloadable programs.
Special interests: Multiple message boards. Categories include General, TRS-80 Model I/II/III/IV.
Comments: This is mid-Michigan's oldest BBS. When I called it, it had just implemented the TBBS software and the sysop was in the process of constructing the system. It will eventually have a library of over 400 programs for downloading for a variety of computers. If you have an interest in public-domain software, this is another resource to tap. Don't forget to leave a message (or thank the sysop).

Michigan (616)

CPBB02680 (616) 241-1971
GRASS 300 bps
Grand Rapids, Michigan 7/1/E or 8/1/N
Open AMIS

Features: Chat, downloading, feedback, messaging, parameters, text files, time/duration.
Special features: Downloadable programs for Atari home computers, text files on various topics.
Special interests: Atari home computers.
Comments: When I called this system, it had just gotten in Tempest to download. (I'm sure, by that, they must have meant a public-domain clone, and not the actual, Copyrighted program!) Another one for Atari owners to call.

Minnesota (612)

CPBB02710 (612) 542-9597
The Job System™ 300/1200 bps
Minneapolis, Minnesota 7/2/N
Password Required Job System

Features: BBS list, chat, mail, messaging, parameters, system information, text files, time/duration, userlog.

Special features: Text files on various topics.
Special interest: Online listings of computer-related job positions.
Notice: A registered password is required to post messages.
Comments: This system uses a very nice new BBS software package called The Job System. On this system, you can find employment opportunity listings for computer-related jobs in the Twin Cities area. The company running the system plans to expand their job listing for positions outside the Twin Cities. All of this adds up to a system that is worth a long-distance call for those looking to get a new job.

CPBB02720   (612) 872-2352
LawSIG   300 bps
Minneapolis, Minnesota   7/1/E
Open   Conference Tree

Features: Conferencing.
Special interest: Computer-related law.
Comments: This system contains conferences on computer-related law, such as software piracy and computer crime. The branch titled Computer Crime was one of the most interesting conferences I have read in quite some time. I have to commend the sysop for organizing a well-run Conference Tree and for having, herself, a professional and highly polished writing style. Well worth a long-distance phone call.

CPBB02730   (612) 571-5965
Loki's Corner   300 bps
Minneapolis, Minnesota   8/1/N
Password Required   Net-Works

Features: BBS list, chat, messaging, parameters, system information, time/duration.
Special interests: Multiple message boards. Categories include Buy/Sell, Chess, Games, General, Jokes, Relatives/Geneology, Risque Jokes, Robotics, Sociology, Video/Videogames.

Notice: Follow signon instructions to log on as a guest account.

Comments: I would not recommend calling this system unless you plan to become a regular user. The passwords are assigned on the basis of people the sysop knows submitting others' names for password privileges. There is a guest account, though, and you are informed of it at signon. However, if you are outside of the local area, you could spend your long-distance dollars in a better way by calling another system.

CPBB02740 (612) 333-8970
MarkeTrak 300 bps
Minneapolis, Minnesota 7/1/N
Open ABBS

Features: BBS list, conferencing, downloading, messaging, parameters, text files, time/duration.

Special features: Downloadable text files that provide an electronic update to a printed commodities newsletter.

Special interests: Commodities. Multiple message boards. Categories include MarkeTrak Analysis, Precious Metals/Futures Markets, VIC-20.

Notice: There is a 14-minute time limit on this system. This system is *unavailable* Mon–Fri 7 AM–9 AM and 1:30–5:30 PM Central Time and has sporadic availability on Saturday mornings.

Comments: "This service is neither an advisory or commodity trading nor a solicitation for commodity transactions," cautions the opening disclaimer on this system. Commodities news is limited to password holders, some of whom must also subscribe to the firm's printed commodities newsletter. Otherwise, this system is a full implementation of ABBS version 4.01 and is open to all users.

CPBB02750 (612) 533-1957
NC Software 300/1200 bps
Minneapolis, Minnesota 8/1/N
Open MCMS

Features: BBS list, catalog, chat, downloading, feedback, messaging, parameters, system information, time/duration, userlog.

Special features: Unspecified downloadable programs.
Special interests: TRS-80 computers.
Comments: A general-interest message system, with an emphasis on TRS-80 computers.

CPBB02760 (612) 929-6699
PMS 300 bps
Minneapolis, Minnesota 7/1/E or 8/1/N
Open PMS

Features: BBS list, downloading, feedback, messaging, parameters, system information, text files, time/duration.
Special features: ALTernate message base, downloadable programs for the Apple II+, text files on various topics.
Comments: A general-interest message system using that fine software, PMS.

CPBB02770 (612) 929-8966
PMS—Twin Cities 300 bps
Minneapolis, Minnesota 7/1/E or 8/1/N
Open PMS

Features: BBS list, feedback, messaging, parameters, system information, text files, time/duration.
Comments: Another fine PMS system for general-interest messages.

CPBB02780 (612) 432-3779
TAIG 300 bps
Minneapolis, Minnesota 7/1/E or 8/1/N
Open AMIS

Features: BBS list, chat, downloading, feedback, messaging, parameters, time/duration, userlog.
Special features: Downloadable programs for Atari home computers.
Special interests: Atari home computers.
Comments: TAIG stands for Twin Cities Atari Interest Group. This is another resource for Atari users and owners to tap.

CPBB02790   (612) 731-1063
United BBS   300 bps
Minneapolis, Minnesota   8/1/N
Password Required   Greene Machine

Features: BBS list, conferencing, downloading, feedback, mail, messaging, parameters, time/duration, userlog.
Special features: Conferencing on various topics, downloadable programs for TRS-80 computers.
Special interests: TRS-80 computers.
Notice: A registered password is required to access the TRS-80 conference and downloading sections.
Comments: A general-interest message system. It acts as a backup to BBS Richfield (see following entry).

CPBB02800   (612) 869-0054
BBS Richfield   300/1200 bps
Richfield, Minnesota   8/1/N
Open   MCMS

Features: BBS list, downloading, feedback, messaging, parameters, system information, text files, userlog.
Special features: Downloadable programs for TRS-80 computers, text files on various topics.
Comments: A general-interest message system.

Mississippi (601)

CPBB02820   (601) 264-2361
Southern Bullet   300 bps
Hattiesburg, Mississippi   8/1/N
Open   Bullet-80

Features: BBS list, chat, downloading, feedback, games, messaging, parameters, system information, time/duration, userlog.

Special features: Downloadable programs for TRS-80 Model I and III computers.
Comments: A general-interest message system and the only one I've found in Mississippi.

Missouri (314)

CPBB02850   (314) 625-4576
Commodore Communications   300 bps
St. Louis, Missouri   7/1/E or 8/1/N
Password Required   CBMBBS

Features: BBS list, chat, downloading, messaging, parameters, text files, time/duration, userlog.
Special features: Downloadable programs for VIC-20, Commodore-64, and Commodore Business Machines computers; text files on various topics.
Special interests: Commodore computers.
Notice: To download programs, you need an authorization code and a special terminal program. Contact the sysop for details.
Comments: This system features an incredible selection of downloadable software. The sysop has made arrangements with TORPET (Toronto PET Users' Group) to offer their program disks for downloading. This is yet another one of the fine CBMBBSs and is definitely worth a long-distance call.

Missouri (816)

CPBB02870   (816) 331-7023
Online II—Amateur Radio BBS   300 bps
Belton, Missouri   7/1/E or 8/1/N
Password Required   Online

Features: BBS list, downloading, feedback, mail, messaging, parameters, userlog.

Special features: Unspecified downloadable programs.
Special interests: Ham radio.
Notice: A registered password is required to access the downloading section and all available system sections.
Comments: Unless you have a User ID on this system all you can do is read the BBS list, help files, for-sale messages from User ID-holders, and send mail to and receive mail from User ID holders. Long-distance callers can skip this one.

CPBB02880   (816) 833-3427
Ham BBS   300 bps
Independence, Missouri   8/1/N
Open   Original

Features: BBS list, downloading, feedback, games, messaging, parameters, system information, userlog.
Special features: Unspecified downloadable programs; games include Biorhythm, Lunar Lander, Mastermind.
Notice: System may be unavailable from 6 PM to midnight *Central Time.*
Comments: A general-interest message system that looks like a Forum-80 but runs faster. Give it a call.

CPBB02890   (816) 358-6222
MACC-Net   300 bps
Independence, Missouri   8/1/N
Open   OCCCS

Features: BBS list, catalog, chat, downloading, feedback, messaging, parameters, userlog.
Special features: Downloadable programs for the Color Computer.
Special interests: Color Computer.
Comments: There were plenty of messages and downloadable programs on this system when I called it, making it worth a long-distance call for CoCo owners.

CPBB02900   (816) 861-7040
Forum-80 #1   300 bps
Kansas City, Missouri   8/1/N
Probationary   Forum-80

Features: BBS list, downloading, messaging, parameters, text files, userlog.
Special features: Downloadable Forum-80 help files.
Notice: Forum-80 has a policy of displaying a long (series of) signon bulletin(s) that you cannot bypass and labeling all new users as "probationary," requiring the sysop to approve any messages new users post before other users may read them (if at all).
Comments: Yep, folks, this is the system behind all of those other Forum-80 systems that drive up your long-distance phone bills with irrelevant, dull, unwanted, unneeded, time-wasting bulletins. That's beside the fact the system itself is slow and inflexible. Forum-80, I have been told, is more successful when sold to businesses.

Montana

At one time there was one BBS in Montana. It was, in fact, one of the first BBSs for IBM PC users and the first BBS running *on* an IBM PC. The sysop moved to California. Montana had a second BBS pop up, only to disappear.

Nebraska (402)

CPBB02950   (402) 571-8942
Dial-Your-Match #23   300 bps
Omaha, Nebraska   7/1/E
Questionnaire/Password Required   DYM

Features: BBS list, chat, feedback, mail, matchmaking, messaging, parameters, time/duration.
Special features: Matchmaking.

Notice: There is a 30-minute time limit on this system. Even to browse a Dial-Your-Match system, you must first fill out a questionnaire. All of your answers will be public, available to other system users. Depending on the individual sysop (called a Matchmaker), the questions could be quite explicit. This is a sexually oriented system.
Comments: Can you beat this? No match.

CPBB02960 (402) 339-7809
ABBS 300 bps
Omaha, Nebraska 7/1/E
Open ABBS

Features: BBS list, downloading, messaging, parameters, system information, text files, time/duration, userlog.
Special features: Downloadable programs for the Apple II+ computer, text files on various topics.
Comments: This is a general-interest message system that is quite active. There are always a variety of topics covered in the messages to make interesting reading. If you can't get on a Conference Tree, a PMS, a CBMBBS, or a CBBS, give this one a call even long distance. It'll be worth it.

CPBB02970 (402) 292-9598
OACPMUG BBS 300 bps
Omaha, Nebraska 8/1/N
Password Required RCP/M RBBS

Features: CP/M, downloading, messaging, userlog.
Special features: Downloadable programs for CP/M-based computers.
Special interest: CP/M.
Notice: This may not be a 24-hour system; no hours posted. New users will only have access to the RBBS; no information was available about gaining access to the downloading section.
Comments: OACPMUG stands for Omaha Area CP/M Users' Group. There were fewer than 10 messages on this system when I called it. Since there was absolutely no information on how a caller may gain access to the downloading section, long-distance callers can bypass this one.

Nevada (702)

CPBB02990   (702) 878-9106
PMS—Century 23   300 bps
Las Vegas, Nevada   7/1/E or 8/1/N
Open   PMS

Features: BBS list, feedback, messaging, parameters, system information, text files, time/duration.
Special features: Text files on various topics.
Comments: A general-interest message system.

CPBB03000   (702) 733-9488
SNACC AMIS   300 bps
Las Vegas, Nevada   7/1/E or 8/1/N
Open   AMIS

Features: Chat, downloading, messaging, parameters, time/duration, userlog.
Special features: Downloadable programs for Atari home computers.
Special interests: Atari home computers.
Comments: SNACC stands for Southern Nevada Atari Computer Club. This is a general-interest message system with a private section for SNACC members.

New Hampshire (603)

CPBB03010   (603) 888-6999
Access-80   300 bps
Nashua, New Hampshire   8/1/N
Password Required   Access-80

Features: Messaging, text files, time/duration.
Special features: Downloadable programs for Apple, Atari, Color Computer, DEC, IBM, Osborne, Sinclair, TRS-80 I/II/III/IV, Xerox computers.

Special interests: Multiple message boards. Categories include Amateur Radio, Apple, Atari, Color Computer, DEC, Heath, IBM PC, Osborne, Personal Finance, Sinclair, TRS-80 I/II/III/IV, Women & Computers, Xerox.
Notice: This system solicits a fee.
Comments: It took me a while to catch onto this system's format, until I exited the signon bulletins, and then discovered that it is aping CompuServe! Now, I automatically have a problem with imitators such as this. You see, I once subscribed to a service that aped The Source—and about all my money bought for me was an account number. Virtually nothing else. The system contained zip, zilch, zero, nada, nil, nothing. This is not to say that *this* system is a rip-off—just to caution you to the fact that a system with 100 menus does not necessarily mean there is any information worth your money behind them.

CPBB03020
Magazine-80
Peterborough, New Hampshire
Open

(603) 924-7920
300 bps
7/1/E
Connection-80

Features: Catalog, chat, downloading, feedback, messaging, parameters, text files, time/duration, userlog.
Special features: Downloadable programs for TRS-80 Model I and III computers; text files contain original fiction, movie & software reviews, and TRS-80 information from Captain-80.
Special interests: Online fiction, TRS-80 computers.
Notice: While there is no official time limit, the sysop hopes you will keep your sessions to 20 minutes maximum.
Comments: "This system is running on a 48K TRS-80 Mod I (paid for in blood)," is what you will see when you log on to this special system. This is Magazine-80, up since 1980 and one of the oldest active BBSs in the New Hampshire area. The message base is quite active and you're bound to find several messages of praise for the sysop—all of them well deserved. Under ⟨B⟩*ulletins*, you will find the Magazine Section. It had 32 items when I accessed it, with a variety of stories (for children and general audiences), movie and

software reviews, and several Captain-80 columns. This is quite an imaginative system and definitely worth a long-distance call.

CPBB03030 (603) 888-4488
C/80 & RCP/M 300 bps
Nashua, New Hampshire 8/1/N
Open C/80

Features: CP/M, downloading, messaging, parameters, userlog.
Special features: Downloadable programs for CP/M-based computers.
Special interests: CP/M.
Comments: A typical RCP/M system.

New Jersey (201)

CPBB03050 (201) 291-8319
KUGNJ BBS 300/1200 bps
Atlantic Highlands, New Jersey 8/1/N
Password Required RCP/M RBBS

Features: CP/M, downloading, messaging, userlog.
Special features: Downloadable programs for Kaypro computers.
Special interests: Kaypro computers.
Notice: To logon this system as a first-time user, type **KUGNJ1** as the password.
Comments: There weren't many programs on this system when I called it, but it did have an enthusiastic user base and a friendly sysop. It's a good system to call if you have a Kaypro.

CPBB03060 (201) 528-6623
Forum-80 300 bps
Brielle, New Jersey 7/2/N
Open Forum-80

Features: BBS list, downloading, feedback, messaging, system information, userlog.

Special features: Downloadable programs for TRS-80 Model I and III computers.
Notice: This is a Forum-80 that does not adhere to either the time-wasting signon bulletins nor the probationary branding of new users.
Comments: In the land of Uncle Floyd there lies a Forum-80 that is not hostile to new users. For that alone, it deserves your call.

CPBB03070 (201) 790-6795
Photo-80 300/1200 bps
Haledon, New Jersey 7/1/E
Open Connection-80

Features: BBS list, chat, downloading, feedback, messaging, parameters, system information, time/duration, userlog.
Special features: Downloadable Orchestra 80/85/90 programs.
Special interests: Orchestra 80/85/90, photography.
Comments: A general-interest message system that could use quite a few callers interested in photography.

CPBB03080 (201) 486-2956
CFONJ 300/1200 bps
Linden, New Jersey 8/1/N
Password Required TBBS

Features: Downloading, feedback, mail, messaging, parameters, system information, time/duration.
Special features: Unspecified downloadable programs.
Special interests: Multiple message boards. Categories include Chatter, Chess, For Sale, Hardware, Help!, Languages, System Bulletins.
Notice: There is a 30-minute time limit on this system. Access to the downloading section is restricted to registered password holders. Read New User Registration for details.
Comments: CFONJ stands for Computer Forum of New Jersey. The sysop of this system is very dedicated and will be placing a large library of TRS-80 programs online for downloading. The system is

running on a 10-megabyte hard disk, so that should give you an idea of what a wealth of material will be available. This could turn out to be one of the foremost TBBSs in the nation; well worth a long-distance call.

CPBB03090 (201) 494-3649
TBBS 300 bps
Metuchen, New Jersey 8/1/N
Password Required TBBS

Features: BBS list, chat, downloading, feedback, mail, messaging, parameters, system information, text files, time/duration.
Special features: Downloadable programs for Apple, Atari, Color Computer, Commodore-64, TRS-80 Model I and III, VIC-20 computers, text files on various topics.
Special interests: Multiple message boards. Categories include Apple, Atari, Commodore/VIC, CompuServe, For Sale, Issues, Jokes/Humor, Ham Radio, TBBS, TRS-80/CoCo, Wanted To Buy.
Notice: This system has a 30-minute time limit. A registered password is required to access all system features.
Comments: This is a very active system with a lot to offer. Worth a long-distance call.

CPBB03100 (201) 783-6976
NYC IBMPCUG 300/1200 bps
Montclair, New Jersey 7/1/E
Open Hostcomm

Features: Chat, downloading.
Special features: Downloadable programs for the IBM PC.
Special interests: IBM PC.
Notice: A password may be needed by the time you read this.
Comments: This is run by the New York City IBM PC User's Group and features nine levels of menus for downloadable programs representing a variety of applications. At the time I called this system, I was allowed free access to six of the nine menus; that's quite a

few more than most Hostcomm systems will permit a first-time caller. For IBM PC owners, this is the cream of the crop and well worth a long-distance call.

CPBB03110   (201) 249-0691
CP/M-Net™ East   300/1200 bps
New Brunswick, New Jersey   8/1/N
Password Required   RCP/M RBBS

Features: CP/M, downloading, messaging.
Special features: Downloadable programs for CP/M-based computers.
Special interests: CP/M.
Comments: Although there weren't many messages on this system when I called it, there were plenty of downloadable programs.

CPBB03120   (201) 572-0617
Limericks BBS   300 bps
New Brunswick, New Jersey   8/1/N
Open   CoCo Board

Features: Chat, feedback, graphics, messaging, parameters, system information, userlog.
Special features: Online graphics for the Color Computer.
Special interests: Limericks, trivia, quotations.
Notice: To view online graphics, you must be using a Color Computer and a terminal program such as Colorcom/E.
Comments: This is a painfully slow system. On the other hand, it offers some hilarious limericks, intriguing trivia, and a wide variety of quotations. This system is only worth a long-distance call to diehard fans of limericks, trivia, and/or quotations.

CPBB03130 (201) 667-2504
Connection-80 300 bps
Nutley, New Jersey 7/1/E
Open Connection-80

Features: Chat, downloading, feedback, messaging, parameters, system information, time/duration, userlog.
Special features: Downloadable programs for the Color Computer, TRS-80 Model I and III computers.
Comments: A general-interest message system.

CPBB03140 (201) 775-8705
SHUG BBS 300/1200 bps
Ocean, New Jersey 8/1/N
Open HBBS

Features: Downloading, messaging, text files.
Special features: Downloadable programs for Heath/Zenith computers, text files on various topics.
Special interests: Heath/Zenith computers.
Comments: SHUG stands for Shore Heath User's Group. If you are an owner or a user of a Heath/Zenith computer, this is one of but a few systems you can call to meet other owners.

CPBB03150 (201) 627-5151
Conference Tree 300 bps
Rockaway, New Jersey 7/1/E
Open Conference Tree

Features: Conferencing.
Comments: This tree has its moments—but it can use more of them. It seems that there will be a flurry of new messages then nothing. Add a message and help make this system worth a long-distance call.

CPBB03160 (201) 467-1303
Oriental Express 300 bps
Short Hills, New Jersey 8/1/N
Password Required Greene Machine/RATS

Features: BBS list, chat, downloading, feedback, mail, messaging, system information, time, userlog.
Special features: Unspecified downloadable programs.
Notice: A registered password is required to access all system sections.
Comments: Choo! Choo! The Oriental Express's ads for itself, posted on other BBSs, featured an imaginative graphic of a locomotive. This system uses a modified version of Greene Machine and RATS and looks it: There were very few public messages on the system when I called it.

CPBB03170 (201) 694-7425
Ed Gelb's Data Base 300/1200 bps
Wayne, New Jersey 8/1/N
Open HBBS

Features: Downloading, messaging, text files, userlog.
Special features: Downloadable programs for various computers; text files on various topics.
Special interests: Multiple message bases. Categories include Games, Real Estate, Used Equipment.
Comments: Although this system offers fewer commands than most other systems, it is one of the busiest systems in the nation. Why? Simply because the sysop is attempting to compile an up-to-date worldwide listing of all BBSs. Even in electronic form, the list is constantly filled with disconnected or erroneous numbers. Still, people from all over the country and the world dial into this system to download the lists. You should, however, be warned about two things: (1) some of the lists are quite long and all of them contain excess text at the beginning, and (2) if you lose your connection during a download of a list, you will have to start from the beginning. Is it worth a long-distance call? If you, quite literally, can afford up to an hour of phone costs, certainly. Remember, though,

it is only in your imagination if you hear an author's voice in one ear whispering, "I told you so. . ."

New Jersey (609)

CPBB03190   (609) 261-5498
RATS   300 bps
Mt. Holly, New Jersey   8/1/N
Open   RATS

Features: Chat, conferencing, downloading, feedback, mail, messaging, system information, text files, time/duration, userlog.
Special features: Conferencing on various topics; downloadable programs for TRS-80 Model I and III computers; text files on various topics.
Notice: This system was due to be upgraded, so the comments below may be inapplicable.
Comments: RATS stands for Remote Access Terminal System. It may as well stand for the rodent because this system was a beast to use. Although it had 8/1/N protocol, my terminal went into apoplexy trying to communicate with it. The message base was small and stale when I called, although the conference section, particularly the sysop's plans for his next BBS, provided lively reading. His plans sounded quite ambitious, so you may be in for a treat in calling his new system at the above phone number.

CPBB03200   (609) 894-4366
N2EHM BBS   300/1200 bps
Pemberton, New Jersey   7/1/E
Open   HBBS

Features: BBS list, downloading, feedback, messaging, text files.
Special features: Unspecified downloadable programs; text files on Ham radio topics.
Special interests: Ham radio.

Comments: This is an excruciatingly slow system at 300 bps and may not be much better at 1200 bps. Even if you are a Ham radio enthusiast, you could do better by radio than data. If you must use data, though, you'll find plenty of other Hams here.

CPBB03210 (609) 468-3844
CoCoMat 300 bps
Wenonah, New Jersey 8/1/N
Open Original

Features: Chat, downloading, feedback, messaging.
Special features: Downloadable programs for the Color Computer.
Special interests: Color Computer.
Comments: This is a simple system, primarily of interest to local callers who own CoCos. The system could use some public-domain programs for its downloading section. If you have any to share, give this system a call. The sysop is a very amiable fellow.

New Mexico

To the best of my knowledge, there has never been a BBS in New Mexico.

New York (212)

CPBB03240 (212) 799-4649
AstroCom 300 bps
New York, New York 7/1/E
Password Required TCBBS

Features: Chat, downloading, messages, system information, text files, time/duration.
Special features: Unspecified downloadable programs, unspecified text files.

Special interests: Multiple message boards. Categories include Apple, Astronomy/Science-Fiction, Atari, BBSs, Commodore, Dating, For Sale/Wanted, Games, General, IBM PC, Jokes, Movies, Music, Restaurant.
Notice: This system solicits a subscription fee for full system access.
Comments: An interesting system that is designed as a sort of electronic city. The multiple message boards listed above are categories only. The actual name of the IBM PC board, for instance, is The Charlie Chaplin Cinema; the Atari board is called Uncle Nolan's Atari Cafe. This system is formatted in 40 columns and sends plenty of linefeeds, so beware if you use a printing terminal or plan to capture and print your session. This system would get a long-distance call recommendation from me except for the fact that you cannot retrieve individual (or a string of individual) messages; only forward or reverse multiple retrievals are allowed. In a word: Ugh.

CPBB03250 (212) 490-1146
Bull-PC 300 bps
New York, New York 8/1/N
Open Original

Features: Chat, downloading, feedback, messaging, parameters, time/duration.
Special features: Downloadable programs for the IBM PC.
Special interests: IBM PC.
Comments: Interested in IBM PCs? Give this system a call. There are plenty of messages about different aspects of using the IBM PC and over 50 downloadable programs. This system is fast and worth long-distance call.

CPBB03260 (212) 541-5975
MMMMMM #2 300/1200 bps
New York, New York 8/1/N
Questionnaire/Password Required MMMMMM

Features: BBS list, chat, feedback, mail, matchmaking, messaging, system information, time/duration.

Special features: Matchmaking.
Comments: One of the fastest matchmaking systems in the nation, with close to 1000 callers in the database. As usual, Cupid got in his two cents: I was matched to a woman who stated in an early question that she was "married but available," then stated in a later question that she thought "both should be faithful" in a relationship!

CPBB03270 (212) 512-2488
PMS—McGraw-Hill Book Company 300 bps
New York, New York 7/1/E or 8/1/N
Open PMS

Features: BBS list, catalog, feedback, messaging, parameters, time/duration.
Special features: McGraw-Hill Book Company's Electronic Bookshelf™, a catalog of over 100 McGraw-Hill books about computers and electronics. If you have a credit card, you can order a book online. Type **F** to enter the catalog.
Notice: This is a *part-time* system. Its operating hours are Mon–Thurs 6 PM–8 AM and Fri 6 PM–Mon 8 AM *Eastern Time.*
Comments: Please note, first of all, that this system is *not* run by the McGraw-Hill Bookstore. This is one of the most active systems in the NYC area. It has evolved into more of a mail system—with callers leaving private messages for one another—than a general-interest message system. The Electronic Bookshelf is in itself interesting reading, and you can order any book with your credit card. This is the only NYC system I frequent, and I can be reached there via messages (please make them private).

CPBB03280 (212) 543-9033
Stewart/Finnco On-Line 300 bps
New York, New York 7/1/E
Open Original

Features: Demonstration, mail, text files.
Special features: Online demonstration of the Stewart/Finnco Stock/Option Databank (CPBN00875, page 162).

Comments: If you want to see what your money will buy you before signing up for the Stewart/Finnco Databank, this is the system to call. It's free and it's formatted for a 40-column screen.

CPBB03290 (212) 986-1660
Tickerscreen 300 bps
New York, New York 7/1/E
Open Connection-80

Features: Catalog, chat, feedback, mail, messaging, parameters, system information, text files, time/duration.
Special features: Online demonstration of Tickerscreen stock market system, text files on various financial-related topics.
Notice: This is a *part-time* system. Its operating hours are Mon–Thurs 6 PM–8 AM *Eastern Time* and Fri 6 PM–Mon 8 AM *Eastern Time*. This system also has local access lines in the (516) and (914) area codes. Dial (516)794-1707 or (914)997-1277.
Comments: This system is run by Max Ule and Company. If you have an interest in using your microcomputer to help you keep up with the stock market, this is a system you must call. It is filled with information for those interested in maintaining their financial portfolios. Worth a long-distance call.

CPBB03300 (212) 441-3755
Rainbow Connection #1 300 bps
Woodland Hills, New York 8/1/N
Password Required TBBS

Features: BBS list, catalog, downloading, mail, messaging, parameters, system information, text files, time/duration, userlog.
Special features: Downloadable programs for Apple, Atari, Color Computer, Commodore-64, IBM PC, TI-99/4A, TRS-80 Model I, III, and 100 computers; text files on various topics.
Special interests: Color Computer. Multiple message boards. Categories include Apple, Atari, Color Computer, Commodore/VIC, Dealer Ads, General, Ham/Scanners, IBM PC, Magazines/Comics, Sports, TI/99, TRS-80 Model I/III, TRS-80 Model 100, Want Ads.

Notice: There is a 30-minute time limit on this system. There are actually three systems running at this location; see two listings following for phone numbers.

Comments: This system just missed being classified as a Local-Area Service in this edition of *The Computer Phone Book*. It is the sysop's plans, however, to provide a multiuser system. By the time you read this, his plans should be implemented and additions to the system will include DFT; Rainbow Connection #4; and sections for Adventurers, Arcade Games, Astrology/Astronomy, Auto Care, Barter, Entertainment, Graphics, Hobby, Investors, Magazines, Programming, Shop-at-Home, and Women. This system is the handiwork of its founder, Bob Rosen, and a gaggle of co-sysops. Definitely worth a long-distance call.

CPBB03301   (212) 441-3766
Rainbow Connection #2   300 bps
Woodland Hills, New York   8/1/N
Password Required   TBBS

Notice: See above listing for details. A multiplexor is used to switch callers to whichever one of the three systems is not currently in use; in other words, you may not get RC #2 by calling this number. But that's the chance you take.

CPBB03302   (212) 441-5719
Rainbow Connection #3   300 bps
Woodland Hills, New York   8/1/N
Password Required   TBBS

Notice: See CPBB03300 and CPBB03301 for details.

New York (516)

CPBB03310   (516) 561-6590
LICA   300 bps
Bethpage, New York   8/1/N
Open   CBBS

Features: BBS list, downloading, feedback, messaging, polling, parameters, time/duration.
Special features: Instapoll®.
Comments: LICA stands for Long Island Computer Association. This system has the largest message base of any BBS in the nation—over 600 messages online at any one time. They go back over a year and a good deal of them should be deleted, but there is loads of interesting reading here. This system is worth a long-distance call if you just want to sit at your terminal and wade through messages.

CPBB03320   (516) 588-5836
Connection-80 #1   300 bps
Centereach, New York   7/1/E
Open   Connection-80

Features: Chat, downloading, feedback, messaging, parameters, system information, time/duration.
Special features: Downloadable programs for the Color Computer, TRS-80 Model I and III computers.
Comments: This is the headquarters system of Connection-80. It has quite a selection of downloadable programs and a general-interest message base.

CPBB03330 (516) 536-3510
South Shore Connection-80 300/1200 bps
Oceanside, New York 7/1/E
Open Connection-80

Features: BBS list, chat, downloading, feedback, games, messaging, parameters, system information, time/duration, userlog.

Special features: Downloadable programs for TRS-80 Model I and III computers; games include Football, Gargoyle Castle Adventure, Ice World Adventure, Kingdom Adventure, Space Empire, Star Trek.

Notice: There is a 20-minute time limit in the games section of this system; once you enter the game section you cannot return to the message base. A registered password is required to access the downloading section.

Comments: An active general-interest message system with a friendly sysop.

CPBB03340 (516) 924-8115
IBM/LNW User Groups 300/1200 bps
Yaphank, New York 8/1/N
Open TBBS

Features: Catalog, chat, downloading, feedback, mail, messaging, parameters, system information, text files, time/duration.

Special features: Downloadable programs for IBM and LNW computers.

Special interests: Multiple message boards. Categories include Hires 1,2,3; IBM PC; LNW; Swap & Shop.

Comments: If you are an LNW owner, this is another of a handful of systems designed for your enjoyment. It seems that not too many LNW owners have modems since this system had only a few downloadable programs and messages. Give it a try.

New York (518)

CPBB03350   (518) 346-3596
Access-80   300 bps
Schenectady, New York   8/1/N
Password Required   Access-80

Features: Chat, downloading, mail, messaging, parameters, system information, text files, time/duration, userlog.
Special features: Unspecified downloadable programs; text files on various topics.
Special interests: Multiple message boards. Categories include Arcades, Color Computer, Heath, IBM, Osborne, TI, Timex-Sinclair, TRS-80 Model I/II/III/IV/12/16, VIC/64, Women.
Notice: This system solicits a fee for full access.
Comments: Another Access-80 system, aping CompuServe. I would very carefully check out this system before sending in money for a subscription. I searched the downloadable program database for all available programs; the system said there were "81 entries" then contradicted itself and said there were no programs to list! You will have to spend about 5 minutes online when you first call to go through a tedious and nonsensical screening process before you are allowed on the system. Once on you won't be able to see much until you cough up and send in some dough. Caveat emptor and long-distance callers can definitely skip this one.

New York (607)

CPBB03370   (607) 797-6416
SJBBS   300 bps
Johnson City, New York   8/1/N
Open   RCP/M RBBS

Features: CP/M, downloading, messaging, userlog.
Special features: Downloadable programs for CP/M-based computers.

Special interest: CP/M.
Comments: A typical RCP/M system.

CPBB03380 (607) 754-2910
Vestal BBS 300 bps
Vestal, New York 8/1/N
Password Required RCP/M RBBS

Features: CP/M, downloading, feedback, messaging.
Special features: Downloadable programs for CP/M-based computers.
Special interests: CP/M.
Notice: A registered password is required to access the downloading section.
Comments: There were only nine messages on the RBBS when I called. Since downloading is restricted, long-distance callers can skip this one.

New York (914)

CPBB03400 (914) 297-0665
Bullet-80 300/1200 bps
Poughkeepsie, New York 8/1/N
Open Bullet-80

Features: BBS list, catalog, chat, downloading, feedback, messaging, parameters, system information, time/duration, userlog.
Special features: Downloadable programs for TRS-80 Model I and III computers.
Comments: A general-interest message system with quite a few downloadable programs.

North Carolina (704)

CPBB03450 (704) 364-5245
ABBS 300 bps
Charlotte, North Carolina 7/1/E
Open ABBS

Features: Downloading, messaging, parameters, text files, time/duration.
Special features: Downloadable programs for the Apple II+ computer; text files on various topics.
Special interests: Charlotte Apple Computer Club.
Notice: There is a 30-minute time limit on this system.
Comments: There weren't many messages on this system when I called it. There were rumors that 1200 bps service may be added and that the system software also might be changed.

CPBB03460 (704) 365-4311
PC-BBS™ 300 bps
Charlotte, North Carolina 7/1/E
Password Required Original

Features: Chat, downloading, mail, messaging, time/duration.
Special interests: Downloadable programs for Apple II+, Commodore-64, CP/M, IBM, and TRS-80 computers.
Special interests: Multiple message boards. Categories include Apple, Apple //e, CPM, General, IBM PC, Q/A, TRS-80, VIC/PET/CBM.
Notice: A registered password is required to post messages.
Comments: This is a very nice system with very active message bases. The system's commands aren't immediately clear, but if you think of Net-Work software, things will become apparent to you. There are plenty of messages and plenty of downloads, making this system worth a long-distance call.

North Carolina (919)

CPBB03470 (919) 362-0676
Dial-Your-Match #20 300 bps
Cary, North Carolina 7/1/E
Questionnaire/Password Required DYM

Features: BBS list, chat, feedback, mail, matchmaking, messaging, parameters, time/duration.
Special features: Matchmaking.
Notice: Even to browse a Dial-Your-Match system, you must first fill out a questionnaire. All of your answers will be public, available to other system users. Depending on the individual sysop (called a Matchmaker), the questions could be quite explicit. This is a sexually oriented system.
Comments: This system has the standard DYM questionnaire, that is, pretty innocuous. Even with that—or because of it—my highest match was 64 percent to a woman 26 to 30 years old.

CPBB03480 (919) 758-5261
Sangarnet™ 300 bps
Greenville, North Carolina 7/1/E
Open Superhost

Features: Catalog, chat, downloading, feedback, messaging, text files, time/duration.
Special features: Downloadable programs for TRS-80 Model I and III.
Notice: There is a 10-minute time limit on this system for first-time callers.
Comments: This is quite a nice little system. It's faster than Bullet-80, Connection-80, and Forum-80 and has a command structure that users of those systems will feel at home with. The sysop should be proud of this system. Worth a long-distance call.

CPBB03490 (919) 353-0610
TBBS 300 bps
Jacksonville, North Carolina 8/1/N
Password Required TBBS

Features: Chat, downloading, mail, messaging, parameters, system information, time/duration, userlog.
Special features: Broadcasting-related downloadable programs for TRS-80 Model I and III computers.
Special interests: Radio broadcasting.
Notice: There is a 40-minute time limit on this system.
Comments: If you have an interest in or are employed by the radio broadcasting industry, this system is dedicated to the exchange of ideas and opinions in that field.

North Dakota

The only operating BBS in the entire state of North Dakota is no longer online. Anyone care to start a new system?

Ohio (216)

CPBB03510 (216) 745-7855
Akron Digital Group 300 bps
Akron, Ohio 7/1/E
Open ABBS

Features: BBS list, messaging, parameters, text files, time/duration.
Special features: Text files on various topics.
Comments: Believe it or not, this system had messages dating back to 1979 on it when I called. I think it could use some more callers.

CPBB03520 (216) 645-0827
Commnet-80 300/1200 bps
Akron, Ohio 8/1/N
Open Commnet-80

Features: BBS list, chat, downloading, feedback, games, messaging, system information, time/duration, userlog.
Special features: Downloadable programs for TRS-80 Model I and III computers; games include CIA, Dogstar, Isle.
Notice: There is a 30-minute time limit in the games section.
Comments: A general-interest message system.

CPBB03530 (216) 867-7463
PMS—RAUG 300 bps
Akron, Ohio 7/1/E
Open PMS

Features: BBS list, downloading, feedback, messaging, parameters, system information, text files, time/duration.
Special features: ALTernate message base; downloadable programs for the Apple II+ computer; text files on various topics.
Comments: RAUG stands for Rubber Apple User's Group. This system has 16 megabytes of online storage; that means a lot of downloadable programs and text files to read. The sysop is friendly and his system is worth a long-distance call.

CPBB03540 (216) 724-2125
TBBS 300 bps
Akron, Ohio 8/1/N
Open TBBS

Features: Chat, downloading, feedback, mail, messaging, parameters, text files, time/duration, userlog.
Special features: Downloadable programs for TRS-80 computers.
Special interests: Multiple message boards. Categories include Apple, Atari, Commodore, Max-80, TRS-80.

Notice: There is a 30-minute time limit on this system.
Comments: A general-interest message system.

CPBB03550   (216) 932-9845
Dial-Your-Match #34   300 bps
Cleveland, Ohio   7/1/E
Questionnaire/Password Required   DYM

Features: BBS list, chat, feedback, mail, matchmaking, messaging, parameters, system information, text files, time/duration, userlog.
Special features: Matchmaking, text files on various topics.
Special interests: Jokes and X-rated boards.
Notice: This system requires your full name, address, and phone number for password validation. Even to browse a Dial-Your-Match system, you must first fill out a questionnaire. All of your answers will be public, available to other system users. This is a sexually oriented system.
Comments: My highest match was 66 percent to two women who gave identical answers to the questionnaire. That is a first in my experience and, if you ask me, cause for suspicion. Ah, but Cupid gets his on this system in the form of a text file called Oscar's Guide to DYMs. If you call this system you must read that file.

CPBB03560   (216) 875-4582
Micro-Com   300 bps
Louisville, Ohio   7/1/E
Password Required   Micro-Com

Features: BBS list, chat, mail, messaging, system information, text files, userlog.
Special features: Unspecified text files.
Notice: A registered password is required for full system access.
Comments: Of local interest only.

CPBB03570 (216) 832-8392
PMS 300 bps
Massillon, Ohio 7/1/E or 8/1/N
Open PMS

Features: BBS list, feedback, messaging, parameters, system information, text files, time/duration.
Special features: Text files on various topics.
Comments: A general-interest message system.

CPBB03580 (216) 788-7910
CoCo-Nut Tree (Color-80 #17) 300 bps
Youngstown, Ohio 8/1/N
Open Color-80

Features: BBS list, catalog, chat, downloading, feedback, messaging, parameters, text files, time/duration.
Special features: Downloadable programs for the Color Computer.
Special interests: Color Computer.
Notice: To download programs, you must be using a Color Computer and a terminal program such as Colorcom/E.
Comments: This system didn't seem to be as active as other Color-80s when I called it. Give it a ring and post some messages.

Ohio (419)

CPBB03600 (419) 729-4221
Independent BBS 300 bps
Toledo, Ohio 8/1/E
Password Required Original

Features: BBS list, chat, downloading, feedback, messaging, parameters, text files, userlog.
Special features: Unspecified downloadable programs; text files on various topics.

Comments: What a pleasant surprise to find such a nice system in Ohio—and with original software, too. Although it is a bit on the slow side, this system is worth a long-distance call.

Ohio (513)

CPBB03620 (513) 522-8227
CINTUG 300 bps
Cincinnati, Ohio 8/1/N
Password Required TBBS

Features: Downloading, feedback, mail, messaging, parameters, system information, time/duration.
Special features: Downloadable programs for the Color Computer, TRS-80 Model I and III computers.
Special interests: Message boards for Color Computer and Games.
Comments: This is a very verbose TBBS system. It has, in fact, the longest-winded menu headers and selection descriptions of any BBS I've been on. Apparently, telecommunications is so new to Cincinnati that everything has to be spelled out. If you've had problems using TBBSs, you should give this system a call. The handholding is so tight that you'll never get lost in the system (although your hand may turn blue in the process).

CPBB03630 (513) 631-3332
Komputer Klassified® 300 bps
Cincinnati, Ohio 8/1/N
Password Required TBBS

Features: Catalog, chat, downloading, mail, messaging, parameters, system information, text files, time/duration, userlog.
Special features: Downloadable programs for Apple, Atari, IBM, TRS-80 Model I and II, VIC-20 computers.
Special interests: Multiple message boards. Categories include Apple, Atari, Games, General, IBM, Model IV, Swap, TRS-80, VIC.
Comments: A general-interest message system.

CPBB03640   (513) 277-3019
The Choyce BBS   300 bps
Dayton, Ohio   8/1/N
Password Required   Trade-80

Features: BBS list, chat, downloading, feedback, messaging, parameters, system information, userlog.

Special features: Downloadable programs for Apple, Atari, CP/M, IBM. Northstar, Pocket Computer, TRS-80 Model I and II, and VIC-20 computers.

Comments: There are over 100 downloadable programs on this system. It is up to you, though, as to whether or not you want to call this system long-distance and wrestle with the Trade-80 software.

CPBB03650   (513) 435-5201
Drake RCP/M RBBS   PMMI
West Carrollton, Ohio   8/1/N
Password Required   RCP/M RBBS

Features: CP/M, downloading, feedback, messaging, parameters.
Special features: Downloadable programs for CP/M-based computers.
Special interests: CP/M.
Comments: What is the name of Digital Research's standard debugger? is the question you must answer to get into this system. If you can't answer it, you are out of luck.

Oklahoma (405)

CPBB03680   (405) 722-6809
Flexnet   300 bps
Oklahoma City, Oklahoma   8/1/N
Open   Unknown

Features: Chat, downloading, messaging, parameters, text files.
Special features: Downloadable programs for the Color Computer; text files on Color Computer-related topics.

Special interests: Color Computer.

Comments: I do *not* recommend that you call this system as your first encounter with a BBS because this is not a typical BBS; it resembles a CP/M downloading system on which all of the text files have to be LISTed. While this in itself is easy enough, the files are not arranged in an easy-to-find logical order. Although I've called hundreds of systems, I still had some problems in discovering all of the hiding places where text files were stashed in this system. All the same, this system provides a large variety of downloadable programs that I haven't seen anywhere else for the CoCo. Worth a long-distance call for CoCo owners.

CPBB03690   (405) 949-2815
Mid-America Data   300 bps
Oklahoma City, Oklahoma   8/1/N
Open   Unknown

Features: Catalog, mail.
Special features: Online ordering of computer-related merchandise.
Comments: Any system that opens with, "PLEASE HAVE PATIENCE. This system was built from a kit in 1976. It is old, tired, and slow," is more frank than most! If you're looking for computer supplies or just want to compare prices, give this system a call.

CPBB03700   (405) 636-0218
Software Safaris   300 bps
South Oklahoma City, Oklahoma   7/1/E or 8/1/N
Open   AMIS

Features: BBS list, chat, downloading, messaging, parameters, text files, time/duration.
Special features: Downloadable programs for Atari home computers.
Special interests: Atari home computers.
Comments: Another Atari system; nothing more or less.

Oklahoma (918)

CPBB03730 (918) 749-0059
TBBS 300 bps
Tulsa, Oklahoma 8/1/N
Password Required TBBS

Features: BBS list, chat, downloading, mail, messaging, parameters, system information, time/duration.
Special features: Downloadable programs for the VIC-20 computer.
Special interests: Multiple message boards. Categories include Apple, Atari, Color Computer, CP/M, Dear Gabby, General, IBM, Investments, Music, Photography, Politics, TRS-80 Model I/III, X-rated.
Notice: There is a 25-minute time limit on this system. There is an X-rated section on this system. A registered password is required to access all system sections.
Comments: This system has a friendly atmosphere and, aside from the X-rated section, is a general-interest message system.

CPBB03740 (918) 438-3363
T.I.E. 300 bps
Tulsa, Oklahoma 8/1/N
Password Required TBBS

Features: Chat, downloading, feedback, mail, messaging, parameters, time/duration.
Special features: Downloadable programs for Apple, Color Computer, IBM, TRS-80 Model I and III, Model 100 and VIC-20 computers.
Special interests: Multiple message boards. Categories include Apple, Color Computer, General, For Sale, IBM, TRS-80 Model I/III, TRS-80 Model 100, VIC-20.
Notice: There is a 30-minute time limit on this system.
Comments: Aside from serving the above computers, if you own a VIC-20, this system is of particular interest. There is a sub-BBS

that is totally dedicated to the VIC-20 and features quite a few downloadable programs. This system has been known to get very busy from VIC-20 owners calling it from all across the country. It's worth the long-distance charges.

Oregon (503)

CPBB03760   (503) 641-7276
RCP/M   300 bps
Beaverton, Oregon   8/1/N
Open   RCP/M RBBS

Features: CP/M, downloading, messaging, time/duration.
Special features: Downloadable programs for CP/M-based computers.
Special interests: CP/M.
Notice: There is a 1-hour time limit per day per person on this system.
Comments: A typical RCP/M system.

CPBB03770   (503) 883-3735
Bullet-80   300/1200 bps
Klamath Falls, Oregon   8/1/N
Open   Bullet-80

Features: BBS list, catalog, chat, downloading, games, feedback, messaging, parameters, system information, time/duration.
Special features: Downloadable programs for TRS-80 Model I and III computers; games include CIA, Dogstar, Thunder.
Comments: A general-interest message system.

CPBB03780   (503) 535-6883
Forum-80   300/1200 bps
Medford, Oregon   8/1/N
Probationary   Forum-80

Features: BBS list, downloading, feedback, messaging, parameters, system information.

Special features: Unspecified downloadable programs.
Notice: Forum-80 has a policy of displaying a long (series of) signon bulletin(s) that you cannot bypass and labeling all new users as "probationary," requiring the sysop to approve any messages new users post before other users may read them (if at all).
Comments: When I called this system there were four slow minutes of signon bulletins—all of them unwanted, all of them unnecessary. Long-distance callers can skip this one, and local callers should have a high tolerance.

CPBB03790   (503) 761-6345
Bit Bucket BBS   300 bps
Portland, Oregon   8/1/N
Password Required   Original

Features: BBS list, messaging, system information, text files, time/duration, userlog.
Special features: Text files on various topics.
Comments: An interesting system, albeit on the slow side. It has a good message editor, a lot of text files, and plenty of messages on different topics. It is worth a long-distance call.

CPBB03800   (503) 245-2536
PMS   300 bps
Portland, Oregon   7/1/E or 8/1/N
Open   PMS

Features: BBS list, feedback, messaging, parameters, system information, text files, time/duration.
Special features: Text files on various topics.
Comments: As with all PMSs, the worth of the system is based on the messages posted by its users. In general, there are always a variety of interesting messages on board a PMS, and this one is no exception. There are also quite a few text files of interest.

CPBB03810 (503) 621-3193
RCP/M PMMI
Portland, Oregon 8/1/N
Open RCP/M BBS

Features: CP/M, downloading, messaging.
Special features: Downloadable programs for CP/M-based computers.
Special interests: C programming language, CP/M.
Comments: This system admits, and warns, up front that it is not designed for novice users but for experienced RCP/M callers. If you are a novice RCP/M user, you are advised to call elsewhere, and I agree. On the other hand, if you are a C hacker, this is a system you can call to download some programs of use to C explorers.

Pennsylvania (215)

CPBB03830 (215) 434-3998
Hermes-80 300 bps
Allentown, Pennsylvania 8/1/N
Password Required Unknown

Features: Chat, downloading, messaging, time/duration.
Special features: Unspecified downloadable programs.
Comments: This may or may not be an X-rated system. When I called it, there were several X-rated messages but no signon notice saying that the system itself was X-rated. If it isn't X-rated, the sysop should police the message base more carefully. If it is an X-rated system, be prepared.

CPBB03835 (215) 868-1230
Microline[sm] 300 bps
Bethlehem, Pennsylvania 8/1/N
Open Original

Features: Catalog, mail.
Special features: Online ordering of computer-related products.

Comments: This system is run by Microhouse, a supplier of computer hardware, software, firmware, and peripherals. This is another system on which you can shop using your credit card. Or you can use the system to compare prices.

CPBB03840   (215) 836-5116
RCP/M   300/1200 bps
Cheltenham, Pennsylvania   8/1/N
Open   RCP/M RBBS

Features: CP/M, downloading, feedback, messaging, time/duration.
Special features: Downloadable programs for Atari home computers.
Special interest: Atari home computers.
Comments: This system is both a surprise and a rarity—an RCP/M that caters to Atari owners. Worth a long-distance call to Atari owners.

CPBB03850   (215) 855-3809
Drucom   300 bps
North Wales, Pennsylvania   8/1/N
Password Required   Commnet-80

Features: BBS list, catalog, chat, downloading, feedback, games, messaging, parameters, system information, time/duration.
Special features: Unspecified downloadable programs; unspecified games.
Special interests: X-rated.
Notice: This is an X-rated system.
Comments: Not worth a long-distance call.

Pennsylvania (412)

CPBB03870 (412) 655-2652
Acenet 300 bps
Pittsburgh, Pennsylvania 7/1/E
Open Armudic

Features: BBS list, downloading, messaging, text files.
Special features: Downloadable programs for Atari home computers.
Special interests: Atari home computers.
Comments: This system would be of interest only to local callers.

Pennsylvania (717)

CPBB03880 (717) 774-6543
CAPATUG 300 bps
Camp Hill, Pennsylvania 8/1/N
Password Required TBBS

Features: BBS list, downloading, feedback, mail, messaging, parameters, system information, text files, time/duration, userlog.
Special features: Downloadable programs for TRS-80 Model I and III computers, text files on various topics.
Special interests: TRS-80 computers.
Notice: There is a 25-minute time limit on this system.
Comments: This is mainly a club system for TRS-80 owners. If you live in the area, give it a call and join.

Rhode Island (401)

CPBB03900   (401) 944-4689
RITUG BBS   300 bps
Cranston, Rhode Island   8/1/N
Open   Original

Features: Downloading, mail, messaging, userlog.
Special features: Unspecified downloadable programs.
Special interests: Apple, Color Computer, TRS-80 Model I and III computers.
Comments: This system claims to have 10 megabytes of downloadable programs. Not one program was available when I called it. Further, the system's software was overrun with bugs. By the time you read this, the system may be fixed—or offline.

CPBB03910   (401) 521-1998
AMIS   300/1200 bps
Providence, Rhode Island   7/1/E or 8/1/N
Open   AMIS

Features: Chat, downloading, feedback, messaging, parameters, system information, text files, time/duration.
Special features: Downloadable programs for Atari home computers, text files on various Atari-related topics.
Special interests: Atari home computers.
Comments: This is the fastest AMIS in existence, featuring one-touch commands. The downloading and messages sections were rather slim when I called it, and if they haven't filled by the time you read this, help fill them.

South Carolina (803)

CPBB03920   (803) 548-0900
RBBS   300 bps
Ft. Mill, South Carolina   7/1/E
Password Required   RCP/M RBBS

Features: Downloading, feedback, messaging, userlog.
Special features: Downloadable programs for CP/M-based, Osborne, and TRS-80 Model 100 computers.
Special interests: CP/M.
Comments: When I called this system, it was a virtual electronic ghost town. If you live in the area, give it a call and help bring it to life. Incidentally, this is the first RCP/M I've come across that is running on an Apple //e.

CPBB03930   (803) 884-8531
Mt. Pleasant-80   300 bps
Mt. Pleasant, South Carolina   8/1/N
Password Required   Greene Machine

Features: BBS list, chat, conferencing, downloading, feedback, mail, messaging, parameters, system information, text files, time/duration, userlog.
Special features: Unspecified downloadable programs, unspecified text files.
Notice: A registered password is required to access all system sections.
Comments: This is an OK system; there were a variety of interesting conferences taking place when I called. This system is scheduled to be running on a TRS-80 Model IV.

CPBB03940 (803) 279-5392
Forum-80 300/1200 bps
North Augusta, South Carolina 8/1/N
Open Forum-80

Features: BBS list, chat, downloading, feedback, messaging, parameters, userlog.
Special features: Downloadable programs for TRS-80 computers.
Comments: Unlike most Forum-80s, this one welcomes all callers with hospitality. Call this system and chat with the friendly, dedicated sysop, as well as upload a program or two.

CPBB03950 (803) 873-8544
Summerville-80 300 bps
Summerville, South Carolina 8/1/N
Password Required Greene Machine

Features: BBS list, chat, conferencing, downloading, mail, messaging, parameters, system information, text files, userlog.
Special features: Unspecified downloadable programs, unspecified text files.
Notice: A registered password is required to access all system sections.
Comments: For the short time that I was able to stay on this system, I got to see that it was quite active with a variety of messages on it. Long-distance callers should be warned that I had a difficult time in grabbing and holding this system's carrier signal. Apparently, the sysop needs to increase his modem carrier–loss detection delay. I was thrown off the system three times; I did not go back for a fourth round.

CPBB03960 (803) 871-3468
Tinbrain's BBS 300 bps
Summerville, South Carolina 8/1/N
Password Required TBBS

Features: Chat, mail, messaging, parameters, time/duration, userlog.
Special features: Message base for role-playing games.

Special interests: Role-playing games. Multiple message boards. Categories include Apple, Atari, Color Computer, Commodore, CP/M, Games, Ham Radio, IBM, Science-Fiction, Swap Shop, Timex-Sinclair, TRS-80 Model I/III.
Notice: There is a 30-minute time limit on this system.
Comments: This is a very good system, showing imagination, initiative, and supported by active users. Worth a long-distance call.

South Dakota

This is another state without a BBS systems.

Tennessee (615)

CPBB03980 (615) 842-6809
Bulletin/68 300 bps
Hinson, Tennessee 8/1/N
Open Bulletin/68

Features: Downloading, messaging, text files.
Special features: Downloadable programs for the Color Computer, text files on Color Computer-related topics.
Special interests: Color Computer.
Comments: This system has the worst phone line I encountered in calling any type of system; in fact, I had a better trans-Atlantic connection to England. It took five tries before I was able to stay on the system long enough to tour it—then I was dropped again. If you can get a good line, it's worth the call.

CPBB03990 (615) 847-8930
Forum-80 300 bps
Nashville, Tennessee 8/1/N
Probationary Forum-80

Features: BBS list, downloading, feedback, messaging, parameters, system information, userlog.

Special features: Downloadable programs for TRS-80 Model I and III computers.

Notice: This system solicits a fee for regular use. Forum-80 has a policy of displaying a long (series of) signon bulletin(s) that you cannot bypass and labeling all new users "probationary," requiring the sysop to approve any messages new users post before other users may read them (if at all).

Comments: With all of the time that is wasted by Forum-80s in displaying useless signon bulletins, I would think that sysops would be giving their callers a rebate on their phone costs rather than asking their users to be an accomplice in the act as this one is doing. Long-distance callers can skip this one. Local users should be insulted.

Tennessee (901)

CPBB04010 (901) 276-8196
Forum-80 300 bps
Memphis, Tennessee 8/1/N
Probationary Forum-80

Features: BBS list, downloading, feedback, messaging, parameters, system information, userlog.

Special features: Downloadable programs for TRS-80 Model I and III computers.

Notice: See previous listing, re: bulletins—this system does *not* solicit a fee.

Comments: This system needs public-domain programs for its downloading section. If you have any and are in the area, give the system a call and make some arrangements.

CPBB04020 (901) 743-0016
Microserve Information Service 300 bps
Memphis, Tennessee 8/1/N
Password Required Original

Features: BBS list, downloading, messaging, parameters, userlog.

Special features: Downloadable programs for TRS-80 Model I and III computers.

Special interests: Multiple message boards. Categories include All Others (computers), Apple II/III, Color Computer, Games & Adventures, General Interest, Model I/III, Model II/12/16.
Comments: Well, well, well. . . if the name sounds familiar, it should. This is another would-be CompuServe micro clone. However, unlike both Access-80 and Micro-80, this system is easy to use, is free, and welcomes new callers to look around. About all the system can be used for is messaging, and the message base looks like a CompuServe SIG. It's worth a long-distance call to satisfy your curiosity.

CPBB04030 (901) 761-5018
On-Line 80 #1 300 bps
Memphis, Tennessee 8/1/N
Open On-Line 80

Features: BBS list, catalog, chat, downloading, feedback, games, messaging, parameters, text files, userlog.
Special features: Downloadable programs for TRS-80 Model I and III computers; text files updating Stewart Software products.
Notice: New callers will not be able to post a message until their second call.
Comments: This is the headquarters system of On-Line 80, from Stewart Software, Inc. It is similar to Bullet-80 and Forum-80 but is faster than both. If you're looking for BBS software for your TRS-80, give this system a call and look around. This is a general-interest message system that is quite busy during the day, so try calling at night.

CPBB04040 (901) 358-8227
Tennessee BBS 300 bps
Memphis, Tennessee 8/1/N
Password Required TBBS

Features: Feedback, messaging.
Notice: There is a 30-minute time limit on this system.
Comments: The only thing a new user can do on this system is read messages. The ads I've seen for this system don't mention any

special features; that may be because of the system's and sysop's newness. If you live in the area, give the system a call and help get things moving.

Texas (214)

CPBB04080 (214) 742-1380
Dallas Heathkit 300 bps
Dallas, Texas 8/1/N
Open HBBS

Features: Downloading, feedback, messaging, userlog.
Special features: Downloadable programs for Heath/Zenith computers.
Special interests: Heath/Zenith computers.
Comments: If you own a Heath/Zenith computer, this is a system to help you use it to its fullest.

CPBB04090 (214) 248-7757
Software Exchange 300/1200 bps
Dallas, Texas 8/1/N
Password Required Trade-80

Features: BBS list, downloading, feedback, mail, messaging, parameters, system information, time/duration.
Special features: Downloadable programs for Apple, Atari, TRS-80 computers.
Notice: There is a 30-minute time limit on this system. To use this system, you must upload a public-domain program or pay a fee.
Comments: This system boasts over 600 downloadable programs but does not allow new callers to see even a menu of said programs; this is a practice that I find to be reprehensible. Since this system was publicized on a national network and the sysop knew he would get long-distance callers, it would be natural to expect at least a menu of available programs. Such was not the case. What is my opinion of systems that do business in this manner? Not much. Save your phone call.

CPBB04100 (214) 769-3036
MicroServe 300/1200 bps
Hawkins, Texas 8/1/N
Password Required TBBS

Features: BBS list, chat, downloading, feedback, mail, messaging, parameters, system information, text files, time/duration.
Special features: Downloadable programs for the Color Computer, TRS-80 Model I and III computers.
Special interests: Multiple message bases. Categories include Atari, Color Computer, Commodore, CP/M, IBM, Osborne, RCA, TI, Timex-Sinclair, TRS-80 Model I/III, TRS-80 Model II, VIC-20, Xerox.
Notice: There is a 20-minute time limit on this system. To access the library of downloadable programs, you must pay a fee.
Comments: The sysop of this system has been running a BBS for several years. As a first-time caller, you are not allowed to see a menu of available programs, and this does not please me (nor long-distance callers, I suspect). If you want to expand your TRS-80 software library, consider MicroServe.

CPBB04110 (214) 657-8147
International Color BBS (Color-80 #5) 300 bps
Henderson, Texas 8/1/N
Password Required Color-80

Features: BBS list, catalog, chat, downloading, feedback, graphics, messaging, parameters, system information, time/duration, user-log.
Special features: Downloadable programs for the Color Computer, online graphics for the Color Computer, text files on Color Computer-related topics.
Special interests: Color Computer.
Notice: This system is run by the International Color Computer Club for its membership. To be able to download programs from this system, you will need to be a member of the ICCC.
Comments: Unless you are an ICCC member, you can do better by calling one of the many other Color-80 systems available.

CPBB04120   (214) 566-1374
TBBS   300 bps
Tyler, Texas   8/1/N
Password Required   TBBS

Features: BBS list, chat, downloading, feedback, mail, messaging, parameters, system information, time/duration, userlog.
Special features: Downloadable programs for the Color Computer, TRS-80 Model I, II, and III computers; including Orchestra 85-90 and Piano 85-90 programs.
Special interests: Multiple message boards. Categories include Color Computer, Orchestra 85-90, Piano 85-90, Software Reviews, TRS-80 Model I/II/III.
Notice: There is a 45-minute time limit on this system.
Comments: This system is dedicated to TRS-80 computers in a big way. Unlike most TBBSs, it seems that everything offered is available to first-time callers. If that is so, this system is definitely worth a long-distance call for all TRS-80 owners.

Texas (512)

CPBB04140   (512) 385-1102
TBBS   300 bps
Austin, Texas   8/1/N
Open   TBBS

Features: Downloading, feedback, mail, messaging, parameters, system information.
Special features: Downloadable programs for Apple, Atari, TRS-80 computers.
Special interests: Multiple message boards. Categories include Apple, Atari, Humor, TRS-80, Women.
Notice: There is a 30-minute time limit on this system.
Comments: A general-interest message system.

CPBB04150   (512) 285-5028
Color Connection   300 bps
Elgin, Texas   7/1/E
Password Required   Connection-80

Features: BBS list, catalog, chat, downloading, feedback, games, graphics, messaging, parameters, text files, time/duration.
Special features: Downloadable programs for the Color Computer, online graphics for the Color Computer, text files on Color Computer-related topics.
Special interest: Color Computer.
Notice: To download programs and view online graphics, you must be using a Color Computer and a terminal program such as Colorcom/E.
Comments: Morris is back and the Color Connection's got him. Morris who? Morris the cat, of course! What's that? You don't believe me? Well, get the moths out of your wallet and give this system a call—you'll hear Morris greet you after you pat him on the back with a few C/Rs. This system has a hilarious set of menu selections and a large and varied library of downloadable CoCo programs. It's worth a long-distance call. Tell Morris that my cat, Backspace, says hello. Chow-chow-chow! (Or is that Co-Co-Co on this system?)

Texas (713)

CPBB04170   (713) 471-7117
Apex BBS   300 bps
Laporte, Texas   7/1/E or 8/1/N
Open   AMIS

Features: BBS list, chat, downloading, feedback, messaging, parameters, system information, text files, time/duration.
Special features: Downloadable programs for Atari home computers; text files on Atari-related topics.
Special interests: Atari home computers.
Comments: There were only a few messages on this system when I called it, but there were a variety of programs to download.

Texas (806)

CPBB04190 (806) 374-9711
Burg Board 300 bps
Amarillo, Texas 8/1/N
Password Required TBBS

Features: Chat, downloading, feedback, games, mail, messaging, parameters, system information, text files, time/duration.
Special features: Downloadable programs for the Color Computer, IBM PC, and TRS-80 Model I and III computers.
Special interests: Multiple message boards. Categories include Apple, Atari, Commodore, IBM PC, TRS-80.
Notice: There is a 30-minute time limit on this system.
Comments: This is an amazing system. Designed as an electronic town (not a new idea), this system has an incredible amount of information and features on it. Aside from the multiple message boards, there is some very imaginative interactive fiction games (try Spy, Deal, and Air). I have to commend the sysop for putting so much effort into this system—every bit of it shows. This is one system that is worth every cent of a long-distance call.

Texas (817)

CPBB04220 (817) 767-5847
Commnet-80 300 bps
Wichita Falls, Texas 8/1/N
Open Commnet-80

Features: BBS list, catalog, chat, downloading, feedback, games, messaging, parameters, system information, time/duration, userlog.
Special features: Downloadable programs for Apple, Atari, Color Computer, and CP/M-based computers; games include Biorhythm, CIA, Deadly, Journey, Kingtut, Thunder.

Comments: This is another Commnet-80 system that has an Eliza-type program kick in if the sysop is not available to chat; you will meet "Goonhilda" the computer.

Texas (915)

CPBB04250	(915) 755-1000
Forum-80	300 bps
El Paso, Texas	8/1/N
Probationary	Forum-80

Features: Chat, downloading, feedback, messaging, parameters, text files, time/duration, userlog.
Special features: Unspecified downloadable programs, text files on various topics.
Notice: Forum-80 has a policy of displaying a long (series of) signon bulletin(s) that you cannot bypass and labeling all new users as "probationary," requiring the sysop to approve any messages new users post before other users may read them (if at all).
Comments: More proof to substantiate the above notice.

CPBB04260	(915) 942-8035
TBBS	300 bps
San Angelo, Texas	8/1/N
Password Required	TBBS

Features: BBS list, catalog, chat, downloading, feedback, mail, messaging, parameters, system information, text files, time/duration, userlog.
Special features: Downloadable programs for the Color Computer, TRS-80 Model I and III computers.
Notice: There is a 45-minute time limit on this system.
Comments: A general-interest message system.

Utah (801)

CPBB0428Ø (801) 277-3913
Commodore Central 300 bps
Holladay, Utah 7/1/E or 8/1/N
Password Required CBMBBS

Features: BBS list, downloading, messaging, parameters, time/duration, userlog.
Special features: Downloadable programs for VIC-20, Commodore-64, and Commodore Business Machines computers.
Special interests: Commodore computers.
Notice: To download programs, you will need an authorization code and a special terminal program. Contact the sysop for details.
Comments: This is another fine CBMBBS with quite a selection of downloadable programs. Like any other CBMBBS, to a Commodore owner it is worth a long-distance call.

CPBB0429Ø (801) 776-5029
North Utah Exchange RBBS 300 bps
Roy, Utah 8/1/N
Password Required RCP/M RBBS

Features: CP/M, downloading, messaging, userlog.
Special features: Downloadable programs for CP/M-based computers.
Special interests: CP/M.
Notice: A registered password is required to access all system features.
Comments: A typical RCP/M system.

Vermont (602)

CPBB04320 (602) 862-7023
Mouse-Net™ 300 bps
Burlington, Vermont 8/1/N
Open Mouse-Net

Features: Catalog, chat, downloading, messaging, system information, text files.
Special features: Downloadable programs for CP/-based computers and TRS-80 Model I and III computers.
Comments: If you're looking for TRS-80 communications software, look into ST80™ from Lance Miklus, Inc., the operator and author of this system. If you're not looking for communications software, give this system a call anyway. There's plenty of interesting messages and text files.

Virginia (703)

CPBB04350 (703) 524-7006
Best Little BBS 300 bps
Arlington, Virginia 7/1/E or 8/1/N
Password Required FoReM

Features: BBS list, chat, downloading, messaging, parameters.
Special features: Downloadable programs for Atari home computers.
Special interests: Atari home computers.
Notice: A registered password is required to access all system sections.
Comments: Say hello to Monica the Sysopette (as she calls herself). An OK system but not for long-distance callers, since at least two calls are required to gain full system access.

CPBB04360 (703) 670-5881
Forum-80 300/1200 bps
Dale City, Virginia 8/1/N
Probationary Forum-80

Features: BBS list, downloading, feedback, messaging, parameters, system information, text files, userlog.
Special features: Unspecified downloadable programs, text files of local user group newsletters for Atari, Commodore, and Ham Radio.
Notice: Forum-80 has a policy of displaying a long (series of) signon bulletin(s) that you cannot bypass and labeling all new users as "probationary," requiring the sysop to approve any messages new users post before other users may read them (if at all).
Comments: This system runs on NewDOS80, and that apparently helps speed it up. Local user-group newsletters are featured on this system, and all make for fascinating reading. If you aren't a member of a user group, you can see what you're missing by reading these newsletters; it'd be worth the price of a long-distance call. But, unfortunately, the sysop is considering restricting access to them to registered users.

CPBB04370 (703) 360-3812
C-HUG 300 bps
Fairfax, Virginia 8/1/N
Open Unknown

Features: Downloading, messaging, system information.
Special features: Downloadable programs for Heath/Zenith computers.
Special interests: Heath/Zenith computers.
Comments: C-HUG stands for Capital Heath User's Group, which happens to be the largest Heath user's group in the world. This is the prime system for Heath/Zenith owners to call.

CPBB04371   (703) 759-2072
C-HUG GP HBBS   300 bps
Fairfax, Virginia   8/1/N
Password Required   HBBS

Features: Chat, downloading, feedback, messaging, userlog.
Special features: Downloadable programs for Heath/Zenith computers; group purchasing.
Special interests: Group purchasing for C-HUG.
Notice: A password is required for full system access.
Comments: This HBBS facilitates group purchasing for C-HUG (see previous listing). Don't try to enter HDOS if you don't have a password or you will be dropped from the system.

CPBB04380   (703) 425-9452
Hostcomm #1   300 bps
Fairfax, Virginia   8/1/N
Password Required   Hostcomm

Features: Chat, downloading, mail, messaging.
Special features: Downloadable programs for the IBM PC.
Special interest: IBM PC.
Notice: There is a 45-minute time limit on this system. If you are asked for a password at signon, type **IBMPC**.
Comments: This is the headquarters system of Hostcomm, a file transfer facility for IBM PCs.

CPBB04385   (703) 978-0921
Hostcomm   300 bps
Fairfax, Virginia   8/1/N
Password Required   Hostcomm

Features: Chat, downloading.
Special features: Downloadable programs for the IBM PC.
Special interests: IBM PC.

Notice: There is a ½-hour time limit on this system. If you are asked for a password at signon, type **IBMPC**.
Comments: Another Hostcomm.

CPBB04390 (703) 978-9592
Hostcomm 300 bps
Fairfax, Virginia 8/1/N
Password Required Hostcomm

Features: Chat, downloading.
Special features: Downloadable programs for the IBM PC.
Special interests: IBM PC.
Notice: If asked for a password at signon, type **IBMPC**.
Comments: Yet another Hostcomm.

CPBB04400 (703) 734-1387
CBBS AMRAD 300 bps
McLean, Virginia 8/1/N
Open CBBS

Features: Feedback, messaging, parameters, time/duration.
Special interests: Amateur radio.
Comments: This is the AMateur RADio CBBS, featuring all sorts of technical topics from Ham radio to telecommunications for the deaf to packet radio transmission. If you ever need a technical question answered, you can't find a better place to ask. Worth a long-distance call even if you don't have a question.

CPBB04410 (703) 360-5439
Future Tech 300 bps
Springfield, Virginia 7/1/E or 8/1/N
Open Armudic

Features: BBS list, downloading, messaging, system information, text files.
Special features: Downloadable programs for Apple, Atari, CP/M-based, and IBM computers; text files on various topics.
Comments: Of interest mainly to local callers.

Virginia (804)

CPBB04450 (804) 898-7493
Oxgate RBBS 300 bps
Grafton, Virginia 7/1/N
Password Required RCP/M Oxgate

Features: BBS list, chat, CP/M, downloading, feedback.
Special features: Unspecified downloadable programs.
Special interests: CP/M.
Comments: A rather different RCP/M. Worth a long-distance call to see why.

CPBB04460 (804) 838-3973
Dial-Your-Match #32 300 bps
Newport News, Virginia 7/1/E
Questionnaire/Password Required DYM

Features: BBS list, chat, feedback, mail, matchmaking, messaging, parameters, text files, time/duration.
Special features: Matchmaking; joke message board; text files on various subjects.
Notice: There is a 25-minute time limit on this system. Even to browse a Dial-Your-Match system, you must first fill out a questionnaire. All of your answers will be public, available to other system users. Depending on the individual sysop (called a Matchmaker), the questions can be quite explicit. This is a sexually-oriented system.
Comments: When you call this DYM, this is what you will see on your screen:

```
$%ˆ&$&ˆ@*&%ˆ$#!) (&ˆ
&#(*#%$#$@$!(*&#@*%$
There is nothing wrong
with your computer!
We are controlling transmission!

We can control the vertical!
```

```
We can control the horizontal!
>>>>>>>>>>>>>>>>>>>>>>>>>>
>>>>>>>>>>>>>>>>>>>>>>>>>>
For the next 25 minutez
we will control all that
you see & think!
The bologna you are reading
reaches from the inner mind to:
= = > DYM #32 < = =
```

In other words, folks, this is another DYM that is as much fun as *NBC News Overnight*! What, pray tell, was my score this round? My highest was 61 percent to—wait for it—a woman called (I kid you not! This kid *keeps* his printouts!) "Smurf!" Sorry, but I don't mess around with blue-skinned women. Besides, by this time I was turning blue myself. This is the last DYM listed in The Computer Phone Book (thank goodness!), and is well worth a long-distance call.

CPBB04470 (804) 543-7194
T.A.W.B.B.S. 300 bps
Tidewater, Virginia 8/1/N
Password Required Net-Works

Features: BBS list, chat, mail, messaging, parameters, system information, text files, time/duration.

Special features: Text files on various topics.

Notice: Net-Works systems do not allow you to read past the first 10 messages or access certain sections of the system until your password is validated. Your telephone number will become part of your password, so don't give a false one.

Comments: A general-interest message system. Plans are for 1200 bps service and a hard disk, which may be realized by the time you read this.

Washington (206)

CPBB04490 (206) 453-0596
NRCS Buying Service 300 bps
Bellevue, Washington 8/1/N
Password Required Net-Works

Features: BBS list, chat, downloading, mail, messaging, parameters, system information, time/duration.
Special features: Unspecified downloadable programs.
Notice: Net-Works systems do not allow you to read past the first 10 messages or access certain sections of the system until your password is validated. Your telephone number will become part of your password, so don't give a false one.
Comments: This system is for a buying service. For a one-time fee, you can buy (unspecified) computers and related equipment "at 10% over cost, this could mean a 30% discount over retail." There weren't many messages on this system. Long-distance callers can skip this one, and local callers should be wary.

CPBB04500 (206) 692-8408
U.S.—Online 300 bps
Bremerton, Washington 8/1/N
Password Required TBBS

Features: Catalog, chat, feedback, mail, messaging, parameters, system information, text files, time/duration, userlog.
Special features: Downloadable programs for TRS Model I and III computers, text files on various topics.
Special interests: Multiple message boards. Categories include Apple, Atari, Commodore-64, IBM PC, TRS-80, VIC-20.
Notice: There is a 30-minute time limit on this system.
Comments: A general-interest message system. It had only a few messages when I called it, so help fill it up.

CPBB04510 (206) 743-6021
Northwest Commodore User's Group 300 bps
Edmonds, Washington 7/1/E or 8/1/N
Password Required CBMBBS

Features: Downloading, messaging, parameters, text files, time/duration, userlog.
Special features: Downloadable programs for VIC-20, Commodore-64, and Commodore Business Machines computers; text files on Commodore-related topics.
Special interests: Commodore computers.
Notice: To download programs, you need an authorization code and a special terminal program. Contact the sysop for details.
Comments: This is another fine CBMBBS, filled to the brim with messages and information of interest to every Commodore user. It is well worth a long-distance call.

CPBB04520 (206) 778-1940
PC BBS 300 bps
Edmonds, Washington 7/1/E
Open PCRBBS

Features: Chat, downloading, feedback, messaging, parameters, system information, time/duration.
Special features: Downloadable programs for the IBM PC.
Special interests: IBM PC.
Comments: Another IBM PC BBS for IBM owners to gather around.

CPBB04530 (206) 883-0403
JCTS Super-System 300 bps
Redmond, Washington 7/1/E
Open Unknown

Features: BBS list, chat, downloading, feedback, mail, messaging, system information, text files, userlog.

Special features: Downloadable programs for TRS-80 computers, text files on various topics.
Comments: When you call this number, you may or may not find the system described above. If you do get the system described, there may not be anything special about it. On the other hand, if you don't get the system described, you will enter a system that deserves something akin to a *Guinness Book of World Records* entry—a tape-based system that was operated for 2 years and contained quizzes and games unlike any other system. If you're not offended by having a system call you a "Turkey" or other such epithets, you'll fall in love with that tape-based system (and will probably wind up calling it a second time—you'll understand why if you get it). So, you may get one system or the other. Before you dial the phone, ask yourself: Do I feel lucky? Worth a long-distance call to find out.

CPBB04540 (206) 527-7638
Eskimo North 300 bps
North Seattle, Washington 8/1/N
Open Minibin

Features: Chat, messaging, parameters, userlog.
Comments: This is a very strange system. Although it is supposed to be designed as a house, it gave me the impression of being more like a closet—and a small one at that. Using this system is confusing at first, and if you are new to BBSs, you should start with a conventional BBS, not this one. Long-distance callers may want to look in on this to see what it's like.

CPBB04550 (206) 527-0897
Mailboard 82.1 300 bps
Seattle, Washington 8/1/N
Password Required Mailboard

Features: BBS list, chat, feedback, messaging, system information, text files, time/duration, userlog.

Special features: Text files on various topics.
Comments: This is a very nice system. Aside from a very good local BBS list and a very funny humor section, there is a text file that is a computer autobiography of the sysop and this system that you must read. Worth a long-distance call.

CPBB04560 (206) 763-8879
Seacomm-80 300 bps
Seattle, Washington 8/1/N
Password Required RACS

Features: BBS list, chat, downloading, feedback, messaging, parameters, polling, text files, time/duration, userlog.
Special features: Downloadable programs for Apple, Atari, Commodore, CP/M, IBM, Model 100 computers; polling of users; text files on various topics.
Special interests: Multiple message bases. Categories include Apple, Atari, Commodore, CP/M, General, Ham-80, IBM, TRS-80.
Comments: RACS was once a nice piece of software, although very complex. Then TBBS came along and RACS was obsoleted overnight. This is the only RACS listed in *The Computer Phone Book,* the last of a dying breed. If you can tolerate the system's slowness, you might want to call it long-distance.

CPBB04570 (206) 334-7394
West Coast Message System 300/1200 bps
Snohomish, Washington 8/1/N
Open Unknown

Features: Chat, games, messaging, system information, time/duration, userlog.
Special features: A variety of online games.

Comments: There weren't many messages on this system when I called it; it could be that everyone signs on just to play games. It's a fast system but of local interest only.

CPBB04580 (206) 535-2837
NW Micronet 300 bps
Tacoma, Washington 8/2/N
Password Required TBBS

Features: Catalog, feedback, mail, messaging, parameters, system information, time/duration.
Special features: Downloadable programs for Atari, Color Computer, and TRS-80 Model I and III computers.
Special interests: Multiple message boards. Categories include Apple, Atari, Color Computer, Heath, IBM PC, Sale/Wanted, TRS-80 Model I/III.
Notice: There is a 30-minute time limit on this system. You will need to register a password to access all system sections.
Comments: There are some very good downloadable programs on this system.

CPBB04590 (206) 756-0448
Tech-BBS 300 bps
Tacoma, Washington 8/1/N
Password Required TBBS

Features: Downloading, feedback, mail, messaging, parameters, system information, text files, time/duration, userlog.
Special features: Various text files provided by *Basic Computing* (formerly *80-U.S.*) magazine.
Special interests: Multiple message boards. Categories include Apple, Color Computer, Commodore, Max-80, TRS-80.
Notice: There is a 30-minute time limit on this system.

Comments: If you read *Basic Computing* magazine, you might want to give this system a call to read corrections to articles and program listings; there is even an index to all published articles on the system.

West Virginia (304)

CPBB04620 (304) 925-3338
21st Century Connection 300 bps
Charleston, West Virginia 8/1/N
Password Required Color-80

Features: BBS list, catalog, chat, downloading, feedback, graphics, messaging, parameters, system information, text files, time/duration, userlog.
Special features: Downloadable programs for the Color Computer, online graphics for the Color Computer, text files on Color Computer-related topics.
Special interests: Color Computer.
Notice: A registered password is required to access the downloading section. To download programs and view online graphics, you must be using a Color Computer and a terminal program such as Colorcom/E.
Comments: Long-distance callers can do better by calling a Color-80 that does not require a password for downloading access.

CPBB04630 (304) 273-4136
TBBS 300 bps
Comet, West Virginia 8/1/N
Password Required TBBS

Features: BBS list, feedback, mail, messaging, parameters, system information, time/duration, userlog.

Special interests: Multiple message boards. Categories include Amateur Radio, Apple, Atari, IBM, Swap & Shop, TRS-80.
Notice: There is a 30-minute time limit on this system.
Comments: A general-interest message system.

CPBB04640 (304) 372-9654
Bullet-80 300 bps
Evans, West Virginia 8/1/N
Open Bullet-80

Features: BBS list, catalog, chat, feedback, messaging, parameters, system information, time/duration, userlog.
Special features: Downloadable programs for TRS-80 Model I and III computers.
Special interests: Multiple message boards. Categories include Apple, Color Computer, CP/M & S-100, General, IBM PC, TRS-80 Model I/III.
Comments: A general-interest message system.

CPBB04650 (304) 599-0760
Mountaineer Softline #1 300 bps
Morgantown, West Virginia 8/1/N
Open Color-80

Features: BBS list, catalog, chat, downloading, feedback, graphics, messaging, parameters, system information, text files, time/duration, userlog.
Special features: Downloadable programs for the Color Computer, online graphics for the Color Computer, text files on Color Computer-related topics.
Special interests: Color Computer.
Notice: To download programs and view online graphics, you must be using a Color Computer and a terminal program such as Colorcom/E.
Comments: This Color-80 has a larger downloading section than others.

Wisconsin (414)

CPBB04690 (414) 281-0545
Canopus 300 bps
Greenfield, Wisconsin 8/1/N
Password Required TBBS

Features: Chat, feedback, mail, messaging, parameters, system information, time/duration.
Special interests: Multiple message boards. Categories include Apple, Color Computer, Commodore/VIC, DOS, Jokes, Reviews (books, movies, records, Milwaukee), Teenagers, TI, TRS-80.
Notice: There is a 35-minute time limit on this system.
Comments: Here is a TBBS that has been intelligently produced by a firm called Canopus Systems. It has sections for local discussions and a range of interests, yet the system lies fallow. Come on, Greenfield, get to your computers and start filling up this system.

CPBB04700 (414) 355-8839
Beer City BBS 300/1200 bps
Milwaukee, Wisconsin 7/1/E
Password Required TBBS

Features: Chat, downloading, feedback, mail, messaging, parameters, system information, time/duration.
Special features: Downloadable programs for the Osborne, TRS-80 computers.
Notice: There is a 30-minute time limit on this system. A registered password is required to post messages; access to the downloading section is restricted to those who upload a public-domain program.
Comments: Unfortunately, someone tried to harass this system with prejudice, so the sysops had to restrict public message entry to

registered password holders. You can't even take a look at the downloading menu until you have uploaded a public-domain program. This is a practice I am against and have asked the sysops to reconsider. By the time you read this, let's hope they have changed it.

CPBB04710   (414) 554-9520
C.U.S.S.H.   300 bps
Milwaukee, Wisconsin   7/1/E or 8/1/N
Password Required   CBMBBS

Features: BBS list, downloading, messaging, parameters, text files, time/duration, userlog.
Special features: Downloadable programs for VIC-20, Commodore-64, and Commodore Business Machines computers; text files on Commodore-related topics.
Special interests: Commodore computers.
Notice: To download programs, you need an authorization code and a special terminal program. Contact the sysop for details.
Comments: C.U.S.S.H. stands for Commodore Users of Systems, Software, and Hardware. This is another of several CBMBBSs that is worth a long-distance call for all Commodore owners.

CPBB04720   (414) 241-8364
MAUDE   PMMI
Milwaukee, Wisconsin   8/1/N
Open   CBBS

Features: Feedback, messaging, parameters, time/duration.
Comments: MAUDE stands for Milwaukee Area Utility for Digital Exchanges, a system that is going on 4 years old and is the most

active system in Wisconsin. This system is run by the same firm that provides MicroShare (CPBL00750, page 172), and you can get additional information about MicroShare by reading messages 19 and 20 here. Worth a long-distance call.

CPBB04730   (414) 637-9990
Colortron ABBS   300 bps
Racine, Wisconsin   7/1/E
Open   ABBS

Features: Downloading, messaging, text files, time/duration.
Special features: Downloadable programs for the Apple II+ computer; text files on various topics.
Comments: A general-interest message system mainly for local use.

Wisconsin (608)

CPBB04760   (608) 752-7840
JADE   300 bps
Janesville, Wisconsin   8/1/N
Password Required   TBBS

Features: Downloading, feedback, mail, messaging, parameters, system information.
Special features: Downloadable programs for the TRS-80 Model 100 computer.
Special interests: Multiple message boards. Categories include Hippo House, Model 100, News & Views.
Notice: There is a 30-minute time limit on this system.
Comments: JADE stands for Janesville Area Data Exchange. A general-interest message system that had only a few messages when I called it.

Wisconsin (715)

CPBB04780 (715) 848-3415
Personal Computer Communications 300 bps
Wausau, Wisconsin 8/1/N
Password Required TBBS

Features: Downloading, feedback, messaging, parameters, system information, time/duration.
Special features: A second subsystem with TRS-80 Model 100 downloadable programs.
Special interests: TRS-80 Model I/III, Model 100.
Notice: There is a 25-minute time limit on this system. A registered password is required to enter the Model 100 subsystem.
Comments: This system looked like it could use callers.

CPBB04790 (715) 352-2093
TBBS 300 bps
Wausau, Wisconsin 8/1/N
Password Required TBBS

Features: Feedback, mail, messaging, parameters, time/duration.
Special features: Unspecified downloadable programs.
Special interests: TRS-80, VIC-20.
Notice: A registered password is required to access the downloading section.
Comments: This is another TBBS with the inane policy of not letting first-time callers see even a downloading section menu. If you call this system, ask the sysop to reconsider his policy. Until that time, long-distance callers can skip this one.

Wyoming (307)

CPBB04850 (307) 637-6045
Commodore Bulletin-Board 300 bps
Cheyenne, Wyoming 7/1/E or 8/1/N
Password Required CBMBBS

Features: BBS list, chat, downloading, messaging, parameters, text files, time/duration, userlog.

Special features: Downloadable programs for VIC-20, Commodore-64, and Commodore Business Machines computers; text files on Commodore-related topics.

Special interests: Commodore computers.

Notice: To download programs, you need an authorization code and a special terminal program. Contact the sysop for details.

Comments: The amount of information on this system is truly staggering. This system features complete documentation for CBMBBSs—but be forewarned that it will take approximately a ½ hour to print out! It's fitting that this wonderful system should be the last U.S. BBS listed in *The Computer Phone Book*. I like saving some of the best for last.

CHAPTER 7

Directory Section: Canadian Bulletin-Board Systems

If, from the slimness of this chapter, you are thinking that Canada is underrepresented, you are correct. Unfortunately, of all the operating BBS numbers I had at my disposal, very few answered with a carrier signal, far too many of them were only part-time systems, and only a small percentage looked to be lively enough to still be operational by the time *The Computer Phone Book* finds its way into your hands. Explanation over, here are the listings.

Alberta (403)

CPBBC00050 (403) 482-6854
Computron RBBS PMMI
Edmonton, Alberta, Canada 8/1/N
Open RCP/M RBBS

Features: BBS list, CP/M, downloading, feedback, messaging, parameters, userlog.
Special features: Downloadable programs for CP/M-based machines.
Special interests: CP/M.
Comments: A typical RCP/M system, with an expected Canadian touch.

CPBBC00075 (403) 454-6093
Edmonton RCP/M 300/1200 bps
Edmonton, Alberta, Canada 8/1/N
Open RCP/M RBBS

Features: BBS list, CP/M, downloading, feedback, messaging, parameters, userlog.
Special features: Downloadable programs for CP/M-based computers.
Special interests: CP/M.
Comments: Another RCP/M, with more of a Canadian touch, and 35 megabytes of online storage.

CPBBC00125 (403) 463-5774
Southside RCP/M 300 bps
Edmonton, Alberta, Canada 8/1/N
Open RCP/M RBBS

Features: BBS list, CP/M, downloading, feedback, messaging, parameters, userlog.
Special features: Downloadable programs for CP/M-based computers.
Special interests: CP/M.
Comments: Another RCP/M.

British Columbia (604)

CPBBC00350 (604) 438-2468
Satyricon CBBS RCP/M 300 bps
Burnaby, British Columbia, Canada 8/1/N
Open RCP/M CBBS

Features: Chat, CP/M, downloading, feedback, games, messaging, parameters, time/duration.
Special features: Downloadable programs for CP/M-based computers.
Special interests: CP/M.
Comments: An interesting system, run by a computer dealer.

Quebec (514)

CPBBC00700 (514) 622-1274
B.E.L.E. 300/1200 bps
Laval, Quebec, Canada 7/1/E
Open Connection-80

Features: Catalog, chat, downloading, feedback, messaging, parameters, system information, time/duration, userlog.

Special features: Downloadable programs for Color Computer, IBM PC, other computers.

Notice: This is a bilingual system.

Comments: "⟨F⟩rancais ou/or ⟨E⟩nglish" is the first thing you will see when you sign on to this system. Although, when selecting *Anglais*, you are only supposed to see English menus, the system slips back into Francais when the downloading menu is selected.

CHAPTER 8

Directory Section: Overseas Bulletin-Board Systems

Here are the overseas listings of Bulletin Board Systems, mainly drawn from previously published sources that, at the time I was compiling this section, still seemed fresh.

Please note, in the bits-per-second category, that most of these systems run on CCITT modem tones. These are different from Bell 103-, 212A-, and 202-modem frequencies, and a dedicated CCITT-standard modem is required to sign on to these systems. In any instance where Bell 103 frequencies are available, you will be able to dial the system with your 300-bps modem and log on to it.

Further, note that all phone numbers are in the original country format. This means you will have to do some "translating" if you plan to call them from the United States. The numbers in parentheses next to each country's name is the telephone country code required as part of the phone number's prefix if you are going to dial it from the United States. In some cases, all you need to do is dial the international access code (01), plus the country code, drop the first zero from the numbers listed, and dial the remaining numbers. Check with your telephone operator before doing so.

If you are a sysop of one of the systems listed, please furnish me with additional information about your system. If you are a sysop whose system is not listed, please use the form in Appendix 9 of *The Computer Phone Book* to supply your information and a printout (with English translation, if necessary).

Australia (61)

CPBBA000100   2-762-5088
Micom CBBS   300 bps CCITT v21
Melbourne, VIC, Australia   Unknown
Unknown   CBBS

Comments: If anyone could supply me with a printout of this system, I would appreciate it.

CPBBA000300   2-997-1018
Software Tools RCP/M   300 bps CCITT v21
Sydney, Australia   Unknown
Unknown   RCP/M

Comments: A printout from this system would be greatly appreciated.

Great Britain (44)

CPBBB000200   02707-43555
CBBS North-East   300 bps CCITT
Unknown, Unknown, Great Britain   Unknown
Unknown   CBBS

Comments: Operating hours of record are 2:30 PM–9 AM local country time. Additional information and a printout would be appreciated.

CPBBB000300   01-902-2546
Forum-80   300 bps CCITT
Wembley, London, Great Britain   Unknown
Unknown   Forum-80

Comments: Operating hours are unknown. Additional information and a printout would be appreciated.

CPBBB000350 0482-859169
Forum-80 300 bps Bell 103
Hull, Great Britain 8/1/N
Probationary Forum-80

Features: BBS list, downloading, feedback, messaging, parameters, system information, userlog.
Special features: Bell 103 modem standard; may be called from the United States directly.
Comments: This is one Forum-80 that doesn't have a lengthy signon bulletin (at the rates it costs Americans to call it, it can't afford to have them). It bills itself as "The World's First International Bulletin Board." It may well be, but it seems only to be used by Britons and Americans with too little information about telecommunications systems in its native land and too many "Gee whiz, Ma, lookit me!" messages from Americans. One thing hasn't changed, though; this system still insists on that annoying "probationary" policy. Worth a (very) long-distance call if you can stand the probationary policy.

CPBBB000400 0908-566660
Forum-80 300 bps CCITT
Milton, Great Britain Unknown
Unknown Forum-80

Comments: Again, I would appreciate additional information and a printout. Recorded operating hours are 7 AM–10 PM local country time.

CPBBB000500 051-428-8924
Mailbox-80 300 bps CCITT
Liverpool, Great Britain 8/1/N
Unknown TBBS

Comments: Operating hours of record are 9 AM–11 PM local country time. Additional information and a printout would be welcomed.

CPBBB000600   038-482-7868
Mailbox-80   300 bps CCITT
Stourbridge, Great Britain   Unknown
Unknown   Unknown

Comments: I would appreciate additional information and a printout.

CPBBB000700   02993-2853
Mailbox-83   300 bps CCITT
West Midlands, Great Britain   Unknown
Unknown   Unknown

Comments: Additional information and a printout would be appreciated.

Netherlands (21)

CPBBH00050   01-313-512533
Forum-80   300 bps CCITT
Holland, Netherlands   Unknown
Unknown   Unknown

Comments: Recorded operating hours are Tues–Sat 6 PM–7 AM, Sat 6 PM–Tues 7 AM, all local country time. I would very much appreciate additional information and a printout (and, if the output isn't in English, at least a rough translation).

Sweden (46)

CPBBS00050   010-468-190522
ABC-80   300 bps CCITT
Stockholm, Sweden   Unknown
Unknown   Unknown

Comments: Operating hours are unknown. Additional information and a printout (and a rough translation, if necessary) would be appreciated.

CPBBS00100   010-468-7300-706
Elfa   300 bps CCITT
Unknown, Sweden   Unknown
Unknown   Unknown

Comments: Operating hours unknown. Additional information and a printout (and any needed translation) would be appreciated.

CHAPTER 9
Special Services: Domestic and Foreign

What are Special Services? Simply put, they are information, entertainment, or transactional services delivered over the telephone that do not fit into any of the categories in this edition of *The Computer Phone Book*. One special service is for videogame owners, the other two are videotex systems.

In the next edition of *The Computer Phone Book*, I anticipate including most operating videotex systems. This will be possible because of the availability of firmware and software for personal computers that will allow them to access Telidon and PLP/NAPLP videotex systems and services. Videotex operators (and would-be operators) should contact me at the address listed in *The Computer Phone Book* so that I may gather the necessary information to make such inclusion possible. Please do *not* use the form at the back of *The Computer Phone Book*; instead, write me for details.

United States

CPBC00050
GameLine

Operating hours: 24 hours/day, 7 days/week.
Registration fee: $15.
Minimum: None.
Billing: Credit card.
Contact: Control Video Corporation, 8620 Westwood Center Drive, Vienna, VA, 22180, (703)448-8700.

Contents: Downloadable videogames for Atari VCS and VCS-compatible home videogame consoles.
Comments: I have not used this service. You must also purchase, for $49.95, a Master Module at a retail store. This cartridge contains the necessary RAM, modem, and telephone interface to allow VCS and VCS-compatible consoles to use the service over the telephone.

CPBV00500   300/1200 bps
Citylink   Prestel

Operating hours: 24 hours/day, 7 days/week.
Registration fee: Not available at press time.
Minimum: Not available at press time.
Connect-time: Not available at press time.
Billing: Not available at press time.
Contact: Torch Computers, 61 Commerce Way, Woburn, MA, 01801, (617)935-2575.
Contents: Not available at press time.
Comments: Citylink was planned to be operational at the time *The Computer Phone Book* went to press. At press time, however, all of the necessary software had yet to be delivered to Torch Computers. The service is envisioned as providing information and services for metropolitan Boston in the Prestel videotex format. Contact Torch Computers for additional information.

Great Britain

CPBVB00100   75 bps to/–1200 bps from
Prestel World Service   Prestel

Networks: Direct-dial, Telenet.
Operating hours: Prime time: Mon–Fri 3 AM–1 PM U.S. Eastern time; Sat 3 AM–8 AM U.S. Eastern time. Non-prime time: Mon–Fri 1 PM–3 AM U.S. Eastern time; Sat 8 AM to midnight U.S. Eastern time; Sun all day.
Registration fee: $80 for 3 months, $320 a year; prepaid.
Minimum: Registration fee.

Connect-time: Prime time: $6/hour*; Non-prime time: free.* (*Direct-dial rates; phone costs not included.)

Billing: Registration fee must be prepaid; connect time is direct billing to businesses.

Contact: Torch Computers, 61 Commerce Way, Woburn, MA, 01801 (617)935-2575.

Contents: Prestel contains shopping services, travel services, information resources, and much more. Of interest to microcomputer owners is Micronet 800, a portion of the system designed to provide information from and about users' groups; downloadable software for a variety of computers; and games. To access Prestel, you must use either a dedicated Prestel terminal or, with your microcomputer, special firmware and software. To access Prestel via Telenet, you will need a Telenet account number and password. Contact Torch Computers for full details.

APPENDIX 1
Bulletin-Board System Help Files

Although not every BBS software format is represented in this section, enough are to give you a solid understanding of all of the commands available to you on all of the software formats. You will be able to refer to this section for particular menu selections should you find yourself somehow stranded in Expert Mode.

ABBS: Apple Bulletin Board System
Main menu:
A = Apple 40 column
B = Print Bulletin
C = Case switch
D = Duplex switch (Echo/No Echo)
E = Enter message into system
G = Good-bye (leave system)
H = Help with functions
K = Kill (erase) a message
L = Line feed (on/off)
N = Nulls (set as req'd)
Q = Quick summary of msg's
R = Retrieve msg
S = Summary of msg's
T = Time of day
V = Toggle video/printer terminal mode
W = Print Welcome message
? = Prints Functions Supported
DOWNLOAD = Download software to your Apple
UPLOAD = Upload files/software to this system

NEWS = Info of interest to system users
CONF = Switch conferences

Main prompt:
FUNCTION:
(A,B,C,D,E,G,H,K,L,N,Q,R,S,T,V,W,X,
DOWNLOAD, UPLOADED, NEWS, CONF,?)

Message entry menu:
Entry Functions:
A = Abort
C = Continue Entry
D = Delete a line
E = Edit line
L = List line(s)
R = Restart from beginning
S = Save message to disk

Message entry prompt:
(A,C,D,E,L,R,S,?)?

Help file:
Ctrl C -- Cancels printing of the current line being output.

Ctrl H (Backspace) -- Allows you to backspace one character at a time and prints a '/' followed by the character you are backspacing over. This is the same routine that is used for Delete or Rubout instead of true Delete (for the benefit of printers).

Ctrl K -- Cancels current function.

Ctrl U (Forward Arrow) -- Starts you back at the beginning of the current line being typed (ie: start over).

A -- Toggle display mode between 64 and 40 column mode. When you sign on, you are allowed to put up to 64 characters/line. A bell will sound at 59 and on, up to 64 columns, at which point you would be forced onto the next line of text. In the Apple 40 column mode, the bell will ring at 35, then again at 38 and 39, dropping you to the next line at 39. 39 was used instead of 40 to avoid an extra blank line because of the 40th character.

B -- Print Bulletin. Reprints Bulletins that you see when you sign on.

C -- Case Switch. When you sign on, the system defaults to UPPER CASE input and output. The "C" command allows you to switch between UPPER CASE ONLY and UPPER/lower case mode.

D -- Duplex Switch. Alternately selects full or half duplex operation and informs you of current status.

E -- Enter Message. Allows you to enter a message into the system. Entry commands are basically self-explanatory. A carriage return (C/R) at this point will list out the command menu for entries. The "change" command allows you to change an entire line or just part of it. To change just part of a line, enter the following:

/string to change/replacement string

You will then be shown the new version of the line and you should hit Return to leave the change mode. You can exit the Enter mode entirely by entering the 'A' command. You should be sure to enter an 'S' to Save a message to disk.

G -- Good-bye. Exits system and hangs up the phone at the ABBS end of the connection.

H -- Help. Prints this documentation.

K -- Kill a message. Enter this to delete a message from the system. A password may be necessary if one was used at the time of message entry.

L -- Line Feed On/Off. Normally on. For terminals that need an extra line feed character to advance to the next line

N -- Nulls. Adds an extra delay after a carriage return, to allow printers time to move the printhead back to the starting position. This option only works with the line feed option on. Each null is equivalent to a 30-millisecond delay and is adjustable from 1 to 30 nulls. It defaults to 1.

Q -- Quick Scan. An abbreviated Scan, showing only a message's number, its subject, and date. See "S" for Scan.

R -- Retrieve Message. Allows you to retrieve a message from the system. You can specify a single message, multiple messages, or all of the messages from a given number on up. To specify a single message, enter R;N, where "N" is the number of the message you wish to read. To read multiple messages, separate each message number with a ";" (semicolon; ie : R;1;2;3;7;8). To retrieve all of the messages starting from a certain message number, enter 'R' followed by a ";" then the starting message number, followed by "^" (an up-arrow; ie : R;101;^). (In some cases you may replace an up-arrow with an at-sign, "@.")

S -- Scan Messages. Allows you to scan over messages starting at the message number that you specify. You will be able to see who the message is from, who it is addressed to, its subject, and the date it was posted.

T -- Time and Date. Gives you the current time and date. This is automatically used during login.

W -- Welcome. Prints Welcome message at the beginning of the system.

X -- Expert User. Does away with certain explanatory messages. It also allows certain C/R defaults. Example: a C/R in response to "FUNCTION:" will print functions supported by this system.

? -- Prints functions supported in that current mode of operation.

CONF -- Allows you to switch between sets of messages. This feature operates only if the optional Conference module has been installed.

NEWS -- Displays a list of text files that are available for reading. This feature operates only if the optional News module has been installed.

DOWNLOAD -- Gives you access to a library of software that can be downloaded to your system. This feature operates only if the optional Download module has been installed.

UPLOAD -- Allows you to transfer a file (text or program) to this system. This feature operates only if the optional Upload module has been installed.

In addition to the above documentation, an ABBS sysop provides this information:

- Please kill old messages that are addressed to you when you no longer need them. This will allow the general interest messages to stay on the system longer.
- There is a feature in this system that will not permit you to erase too many of your old messages at one time. If you have many old messages to erase, you may not be able to do so all at one time. This feature is to protect someone from erasing all of the messages on the system.
- When you enter a message, the system will ask you if you would like to "lock" it with a password, so that only you may erase the messages you have left, using your password. The password may be any four characters you wish. The system will then ask you if you would like the message marked as "private mail." If you reply "Yes" to this, the person the message is addressed to must also

know the password in order to read the message and erase it. Although you may address your message to a particular person, it will not be treated as a private message -- anyone can read it -- unless you specify it as such.
- The upload function of this system will only accept one line at a time. You must wait for the "?" prompt before sending a line. The system is writing each line to the disk as it is received, and there may be a delay ranging from 1 to 20 seconds.

AMIS: Atari Message and Information System

Main menu (representative):
(^ = CTRL, ^S PAUSE, ^Q RESUME, ^X QUIT)
A = ASCII/ATASCII mode
B = Bulletin reprint
C = Callers listing
D = Download file
F = File listing for download
G = Good-bye (leave system)
H = Help with functions
I = Index of download programs
L = Line feed (ON/OFF) switch
M = Message base
N = New user information
O = Other BBS list
T = Time, day and date
U = Upload file
W = Welcome message reprint
X = eXpert user
Y = Yell for sysop (chat)
? = This list
^ = Control key
^S = Suspend display
^Q = Resume display
^X = Abort function

Main prompt (representative):
A,B,C,D,F,G,H,I,L,M,N,O,T,U,W,X,Y,
or ? >

Message base functions (representative):
E = Enter message
K = Kill message
M = Main menu
Q = Quick scan
R = Retrieve message
S = Summary

Message entry functions (representative):
A = Add line(s)
E = Edit message
L = List line(s)
Q = Quit entry (abort)
R = Read message entered
S = Save message on system

AMIS is similar to the other BBSs in format. Its differences arise when downloading files. You must use the ATASCII function in order to receive programs and run a communications program such as AMODEM, JMODEM or XMODEM. Also, Atari computers do not require line feeds.

Bullet-80

Main menu (version 8.0)

<A>utolog	<B>ulletins
<C>lub	<D>irections
<E>lec-Shopping	<F>ile-Transfer
<G>ames	<H>ow-Long
<I>nterests	<L>ine-test
<M>essage-Center	<O>ther-Systems
<R>equest-Chat	<S>ystem-Config
<T>erminate	<U>sers-Log
<V>iew-System	<X>pert-User

Message-Center menu:
<C>hange Section #
<H>elp With Functions
<L>eave Message
<R>ead Messages
<S>can Messages
<T>erminate Session
<A>bort to Bullet-80

Message entry commands:
<I> -- Insert a new line before the current line, or to begin to enter message
<D>+Line Number -- deletes that line (D3 will delete line 3)
<+> -- Step forward one line
<-> -- Step backward one line
<R> -- Replace word, ex: r/word1/word2
<RG> -- Global Replace
<B> -- Position to <B>eginning
<E> -- Position to <E>nd of text
<C> -- Continue message entry
<K> -- Kill Editing Session (Return to module menu)
<H> -- Prints this HELP screen
<L> -- Lists all lines in buffer
<L>+Line Number -- List That Line (L3 Will List Line 3
<S> -- Send Message
<A> -- Abort, return to Bullet-80
<T> -- Terminate Session
<?> -- To read instructions.
End ALL Inserts With A Blank Line

Help file (<D>irections):
  To use this system is simple, just press the FIRST letter of any command you care to execute. Entering a Carriage Return, <C/R>, or pressing <ENTER> at an abbreviated menu will display an expanded menu if you're not sure what to do.
  Note ** You can also press <S> to stop or CONTROL-S or <P> to pause during the print out of module instructions, and MESSAGE-CENTER messages. Any input will restart the display.
  Here is an explanation of the commands:
  <A>utolog -- In the past, the sysop had to activate your logon password. Now it becomes active immediately. Please note that passwords must begin with a number from 0 to 9, followed by up to 8 characters. Passwords must be at least 6 characters long.
  <B>ulletins -- This command will display the current system <B>ulletins. I try to update them periodically.
  <C> -- This command will activate our <C>lub module. It's easy to join and fun to belong. To get more information, run <C>lub and read instructions.

Message base functions (representative):
E = Enter message
K = Kill message
M = Main menu
Q = Quick scan
R = Retrieve message
S = Summary

Message entry functions (representative):
A = Add line(s)
E = Edit message
L = List line(s)
Q = Quit entry (abort)
R = Read message entered
S = Save message on system

   AMIS is similar to the other BBSs in format. Its differences arise when downloading files. You must use the ATASCII function in order to receive programs and run a communications program such as AMODEM, JMODEM or XMODEM. Also, Atari computers do not require line feeds.

Bullet-80

Main menu (version 8.0)
<A>utolog   <B>ulletins
<C>lub   <D>irections
<E>lec-Shopping   <F>ile-Transfer
<G>ames   <H>ow-Long
<I>nterests   <L>ine-test
<M>essage-Center   <O>ther-Systems
<R>equest-Chat   <S>ystem-Config
<T>erminate   <U>sers-Log
<V>iew-System   <X>pert-User

Message-Center menu:
<C>hange Section #
<H>elp With Functions
<L>eave Message
<R>ead Messages
<S>can Messages
<T>erminate Session
<A>bort to Bullet-80

368 APPENDIX 1

Message entry commands:
<I> -- Insert a new line before the current line, or to begin to enter message
<D>+Line Number -- deletes that line (D3 will delete line 3)
<+> -- Step forward one line
<-> -- Step backward one line
<R> -- Replace word, ex: r/word1/word2
<RG> -- Global Replace
<B> -- Position to <B>eginning
<E> -- Position to <E>nd of text
<C> -- Continue message entry
<K> -- Kill Editing Session (Return to module menu)
<H> -- Prints this HELP screen
<L> -- Lists all lines in buffer
<L>+Line Number -- List That Line (L3 Will List Line 3
<S> -- Send Message
<A> -- Abort, return to Bullet-80
<T> -- Terminate Session
<?> -- To read instructions.
End ALL Inserts With A Blank Line

Help file (<D>irections):
  To use this system is simple, just press the FIRST letter of any command you care to execute. Entering a Carriage Return, <C/R>, or pressing <ENTER> at an abbreviated menu will display an expanded menu if you're not sure what to do.
  Note ** You can also press <S> to stop or CONTROL-S or <P> to pause during the print out of module instructions, and MESSAGE-CENTER messages. Any input will restart the display.
  Here is an explanation of the commands:
  <A>utolog -- In the past, the sysop had to activate your logon password. Now it becomes active immediately. Please note that passwords must begin with a number from 0 to 9, followed by up to 8 characters. Passwords must be at least 6 characters long.
  <B>ulletins -- This command will display the current system <B>ulletins. I try to update them periodically.
  <C> -- This command will activate our <C>lub module. It's easy to join and fun to belong. To get more information, run <C>lub and read instructions.

<D>irections -- This command will print out these directions on how to use Bullet-80 Version 8.0

<E>lectronic Shopping -- This module opens up for use a new use for your home or business computer. It offers you a selection of items that you could purchase and bill to your charge card. It's easy and fun!!

<F>ile-Transfer -- This command combines 2 functions into one. <D>ownloading and <U>ploading. Bullet-80 also supports 4 kinds of file transfer, Standard ASCII, DFT, XModem, and Modem. Be sure you know which method you support before selecting your option. Modem not available at 1200 baud.

<D>ownload: This module allows you to get programs from our database for free. I will only keep this section open as long as I get support from my users. If you care to donate programs to the database, you can use our <U>pload module or call our voice line to make arrangements.

<P>rogram Uploading: This module will allow you to upload programs to Bullet-80 so others can enjoy your ORIGINAL or PUBLIC DOMAIN programs. After review they will be placed in our downloading section.

<G>ames -- This module allows you to play assorted games online. These may change for variety from time to time. Please try to limit your game playing to 30 minutes or less, so Bullet-80 will be available to other users for their needs.

<H>ow-Long -- This function will tell you how long you've been on Bullet-80 for this session. It will also give you the current local time and date.

<I>nterests -- This module will allow you to enter any interests or hobbies you have, or things you like to do. This information will be made available to other Bullet-80 users to read and see if you have anything in common. This is a great way to get to know each other.

<M>essage-Center -- This module is where you gain access to the <M>essage Center on Bullet-80. Here you have the option of <R>eading, <S>canning, or <L>eaving mail for Bullet-80's other users. Each section of the message center has help menus for full instructions.

<O>ther Network Phone Numbers -- Prints out a list of many online systems. This option allows you to search for any BBS by city,

state, area code, or network name. If you know of any not listed, leave me a message as you terminate and I will add it.

<R>equest-Chat -- This will allow you to chat with the sysop via the TRS-80. Generally available from 12PM on, for this particular system. If the sysop isn't available, leave him a private message as you terminate.

<S>ystem Configuration -- This function allows you to customize Bullet-80 to your terminal by letting you adjust screen width, line feeds, upper and lower case, nulls and your bell code.

<T>erminate -- Logs you off of Bullet-80. At this time you can leave a private message to the sysop or be placed on our mailing list. Always use this option so your information can be recorded.

<U>sers Log -- Will display Bullet-80 users for you. You can scan <F>orward or <R>everse or <S>earch for a certain user.

<V>iew System Configuration -- Will tell you about the hardware Bullet-80 uses and a bit about its development.

<X>pert User -- The first time you call Bullet-80, you will be considered a novice user and all menus will be printed out in full. On all future calls, you will be in expert mode with short menus. You can always have the option of toggling your <X>pert status with the <X> command.

Bullet-80 Message Center Instructions
Version 3.0

To leave mail for other users, enter <L> from the main menu. When in that section, at the EDIT prompt, enter <?> for help.

To read mail, you have several new options. You now have the ability to read selectively by sections. When you enter the message center, Section 0 is activated. This means that all open mail in all the public sections is available for you to read. If you would like to read mail for a certain section, use the <C>hange Section # option. At that time, you can view the available sections by entering a C/R at the section # question. Club members with Level 2 clearance will need to enter the <C>lub module to establish their identity, and then will be able to select Section 8, which is the private club mail call. Bullet-80 sysops need to enter the Bullet-80 sysop section for the same reason, and then can select Section 9, which is the sysop mail section.

The message center offers you many ways to read the mail:

Full messages forward and reverse
Scan headers forward and reverse without passes

Scan headers forward and reverse with marking option
Individually by message number

The message center is fully menu-driven. At short menus, pressing <ENTER> will display the expanded menu. Please leave any questions or suggestions you may have addressed to the SYSOP of this system.

Bullet-80 Download Instructions

Bullet-80 version 8.0 supports 4 different kinds of downloading. Here are the download protocols we support:

Standard ASCII
DFT
Modem (300 baud only)
XModem

Most terminal programs will support ASCII file transfers. They are the most common type available.

DFT (Direct File Transfer) requires that you purchase the DFT package if you want to transfer files a sector at a time with error-checking. The advantage of DFT is that the program re-sends each sector until it's told by your computer that it's been received and has been verified. DFT works with tape and disk. It is available for purchase in the shopping section.

Modem file transfer is a disk-based program and is one in the public domain. It is also a sector-by-sector file transfer program that writes to your disk automatically after its buffer is full. Has some error-checking. 300 baud only.

XModem file transfer is similar to Modem, except it works at both 300 and 1200 baud.

WARNING!!!

DON'T ATTEMPT TO USE ANY STYLE YOU DON'T HAVE THE PROPER SOFTWARE FOR. YOU WILL HAVE A LONG WAIT BEFORE THE SYSTEM REALIZES YOU HAVE SELECTED IT IN ERROR!!

Modem and XModem, along with their documentation, should be in the download section in this system. If not, please leave a message for the SYSOP asking him to place it there.

If you experience any problems with any form of download, please notify the SYSOP. His goal is to keep this Bullet-80 system running as smoothly as possible.

CBBS: Computerized Bulletin-Board System

Main menu (Version 3.6):
    MAJOR FUNCTIONS:

(E)nter message	:	(H)elp <= =	:	(Q)uick summary	
(G)ood bye	:	(R)etrieve msg	:	(S)ummarize msgs (see also (O) below)	

    MINOR FUNCTIONS:

# Print caller # etc		(P)rompt bell off :	:	(U)ser update (password, etc)
(A)lter Baud rate	:	(K)ill message	:	(V)ideo backspace
(B)ulletin reprint	:	(N)ulls: How many?	:	(W)elcome reprint
(C)ase upper/lower	:	(O)ne line summary:		e(X)pert user mode
(D)uplex echo off	:	(T)ime/date/E.T.	:	

] >> For details, type H, press return, then type the letter. <<
CHAT See if Randy is available to talk via the keyboard.
  (Please don't abuse this for for "Hi, how are you" -- it's meant to be used to report bugs, seek advice on CBBS usage, etc.)
HELP New user help; (vs. H: keyword based help)
MINE find my messages
NEWS What's new on CBBS
SHORT Shorten output; no dup spaces, etc.

Main prompt:
    Function:A,B,C,D,E,G,H,K,N,O,P,Q,R,S,T,U,V,W,X,# (OR ? IF NOT KNOWN)?

Keyword help list:

HISTORY	KEYWORDS	MINE	STAT	CHAT
OTHER	PARITY	COMMANDS	MAIN	INFO
MENU	MESSAGES	SIGNON	USER	*
U	NULL	GAMES	-	LINEFEEDS
SALE	SELL	CLUB	CLUBS	CBBS
OVERVIEW	SHORT	LONG	BRIEF	NEXT
#	MARK	NEW	MAIL	FUNCTIONS
HELP	H	CTL CHARS	^C	^E
^H	^K	^L	^N	^R
^S	^W	^X	HEADLINES	NEWS
C	CASE	ENTER	MESSAGE	E
INPUT	ESUB	EDIT	LEAVE	PASSWORD
KILL	DELETE	ERASE	K	SUMMARY

O	S	Q	SR	QR
QUICK	SEARCH	FIND	SCAN	BOOLEAN
AND	OR	RETRIEVE	READ	R
FLAG	F	M	STOP	END
EXIT	OFF	QUIT	GOODBYE	G
BYE	COMMENTS	NULLS	N	PHONE
BULLETIN	B	WELCOME	W	DUPLEX
D	ECHO	DOUBLE	BELL	PROMPT
P	EXPERT	X	USE	NEWBAUD
ALTER	BAUD	1200 BAUD	SPEED	A
TIME	T	VIDEO	BACKSPACE	V
TABS	FILES	SOFTWARE	FLIP	OTHER
CPM	CP/M	CPMUG	HARDWARE	OPERATOR
OPERATORS	WHY			

Control Functions:

ASCII	CONTROL	
	DEL/BS	Character delete
C	C	Cancel output (*)
	I	Tab (Tabs set every 8)
K	K	Function abort (*)
N	N	Send 5 more nulls (*)
	R	Retype input line
S	S	Stop/start output (*)
ESC	U	Line delete
	W	Video word backspace
	X	Video line delete

(*): Use while CBBS types to you.

Conference Tree

A hierarchical conferencing system. No menus as such, although the trunk and branches are in this format:

```
*** CONFERENCES      0-JAN-80
   PARENT= NONE       USAGE1500
      +++ SUBMESSAGES +++
HELP                 0-JAN-80
ANNOUNCEMENTS        0-JAN-80
FLAGSHIP             0-JAN-80
SYSOP                0-JAN-80
USERS                0-JAN-80
```

374 APPENDIX 1

Retrieval commands:
Read Conference-name options
Browse Conference-name options
Index Conference-name options

Retrieval options:
Starting (date)
Find (string)
Beyond Conference-name
Exiled
Onlyexiled

Message entry command:
Addto Conference-name

Message edit commands:
List
Replace
Quit
Savepermanent

Help file (READ HELP COMPLETE):
   *** HELP   16-JUL-81
     PARENT = CONFERENCES   USAGE1750
  "READ CONFERENCES" for current subjects.
  "READ <NAME>" where <NAME> is any message or submessage.
  "BROWSE CONFERENCES COMPLETE" to skim.
  "INDEX <NAME>" for index of subtree.
  Commands and options may be abbreviated to their first letters.
  Press "S" key to pause or resume printing.
  Press "K" key to stop message listing.
  Press "C" key to kill current command.
  Control-H or DEL key for backspace.
  To leave system, just hang up!
  "READ HELP-COMMANDS" for more features.
  "READ HELP COMPLETE" for all help documentation.
     + + + SUBMESSAGES + + +
   *** HELP-COMMANDS   16-JUL-81

```
    PARENT=HELP                USAGE1200
```
The commonly-used commands are:
```
  READ <NAME> <OPTIONS>
  BROWSE <NAME> <OPTIONS>
  INDEX <NAME> <OPTIONS>
  ADDTO <NAME> <OPTIONS
```
The other commands, used less often, are:
```
  TERMINAL
  EXILE <NAME>
  UNEXILE <NAME>
  +ADDTO <NAME>
  SERIAL
```

The <NAME> above refers to any message name; for example, "CONFERENCES" or "HELP." <OPTIONS> are optional search techniques described later -- they can be ignored for now.

The "READ" command prints out the named message and then lists its submessages (children) if any -- i.e., all other messages directly attached to it. A message can have any number of submessages, limited only by the system's capacity, and each can have children of its own, to almost any depth. Therefore, the whole structure of messages forms a tree, which grows as users add new items to it.

The "READ" command also shows the message creation date, its parent, and the number of times it has been read (its usage count).

The "BROWSE" command is like "READ" except that it only prints the first line of the message. It is usually used with search options to skim sections of the message tree.

The "INDEX" command shows the name, creation date, and usage count of the message and its complete subtree (the names of all of its children and grandchildren), each properly indented on the printout. It gives a quick overview of what is going on in a section of the tree or the whole tree. For example, try "INDEX HELP" or "INDEX CONFERENCES" (you can abort the command by typing "C" or Control-C while it is printing).

"ADDTO" allows you to add a new message. It must always be added to a message which already exists in the system. "READ HELP-ADDTO" for more details.

The remaining commands are used less often:

"TERMINAL" lets you request special options -- half-duplex, carriage return nulls, and linefeed suppress -- which some terminals require.

"EXILE" and "UNEXILE" are used mainly by the system operator, to control outdated or inappropriate messages without deleting them. Messages that have been exiled are ignored by "READ," "BROWSE," and "INDEX" unless they are requested by name or unless special options (described later) are used. The system operator can avoid clutter such as unwelcome advertising messages, but the reader has the ultimate choice of what to see—a form of soft censorship.

   *** HELP-COMMANDS-2   16-JULY-81
      PARENT = HELP-COMMANDS   USAGE = 600

Eventually, the exiled messages, and any others attached to them, go away when the system operator "squeezes" the disk to reclaim the space they had used. Usually, "EXILE" and "UNEXILE" will require a password.

The " + ADDTO" command is also used mainly by the system operator. It works like "ADDTO" except that the last message read or browsed is retained for re-editing. Usually, a password is required for this command, also

"SERIAL" prints out a Copyright notice and the serial number of the particular CommuniTree system. This is primarily a software protection feature, although it may be helpful in cases when one can't recall which system one is currently using.

All the commands, except for " + ADDTO" and "SERIAL" can be abbreviated to their first letters only: R, B, A, and I.

   *** HELP-OPTIONS   16-JUL-81
      PARENT = HELP   USAGE = 400

The following options can be used with the "READ," "BROWSE," and "INDEX" commands:
   COMPLETE
   STARTING <DATE>
   FIND <STRING>
   BEYOND <NAME>
   EXILED
   ONLYEXILED

These can be used in any combination and in any order. They are entirely optional, but if they are used, they must appear after the <NAME> argument of the command.

"COMPLETE" causes the entire subtree to be printed -- all submessages and their children, etc. -- not just the individual message named. It is automatic with the "INDEX" command, so it needn't be specified. It is also automatic with all other options, i.e., they cause "COMPLETE" to be assumed.

"STARTING" must be given a date in the exact form DD-MMM-YY or D-MMM-YY, where MMM is the first three letters of the month name. "READ CONFERENCES STARTING 6-JUL-81" will skip all messages created before that date. "STARTING" is commonly used in each session to check what's new since the last time you were on the system.

"FIND" must be given a search string. "READ GAMES FIND ROLE" will print any message in a game conference (subtree) with "role" in it: "role playing," etc.

A "FIND" search of the complete "CONFERENCES" can take a long time, up to 15 minutes or more for a large data base. All the other options are much faster because they use data which are always kept in the computer's memory and do not need to be read from the disk. To make "FIND" searches run faster, search only the subtrees of interest, not all of "CONFERENCES," and/or use "STARTING" or other options to limit the search. Or use "FIND" with the "INDEX" command, which is fast because only titles are searched, not the full text, and the disk is not involved. A search can be interrupted by typing "C" or Control-C.

To search for a string that includes spaces, enclose the string in double quotes: 'READ GAMES FIND "ROLE PAYING".' It is usually better to search for single words or parts of words instead, to get spelling and phrasing variations: "comput" gets "computer," "computing," etc.

The "BEYOND" option suppresses printing until the named message has been seen. It is used mainly to continue a printout which has been interrupted.

"EXILED" includes messages which the system operator or others have exiled for some reason. "ONLYEXILED" will display only those messages.

All options can be abbreviated to their first letters. "READ CONFERENCES STARTING 10-JUL-81 FIND GAME EXILED" could be written "R CONFERENCES S 10-JUL-81 F GAME E."

   *** HELP-ADDTO   16-JUL-81
    PARENT=HELP   USAGE=375
     ADDTO COMMAND

"ADDTO <NAME>" lets you enter your own message to the system. You will be asked to confirm the date setting, and to give your message a name. Try to pick a name that is somewhat descriptive of content, and unlikely to be used elsewhere on the tree, to avoid confusion when searching by message name. You may "ADDTO" any message. On some systems, you may need a password to "ADDTO" messages; on others, you may need a password in order to "ADDTO PRIVATE" or "ADDTO CONFERENCES." These variations depend on the system operator and the application. You can experiment with the "ADDTO" command, as long as you don't use the "SAVE-PERMANENT" word, which will save your experiment permanently.

*** EDITOR   16-JUL-81
   PARENT=HELP-ADDTO   USAGE=275
   THE EDITOR

When you use the "ADDTO NAME" command, you are given a simple line-oriented editor with which to enter your text. You may enter up to 50 lines of text with up to 80 characters in each line. The editor prompts are self-descriptive. To help keep the text readable, you should avoid ending lines with parts of words or hyphenated words. You will be able to "LIST" and "REPLACE" lines that are erroneous before you save them permanently. When typing a line, you may type the entire 80 character line before hitting Return. If you go over, the system will give you a "bell" warning. To get out of the editor, simply type "QUIT" when the editor prompt line appears, and this will put you back into the main command mode.

*** MISC-HELP   16-JUL-81
   PARENT=HELP   USAGE=300

These tips will help you get the most out of the system, and will also prove beneficial to all if they are heeded.

1) Descriptive message names, preferably unique, are recommended. The use of hyphens is preferred over the use of periods to separate words in message titles.

2) Children of exiled messages will go away when the disk is squeezed, so be careful not to add valued messages to messages that are dated.

3) There is a limit of 321 messages that can be in the system at any given time, so one big message is preferred to several small ones.

4) "BROWSE" returns the first line of a message, so it is helpful to make that first line as descriptive as possible of the message's content.

*** SYSTEM-PASSWORD   16-JUL-81
    PARENT = HELP   USAGE = 290

The system operator can choose from seven levels of password protection—from none at all, to requiring a password just to log on. At any time, there is only one password, which is usually given to anyone who is a Fairwitness of a conference. The default is medium protection, with the password required for "+ADDTO," "EXILE," "UNEXILE" and starting a new private conference.

A higher password level allows the public to read only and not enter any new messages; this level might be used for a commercial movie guide or similar service. In this case you can still add messages to the "GUEST" message (if the system operator has provided one), to give feedback to the system operator on an otherwise read-only system.

The system operator does not see what you are writing or reading, but does see erroneous command names and erroneous passwords on a log. This can allow you to communicate with the system operator (say, to send a phone number to him or her privately . . . since the phone number is not a valid command name, it will show up on the log). But this channel is unreliable, as the information may be dropped off the screen before it is seen.

PMS (People's Message Service)

Main menu:
---->> System Commands
E = Enter a message into system.
F = Features, articles, excerpts.
G = Goodbye. Leave system. (Hangup)
H = Help with various functions.
I = Information about system.
K = Kill a message from the files.
M = Message alert. Messages for you?
N = News -- System news.
O = Other systems current summary.
Q = Quickscan of all message headers.
QP = Quickscan of private msg headers.
R = Retrieve a message from the files.
S = Scan of all message headers.
SP = Scan of private message headers.

380 APPENDIX 1

SR = Selective message retrieval.
T = Time, date and connect-time.
U = User modifiable system functions.
X = eXpert user mode (On/Off toggle).
Z = Continue message entry after abort.
? = Prints this list of commands.
* = Flagged message memory retrieval.
TALK = Lets you talk to the sysop.
TEST = Modem continuous test loop.
NEWCALL = Information for new callers.
ALT = Switch message bases.
GENERAL14 = File Transfer -- Download files.
GENERAL15 = File Transfer -- Upload files.

Main prompt:
Command?

Message entry menu:
---->> Message entry commands
A = Abort message.
C = Continue entry.
D = Delete line (Dx).
E = Edit line (Ex).
H = Help with message entry functions.
I = Insert a line (Ix).
L = List lines from specified # (Lx).
S = Save completed message to disk.<<<
W = reWrite an old message.

Message entry prompt:
(A,C,D,E,H,I,L,S,W,?)?

Help file:
   * * SYSTEM CONTROL FUNCTIONS AND CODES * *

There are certain characters which cause specific functions to occur while system is printing to you, NOT when waiting for input. These may be Control, lower or upper case characters.

-- C -- Stops printing the current line up to carriage return. Use this if you want to skip over several lines of text without aborting the function. Use one 'C' for each line you want to jump over.

-- K -- Causes a jump to the next logical operation. As an example, if you were retrieving several messages, it would cause a jump to the next message. During message entry listing, will return you to the message entry command level. The ONLY time this command will return to main COMMAND level is if there is no logical next function.

-- N -- Adds to nulls for each 'N' types. Use this when you have a printer online, which needs nulls (is dropping first characters of lines). May be used at any time in system operation. Up to 100 nulls can be added, but in practice no more than 20 should ever be needed, and even that is extreme.

-- P -- Cancels nulls to zero. Regardless of current null setting, resets nulls to zero. You can then add again with 'N' if you wish.

-- R -- Flags messages during a scan or quickscan to be later retrieved with the * command. Type an 'R' at the NEXT message header. It will always be one message behind. There is usually not time to comprehend a message header and type the 'R' before that header is done being printed. Just pause slightly and then type it. At the end of that next message header, you will see an "**OK** <xxxx> verification. The 'xxxx' will contain the number of the message actually flagged.

-- S -- Stops text output until any other character is sent.

-- X -- This guy causes an unconditional abort of whatever function you're in, and an immediate jump to main COMMAND level.

In addition, there are three other Control characters that are used during text entry. They are:

-- ^I -- Tab to next column (mod eight)

-- ^R -- Retype the line up to current position. Use this to verify what you have typed so far.

-- ^X -- Abort and start current line over.

* * SYSTEM COMMANDS * *

All system commands are input to the main COMMAND level. Certain commands (H, K, O, R, S, SR, and others) may also have extenders describing or anticipating the next question asked. As an example: Since H is for help, if you wanted help on everything, you could type H;ALL. Using R as another example, if you wanted to retrieve message #1937, you could type R;1937. More examples of various multiple parameters are explained for each individual command.

-- E -- Enter a message into the system. Pretty self-explanatory, just follow the prompting. You must enter a password when asked. This is the password used to kill the message. There are also two levels of security messages available. If you type LOCK as your password (you will be asked again for the password for killing), the message will be marked as private, and will automatically open for the person to whom it's addressed or who wrote it. Others will be asked for a password which will be the same as the password for killing it. If you enter LOCX instead of LOCK, the message can be read ONLY with the password unless the caller has signed in with a USERID. If you decide you're not done with the message and want to continue instead of saving, just type R in response to password.

-- F -- Features. Articles on interest. To read an article, type the name of the article as a command. Do not use F.

-- G -- Goodbye. Exit the system and hang up the phone. Files will be updated at this time. System will also respond to: END, OFF, BYE, and a few others. Comments can be left or type R to return to program.

-- H -- System help files. Typing an H by itself will print out all the possible areas you can obtain help for. Typing H; (character) will print help on a specific function.

-- K -- Kill a message. This will remove a message from the system files. You must have the password (entered during message entry) to use it. You also have the option of automatically killing messages that are addressed to you at the time you read them. See more details in 'R' command.

-- M -- Message alert. This command is issued directly after you're logged on. It allows you to automatically retrieve all messages addressed to you. You may use it at any time in the program. One word of caution: If you have flagged messages for retrieval and use this command, all the flagged messages will be lost. If you do use it, and don't retrieve all the messages to you, you can continue with the * command (same as flagged retrieval).

-- N -- News. Display system news, highlights.

-- O -- Other systems list. Updated regularly, is the nationally distributed P.A.M.S. list, a summary of all known Public Access Message Systems of all types, in alphabetical order. It can also be printer formatted by following the prompting. When asked to format, and your printer is not the standard 66 lines per page default of PMS but you still want to format to your printer, type the effective number of lines per page for your printer INSTEAD of a 'Y' response. You can also specify a string to look for within this file by typing O;search, where 'search' is the area code, or system name in question. All lines containing appropriate information will be displayed.

-- Q -- Quickscan of message headers. Not that much quicker. See also, 'S.'

--R -- Retrieve messages from the files. There are several modes here. You can select messages singly or in multiples. Examples of entries: R;381 or R381 or R381; R560;etc. To retrieve all messages starting from a certain point, type: R;555^ or R;1010+ (for example). See also the * command for flagged messages.

When you retrieve a message that is addressed to you, at the end of it, you'll drop to a secondary level with the option "Kill this message (y/n/a/u)." 'Y' means, yes, kill the message. 'N' means, no, don't kill it. 'A' means read it again. 'U' means to Unmark it. Unmarking a message removes it from your message alert section, but leaves it for others to read. You would use this if you wanted to leave a message containing useful information for others to read. You cannot, however, Unmark a private message, as others couldn't read it anyway.

You'll then be asked if you have a reply. If you do, answer yes, otherwise answer no. The automatic reply does some of the busywork for you (To: From: etc) and upon completion of the reply and saving the message, will continue with retrieving other messages you may have specified. During auto-reply, if you just type carriage return in response to 'Subject?', it will take the subject of the message that was to you and add a 'r/' to it, meaning reply to the previous message.

-- S -- Scan message headers. Here you specify a starting message number to start the scan. S;500 would start scanning at message 500 or the next highest if there is no message 500. You can also scan in reverse order by either specifying a number greater than or equal to the highest message number, or by adding a '–' (minus sign) directly AFTER the message number to start. Examples: S;500 S1200 S;1040– etc. As you are scanning you use 'R' to flag messages you want to read later with the * command. (See *.)

-- SR -- Selective retrieval. Use this command to retrieve all messages whose headers contain data you are looking for. As an example, if you enter FOR SALE, it would automatically retrieve all messages with FOR SALE in the header. This will work for ALL aspects of the header. FROM, TO, DATE, SUBJECT and LOCATION. All messages that meet these parameters are put in flagged memory and automatically retrieved. If there are no matches, it will tell you.

-- T -- Prints current local time and date, and the length of time since you logged on.

-- U -- User modifiable functions. These are parameters which affect certain default conditions of the system. You modify them to your current needs.

A) Apple 40 mode. Toggles between Apple 40 and 64 column message entry mode. Does not affect text output.

C) Case switch. Toggles between UPPER ONLY and UPPER/lower case text output. Lower case text is accepted during message entry and comments in either mode.

CS) Clear screen. Allows setting the character or sequence of characters that will cause the local terminal to clear its screen. In this mode, after each message has been displayed, the string 'more--' will display. The system will sit there and wait for a response from you. This is to keep the screen from clearing before you are ready to move on to the next message. Should you want to temporarily remove this option for the retrieval of a particular string of messages (say for printing them), you can type the letter 'N' at 'more--'. If you wish to abort the string of messages altogether, you can type 'K' or 'X.' You can then continue with *.

D) Duplex switch. Toggles between full (echo) and half (no echo) duplex modes.

L) Line feed switch. Turns linefeeds on or off. System default when your call is on.

N) Nulls. Displays the current number of nulls in effect, and allows you to modify them directly.

P) Prompt. Allows you to change the current system prompt, which is usually a '?' (a question mark). Here you can enter either the character you want the prompt to be or the ASCII value of it. The prompt will stay defined as such through all system functions, until you change it again, or log off. This feature can be used to good advantage with automatic upload or download programs (automatic message entry, etc).

T) Term - video/printer mode toggle. In the video mode, recognizes Control-H (backspace), delete (underscore) and rubout (ASCII 08,

95 and 127, respectively) as backspace characters and echoes backspace-space-backspace as destructive backspace. In the printer mode, the same characters are recognized, but during the backspacing additional reverse slashes and the characters being backspaced over will appear in reverse order.

PAR) Parity. Allows you to modify the word length, parity, and number of stop bits employed. Displays a little chart with 8 positions. One of them will have a circumflex (^) under it, indicating the current system default at that time. Examples of numbers could be: 7E1 or 8N2, etc. 7E1 means 7 bit word, even parity, and 1 stop bit. 8N2 would mean 8 bit word, no parity, and 2 stop bits, etc. Enter the position number 1-8 of the mode you need to use.

STAT) Displays current system status of all the modes covered by the 'U' function, so you can see your current setup.

-- X -- eXpert user mode. System default is on. Does away with the additional prompting at command level, the pausing between messages during a multiple retrieval and allows certain other privileges. However, when clear screen option is in effect (U;CS), the pausing beteen messages will return.

-- Z -- Allows you to resume entering a message after you have aborted it. Let's say you were entering a message and realized you had forgotten something relevant to that message and needed to reread an earlier message or article. You can abort the message, reread the other messages or articles and then re-enter your message with all data intact, and continue. Should you be disconnected while entering a message, and you are the very next caller calling back, the system will ask if you want to continue the message. Answering 'yes' will list the message so far and allow you to pick up from there. If you were in abort when carrier was lost and call right back, the system will not ask about continuing the message, but you can with the 'Z' command. Also your flagged messages will be preserved if losing carrier occurs during flagged retrieval. Just continue with*.

-- ? -- Prints a list of all commands available at your current level of operation.

-- * -- Retrieve messages in flagged memory. This can be messages flagged during a scan or using the 'M' or 'SR' function. You may pick up where you left off with this command, if you ended your retrieval for any reason. Using this command with scanning messages (such as S;1000*) will clear the flagged memory completely for starting fresh.

386   APPENDIX 1

Those calling with USERIDs will be able to retain various parameters of their last visit to the system automatically. All parameters set by U;STAT except nulls are retained in the USERID system plus the highest message number of each visit. After logging in, if you would like to scan messages starting from the highest of the last visit, type 'S;!'. If you would rather just retrieve all those messages, type 'R;!'. If you do not access S;! or R;!, your message marker will not be updated.

* * MESSAGE ENTRY COMMANDS * *

Note: All the following commands can be issued as DOT commands. A dot command may be entered as '.A' or '.E' or whatever the desired command is, as long as the dot is the first character throughout message entry.

-- A -- Abort message and return to command level. You may continue your message with the 'Z' command.

-- C -- Continue with message entry. Allows you to continue your message at whatever the next line in succession would be.

-- D -- Delete a line. Specify the number of the line you wish to delete. D;x and Dx are legal here. (x = line number.)

-- E -- Edit or retype a mesage line (Ex or E;x also legal). To replace the line, just enter the new line. Editing a line is accomplished by specifying a string you want to replace with what you want to replace it with, in this form: OLD/NEW with old and new string separated by a slash. You can also use three slashes as in the old editing routine: /OLD/NEW/. To remove a section of text, type: OLD// or /OLD//.

To insert text at the beginning of a line, type: <this is new text. The left arrow means insert at the beginning. To append text at the end of a line, type: >this is new text. The right arrow means append at the end. If you type a Control-S (Control-S only) as the first character of the line, the contents of the line will be automatically centered. If you are modifying an existing line and just type a Control-S by itself, whatever is already on that line will be centered. Control-S as the first character of a line will also work during regular line entry (not just during edit).

One eccentricity of this type of editing is that the '/' (slash) character cannot be contained within the text you are actually editing. It would be necessary to retype the new line up to the '/' and then append ('>') at the end of that section.

Should the line you are editing get mangled beyond recognition, you can type '!' (exclamation point) on the line by itself, and the original line will be reinstated as it was when you first started the edit.

-- I -- Insert a line (Ix or I;x also legal). Allows you to insert a line directly BEFORE whatever line # you specify.

-- S -- Save the completed masterpiece to disk. You MUST use this command for your message to be saved!

-- W -- reWrite an old message. Using this command, you can kill an older message (with the correct password, of course) with the contents of it appearing in the message you are currently entering. The old message lines will be appended to your current position in the message. As an example, if you were at line 10 of a message, and wanted some data that was in an old message, use 'W.' The contents of the message you killed will start at line 10. You can then edit or modify as required, then save it.

APPENDIX 2
State, City, Area Code Guide

STATE, CITY	AREA CODE	CPB NUMBER	PAGE
Alabama			
Gadsden	205	CPBB00030	180
Montgomery	205	CPBB00040	180
Montgomery	205	CPBB00050	181
Montgomery	205	CPBB00060	181
Alaska			
Anchorage	907	CPBB00070	182
Arizona			
Phoenix	602	CPBB00090	182
Phoenix	602	CPBB00100	183
Phoenix	602	CPBB00110	183
Phoenix	602	CPBB00120	183
Sierra Vista	602	CPBB00130	184
Tucson	602	CPBB00140	184
Arkansas			
Ft. Smith	501	CPBB00150	184
Little Rock	501	CPBB00160	185
California			
Clovis	209	CPBB00170	185
Beverly Hills	213	CPBB00180	186
Burbank	213	CPBB00190	186
Granada Hills	213	CPBB00200	187
Hollywood	213	CPBB00210	187
Hollywood	213	CPBB00220	188
Hollywood	213	CPBB00230	188
Huntington Park	213	CPBB00240	189

State, City, Area Code Guide

STATE, CITY	AREA CODE	CPB NUMBER	PAGE
Long Beach	213	CPBB00250	189
Long Beach	213	CPBB00260	190
Los Angeles	213	CPBB00270	190
Los Angeles	213	CPBB00280	191
Los Angeles	213	CPBB00290	191
Los Angeles	213	CPBB00300	192
Los Angeles	213	CPBB00310	192
Los Angeles	213	CPBB00320	192
Los Angeles	213	CPBB00330	193
Los Angeles	213	CPBB00340	193
Pasadena	213	CPBB00350	194
San Fernando	213	CPBB00360	194
Sherman Oaks	213	CPBB00370	194
Sherman Oaks	213	CPBB00380	195
Southgate	213	CPBB00390	195
Sylmar	213	CPBB00400	196
Tarzana	213	CPBB00410	196
Torrance	213	CPBB00420	197
Torrance	213	CPBB00430	197
Venice	213	CPBB00440	198
Aptos	408	CPBB00450	198
Berkeley	415	CPBB00460	199
Campbell	408	CPBB00470	199
Cupertino	408	CPBB00480	200
Milpitas	408	CPBB00490	200
San Jose	408	CPBB00500	200
San Jose	408	CPBB00510	201
San Jose	408	CPBB00520	201
Saratoga	408	CPBB00530	202
Sunnyvale	408	CPBB00540	202
Sunnyvale	408	CPBB00550	203
Berkeley	415	CPBB00560	203
Berkeley	415	CPBB00570	203
Daly City	415	CPBB00580	204
Forest Knolls	415	CPBB00590	204
Fremont	415	CPBB00600	205
Los Altos	415	CPBB00610	205

APPENDIX 2

STATE, CITY	AREA CODE	CPB NUMBER	PAGE
Mountain View	415	CPBB00620	206
Novato	415	CPBB00630	206
Oakland	415	CPBB00640	206
Oakland	415	CPBB00650	207
San Carlos	415	CPBB00660	207
San Francisco	415	CPBB00670	207
San Francisco	415	CPBB00680	208
San Francisco	415	CPBB00690	208
San Francisco	415	CPBB00700	209
San Francisco	415	CPBB00710	209
San Leandro	415	CPBB00720	209
San Leandro	415	CPBB00730	210
San Lorenzo	415	CPBB00740	210
Sausalito	415	CPBB00750	211
Carlsbad	619	CPBB00760	211
Chula Vista	619	CPBB00770	212
Lakeside	619	CPBB00780	212
Poway	619	CPBB00790	213
San Diego	619	CPBB00800	213
San Diego	619	CPBB00810	214
San Diego	619	CPBB00820	214
San Diego	619	CPBB00830	215
San Diego	619	CPBB00840	215
San Marcos	619	CPBB00850	215
Santee	619	CPBB00860	216
Santee	619	CPBB00870	216
Solana Beach	619	CPBB00880	217
Napa	707	CPBB00890	217
Napa	707	CPBB00900	218
Napa	707	CPBB00910	218
Santa Rosa	707	CPBB00920	218
Yountville	707	CPBB00930	219
Anaheim	714	CPBB00940	219
Anaheim	714	CPBB00950	220
Anaheim	714	CPBB00960	220
Fontana	714	CPBB00970	221
Fullerton	714	CPBB00980	221

State, City, Area Code Guide

STATE, CITY	AREA CODE	CPB NUMBER	PAGE
Garden Grove	714	CPBB00990	221
Highland	714	CPBB01000	222
Ontario	714	CPBB01010	222
Riverside	714	CPBB01020	223
Riverside	714	CPBB01030	223
Goleta	805	CPBB01040	224
Santa Barbara	805	CPBB01050	224
Santa Barbara	805	CPBB01060	224
Sacramento	916	CPBB01070	225
Sacramento	916	CPBB01080	225
Colorado			
Colorado Springs	303	CPBB01110	226
Denver	303	CPBB01120	226
Denver	303	CPBB01130	226
Denver	303	CPBB01140	227
Denver	303	CPBB01150	227
Denver	303	CPBB01160	228
Ft. Collins	303	CPBB01170	228
Golden	303	CPBB01180	229
Lakewood	303	CPBB01190	230
Lakewood	303	CPBB01200	230
Connecticut			
Danbury	203	CPBB01250	230
Greenwich	203	CPBB01260	231
Hartford	203	CPBB01270	231
New Canaan	203	CPBB01280	232
New Fairfield	203	CPBB01290	232
Norwalk	203	CPBB01300	233
Windsor	203	CPBB01310	233
Delaware			
Wilmington	302	CPBB01330	233
District of Coumbia			
Washington, D.C.	202	CPBB01350	234

STATE, CITY	AREA CODE	CPB NUMBER	PAGE
Florida			
Deerfield Beach	305	CPBB01390	234
Ft. Lauderdale	305	CPBB01400	235
Ft. Lauderdale	305	CPBB01410	236
Orlando	305	CPBB01420	236
W. Palm Beach	305	CPBB01430	237
Tampa	813	CPBB01450	237
Tampa	813	CPBB01460	238
Tampa	813	CPBB01470	238
Jacksonville	904	CPBB01490	238
Jacksonville	904	CPBB01500	239
Orange Park	904	CPBB01510	239
Pensacola	904	CPBB01520	240
Georgia			
Atlanta	404	CPBB01550	240
Atlanta	404	CPBB01560	241
Atlanta	404	CPBB01570	241
Atlanta	404	CPBB01580	241
Atlanta	404	CPBB01590	242
Ringgold	404	CPBB01600	242
Albany	912	CPBB01620	243
Savannah	912	CPBB01630	243
Hawaii			
Honolulu	808	CPBB01650	244
Honolulu	808	CPBB01660	244
Illinois			
Springfield	217	CPBB01690	245
Argonne	312	CPBB01720	245
Chicago	312	CPBB01730	246
Chicago	312	CPBB01740	246
Chicago	312	CPBB01750	246
Chicago	312	CPBB01759	247
Chicago	312	CPBB01760	247
Chicago	312	CPBB01770	247
Chicago	312	CPBB01780	248
Chicago	312	CPBB01790	248

State, City, Area Code Guide 393

STATE, CITY	AREA CODE	CPB NUMBER	PAGE
Chicago	312	CPBB01800	249
Chicago	312	CPBB01810	249
Chicago	312	CPBB01820	250
Chicago	312	CPBB01830	250
Chicago	312	CPBB01840	251
Chicago	312	CPBB01850	251
Chicago	312	CPBB01860	251
Chicago	312	CPBB01870	252
Chicago	312	CPBB01880	252
Chicago	312	CPBB01890	252
Downers Grove	312	CPBB01900	253
Glen Ellyn	312	CPBB01910	253
Lake Forest	312	CPBB01920	253
Lincolnwood	312	CPBB01930	254
Niles	312	CPBB01940	254
Palantine	312	CPBB01950	255
Wheaton	312	CPBB01960	255
Lockport	815	CPBB01980	255
Indiana			
Indianapolis	317	CPBB02000	256
Indianapolis	317	CPBB02020	256
Iowa			
Cedar Rapids	319	CPBB02040	257
Cedar Raids	319	CPBB02050	257
Iowa City	319	CPBB02060	258
Kansas			
Hutchinson	316	CPBB02090	258
Mission	913	CPBB02110	259
Overland Park	913	CPBB02120	259
Overland Park	913	CPBB02130	260
Overland Park	913	CPBB02140	260
Louisiana			
Shreveport	318	CPBB02200	261
Shreveport	318	CPBB02210	261
Baton Rouge	504	CPBB02230	262

STATE, CITY	AREA CODE	CPB NUMBER	PAGE
Baton Rouge	504	CPBB0224Ø	262
Baton Rouge	504	CPBB0225Ø	263
Maine			
Gorham	207	CPBB0227Ø	263
Maryland			
Baltimore	301	CPBB0229Ø	263
Beltsville	301	CPBB0230Ø	264
Bethesda	301	CPBB0231Ø	264
Bethesda	301	CPBB0232Ø	265
Forest Glen	301	CPBB0233Ø	265
Gaithersburg	301	CPBB0234Ø	265
Silver Spring	301	CPBB0235Ø	266
Upper Marlboro	301	CPBB0236Ø	266
Massachusetts			
Springfield	413	CPBB0238Ø	267
Andover	617	CPBB0240Ø	267
Arlington	617	CPBB0241Ø	268
Bellingham	617	CPBB0242Ø	268
Boston	617	CPBB0243Ø	268
Boston	617	CPBB0243S	269
Boston	617	CPBB0244Ø	269
Chelmsford	617	CPBB0245Ø	270
Lincoln	617	CPBB0246Ø	270
Lynfield	617	CPBB0247Ø	270
Milford	617	CPBB0248Ø	271
Newton	617	CPBB0249Ø	271
Peabody	617	CPBB0250Ø	272
Waltham	617	CPBB0251Ø	272
Michigan			
Ann Arbor	313	CPBB0253Ø	273
Detroit	313	CPBB0254Ø	273
Detroit	313	CPBB0255Ø	274
Detroit	313	CPBB0256Ø	274
Hazel Park	313	CPBB0257Ø	274
Livonia	313	CPBB0258Ø	275

State, City, Area Code Guide

STATE, CITY	AREA CODE	CPB NUMBER	PAGE
Plymouth	313	CPBB02590	275
Plymouth	313	CPBB02600	276
Southfield	313	CPBB02610	276
Warren	313	CPBB02620	276
Waterford	313	CPBB02630	277
Lansing	517	CPBB02650	277
Lansing	517	CPBB02660	277
Grand Rapids	616	CPBB02680	278
Minnesota			
Minneapolis	612	CPBB02710	278
Minneapolis	612	CPBB02720	279
Minneapolis	612	CPBB02730	279
Minneapolis	612	CPBB02740	280
Minneapolis	612	CPBB02750	280
Minneapolis	612	CPBB02760	281
Minneapolis	612	CPBB02770	281
Minneapolis	612	CPBB02780	281
Minneapolis	612	CPBB02790	282
Richfield	612	CPBB02800	282
Mississippi			
Hattiesburg	601	CPBB02820	282
Missouri			
St. Louis	314	CPBB02850	283
Belton	816	CPBB02870	283
Independence	816	CPBB02880	284
Independence	816	CPBB02890	284
Kansas City	816	CPBB02900	285
Nebraska			
Omaha	402	CPBB02950	285
Omaha	402	CPBB02960	286
Omaha	402	CPBB02970	286
Nevada			
Las Vegas	702	CPBB02990	287
Las Vegas	702	CPBB03000	287

STATE, CITY	AREA CODE	CPB NUMBER	PAGE
New Hampshire			
Nashua	603	CPBB03010	287
Peterborough	603	CPBB03020	288
New Jersey			
Atlantic Highlands	201	CPBB03050	289
Brielle	201	CPBB03060	289
Haledon	201	CPBB03070	290
Linden	201	CPBB03080	290
Metuchen	201	CPBB03090	291
Montclair	201	CPBB03100	291
New Brunswick	201	CPBB03110	292
New Brunswick	201	CPBB03120	292
Nutley	201	CPBB03130	293
Ocean	201	CPBB03140	293
Rockaway	201	CPBB03150	293
Short Hills	201	CPBB03160	294
Wayne	201	CPBB03170	294
Mt. Holly	609	CPBB03190	295
Pemberton	609	CPBB03200	295
Wenonah	609	CPBB03210	296
New York			
New York	212	CPBB03240	296
New York	212	CPBB03250	297
New York	212	CPBB03260	297
New York	212	CPBB03270	298
New York	212	CPBB03280	298
New York	212	CPBB03290	299
Woodland Hills	212	CPBB03300	299
Woodland Hills	212	CPBB03301	300
Woodland Hills	212	CPBB03302	300
Bethpage	516	CPBB03310	301
Centereach	516	CPBB03320	301
Oceanside	516	CPBB03330	302
Yaphank	516	CPBB03340	302
Schenectady	518	CPBB03350	303
Johnson City	607	CPBB03370	303

STATE, CITY	AREA CODE	CPB NUMBER	PAGE
Vestal	607	CPBB0338Ø	304
Poughkeepsie	914	CPBB0340Ø	304
North Carolina			
Charlotte	704	CPBB0345Ø	305
Charlotte	704	CPBB0346Ø	305
Cary	919	CPBB0347Ø	306
Greenville	919	CPBB0348Ø	306
Jacksonville	919	CPBB0349Ø	307
Ohio			
Akron	216	CPBB0351Ø	307
Akron	216	CPBB0352Ø	308
Akron	216	CPBB0353Ø	308
Akron	216	CPBB0354Ø	308
Cleveland	216	CPBB0355Ø	309
Louisville	216	CPBB0356Ø	309
Massillon	216	CPBB0357Ø	310
Youngstown	216	CPBB0358Ø	310
Toledo	419	CPBB0360Ø	310
Cincinnati	513	CPBB0362Ø	311
Cincinnati	513	CPBB0363Ø	311
Dayton	513	CPBB0364Ø	312
W. Carollton	513	CPBB0365Ø	312
Oklahoma			
Oklahoma City	405	CPBB0368Ø	312
Oklahoma City	405	CPBB0369Ø	313
S. Oklahoma City	405	CPBB0370Ø	313
Tulsa	918	CPBB0373Ø	314
Tulsa	918	CPBB0374Ø	314
Oregon			
Beaverton	503	CPBB0376Ø	315
Klamath Falls	503	CPBB0377Ø	315
Medford	503	CPBB0378Ø	315
Portland	503	CPBB0379Ø	316
Portland	503	CPBB0380Ø	316
Portland	503	CPBB0381Ø	317

APPENDIX 2

STATE, CITY	AREA CODE	CPB NUMBER	PAGE
Pennsylvania			
Allentown	215	CPBB03830	317
Bethlehem	215	CPBB03835	317
Cheltenham	215	CPBB03840	318
North Wales	215	CPBB03850	318
Pittsburgh	412	CPBB03870	319
Camp Hill	717	CPBB03880	319
Rhode Island			
Cranston	401	CPBB03900	320
Providence	401	CPBB03910	320
South Carolina			
Ft. Mill	803	CPBB03920	321
Mt. Pleasnat	803	CPBB03930	321
North Augusta	803	CPBB03940	322
Summerville	803	CPBB03950	322
Summerville	803	CPBB03960	322
Tennessee			
Hinson	615	CPBB03980	323
Nashville	615	CPBB03990	323
Memphis	901	CPBB04010	324
Memphis	901	CPBB04020	324
Memphis	901	CPBB04030	325
Memphis	901	CPBB04040	325
Texas			
Dallas	214	CPBB04080	326
Dallas	214	CPBB04090	326
Hawkins	214	CPBB04100	327
Henderson	214	CPBB04110	327
Tyler	214	CPBB04120	328
Austin	512	CPBB04140	328
Elgin	512	CPBB04150	329
Laporte	713	CPBB04170	329
Amarillo	806	CPBB04190	330
Wichita Falls	817	CPBB04220	330
El Paso	915	CPBB04250	331
San Angelo	915	CPBB04260	331

State, City, Area Code Guide

STATE, CITY	AREA CODE	CPB NUMBER	PAGE
Utah			
Holladay	801	CPBB04280	332
Roy	801	CPBB04290	332
Vermont			
Burlington	602	CPBB04320	333
Virginia			
Arlington	703	CPBB04350	333
Dale City	703	CPBB04360	334
Fairfax	703	CPBB04370	334
Fairfax	703	CPBB04371	335
Fairfax	703	CPBB04380	335
Fairfax	703	CPBB04385	335
Fairfax	703	CPBB04390	336
McLean	703	CPBB04400	336
Springfield	703	CPBB04410	336
Grafton	804	CPBB04450	337
Newport News	804	CPBB04460	337
Tidewater	804	CPBB04470	338
Washington			
Bellevue	206	CPBB04490	339
Bremerton	206	CPBB04500	339
Edmonds	206	CPBB04510	340
Edmonds	206	CPBB04520	340
Redmond	206	CPBB04530	340
N. Seattle	206	CPBB04540	341
Seattle	206	CPBB04550	341
Seattle	206	CPBB04560	342
Snohomish	206	CPBB04570	342
Tacoma	206	CPBB04580	343
Tacoma	206	CPBB04590	343
West Virginia			
Charleston	304	CPBB04620	344
Comet	304	CPBB04630	344
Evans	304	CPBB04640	345
Morgantown	304	CPBB04650	345

STATE, CITY	AREA CODE	CPB NUMBER	PAGE
Wisconsin			
Greenfield	414	CPBB04690	346
Milwaukee	414	CPBB04700	346
Milwaukee	414	CPBB04710	347
Milwaukee	414	CPBB04720	347
Racine	414	CPBB04730	348
Janesville	608	CPBB04760	348
Wausau	715	CPBB04780	349
Wausau	715	CPBB04790	349
Wyoming			
Cheyenne	307	CPBB04850	350

APPENDIX 3
Downloadable Software

CPB NUMBER	SYSTEM NAME	PAGE
Apple		
CPBB00260	TKM's Mini BBS	190
CPBB00340	PMS	193
CPBB00430	Telephone Software Connection	197
CPBB00780	Online/PMS	212
CPBB00870	PMS #1	216
CPBB01410	Colorburst/Trade-80 #1	236
CPBB01730	Aurora Computers	246
CPBB01880	PMS—CRT	252
CPBB01920	PMS—IAC	253
CPBB02130	PMS—Apple Bits	260
CPBB02140	PMS—Your Computer Connection	260
CPBB02210	TBBS	261
CPBB02350	Computer Age BBS	266
CPBB02450	Chelmsford Exchange	270
CPBB02630	Bullet-80	277
CPBB02760	PMS	281
CPBB02960	ABBS	286
CPBB03010	Access-80	287
CPBB03090	TBBS	291
CPBB03300	Rainbow Connection #1	299
CPBB03301	Rainbow Connection #2	300
CPBB03302	Rainbow Connection #3	300
CPBB03450	ABBS	305
CPBB03460	PC-BBS	305
CPBB03520	PMS—RAUG	308
CPBB03630	Komputer Klassified	311

402 APPENDIX 3

CPB NUMBER	SYSTEM NAME	PAGE
CPBB03640	The Choyce BBS	312
CPBB03740	T.I.E.	314
CPBB04090	Software Exchange	326
CPBB04140	TBBS	328
CPBB04220	Commnet-80	330
CPBB04410	Future Tech	336
CPBB04560	Seacomm-80	342
CPBB04730	Colortron ABBS	348

Atari

CPB NUMBER	SYSTEM NAME	PAGE
CPBB00400	Interact	196
CPBB00480	GFxBBS	200
CPBB00520	IBBS	201
CPBB01070	Bullet-80	225
CPBB01730	Aurora Computers	246
CPBB02240	RCP/M	262
CPBB02610	M.A.C.E. West	276
CPBB02630	Bullet-80	277
CPBB02680	GRASS	278
CPBB02780	TAIG	281
CPBB03000	SNACC AMIS	287
CPBB03010	Access-80	287
CPBB03090	TBBS	291
CPBB03300	Rainbow Connection #1	299
CPBB03301	Rainbow Connection #2	300
CPBB03302	Rainbow Connection #3	300
CPBB03630	Komputer Klassified	311
CPBB03640	The Choyce BBS	312
CPBB03700	Software Safaris	313
CPBB03840	RCP/M	318
CPBB03870	Acenet	319
CPBB03910	AMIS	320
CPBB04090	Software Exchange	326
CPBB04140	TBBS	328
CPBB04170	Apex BBS	329
CPBB04220	Commnet-80	330
CPBB04350	Best Little BBS	333
CPBB04410	Future Tech	336

Downloadable Software 403

CPB NUMBER	SYSTEM NAME	PAGE
CPBB04560	Seacomm-80	342
CPBB04580	NW Micronet	343

Color Computer

CPB NUMBER	SYSTEM NAME	PAGE
CPBB00390	L.A. Color Exchange (Color-80 #4)	195
CPBB00510	Computers For Christ	201
CPBB00540	Color-80 #1	202
CPBB00630	Golden State BBS	206
CPBB00730	System/80	210
CPBB00870	Color Corner	216
CPBB00890	6809 Morningstar BBS (Color-80 #3)	217
CPBB01050	CoCo corner	224
CPBB01070	Bullet-80	225
CPBB01260	Education-80	231
CPBB01270	Bullet-80	231
CPBB01410	Colorburst/Trade-80 #1	236
CPBB01510	Colour-80	239
CPBB01520	Dr. D's CoCo Corner	240
CPBB01570	CoCo Board II	241
CPBB02120	Online Beta Sigma Phi	259
CPBB02360	Color-80 #25	266
CPBB02410	Color-80 #16	268
CPBB02540	Detroit Download	273
CPBB02550	Bit Bucket	274
CPBB02630	Bullet-80	277
CPBB02890	MACC-Net	284
CPBB03010	Access-80	287
CPBB03090	TBBS	291
CPBB03130	Connection-80	293
CPBB03170	Ed Gelb's Data Base	294
CPBB03210	CoCoMat	296
CPBB03300	Rainbow Connection #1	299
CPBB03301	Rainbow Connection #2	300
CPBB03302	Rainbow Connection #3	300
CPBB03320	Connection-80 #1	301
CPBB03580	CoCo-Nut Tree (Color-80 #17)	310
CPBB03620	CINTUG	311
CPBB03680	Flexnet	312

APPENDIX 3

CPB NUMBER	SYSTEM NAME	PAGE
CPBB03740	T.I.E.	314
CPBB03980	Bulletin/68	323
CPBB04100	MicroServe	327
CPBB04110	International Color BBS (Color-80 #5)	327
CPBB04120	TBBS	328
CPBB04150	Color Connection	329
CPBB04190	Burg Board	330
CPBB04220	Commnet-80	330
CPBB04260	TBBS	331
CPBB04580	NW Micronet	332
CPBB04620	21st Century Connection	344
CPBB04650	Mountaineer Softline #1	345

Commodore (CBM/C64/Vic-20)

CPB NUMBER	SYSTEM NAME	PAGE
CPBB01170	Front Range Commodore Bulletin-Board	228
CPBB01800	Commodore Public Bulletin Board	249
CPBB01930	Video King BBS	254
CPBB02000	AVC—Commodore Bulletin Board	256
CPBB02630	Bullet-80	277
CPBB02850	Commodore Communications	283
CPBB03090	TBBS	291
CPBB03300	Rainbow Connection #1	299
CPBB03301	Rainbow Connection #2	300
CPBB03302	Rainbow Connection #3	300
CPBB03460	PC-BBS	305
CPBB03630	Komputer Klassified	311
CPBB03640	The Choyce BBS	312
CPBB03730	TBBS	314
CPBB03740	T.I.E.	314
CPBB04280	Commodore Central	332
CPBB04510	Northwest Commodore User's Group	340
CPBB04560	Seacomm-80	342
CPBB04710	C.U.S.S.H.	347
CPBB04850	Commodore Bulletin-Board	350

CPB NUMBER	SYSTEM NAME	PAGE
CP/M		
CPBB00200	Mog-Ur HBBS	187
CPBB00220	Hollywood RCP/M RBBS	188
CPBB00310	Granada Engineering	192
CPBB00320	LA-KUG	192
CPBB00350	RBBS	194
CPBB00420	South Bay RCP/M RBBS	197
CPBB00440	PatVac	198
CPBB00470	Computer Systems Design	199
CPBB00490	Colossal Oxgate #2	200
CPBB00500	Data Tech Node 007/Servu	200
CPBB00530	Oxgate Message System 001	202
CPBB00620	Piconet Node #1	206
CPBB00660	DataTech Node 001	207
CPBB00840	RCP/M	215
CPBB00910	Napa Valley RBBS RCP/M	218
CPBB00940	Anahug	219
CPBB01130	CNode	226
CPBB01190	RCP/M	230
CPBB01500	JUG RBBS	239
CPBB01720	EL Division Bulletin Board	245
CPBB01740	Bridgeport RCP/M	246
CPBB01840	Logan Square RCP/M	251
CPBB01910	RCP/M	253
CPBB01940	A.B. Dick RCP/M RBBS	254
CPBB02290	BHEC RCP/M RBBS	263
CPBB02400	CNode	267
CPBB02420	RCP/M	268
CPBB02430	BIN-EX	268
CPBB02480	RCP/M	271
CPBB02560	Technical CBBS	274
CPBB02970	OACPMUG BBS	286
CPBB03110	CP/M-Net East	292
CPBB03170	Ed Gelb's Data Base	294
CPBB03370	SJBBS	298
CPBB03380	Vestal BBS	304
CPBB03460	PC-BBS	305

APPENDIX 3

CPB NUMBER	SYSTEM NAME	PAGE
CPBB03640	The Choyce BBS	312
CPBB03650	Drake RCP/M RBBS	312
CPBB03760	RCP/M	315
CPBB03810	RCP/M	317
CPBB03920	RBBS	321
CPBB04220	Commnet-80	330
CPBB04290	North Utah Exchange RBBS	332
CPBB04320	Mouse-Net	333
CPBB04560	Seacomm-80	342

Heath/Zenith

CPBB00940	Anahug	219
CPBB01140	MUMon	227
CPBB01150	TBBS #1 (HQ)	227
CPBB02500	North Shore HUG BBS	272
CPBB03140	SHUG BBS	293
CPBB03170	Ed Gelb's Data Base	294
CPBB04080	Dallas Heathkit	326
CPBB04370	C-HUG	334

IBM PC

CPBB00740	No-Name IBM RBBS	210
CPBB01070	Bullet-80	225
CPBB01280	Connecticut-PC	232
CPBB01580	MultiLink BBS	241
CPBB01590	N.F. Systems Ltd.	242
CPBB01730	Aurora Computers	246
CPBB01870	P-Chicago	252
CPBB01890	SW PC-Connection	252
CPBB02050	Hawkeye-PC	257
CPBB02210	TBBS	261
CPBB02310	Capital PC	264
CPBB02630	Bullet-80	277
CPBB03010	Access-80	287
CPBB03100	NYC IBMPCUG	291
CPBB03250	Bull-PC	293
CPBB03300	Rainbow Connection #1	299
CPBB03301	Rainbow Connection #2	300

CPB NUMBER	SYSTEM NAME	PAGE
CPBB03302	Rainbow Connection #3	300
CPBB03340	IBM/LNW User Groups	302
CPBB03460	PC-BBS	305
CPBB03640	The Choyce BBS	312
CPBB03740	T.I.E.	314
CPBB04190	Burg Board	330
CPBB04380	Hostcomm #1	335
CPBB04385	Hostcomm	335
CPBB04390	Hostcomm	336
CPBB04520	PC BBS	340

Kaypro

CPBB00220	Hollywood RCP/M RBBS	188
CPBB00320	LA-KUG	192
CPBB00420	South Bay RCP/M RBBS	197
CPBB00880	Kaypro BBS	217
CPBB03050	KUGNJ BBS	289

Osborne

CPBB02270	Programmer's Anonymous	263
CPBB03010	Access-80	287
CPBB03920	RBBS	321
CPBB04700	Beer City BBS	346

TRS-80 Models I and III

CPBB00510	Computers for Christ	201
CPBB00630	Golden State BBS	206
CPBB00730	System/80	210
CPBB00980	RACS V	221
CPBB01030	Growth Net	223
CPBB01250	Bullet-80	230
CPBB01260	Education-80	231
CPBB01410	Colorburst/Trade-80 #1	236
CPBB01690	Word Exchange	245
CPBB01730	Aurora Computers	246
CPBB01960	PCMS	255
CPBB01980	JAMS	255
CPBB02210	TBBS	261

APPENDIX 3

CPB NUMBER	SYSTEM NAME	PAGE
CPBB02380	TBBS	267
CPBB02540	Detroit Download	273
CPBB02550	Bit Bucket	274
CPBB02570	Bullet-80	274
CPBB02630	Bullet-80	277
CPBB02650	Babblenet	277
CPBB02790	United BBS	282
CPBB02800	BBS Richfield	282
CPBB02820	Southern Bullet	282
CPBB03010	Access-80	287
CPBB03020	Magazine-80	288
CPBB03060	Forum-80	289
CPBB03070	Photo-80	290
CPBB03090	TBBS	291
CPBB03190	RATS	295
CPBB03300	Rainbow Connection #1	299
CPBB03301	Rainbow Connection #2	300
CPBB03302	Rainbow Connection #3	300
CPBB03320	Connection-80 #1	301
CPBB03330	South Shore Connection-80	302
CPBB03400	Bullet-80	304
CPBB03460	PC-BBS	305
CPBB03480	Sangarnet	306
CPBB03490	TBBS	307
CPBB03520	Commnet-80	308
CPBB03540	TBBS	308
CPBB03620	CINTUG	311
CPBB03630	Komputer Klassified	311
CPBB03640	The Choyce BBS	312
CPBB03740	T.I.E.	314
CPBB03770	Bullet-80	315
CPBB03880	CAPATUG	319
CPBB03940	Forum-80	322
CPBB03990	Forum-80	323
CPBB04010	Forum-80	324
CPBB04020	Microserve Information Service	324
CPBB04030	On-Line 80 #1	325

CPB NUMBER	SYSTEM NAME	PAGE
CPBB04090	Software Exchange	326
CPBB04100	MicroServe	327
CPBB04120	TBBS	328
CPBB04140	TBBS	328
CPBB04190	Burg Board	330
CPBB04260	TBBS	331
CPBB04320	Mouse-Net	333
CPBB04500	U.S.—Online	339
CPBB04530	JCTS Super System	340
CPBB04580	NW Micronet	343
CPBB04640	Bullet-80	345
CPBB04700	Beer City BBS	346

TRS-80 Model 100

CPB NUMBER	SYSTEM NAME	PAGE
CPBB00420	South Bay RCP/M RBBS	197
CPBB03300	Rainbow Connection #1	299
CPBB03301	Rainbow Connection #2	300
CPBB03302	Rainbow Connection #3	300
CPBB03740	T.I.E.	314
CPBB03920	RBBS	321
CPBB04560	Seacomm-80	342
CPBB04760	JADE	348
CPBB04780	Personal Computer Communications	349

Unspecified

The following systems do not allow first-time callers to access their downloading sections or to view a menu. *The Computer Phone Book* does not support this policy; in our opinion, it would be in the best interests of sysops to allow first-time callers to see a menu of downloads. Since *The Computer Phone Book* was not able to access a download menu, the following systems are classified as have unspecified downloadable programs.

CPB NUMBER	SYSTEM NAME	PAGE
CPBB00030	Bama Bullet	180
CPBB00040	Forum-80	180

APPENDIX 3

CPB NUMBER	SYSTEM NAME	PAGE
CPBB00050	Forum-80	181
CPBB00060	Joe's Computer	181
CPBB00070	Abacus-by-Phone	182
CPBB00130	Forum-80	184
CPBB00160	Ark-Net	185
CPBB00240	California/80	189
CPBB00270	Coin Games Net	190
CPBB00330	Softworx	193
CPBB00360	Data Connection	194
CPBB00450	Mines of Moria	198
CPBB00590	Mojo's Download	204
CPBB00600	Aardwolf-Express	205
CPBB00650	Sunrise Omega-80	207
CPBB00770	CVBBS	212
CPBB00780	Online/PMS	212
CPBB00820	PMS—Gameboard	214
CPBB00830	Sabaline	215
CPBB00860	Online	216
CPBB00900	Greene Machine	218
CPBB00920	Peanut Gallery BBS	218
CPBB00950	CSHC	220
CPBB00990	OCTUG	221
CPBB01010	Computers for Christ	222
CPBB01020	Commnet-80	223
CPBB01140	MUMon	227
CPBB01390	Personal Message System	234
CPBB01400	Forum-80	235
CPBB01420	Orlando Connection	236
CPBB01850	MCMS CAMS #1	251
CPBB01860	Multi Image Information Lin	251
CPBB02090	Forum-80	258
CPBB02110	Dickenson's Movie Guide	259
CPBB02200	Apple Gumbo	261
CPBB02230	LNW TBBS Southeast	262
CPBB02330	Tech-Link	265
CPBB02580	Livonia Download	275
CPBB02590	GBBS	275

CPB NUMBER	SYSTEM NAME	PAGE
CPBB02600	Good News BBS	276
CPBB02620	Tony's Place	276
CPBB02660	CompuNet	277
CPBB02750	NC Software	280
CPBB02870	Online II—Amateur Radio BBS	283
CPBB02880	Ham BBS	284
CPBB03080	CFONJ	290
CPBB03160	Oriental Express	294
CPBB03200	N2EHM BBS	295
CPBB03240	AstroCom	296
CPBB03310	LICA	301
CPBB03350	Access-80	303
CPBB03600	Independent BBS	310
CPBB03780	Forum-80	315
CPBB03830	Hermes-80	317
CPBB03850	Drucom	318
CPBB03900	RITTUG BBS	320
CPBB03930	Mt. Pleasant-80	321
CPBB03950	Summerville-80	322
CPBB04250	Forum-80	331
CPBB04360	Forum-80	334
CPBB04450	Oxgate RBBS	337
CPBB04490	NRCS Buying Service	339
CPBB04590	Tech-BBS	343
CPBB04790	TBBS	349

APPENDIX 4

Special Interests: Computers/Miscellaneous

CPB NUMBER	SYSTEM NAME	PAGE
Apple		
CPBB00060	Joe's Computer	181
CPBB00450	Mines of Moria	198
CPBB00600	Aardwolf-Express	205
CPBB00770	CVBBS	212
CPBB00980	RACS V	221
CPBB01160	TBBS	228
CPBB01180	UFONET	229
CPBB01250	Bullet-80	230
CPBB01270	Bullet-80	231
CPBB01290	Telcom-7	232
CPBB01310	Bullet-80	233
CPBB01420	Orlando Connection	236
CPBB01730	Aurora Computers	246
CPBB01920	PMS—IAC	253
CPBB02210	TBBS	261
CPBB02250	TBBS	263
CPBB02450	Chelmsford Exchange	270
CPBB02530	Barton Data Line	273
CPBB03010	Access-80	287
CPBB03090	TBBS	291
CPBB03240	AstroCom	296
CPBB03300	Rainbow Connection #1	299
CPBB03301	Rainbow Connection #2	300
CPBB03302	Rainbow Connection #3	300

Special Interests: Computers/Miscellaneous

CPB NUMBER	SYSTEM NAME	PAGE
CPBB03450	ABBS	305
CPBB03460	PC-BBS	305
CPBB03540	TBBS	308
CPBB03630	Komputer Klassified	311
CPBB03730	TBBS	314
CPBB03740	T.I.E.	314
CPBB03900	RITTUG BBS	320
CPBB03960	Tinbrain's BBS	322
CPBB04020	Microserve Information Service	324
CPBB04140	TBBS	328
CPBB04190	Burg Board	330
CPBB04500	U.S.—Online	339
CPBB04560	Seacomm-80	342
CPBB04580	NW Micronet	343
CPBB04590	Tech-BBS	343
CPBB04630	TBBS	344
CPBB04640	Bullet-80	345
CPBB04690	Canopus	346

Atari

CPBB00060	Joe's Computer	181
CPBB00450	Mines of Moria	198
CPBB00480	GFxBBS	200
CPBB00520	IBBS	201
CPBB00600	Aardwolf-Express	205
CPBB00770	CVBBS	212
CPBB00980	RACS V	221
CPBB01150	TBBS #1 (HQ)	227
CPBB01180	UFONET	229
CPBB01350	Armudic	234
CPBB01420	Orlando Connection	236
CPBB01730	Aurora Computers	246
CPBB02240	RCP/M	262
CPBB02530	Barton Data Line	273
CPBB02610	M.A.C.E. West	276
CPBB02680	GRASS	278
CPBB02780	TAIG	281

CPB NUMBER	SYSTEM NAME	PAGE
CPBB03000	SNACC Amis	287
CPBB03010	Access-80	287
CPBB03090	TBBS	291
CPBB03240	AstroCom	296
CPBB03300	Rainbow Connection #1	299
CPBB03301	Rainbow Connection #2	300
CPBB03302	Rainbow Connection #3	300
CPBB03540	TBBS	308
CPBB03630	Komputer Klassified	311
CPBB03700	Software Safaris	313
CPBB03730	TBBS	314
CPBB03840	RCP/M	314
CPBB03870	Acenet	319
CPBB03910	AMIS	320
CPBB03960	Tinbrain's BBS	322
CPBB04100	MicroServe	327
CPBB04140	TBBS	328
CPBB04170	Apex BBS	329
CPBB04190	Burg Board	330
CPBB04350	Best Little BBS	333
CPBB04500	U.S.—Online	339
CPBB04560	Seacomm-80	342
CPBB04580	NW Micronet	343
CPBB04630	TBBS	344

Color Computer

CPBB00390	L.A. Color Exchange (Color-80 #4)	195
CPBB00540	Color-80 #1	202
CPBB00890	6809 Morning Star BBS (Color-80 #3)	217
CPBB00970	Color Corner	221
CPBB01050	CoCo Corner	224
CPBB01180	UFONET	229
CPBB01250	Bullet-80 #1	230
CPBB01270	Bullet-80	231
CPBB01290	Telcom-7	232
CPBB01310	Bullet-80	233

CPB NUMBER	SYSTEM NAME	PAGE
CPBB01410	Colorburst/Trade-80 #1	236
CPBB01510	Colour-80	239
CPBB01520	Dr. D's CoCo Corner	240
CPBB01560	Bulletin/68	241
CPBB01570	CoCo Board II	241
CPBB01600	Bulletin/68	242
CPBB02360	Color-80 #25	266
CPBB02410	Color-80 #16	268
CPBB02890	MACC-Net	284
CPBB03010	Access-80	287
CPBB03090	TBBS	291
CPBB03210	CoCoMat	296
CPBB03300	Rainbow Connection #1	299
CPBB03301	Rainbow Connection #2	300
CPBB03302	Rainbow Connection #3	300
CPBB03350	Access-80	303
CPBB03580	CoCo-Nut Tree (Color-80 #17)	310
CPBB03620	CINTUG	311
CPBB03680	Flexnet	312
CPBB03730	TBBS	314
CPBB03740	T.I.E.	314
CPBB03900	RITUG BBS	320
CPBB03960	Tinbrain's BBS	322
CPBB03980	Bulletin/68	323
CPBB04020	Microserve Information Service	324
CPBB04100	MicroServe	327
CPBB04110	International Color BBS (Color-80 #5)	327
CPBB04120	TBBS	328
CPBB04150	Color Connection	329
CPBB04580	NW Micronet	343
CPBB04590	Tech-BBS	343
CPBB04620	21st Century Connection	344
CPBB04640	Bullet-80	345
CPBB04650	Mountaineer Softline #1	345
CPBB04690	Canopus	349

APPENDIX 4

CPB NUMBER	SYSTEM NAME	PAGE
Commodore (CBM/C-64/Vic-20)		
CPBB00060	Joe's Computer	181
CPBB00450	Mines of Moria	198
CPBB00600	Aardwolf-Express	205
CPBB00770	CVBBS	212
CPBB00980	RACS V	221
CPBB01110	Old Colorado City Electronic Cottage	226
CPBB01170	Front Range Commodore Bulletin Board	228
CPBB01200	Petula	230
CPBB01800	Commodore Public Bulletin Board	249
CPBB01930	Video King BBS	254
CPBB02000	AVC—Commodore Bulletin Board	256
CPBB02250	TBBS	263
CPBB02530	Barton Data Line	273
CPBB02740	MarkeTrak	280
CPBB02850	Commodore Communications	283
CPBB03090	TBBS	291
CPBB03240	AstroCom	296
CPBB03300	Rainbow Connection #1	299
CPBB03301	Rainbow Connection #2	300
CPBB03302	Rainbow Connection #3	300
CPBB03350	Access-80	303
CPBB03460	PC-BBS	305
CPBB03540	TBBS	308
CPBB03740	T.I.E.	314
CPBB03960	Tinbrain's BBS	322
CPBB04100	MicroServe	327
CPBB04190	Burg Board	330
CPBB04280	Commodore Central	332
CPBB04500	U.S.—Online	339
CPBB04510	Northwest Commodore User's Group	340
CPBB04560	Seacomm-80	342
CPBB04590	Tech-BBS	343
CPBB04690	Canopus	346

Special Interests: Computers/Miscellaneous

CPB NUMBER	SYSTEM NAME	PAGE
CPBB04710	C.U.S.S.H.	347
CPBB04790	TBBS	349
CPBB04850	Commodore Bulletin Board	350

Heath/Zenith

CPBB00060	Joe's Computer	181
CPBB00200	Mog-Ur HBBS	187
CPBB0940	Anahug	219
CPBB01140	MUMon	227
CPBB01500	JUG RBBS	239
CPBB02290	BHEC RCP/M RBBS	263
CPBB02500	North Shore HUG BBS	272
CPBB03010	Access-80	287
CPBB03140	SHUG BBS	293
CPBB03350	Access-80	303
CPBB04080	Dallas Heathkit	326
CPBB04370	C-HUG	334
CPBB04371	C-HUG GP BBS	335
CPBB04580	NW Micronet	343

IBM PC

CPBB00060	Joe's Computer	181
CPBB00560	Blue Boss	203
CPBB00600	Aardwolf-Express	205
CPBB00740	No-Name IBM RBBS	210
CPBB00770	CVBBS	212
CPBB00980	RACS V	221
CPBB01150	TBBS #1 (HQ)	227
CPBB01160	TBBS	228
CPBB01250	Bullet-80 #1	230
CPBB01270	Bullet-80	231
CPBB01280	Connecticut-PC	232
CPBB01290	Telcom-7	232
CPBB01310	Bullet-80	233
CPBB01420	Orlando Connection	236
CPBB01580	MultiLink BBS	241

APPENDIX 4

CPB NUMBER	SYSTEM NAME	PAGE
CPBB01590	N.F. Systems Ltd.	242
CPBB01730	Aurora Computers	246
CPBB01870	P-Chicago	252
CPBB01890	SW PC-Connection	252
CPBB02050	Hawkeye-PC	257
CPBB02210	TBBS	261
CPBB02310	Capital PC	264
CPBB02340	Capital PC	265
CPBB02530	Barton Data Line	273
CPBB03010	Access-80	287
CPBB03100	NYC IBMPCUG	291
CPBB03240	AstroCom	296
CPBB03250	Bull-PC	297
CPBB03300	Rainbow Connection #1	299
CPBB03301	Rainbow Connection #2	300
CPBB03302	Rainbow Connection #3	300
CPBB03340	IBM/LNW User Groups	302
CPBB03350	Access-80	303
CPBB03460	PC-BBS	305
CPBB03630	Komputer Klassified	311
CPBB03730	TBBS	314
CPBB03740	T.I.E.	314
CPBB03960	Tinbrain's BBS	322
CPBB04100	MicroServe	327
CPBB04190	Burg Board	330
CPBB04380	Hostcomm #1	335
CPBB04385	Hostcomm	335
CPBB04390	Hostcomm	336
CPBB04500	U.S.—Online	339
CPBB04520	PC BBS	340
CPBB04560	Seacomm-80	342
CPBB04580	NW Micronet	343
CPBB04630	TBBS	344
CPBB04640	Bullet-80	345
Kaypro		
CPBB00220	Hollywood RCP/M RBBS	188
CPBB00320	LA-KUG BBS	192

Special Interests: Computers/Miscellaneous 419

CPB NUMBER	SYSTEM NAME	PAGE
CPBB0042Ø	South Bay RCP/M RBBS	197
CPBB0088Ø	Kaypro BBS	217
CPBB0116Ø	TBBS	228
CPBB0183Ø	KUG	250
CPBB0305Ø	KUGNJ	289

Osborne

CPBB0111Ø	Old Colorado City Electronic Cottage	226
CPBB0116Ø	TBBS	228
CPBB0227Ø	Programmer's Anonymous	263
CPBB0335Ø	Access-80	303
CPBB0410Ø	MicroServe	327

Texas Instruments/TI

CPBB0006Ø	Joe's Computer	181
CPBB0111Ø	Old Colorado City Electronic Cottage	226
CPBB0116Ø	TBBS	228
CPBB0330Ø	Rainbow Connection #1	299
CPBB03301	Rainbow Connection #2	300
CPBB03302	Rainbow Connection #3	300
CPBB0410Ø	MicroServe	327

TRS-80 (General/All Models)

CPBB0006Ø	Joe's Computer	181
CPBB0060Ø	Aardwolf-Express	205
CPBB0077Ø	CVBBS	212
CPBB0111Ø	Old Colorado City Electronic Cottage	226
CPBB0115Ø	TBBS #1 (HQ)	227
CPBB0142Ø	Orlando Connection	236
CPBB0173Ø	Aurora Computers	246
CPBB0221Ø	TBBS	261
CPBB0238Ø	TBBS	267
CPBB0253Ø	Barton Data Line	273
CPBB0266Ø	CompuNet	277
CPBB0275Ø	NC Software	280
CPBB0279Ø	United BBS	282

CPB NUMBER	SYSTEM NAME	PAGE
CPBB03010	Access-80	287
CPBB03020	Magazine-80	288
CPBB03350	Access-80	303
CPBB03460	PC-BBS	305
CPBB03540	TBBS	308
CPBB03630	Komputer Klassified	311
CPBB03880	CAPATUG	319
CPBB03960	Tinbrain's BBS	322
CPBB04020	Microserve Information Service	324
CPBB04100	MicroServe	327
CPBB04120	TBBS	328
CPBB04140	TBBS	328
CPBB04190	Burg Board	330
CPBB04500	U.S.—Online	339
CPBB04590	Tech-BBS	343
CPBB04630	TBBS	344
CPBB04690	Canopus	346
CPBB04790	TBBS	349

TRS-80 Models I and III

CPBB01250	Bullet-80 #1	230
CPBB01270	Bullet-80	231
CPBB01290	Telcom-7	232
CPBB01310	Bullet-80	233
CPBB03090	TBBS	291
CPBB03300	Rainbow Connection #1	299
CPBB03301	Rainbow Connection #2	300
CPBB03302	Rainbow Connection #3	300
CPBB03730	TBBS	314
CPBB03740	T.I.E.	314
CPBB03900	RITUG BBS	320
CPBB04020	Microserve Information Service	324
CPBB04100	MicroServe	327
CPBB04120	TBBS	328
CPBB04580	NW Micronet	343
CPBB04640	Bullet-80	345
CPBB04780	Personal Computer Communications	349

Special Interests: Computers/Miscellaneous

CPB NUMBER	SYSTEM NAME	PAGE
TRS-80 Model 100		
CPBB00420	South Bay RCP/M RBBS	197
CPBB01270	Bullet-80	231
CPBB02250	TBBS	263
CPBB03300	Rainbow Connection #1	299
CPBB03301	Rainbow Connection #2	300
CPBB03302	Rainbow Connection #3	300
CPBB03740	T.I.E.	314
CPBB04560	Seacomm-80	342
CPBB04760	JADE	348
CPBB04780	Personal Computer Communications	349

MISCELLANEOUS

CPB NUMBER	SYSTEM NAME	PAGE
Alternate Energy		
CPBB00750	Energy Tree	211
Arms Control		
CPBB00610	SACDF Conference Tree	205
Beta Sigma Phi		
CPBB02120	Online Beta Sigma Phi	259
Boston Computer Society		
CPBB02490	Boston Computer Society	271
Catalogs		
CPBB00120	Micro Systems Services	183
CPBB00280	Computer Conspiracy	191
CPBB01300	Westico	233
CPBB02430	Computer Advertising Network	268
CPBB02510	Computer Bargain Guide	272
CPBB03270	PMS—McGraw Hill Book Company	298
CPBB03690	Mid-America Data	313
CPBB03835	Microline	317
CPBB04490	NRCS Buying Service	339

CPB NUMBER	SYSTEM NAME	PAGE
'C' language		
CPBB02400	CNode	267
CPBB03810	RCP/M	317
Coin Games		
CPBB00270	Coin Games Net	190
Commodities		
CPBB02740	MarkeTrak	280
Computer technology		
CPBB02320	CPEUG & NBS/ICST	265
Consulting		
CPBB01790	CODE	248
dBase II		
CPBB00470	Computer Systems Design	199
Education		
CPBB00110	Conference Tree	183
CPBB00700	Living BBS	209
CPBB01110	Old Colorado City Electronic Cottage	226
CPBB01260	Education-80	231
FORTH language		
CPBB00570	Conference Tree	203
Gay sex		
CPBB00230	Oracle BBS	188
CPBB00690	Drummer Magazine	208
CPBB00710	South of Market	209
CPBB02590	GBBS	275
GameMaster system		
CPBB01820	GameMaster ABBS	250
Ham radio		
CPBB02870	Online II—Amateur Radio BBS	283
CPBB03010	Access-80	287
CPBB03200	N2EHM BBS	295
CPBB03960	Tinbrain's BBS	322

CPB NUMBER	SYSTEM NAME	PAGE
CPBB04400	CBBS AMRAD	336
CPBB04630	TBBS	344

International news

CPBB00670	Clearpoint	207

Investments

CPBB03730	TBBS	314

Law

CPBB02720	LawSIG	279

Limericks

CPBB03120	Limericks BBS	292

Literary

CPBB01180	UFONET	229

LNW Computers

CPBB02230	LNW TBBS Southeast	262
CPBB03340	LNW/IBM User Groups	302

Matchmaking

CPBB00170	Dial-Your-Match #26	185
CPBB00180	Dial-Your-Match #1	186
CPBB00190	Dial-Your-Match #7	186
CPBB00210	Dial-Your-Match #28	187
CPBB00300	Dial-Your-Match #9	192
CPBB00370	MMMMMM #1	194
CPBB00380	Dial-Your-Match #4	195
CPBB00580	Dial-Your-Match #17	204
CPBB00680	Dial-Your-Match #10	208
CPBB00760	Dial-Your-Match #11	211
CPBB00790	Dial-Your-Match #33	213
CPBB01630	Dial-Your-Match #3	243
CPBB01810	Dial-Your-Match #39	249
CPBB02470	Dial-Your-Match #18	270
CPBB02950	Dial-Your-Match #23	285
CPBB03260	MMMMMM #2	297
CPBB03470	Dial-Your-Match #20	306
CPBB03550	Dial-Your-Match #34	309
CPBB04460	Dial-Your-Match #32	337

CPB NUMBER	SYSTEM NAME	PAGE
Medical		
CPBB02040	CBBS	257
CPBB02060	Apple Medical BBS	258
CPBB02440	Lawrence General Hospital	269
Movies		
CPBB02110	Dickenson's Movie Guide	259
Online fiction		
CPBB03020	Magazine-80	288
Orchestra 80/85/90		
CPBB01150	TBBS #1 (HQ)	227
CPBB03070	Photo-80	290
CPBB04120	TBBS	328
Parapsychology		
CPBB01180	UFONET	229
Photography		
CPBB03070	Photo-80	290
CPBB03730	TBBS	314
Radio broadcasting		
CPBB03490	TBBS	307
Real estate		
CPBB03170	Ed Gelb's Data Base	294
Religion		
CPBB00510	Computers for Christ	201
CPBB01010	Computers for Christ	222
Science-Fiction		
CPBB01750	Caverns of Appleville	246
CPBB02460	The Outpost	270
CPBB03240	AstroCom	296
CPBB03960	Tinbrain's BBS	322
Space		
CPBB01180	UFONET	229
CPBB02300	GASNet	264

Special Interests: Computers/Miscellaneous

CPB NUMBER	SYSTEM NAME	PAGE
Stock Market		
CPBB03280	Stewart/Finnco On-Line	298
CPBB03290	Tickerscreen	299
Telco (Telephone company)		
CPBB01180	UFONET	229
TV		
CPBB01860	Multi Image Information Line	251
UFO		
CPBB01180	UFONET	229
Video		
CPBB00060	Joe's Computer	181
CPBB00960	PMS—*IF* Magazine	220
CPBB02730	Loki's Corner	279
Writing		
CPBB01110	Old Colorado City Electronic Cottage	226
CPBB01430	The Notebook	237
X-rated		
CPBB00060	Joe's Computer	181
CPBB00230	Oracle BBS	188
CPBB00300	Dial-Your-Match #9	192
CPBB00690	Drummer Magazine	208
CPBB00710	South of Market	209
CPBB01770	Greene Machine	247
CPBB02590	GBBS	275
CPBB03730	TBBS	314
CPBB03830	Hermes-80	317
CPBB03850	Drucom	318

APPENDIX 5
1200 bps Systems

CPB NUMBER	SYSTEM NAME	PAGE
CPBB00040	Forum-80	180
CPBB00050	Forum-80	181
CPBB00060	Joe's Computer	181
CPBB00090	Arizona Bulletin-Board	182
CPBB00200	Mog-Ur HBBS	187
CPBB00220	Hollywood RCP/M RBBS	188
CPBB00350	RBBS	194
CPBB00370	MMMMMM #1	194
CPBB00420	South Bay RCP/M RBBS	197
CPBB00470	Computer Systems Design	199
CPBB00590	Mojo's Download-80	204
CPBB00600	Aardwolf-Express	205
CPBB00660	DataTech Node 001	207
CPBB00930	Infoex-80	219
CPBB00940	Anahug	219
CPBB00950	CSHC	220
CPBB00970	Color Corner	221
CPBB00990	OCTUG	221
CPBB01020	Commnet-80	223
CPBB01070	Bullet-80	225
CPBB01160	TBBS	228
CPBB01180	UFONET	229
CPBB01190	RCP/M	230
CPBB01250	Bullet-80 #1	230
CPBB01390	Personal Message System	234
CPBB01410	Colorburst/Trade-80 #1	236
CPBB01560	Bulletin/68	241
CPBB01580	MultiLink BBS	241

CPB NUMBER	SYSTEM NAME	PAGE
CPBB01590	N.F. Systems Ltd.	242
CPBB01660	Heathkit RBBS	244
CPBB01830	KUG	250
CPBB01850	MCMS CAMS #1	251
CPBB01870	P-Chicago	252
CPBB01940	A.B. Dick RCP/M RBBS	254
CPBB01960	PCMS	255
CPBB02050	Hawkeye-PC	257
CPBB02230	LNW TBBS Southeast	262
CPBB02250	TBBS	263
CPBB02310	Capital PC	264
CPBB02340	Capital PC	265
CPBB02380	TBBS	267
CPBB02430	BIN-EX	268
CPBB02460	The Outpost	270
CPBB02480	RCP/M	271
CPBB02500	North Shore HUG BBS	272
CPBB02510	Computer Bargain Guide	272
CPBB02620	Tony's Place	276
CPBB02650	Babblenet	277
CPBB02660	CompuNet	277
CPBB02710	The Job System	278
CPBB02750	NC Software	280
CPBB02800	BBS Richfield	282
CPBB03050	KUGNJ	289
CPBB03070	Photo-80	290
CPBB03080	CFONJ	290
CPBB03100	NYC IBMPCUG	291
CPBB03110	CP/M-Net East	292
CPBB03140	SHUG BBS	293
CPBB03170	Ed Gelb's Data Base	294
CPBB03200	N2EHM BBS	295
CPBB03260	MMMMMM #2	297
CPBB03330	South Shore Connection-80	302
CPBB03340	IBM/LNW User Groups	302
CPBB03400	Bullet-80	304
CPBB03520	Commnet-80	308

CPB NUMBER	SYSTEM NAME	PAGE
CPBB03770	Bullet-80	315
CPBB03780	Forum-80	315
CPBB03840	RCP/M	318
CPBB03910	AMIS	320
CPBB03940	Forum-80	322
CPBB04090	Software Exchange	326
CPBB04100	MicroServe	327
CPBB04360	Forum-80	334
CPBB04570	West Coast Message System	342
CPBB04700	Beer City BBS	346

APPENDIX 6
United States National Networks

CPB NUMBER	SYSTEM NAME	PAGE
CPBN00040	BRS After Dark	141
CPBN00060	CompuServe Executive Information Service	144
CPBN00045	CompuServe Information Service	144
CPBN00075	Connexions	148
CPBN00100	Delphi	148
CPBN00125	Dow Jones News/Retrieval Service	151
CPBN00200	EIES	152
CPBN00350	Knowledge Index	153
CPBN00500	NewsNet	154
CPBN00575	OAG EE	158
CPBN00625	Photo-1 Network	158
CPBN00650	Photonet	159
CPBN00800	The Source	159
CPBN00875	Stewart/Finnco Stock/Option Databank	162
CPBN00900	Travelhost Network	163

APPENDIX 7
United States Local-Area Services

CPB NUMBER	SYSTEM NAME	PAGE
CPBL00050	A-T Videotex	167
CPBL00150	Buy-Phone	167
CPBL00250	CLEO	168
CPBL00300	DataTrac Information Service	168
CPBL00350	DEC-Line	169
CPBL00400	Electronic Editions	169
CPBL00450	Fantasy Plaza	170
CPBL00500	GameMaster	170
CPBL00550	Harris Electronic News	171
CPBL00600	HEX2	171
CPBL00750	MicroShare	172
CPBL00800	M-Net	172
CPBL00825	Panatgraph Informant	173
CPBL00950	StarText Metro	173

APPENDIX 8
A Sampling of Communications Software Suppliers

Apple
Link Systems
1640 19 St.
Santa Monica, CA, 90404
Product: DataLink

Southwestern Data Systems
P.O. Box 582
Santee, CA, 92071
Products: ASCII Express, Z-Term

SSM Microcomputer Products, Inc.
2190 Paragon Dr.
San Jose, CA, 95131
Product: Transend

Exec Software, Inc.
201 Waltham St.
Lexington, MA, 02173
Product: TermExec

Atari
Roklan Software
10600 W. Higgins Rd.
Suite 200
Rosemont, IL, 60018
Product: Tele Com

CP/M-based
Compu-Draw
1227 Goler House
Rochester, NY, 14620
Products: COMCOM, CPMCPM

International Software Alliance
1835 Mission Ridge Rd.
Santa Barbara, CA, 93103
Product: E/LYNC, LYNC

Microstuf, Inc.
1845 The Exchange
Suite 205
Atlanta, GA, 30339
Product: Crosstalk

Commodore Business Machines
CGRS Microtech
PO Box 102
Langhorne, PA, 19047
Product: Compack

Commodore-64/VIC-20
Astral*Image
812 B St, Studio A
San Rafael, CA, 94901
Product: SpeedTerm II

Finsen Scientific Co.
14631 Berwick Ave.
Livonia, MI, 48154
Product: terminal program

J & G Software
P.O. Box 146
Pelham, NY, 10803
Products: Commterm-20,
  Commterm-64

MicroTechnic Solutions, Inc.
P.O. Box 2940
New Haven, CT, 06515
Product: Smart 64 Terminal

IBM PC
N.F. Systems, Ltd.
P.O. Box 76363
Atlanta, GA, 30358
Product: Hostcomm

Osborne
C.W.I.
4027 N. Oak
Kansas City, MO, 64116
Product: MDMCOM

TRS-80/Color Computer
Double Density Software
920 Baldwin St.
Denton, TX, 76201
Color Term +Plus+

Eigen Systems
P.O. Box 18006
Austin, TX, 78766
Product: Colorcom/E

Nelson Software Systems
9072 Lyndale Ave. So.
Minneapolis, MN, 55420
Product: Super Color Terminal

TRS-80/Models I and III
Lance Miklus, Inc.
217 S. Union St.
Burlington, VT, 05401
Product: ST80

Micro-Systems Software, Inc.
4301-18 Oak Circle
Boca Raton, FL, 33431
Product: Microterm

Stewart Software
P.O. Box 573
Memphis, TN, 38101
Product: Softcomm

APPENDIX 9
Bulletin-Board System Listing Form

If you are a sysop of a system that is not listed in this edition of *The Computer Phone Book*, you can submit your system for entry into *The Computer Phone Book* newsletter update and the next edition of this book by filling out the sheet that follows. Please give as much detail about your system as possible. If you wish, you may also use a separate sheet of paper to go into more depth.

Aside from the systems I weeded out for this edition, there were several systems that I just could not put in. I know of at least five systems that are operating that I simply could not get onto because of their round-the-clock busy signal. If I can't get on your system, I can't verify that it is still operating or compile a list of its contents. If your system falls into this category, I hope you will welcome this opportunity to help rectify matters.

All of the information supplied will be checked; so try not to exaggerate or give an incorrect listing. This sheet does not take the place of a phone call, but it does cut down on the amount of time I will have to spend on your system and allows you to bring to my attention features of your system I might miss.

If you are a sysop whose system is listed in this edition, please use the sheet to note any corrections to your current listing or to provide updates of additions and deletions to your system.

It is not necessary that *The Computer Phone Book* be complete; to list all operating BBSs would be impossible because of their temporary nature. What counts most is the accuracy of what is listed. This is your opportunity to help. Take it.

APPENDIX 9

SYSTEM SHEET

CPBB Number (if assigned in this edition): _____

System name: _____

Location.   City: _____ Country/State: _____

System telephone number (country/area code): _____

Protocol (word bits/stop bits/parity): _____

BPS rate(s):   ( ) 300 bps   ( ) 1200 bps   ( ) PMMI

BBS software used: _____

Operating hours: _____

Following the classification of features in Chapter 6, please check the currently available features of your system:
- ( ) Advertising (paid)
- ( ) BBS list (national)
- ( ) Chat (w/sysop)
- ( ) CP/M
- ( ) Feedback (at logoff)
- ( ) Mail (menu item)
- ( ) Multiple message boards
- ( ) System Info (hard/software)
- ( ) Time/duration
- ( ) BBS list (local)
- ( ) Catalog (shopping)
- ( ) Conferencing
- ( ) Downloading
- ( ) Graphics
- ( ) Messaging (public/private)
- ( ) Parameters
- ( ) Text files
- ( ) Userlog

( ) Other, specify: _____

Are first-time callers to your system assigned or asked to input a password?   ( ) Yes   ( ) No

Are first-time callers to your system allowed to post public messages?   ( ) Yes   ( ) No

Are first-time callers to your system allowed to see a menu of available downloadable programs?   ( ) Yes   ( ) No

Are first-time callers to your system allowed to download available programs?   ( ) Yes   ( ) No

Below is a list of computer types. Please put a check in column D if your system contains downloadable programs for that computer. Please put a check in column M if your system offers a message base for that computer. You may put checks in both columns D and M if appropriate.

D M		D M	
( )( )	Adam (Coleco)	( )( )	Apple (II+, // e, III)
( )( )	Atari	( )( )	Color Computer
( )( )	Commodore/CBM	( )( )	Commodore-64
( )( )	Commodore VIC-20	( )( )	CP/M-based
( )( )	Franklin ACE	( )( )	Heath/Zenith
( )( )	IBM PC	( )( )	IBM PC XT
( )( )	IBM "Peanut"	( )( )	Kaypro (II/10)
( )( )	LNW Computers	( )( )	Osborne (I/Exec)
( )( )	Texas Instruments 99/4A	( )( )	TI Professional
( )( )	Timex-Sinclair 1000 series	( )( )	Timex-Sinclair 2000 series
( )( )	TRS-80 Model I/III	( )( )	TRS-80 Model IV/12/16
( )( )	TRS-80 Model 100	( )( )	Other

Specify other computer brand(s): _____

Please list on a separate sheet of paper any special interests or topics your system deals with.

APPENDIX 9

Your name: _____

Address: _____

_____

Telephone number: _____
                ( ) Home   ( ) Business

Hours you may be reached by phone: _____

Your phone number is necessary in the event your system is too busy to get through to. It will be necessary to call you to verify that it is still operating.

CIS ID: Delphi ID: Source ID:

_____   _____   _____

All of your personal information will be held in the strictest confidence and will not be divulged to anyone.
    Please feel free to place your system's assigned CPB number prominently on your system. It will aid us in updating your system's listing.
    Do you want your name listed in the next edition of *The Computer Phone Book* as the sysop of your system?
    ( ) No, but thanks for the thought.
    ( ) Yes, and I hereby consent to such publication.
    Please mail your completed form and any separate sheet(s) to Mike Cane, 175 5th Avenue, Suite 3371, New York, NY, 10010.

Index

ABBS software format, 23, 113–21
  userlog, 114
  commands, 116
access requirements, 176
account number, 26
addressable cursor, 10
advertising and marketing databases:
  A–T Videotext, 167
  NewsNet, 20, 155
aerospace databases:
  CIS, 145
  GASNet, 264
  NewsNet, 20, 155
Africa databases, NewsNet, 156
agriculture databases:
  BRS, 142
  CIS, 147
  Knowledge Index, 19, 153
  NewsNet, 156
airlines guides, *see* Official Airlines Guides
alphabet, digital, *see* digital alphabet
AMIS software format, 23
analog signals, modulation and demodulation of, 4

Apple Bulletin-Board System, *see* ABBS
appointment calendar services, Delphi, 18
ASCII, 4
  keyboard, 4
  word-length setting, 7
Atari™ Message and Information Service, *see* AMIS
AtariPost (Columbus, Ohio), 23, 169
A–T Videotext (Tiffin, Ohio), 22, 167
auto-logon feature in software, 10
automotive newsletter, NewsNet, 20, 155
aviation information and services, CIS, 147
  See also Official Airline Guides

banking databases:
  CIS Home Management, 145
  NewsNet, 156
banking services, electronic:
  advantages of, 13
  CIS, 145, 146
  Delphi, 18

Basic Computing magazine, 344
"baud rate," *see* bps
BBSs, *see* Bulletin-Board Systems
Bell modems, 5
Beta Sigma Phi, 259
Bibliographic Retrieval Service, *see* BRS After Dark
biological sciences database, BRS, 142
Bit Bucket BBS (Portland, Oregon), 316
"bits";
  defined, 3
  settings in communications protocol, 7, 176
  transmission and reception rate, *see* bps
Blue, Bill, 216
bond market, *see* financial markets
Books in Print databases
  BRS, 33–39, 143
  Knowledge Index, 154
Boston Computer Society (Newton, Massachusetts), 271
bps (bits-per-second) speeds, 4–5
  of BBS, 175
  control of, 178
  standards for, 5
  Videotex, 24
"brain" (computer central processing unit), 9
British Telecom International, 14
British telecommunications systems, *see* Great Britain
broadcasting industry database, NewsNet, 20, 157
brokerage services, *see* financial markets
BRS After Dark, 15–16, 141–43
  use of services, 29–40
  user's manual, 30
building and construction field database, NewsNet, 20, 155
Bullet–80 software, 20
Bulletin Board Systems (BBSs)
  ABBS, 23, 113–21
  accessing of, 15, 113, 176
  bps rates of, 175–76
  calling etiquette for, 179–80
  catalog features, 177 (*see also* shopping and swapping services
  CIS BULLET, 59–63, 145, 146
  DataPost, 23
  DEC-Line, 23
  Delphi, 18, 149, 151
  local, 175–80 (see also Appendix 1)
  Photonet, 20–21, 159
  Photo–1 Network, 158–59
  PMS, see PMS
  POST (The Source), 21, 102–104, 160–62
  RCP/M, *see* RCP/M
  software formats, 23–24, 176–77
  termination of session, 121, 137
business, telecommunications systems for:
  Citylink (Boston, Mass.), 25, 360
  Prestol World Service, 25, 360

business and financial services:
  A-T Videotext, 167
  BRS After Dark, 16, 142
  CIS, 17, 146, 147
  Dow Jones News/Retrieval Service, 19, 85-87, 152
  Harris Electronic News (local), 23
  Knowledge Index, 19, 154
  NewsNet, 20, 156, 157
  Source, 21, 160, 161
  Stewart/Finnco, 162, 298
  Tickerscreen, 299
  Travelhost, 163
buying and selling programs, see shopping and swapping services
Buy-Phone (Los Angeles, California), 22, 167
"byte," 4

Canada, telecommunication systems in:
  B.E.L.E. (Laval, Quebec), 353
  Computron (Edmonton, Alberta), 351
  Edmonton RCP/M (Edmonton), 352
  Satyricon CBBS RCP/M (Burnaby, British Columbia), 352
  Southside RCP/M (Edmonton), 352
career information, Source, 21, 161
  See also job opportunities; professionals, services for
carrier signal, 8
  jamming of phone handset by, 3

cassette recorder, use of, 2, 9
catalog features of systems, 13, 177
  See also shopping and swapping services
CBBS™ software, 23-24, 135, 136
CBers club, CIS, 145
CB Simulator (CIS), 17, 81, 145, 146
  use of, 51-59
character formation in digital processing, 3-4, 7
charges for telecommunications systems, 12, 14
chat capability of local BBSs, 177
Chat conferencing system, Source, 99-102, 161
chemicals field databases:
  BRS, 142
  NewsNet, 20, 155
CIS, see CompuServe Information Service
Citizen's Band radio
  CIS CB Society, 145
  simulation of, see CB Simulator (CIS)
Citylink (Boston, Massachusetts), 25, 360
CLEO (Computerized Listings of Employment Opportunities) (Torrance, California), 22-23, 168
coding standards, 24
Comlink Network, CIS, 144
command-driven systems, 15
command storage feature in software, 10
commodity markets databases:
  CIS, 146, 147

commodity markets databases: (*Cont.*)
  MarkeTrak, 280
  Source, 160, 161
communications protocol, 7, 176
Communications Industry Forum, CIS-SIG, 142
Communications software package features, *see* software package features
CompuServe Executive Information Service, 76, 144
CompuServe Information Service (CIS), 16–17, 144–48
  BBS, 59–63, 145, 146
  CB Simulator service, 17, 18, 51–59, 145, 146
  EMail service, 46–50, 77–79, 145, 146
  "page" system used by, 16, 40
  Programmers Area, 76–79
  Special Interest Groups (SIGs), *see* Special Interest Groups (SIGs)
  users manual, 44, 75, 145, 146
Computer crime conference, Law SIG, 279
computer-dating services, *see* matchmaking, systems specializing in
Computerized Bulletin-Board System, *see* CBBS™
Computer Phone Book (CPB), use and updating of, 1–2
computer signals:
  generation of, 4
  standardization of, 4 (*see also* standards)

computers in medicine and dentistry, systems specializing in:
  CIS SIGS, 147
Conference Tree software format, 23, 122–24, 177, 279
conferencing systems:
  CompuServe CB Simulator, *see* CB Simulator
  CompuServe SIG, 74
  Delphi, 18, 80–84
  EIES, 19, 152
  Source, *see* Chat conferencing system; PARTICIPATE conferencing system
Connection-80 software format, 23
connect-time, 14
Connexions, 17–18
consumer issues and services:
  A-T Videotext, 167
  CIS, 146
  Source, 160
  See also shopping services
control commands, 27–28
cookbook, NewsNet, 155
cooking club, CIS, 145
copyrights database, Photonet, 159
corporate information and services, *see* business categories
CPB number, 139, 175
CPMUG library, 200

database, defined, 13
DataPac network, systems served by:
  BRS After Dark, 141
  CompuServe systems, 144
  Dow Jones News/Retrieval Service, 151

NewsNet, 154
OAG EE, 158
Source, 159
DataPost (Columbus, Ohio), 23
DEC–Line (Woodland Hills, California), 23, 169
Delphi, 18–19, 79–84
"Guided Tour" of system, 18, 149
user directory, 151
Delphi-Oracle, 149
dental field databases:
BRS, 142
CIS, 147
Dial-Your-Match™ software format, 23, 124–28, 178
direct command method of accessing systems, 15
digital alphabet, 4
digital processing:
character formation, 4, 7
signal modulation, 4
dining, databases for:
NewsNet, 155
Source, 160
Travelhost Network, 163
directories, 10
user, *see* user directories
discussions, online, *see* conference trees
Disearch (Source user directory), 101–102
disk drive, use of, 2, 4, 9
Dow Jones News/Retrieval Service, 19, 84–89
downloading, 10
on local BBSs, 177
of videogames, 25
Dun's Net, Photonet served by 159
DYM, *see* Dial-Your-Match

EIES (Electronic Information Exchange Service), 19, 152
Electronic Information Exchange Service (EIES), 19, 152
electronic journals, user-published, Source, 21–22
Electronic Mail Service
advantages of, 12
BRS, 142
CIS, 42–50, 77, 145, 146, 147
Delphi, 18, 151
editing of message, *see* text editing
EIES, 153
Photonet, 20
Photo-1 Network
SourceMail, 21, 94–99
electronics databases
Knowledge Index, 19
NewsNet, 20, 155
E-Mail (Color–80 systems messaging), 178
employee information, NewsNet, 156, 157
encyclopedia databases:
CIS, 145
Delphi, 18, 19, 150
Dow Jones Information Services, 152
energy resources databases:
BRS, 143
NewsNet, 155–56, 157
engineers, services for:
CIS, 147
Knowledge Index, 20, 154
Sources, 160
entertainment and leisure databases:
A–T Videotext, 167

entertainment and leisure databases: (*Cont.*)
   games, *see* games
   NewsNet, 20
environmental databases:
   CIS, 147
   NewsNet, 20, 156

family life, *see* marriage and family life
farming databases:
   Harris Electronic news, 171
   NewsNet, 20, 156
fashion database, CIS, 145
FDA database, CIS, 147
feedback on local BBSs, 177
fiction, user produced:
   Delphi, 18, 150
   Magazine–80 (New Hampshire), 287
file storage, online, MicroNet, 16
FILGE (CIS text editing), 43–49, 76
financial markets databases, *see* business and financial services
firefighters SIG, CIS, 147
flight information, 20
   see also Official Airline Guides
Food Buyline group (CIS), 145
foreign systems, see Australia; Canada; Great Britain; Netherlands; Sweden
foreign languages, *see* languages
Forum–80™ software format, 23
free programs, 9

French language (bilingual) system (B.E.L.E., Quebec), 353

Gameline™, 25, 359
GameMaster (Chicago, Illinois), 23, 108–13, 170, 250
   addressable cursor used for, 10
   messaging service, 113
   GameMaster ABBS (Chicago, Illinois), 250
General Videotex Corporation, 18
Golf SIG, CIS, 145
Government publications/regulations/grants/contracts databases:
   BRS, 143
   CIS, 145
   NewsNet, 20, 156
   Source, 160
graphic systems, *see* videotex systems
Great Britain, telecommunication systems in:
   CBBS North-East, 355
   Forum–80 systems, 355, 356
   Mailbox–80 systems, 356, 357
   Mailbox–83, 357
   Prestel World Service, 25, 360
Greene Machine software format, 177
GTE Telenet, 14

Hamnet Club, CIS, 145
handicapped, services for:
   BRS, 143

CIS, 146
HEX2, 171
NewsNet, 156
hardcopy mail service, Photonet, 159
Harris Electronic News (Hutchinson, Kansas), 23, 171
health care issues, databases on:
BRS, 142
NewsNet, 20, 156
See also medical field
health guide, Source consumer service, 160
hearing-impaired, HEX2 services for, 171
See also handicapped
Help service, Delphi, 18
high-technology discussion forum, CIS, 146
high-technology employment services:
CLEO, 22, 168
Connexions, 17
Hollywood Hot Line, CIS, 145, 147
home services:
CIS, 17, 145
Source, 21, 160
host, *see* mainframes
hotel guide (U.S.), Source, 160
hotels, Travelhost Network for, 22, 163
Hudson's Washington Directory, NewsNet, 157
humanities, *see* social science and humanities

IBM Personal Computer, CompuServe Executive Information Service customized for, 144

ICS editor, 44, 48
Independent BBS (Toledo, Ohio), 310
Infomania service, Delphi, 18, 150
Information retrieval services:
Dow Jones News/Retrieval Service, 88-89
Knowledge Index, 89-92
Source, 160
information utility, defined, 14
International color Computer Club, 327
international news services:
Clearpoint, 207
NewsNet, 20, 156, 157
ITT-Dialcom network
Delphi "gateway" to, 19, 150
Travelhost abbreviated version of, 163

job opportunities, *see* employment services

keyboard, use of
ASCII, 4
Break command, 28
connectors, 34, 35, 37
control key, 27
Delete command, 28
Escape command, 28
keywords, 33-34
letter key controls, 27-28
Newline key, 29
Return/Enter key, 29, 32, 48, 50, 55, 113-14
Rub-out command, 28
keyword-driven telecommunications systems, 15, 106

Knowledge Index service, 18, 19
  manual, 90, 92
  use of, 89–92

labor database, NewsNet, 156
Lance Miklus, Inc., 333
languages databanks:
  BRS, 143
  Source, 161
  See also programming languages
Latin America, NewsNet databases on, 156
law databases:
  CIS, 147
  NewsNet, 20, 156, 157
  Photonet, 159
leaving a system, proper method of, 121
local area services:
  ABBS, 113–21
  accessing of, 15
  bulletin board systems, 174–80 (see also listings by state)
  charges for, 14
  GameMaster, see GameMaster
  signing on to, 26
  StarText Metro, see StarText Metro
  subscribing to, 26
  users' manuals, 27
long distance calling, timing feature for, 50

magazine database, Knowledge Index, 20, 154
mailgram service, see Electronic Mail Service: SourceMail
mainframes, defined, 14

management, services for:
  BRS, 142–43
  NewsNet, 20, 156
  See also business and financial databases
manuals for network users:
  BRS, 29
  CIS, 44, 75, 147
  Knowledge, Index, 90, 92
  Source, 93, 94, 161
manufacturing databases, NewsNet, 20, 156
marking messages, 128–32
marriage and family life databases:
  BRS, 143
  CIS, 145
  NewsNet, 157
mathematics databases:
  BRS, 142
  Source, 161
medical field, services in:
  BRS, 142
  CIS, 147
  Knowledge Index, 20, 154
  See also science and medicine
memory (RAM), 9, 10
  buffer, 10
menu-driven telecommunication systems, 15, 32–33, 106
messaging, 8, 178
  CompuServe SIG, 65–72
  GameMaster, 113
  private, 178
  See also conferencing systems
Micro Moonlighter™, NewsNet, 155
Micronet 800 (Prestel World Service), 25, 361
MicroNET timesharing service, 16

MicroShare (Milwaukee, Wisconsin), 23, 172, 348
mineral resources database, NewsNet, 20, 155–56, 157
MINICBBS, 135, 136
MINIRBBS, 135, 136
modem:
  acoustic-coupled, 3, 8
  bps speeds, 5
  defined, 3
  direct-connect, 3, 8
  full- and half-duplex operation, 5–6
  modulation and demodulation functions of, 4
  on-board, 3
  originate-answer settings, 6
  selection of, 2
  serial port for, 2
  standalone, 3
MODEM (public-domain communications program, 137
movie databases:
  BRS, 16
  CIS, 145
  Dickenson's Movie Guide, 259
  Dow Jones Information Service, 152
music information and groups: CIS, 145

National Technical Information Service (NTIS) database:
  BRS, 142
  Knowledge Index, 154
Netherlands, telecommunication systems in:
  Forum–80, 357
Netwits club, CIS, 145

networks
  accessing of, 15
  connect–time rates, 14
  local, listings of, see Chapters 5 and 6
  national, listings of, see Chapter 4
  packet-switched, 140
  selection of, 138–39
  signing on to, 26
  subscribing to, 26, 139
  value-added, 14
Net–Works software format, 23, 178
New Jersey Institute of Technology, 19
NewsNet, 20, 154–57
news services and information:
  A–T Videotext, 167
  CIS, 145
  Delphi, 18, 150
  Dow Jones Information Service, 152
  Knowledge Index, 19, 154
  NewsNet, 20, 157
  Pantagraph Informant, 173
  Source, 160
  StarText, 108
Nielsen ratings, CIS, 147
noise control report, NewsNet, 156
notices, user, CIS Bullet, 61–63
Novels, user-written collaboration:
  Delphi, 150
  Magazine–80, 288
NTIS database:
  BRS, 142–43
  Knowledge Index, 153
NW Micronet (Tacoma, Washington), 343

OAG EE (Official Airline guide, Electronic Edition), 20, 22, 158
   Travelhost Network feature, 163
office systems databases, NewsNet, 20, 157
Official Airline Guides, electronic availability of:
   CIS, 146, 147
   EIES, 153
   OAG EE 20, 22, 158, 163
online, defined, 1
online timer, 10
Orchestra 90 club, CIS, 145

packet-switched network, 140
parapsychology feature, UFO-NET, 229
parenting, see marriage and family life
parity setting in communications protocol, 7
PARTICIPATE conferencing system, The Source, 161
passwords, use of, 16, 114, 126, 147, 176, 178
patents databases:
   BRS, 13
   NewsNet, 157
People's Message Service, see PMS
Personal computer databases:
   CIS, 146–47
   NewsNet, 155
personal file space, EIES, 153
personal finance services, Source, 160
personal scheduling system/calendar,

Delphi, 18, 80
Photo-1 Network, 159
pet club, CIS, 145
petroleum databases, NewsNet, 155–56
pharmaceutical abstracts, Knowledge Index, 154
photographers, systems for:
   Photonet, 20, 159
   Photo-1, 158
Photonet, 20, 159
PLP (Presentation-Level Protocol), 24
PMMI 176
PMS software format, 24, 128–35
political information databases:
   NewsNet, 20, 156, 157
   Source, 160
pollution, see environmental databases
Popular Science database, CIS, 145
Post BBS, Source, 21, 102–104, 161
President's schedule, Source, 160
press credential service, Photo-1 Network, 158
Prestel coding standard, 24
   Citylink, 360
   Prestel World Service, 25, 360
Prestel World Service (Great Britain), 25, 360
prime time rates, 14
printers, 2, 4, 9
professionals, services for:
   CompuServe, 17, 147
   Knowledge Index, 154

See also engineers, law, medical field
Profile service, Delphi, 18
Startext Metro, 108
Programmers Area, CIS, 44, 76–79, 147
programming database, Source, 161
programming languages
  CIS, 16, 76
  Delphi, 150
protocol, *see* communications protocol
PSS (British Telecom International), 14
psychology databases:
  BRS, 143
  Knowledge Index, 20, 154
public transit database, NewsNet, 157
publications:
  BRS guide to, 15–16
  Knowledge Index database, 90–92
public relations newsletters, NewsNet, 157
publishing:
  NewsNet database, 20
  user, Source service, 21, 161

radio classics feature, TBBS (North Carolina), 307
radio news service, NewsNet, 157
railroad information, NewsNet, 157
Raylux financial service, Source, 160

RCP/M software format, 24, 135–37, 177
Readers Digest, The Source owned by, 21
real estate database, NewsNet, 20, 157
reference services and libraries:
  BRS, 16, 143
  CIS, 145
  Delphi, 18, 80
  Source, 21, 160
rehabilitation topics database, BRS, 143
religious groups and information:
  Computers for Christ BBSs, 201, 222
  NewsNet, 157
Remote Access Terminal System, *see* RATS
Remote CP/M, *see* RCP/M
Research Monitor database, NewsNet, 157
restaurant guides:
  Source, 160
  Travelhost, 163
resume-sending services:
  Connexions, 17–18
  Travelhost, 22, 163
RJII, phones with, 3
RS-232C, interface, 2, 4

screen size specifications, 29–32
  adjustable parameters for, 107, 178
scrolling, 27–28
selling by computer, *see* shopping and swapping services
serial ports, 2, 4

shopping and swapping services, 13, 178
 A-T Videotext, 167
 BRS, 16, 142
 Buy Phone, 22, 167
 Delphi, 18, 150
 Photonet, 159
 Photo-1 network, 159
 Prestel World Service, 360
 Source, 21, 161
 Travelhost, 22, 163
 Westice, 233
 Word Exchange, 245
SIGM volumes, availability of, 200
SIGS, see Special Interest Groups
simulation database, Source, 160
SMail, 21, 94-99, 162
social science and humanities databases:
 BRS, 16, 143
 NewsNet, 20, 157
software package features, 2
 addressable cursor, 10
 auto logon, 10
 dialing program, 8
 directory, 10
 online timer, 10
 ST 80™, 333
 terminals, smart and dumb, 9
 text editor, 10
 uploading and downloading, 9
solid waste report, Newsnet, 156
solar energy database, NewsNet, 156
Source, The, 21-22, 93-106, 159
 Chat, 99-102
 and Control Data Corporation, 162
 Post BBS, 102-104, 161
 SourceMail, 21, 94-99, 105, 162
 Source*Plus, 161
 user directory, 101-102
 user's manual, 93, 94, 161
 user publishing section, 161
Sourcevoid Dave, 226
Special Interest Groups (SIGs), CIS, 17, 63-75
 commands, CIS file of, 75
 conferencing, 74
 databases available in, 72-74
 games, 145
 groups and clubs (computer), 146-47
 groups and clubs (general), 145
 manual for, 65, 73, 75
 messaging, 64-72
 professional/vocational, 147
sports:
 CIS clubs, 145
 CIS news service, 145
 Delphi games, 149
 Dow Jones Information Service news, 152
 Source news, 160
standards:
 for bps speeds, 5
 and communications protocol, 6-7
 for digital alphabet, 4
 in videotex coding, 22
stock market, see business and financial services
stop bits in communications protocol, 7, 8
storage devices, 2, 9

Sweden, telecommunication systems in:
  ABC-80, 358
  Elfa, 358
sysops, role of, 15, 114–15, 121, 129, 178, 179–80
  in DYMS, 124
  RCP/M, 188
  software used by, 131, 176–77
system operators, *see* sysops

Tandy Videotex Host System, 106, 167
taxation database, NewsNet, 20, 156, 157
technical jobs, *see* high technology jobs
teenagers, *see* young persons' BBSs
telecommunications database, NewsNet, 20, 157
Telecomputing Corporation of America, 21
Telenet network, systems served by:
  BRS, 141
  CompuServe, 14, 144
  Dow Jones New/Retrieval Service, 151
  EIES, 152
  Knowledge Index, 153
  NewsNet, 154
  OAG EE, 157
  Prestel World Service, 360
telephone codes, foreign, use of, 354
telephone information database, NewsNet, 157
telephone-computer connection, 2–3

telephone directory, electronic, 13
Teletext, 24
Television Digest database, NewsNet, 157
Telidon videotex system, 24
terminals:
  dumb, 9
  smart, 9–10
  TRS Videotex, 17
Texnet, 162
text editing:
  ABBS, 120–21
  CIS, 44–49, 69–71, 76
  EIES, 153
  PMS, 133–34
  Source SMail 21, 95–98, 105, 161
text editor software feature, 10
text files, 49–50
  CompuServe, 5–11, 17, 76
  Source, 105
text output of computer, control of, 27
time charges, 10, 14
time limits for BBSs, 15
timesharing service, MicroNET, 16
toll-free numbers, Source Customer service, 160
TORPET (Toronto PET Users Group), 283
toxic materials database, NewsNet, 155, 157
Transcanada Telephone System, 14
transportation database, NewsNet, 157
Travelhost Network, 22, 163
travel services:
  CIS, 145–46

Delphi, 18, 151
Prestel World Service, 360
Source, 160
Travelhost, 22, 163
travel writer market letter, NewsNet, 157
Trimline™ telephone, 3
TRS Videotex terminal, 17
Tymnet, Inc., 14

Ule (Max) & Company, Tickerscreen, 299
Uninet, systems served by:
  BRS, 141
  EIES, 152
  NewsNet, 154
  Source, 159
  Travelhost Network, 163
university timesharing systems, 10
Unix Operating system, 172
uploading, 10
U.S. hotel guide, Source, 160
U.S. census report, NewsNet, 156
user directories, 10
  CompuServe, 44, 75, 145, 146
  Delphi (IamWhois), 150, 151
  Source (Disearch), 101–102

userlogs, 179
user publishing:
  Delphi, 151
  Source, 22, 161

value-added networks, 14
value-added services, Dow Jones Retrieval Service, 88
veterinarians forum, CIS, 147
videotex systems, 24
  Citylink, 25, 360
  coding standards for, 24
  GameLine, 25, 359
  PLP/NAPLP, 359
  Prestel format, 24, 25, 360
  Prestel World Service, 360
  Telidon, 359
  transmission speed of, 24

weather reports;
  CIS, 145
  Dow Jones Information Services, 152
  StarText Metro, 107
wine information, Source, 160
word length in communications protocol, 7
Work-at-Home SIG, CIS, 145

New Systems

Use this section of the book to place new system names and numbers that you discover. You should also make a note of the various User IDs you come across on the National Networks, which will enable you to exchange electronic mail quickly.